Identity and African American Men

Identity and African American Men

Exploring the Content of Our Characterization

Kenneth Maurice Tyler

LEXINGTON BOOKS
Lanham • Boulder • New York • London

Published by Lexington Books
An imprint of The Rowman & Littlefield Publishing Group, Inc.
4501 Forbes Boulevard, Suite 200, Lanham, Maryland 20706
www.rowman.com

16 Carlisle Street, London W1D 3BT, United Kingdom

Copyright © 2014 by Lexington Books

All rights reserved. No part of this book may be reproduced in any form or by any electronic or mechanical means, including information storage and retrieval systems, without written permission from the publisher, except by a reviewer who may quote passages in a review.

British Library Cataloguing in Publication Information Available

Library of Congress Cataloging-in-Publication Data

Tyler, Kenneth Maurice.
Identity and African American men : exploring the content of our characterization / Kenneth Maurice Tyler.
pages cm
Includes bibliographical references and index.
ISBN 978-0-7391-8395-3 (cloth : alk. paper) -- ISBN 978-0-7391-8396-0 (electronic)
1. African American men--Race identity. 2. African American men--Social conditions. 3. African American men--Public opinion. 4. United States--Race relations. I. Title.
E185.625.T95 2014
305.38'896073--dc23
2014020472
ISBN 978-1-4985-0000-5 (pbk : alk. paper)

∞ ™ The paper used in this publication meets the minimum requirements of American National Standard for Information Sciences Permanence of Paper for Printed Library Materials, ANSI/NISO Z39.48-1992.

Printed in the United States of America

Contents

Acknowledgments — vii

Part I: — 1

1. "What's Going On?": Rationalizing an Examination of African American Men's Identity — 3
2. "Why We Can't Wait?": Data on the Psychological and Behavioral Outcomes of Young African American Men — 19
3. "Living in America": Identity, Context, and African American Men's Identity — 29
4. "Don't Call Me Nigger, Whitey!": Racism and the Lives of African American Men — 45
5. "Invisible Man": Intersectionality and Invisibility as Conceptual Frameworks in the Study of African American Men's Identity — 57

Part II: — 81

6. "Guess Who's Coming to Dinner?": Identities of Young African American Men — 83
7. African American Men's Gender Identity: Gender Socialization and Identity Development — 87
8. African American Men's Sexual Identity — 97
9. African American Men's Racial Identity — 115
10. African American Men's Ethnic Identity — 129
11. African American Men's Cultural Identity — 143
12. African American Men's Socioeconomic Identity — 167
13. African American Athletic Identity — 181
14. African American Men's Academic Identity — 199
15. Additional Identity Considerations: Colorism — 211
16. "One Day It'll All Make Sense": Examining a Model of African American Men's Identity — 225
17. "Never Say You Can't Survive": Pragmatics and Future Considerations — 233

References	251
Index	289
About the Author	291

Acknowledgments

I express my sincerest gratitude to those who have supported this work since 2009. First, I want to give all thanks and praise to God who guided me and gave me patience and peace throughout the writing of this text and of course, the course of my life, thus far. I look forward to my journeys with you and for you. Next, I'd like to thank my family, Kevin and Lillian Tyler, Kevin, Jr. Keith, Kristin, Wellington, and Wesley, Aesha, and Paul for being a strong foundation for which this work was produced. Your contributions, support, and love are truly immeasurable. I'd also like to thank my son, Asa McKenzey Tyler. I appreciate the patience and love and support you showed while I was completing this work. The fact that you were continuing to be the great student and athlete and son and my biggest supporter and resident comedian that you are while I was completing this text made my efforts for this book so much easier. *II Chronicles XIV: II.* I love you dearly. Also, I dedicate this book to all the men in my family, including my namesakes, Otis Maurice Redmond, Sr, and Jr, Willie Redmond, John Smith, John D. Smith, Emanuel Tyler, Cornelius Tyler, Andrew Tyler, Marrell Tyler, Ricky Tyler, and Orlando Wilder and countless cousins and kinfolk.

Of course, these men would have and know very little were it not for the presence and contributions of the women who support them. A special thank you goes to my great aunt, Marie Smith. She put in motion all the requirements for this text. In addition, I also acknowledge and thank my grandmothers, Dorothy Redmond and the late Lenore Tyler. Also, I thank my aunts, Kimberly Redmond, Lois and Joyce Tyler, Lisa Tyler, and Catherine Wilder and several cousins (Tonnesia, Kim, Stacy) and their children.

Academically, my family includes Dr. Wade Boykin and Dr. Robert Jagers, along with Dr. Jules Harrell, Dr. Leslie Hicks, Dr. James Jones, and the late Dr. Albert Roberts and late Dr. James Starr. Additionally, I send a special thank you to Dr. David Rice and Dr. Aashir Nasim. I fancy the fact that our young boys have A (Asa), B (Biko), and C (Chedza) names, similar to our constant conjunction days at Howard. Many thanks also to Dr. Sean Coleman, Dr. Eric Hurley, Mr. Oronde Miller, Dr. Monica Dillihunt, Dr. Samantha Francois, Dr. Darla Scott, Dr. Grace Carroll, Dr. Rochelle Brock, and Ms. Sonia Bell. At Kentucky, I received continued support from my Chair and mentor, Dr. Lynda Brown-Wright and Dr. Fred Danner. A special thank you to my research team, who were the first readers of this text: Jennifer Burris, Falynn Thompson, Trisha Clement, and Howard Lloyd. I thank you for your dedication to this work and for making research fun again! Thank you also to Ms. Danielle Herriford, a social worker, Ms. Donna Gay, a middle school social studies teacher, and Dr. Aesha Tyler, a clinical psychologist, for your professional insights and reviews.

In addition to those who shaped me professionally, I thank those women I know personally who do their best to raise their young African American men: Christina Jordan, Kristin Tyler, Kimberly Redmond, Nycole Buckner, Charlene Sanford, Alicia Marsh, Sherry Myart, Danielle Dishman, Anika Simpson, and others whose impromptu discussions about raising young African American men informed my own thinking about raising Asa and the importance of knowing who these young men truly are. I also thank several persons who provided encouraging words through the Word and inspired and supported me when both the times and the writing got tough: Pastor Michael Robinson (Lexington, KY), Pastor Chris Harris (Chicago, IL), Donna Gay, Nitzalis Martinez, Rita Marie Small, Techla Nesbitt, Christine Riley, Tamira Devlin, Tanya Anthony, and Tracy and Maria Santiago.

Finally, I want to acknowledge Tracy Martin and Sybrina Fulton, who lost their son to violence emerging out of a fear of who he might have been rather than an understanding of who he truly was. While they aren't the only parents of young African American men who were slain by guntoting ignorance, their public displays of strength and resolve etched in my mind the power of the human and holy spirits. At one point, Mr. Martin asked the U.S. Congress what could be done to protect others like his son. I write this book with the hope that we, as a society that has grown from his loss as a father, can answer his important question.

Part I

ONE

"What's Going On?"

Rationalizing an Examination of African American Men's Identity

> Who are Black men when they are not victims of oppression?
> —Ratele (2003)

During the writing of this introductory chapter, a young African American man named Trayvon Martin was shot and killed in a gated housing community in Florida. He was 17 years old. He was killed while talking on a cellular phone to his girlfriend. He was outside wearing a hooded sweatshirt because of the rain and carrying a bag of candy and a bottled iced tea purchased at a nearby convenience store. He was killed while many individuals, including other young African American men, were watching the televised National Basketball Association's annual All-Star game, where many young African American men have dominated and made significant careers in the sport. He was killed only yards away from the home of his biological father. He was killed on my own father's sixty-first birthday.

Unfortunately, this problem, homicide among young African American men, is common. What makes this story about Trayvon Martin somewhat unique from most stories of young African American men and their lives being taken away through violence is the fact that the man who shot him—a self-proclaimed neighborhood watchman—was not arrested once local law enforcement arrived at the location where the incident took place. According to the shooter, who remained present at the shooting site, Trayvon Martin looked suspicious. He looked like he was "on drugs" and "was up to no good." He looked like other individuals who had allegedly been involved in property crimes within the specific

Floridian community. While the details of the tragic incident were continuing to emerge at the time of this writing, what was known was that the shooter had a perception, an opinion of this young African American man that cost him his life. It is important to note that on July 13, 2013, the accused shooter was found not guilty of committing second-degree murder and was also not charged with manslaughter.

In reflecting on this powerful and yet unbelievably horrific nightmare, I began to think critically about the entire scenario. Specifically, I wondered if the shooter knew that Trayvon's father had significant involvement in Trayvon's life, even though some stereotypes would have people believe that African American fathers are hardly involved in the upbringing of their offspring. I wondered whether the shooter ever thought that perhaps this young African American man—an "A and B student" with hopes of becoming an aviator—could have been a future U.S. president. At the time of this writing, Barack Obama, an African American man having secured reelection, remained the 44th president of the United States. Thus, Trayvon's possibilities of being a future leader of the free world were not out of the question.

Continuing on, I wanted to know what the shooter saw when he deemed Trayvon was acting suspiciously. Just what did this young African American man do? How was the perception of "on drugs" determined? Was the shooter a medical practitioner (i.e., emergency medical technician, nurse, physician's assistant, physician)? How was Trayvon viewed by this shooter, who, according to evidence, was part of a group of individuals who "always get away"? How did he know that the others "always" get away? Had the shooter chased each one individually and experienced how quickly some can run, especially when being justifiably or unjustifiably pursued? Finally, I thought about the idea that this young man's death seemingly resulted from a set of behaviors stemming from a negative stereotype projected onto him because of how he looked. Trayvon Martin was murdered not because of who he actually was, but because of who he was perceived to be. Trayvon Martin's 17 years of life reached an abrupt and violent end as a result of how he "seemed" to be to a layperson that not only initiated a pursuit with the victim, but also did so while brandishing a loaded firearm.

As a social scientist, I think it is important to begin to promote important dialogue regarding possible ways to resolve such deleterious frames of mind that would ultimately "save" young African American men like Trayvon Martin from being suspected, followed, confronted, and murdered. Should I teach a class on the importance of expressive individualism within African American culture and role that the "hoodie" plays in the perceptions (self and others' perceptions) of young African American men? No. I'm far from an expert on contemporary African American culture. Should I discuss how societal ills such as racism and sexism and classism influence the mindsets of would-be perpetrators like Trayvon's shooter? No, because that doesn't really get at the root of the issue.

The root of the issue is that, to the shooter, Trayvon Martin and everything he was to his family and friends, was invisible. His identity, who he truly was, was unbeknownst to the shooter. The shooter didn't know Trayvon. The shooter had an automatic emotional and behavioral response to Trayvon Martin's presence, to the point where he decided the young African American man ought to be pursued (Mays, Johnson, Coles, Gellene, and Cochran 2013). His understanding of Trayvon as an 6'3" 17-year-old African American male high school student with aspirations of becoming a pilot and heroic stories of saving his own father's life simply did not exist. What did exist in the mind of the shooter was the negative and unfortunately, reigning racist stereotypes regarding African American men. Hostile. Aggressive. Lazy. Docile. Sexually promiscuous. Dishonest. Thieves. Crooks. Convicts. And yes, even exceptional basketball and football players (Howard, 2013).

In my view, Trayvon Martin's killer did not see beyond these societal images of young African American men. For many persons made aware of the Trayvon Martin case, the shooter's media-reported fixation with criminal activity among African American men supported his expectation that African American men commit crimes and evade getting caught. This harmful and myopic perception of Trayvon and most African American men is not entirely surprising. A broader conceptualization of the identities of young African American men has yet to fully emerge within popular culture. That is, we are, more often than not, shown in these ways and doing these things.

Yet, some social science disciplines such as psychology and sociology continue to struggle with the ability to unpack and articulate a conceptual and data-based understanding of the experiences and realities of young African American men. While there has been significant research on this population in the past 40 years—some of which will be reviewed throughout this text—much of this work has not sought to provide a salient and comprehensive picture of who these individuals truly are. Though the late twentieth and first decade of the twenty-first centuries have begun to witness an increasing focus on the academic and social experiences of African American men, to date, overall, there has not been a centralized, interdisciplinary effort to capture conceptually the multiple identities of young African American men, particularly those that go beyond reigning negative stereotypical images of this population.

Yes, upon observation, one can conclude that young African American men are, well, young, male, and of African and American ancestry. That gives an ostensible understanding of who they are, but is there more? What about the beliefs and values and corresponding practices associated with these young, male, and African American demographics? Is there more? What about the idea that they have certain cultural beliefs that may have little to do with issues of racism (i.e., caring about your fellow African American man, not because of racism, but because it's the right thing to do?) Is there more? What about the idea that they may have greater reality-based dilemmas that are further complicated by issues of race (i.e., sexual identity, athletic identity, academic identity) rather than being only the result of race-related issues? Is there more?

As African American men, is there more to our story? Is there more to being a young African American man than what media and society offer for consumption? Are we more than rap artists and basketball players and criminals? And even in those positions, is there more to being that African American male entertainer or professional athlete that is simply misunderstood or unrecognized? Did Trayvon Martin invite suspicion because his physical appearance—which may have been culturally affirming and therefore, purposeful in its own right—may not have fully captured his essence as a human being, as a young African American son, student, brother, equestrian, skier, and dreamer? Was there more to Trayvon Martin that was simply masked and rendered invisible by prejudicial thinking and racial bias? Were negative and racist stereotypes present during the decision to confront and ultimately shoot Trayvon Martin? Was he more than just a tall, African American man looking like he's "up to no good"?

Of course, he was. Of course, there is more to his story and thus, "our" story. The problem is that this story of young African American men and their intersecting identities is not being told or at least is not being communicated as fast as the negative preexisting stereotypes that, in some cases, determine if we live or die. Trayvon Martin died, in part, because the positive images and stories of young African American men seem to place second to those that reinforce simplistic and incendiary stereotypes (i.e., criminal behavior, poor academic performance, athletic prowess). Rather than critically delving into the complexity of our being as African American men, many may believe it's easier to think of us in racist, stereotypical terms and thus, render our lives, expendable and our beings, invisible. Some may even rely on these stereotypes throughout their daily functioning. And yet, there is more. There was "more" to Trayvon Martin. There is "more" to us than being male and African American.

This book has been written to provide a conceptual framework articulating the multiple identities of African American male adolescents and young adults, herein referred to as young African American men. For decades, researchers in the social sciences and education have long sought an understanding of the academic and behavioral outcomes of young African American men. Over several decades, members of the lay and scientific communities have provided data-based and rhetorical works that have sought to better explain the identities (i.e., perceptions of the self) and subsequent activities and mindsets of African American male youth and young adults (Johnson 2010; Madhubuti 1991; Rice 2008).

The literature in education and the social sciences contains several articulations of specific identity development theories, namely racial (Cross 1995; Helms 1990; Sellers et al. 1997) and ethnic identity (Phinney 1996) which has sought to explain behavioral and psychological outcomes of young African American men. More recent work has combined the two constructs and examined their impact on behavioral outcomes (Umana-Taylor, Quintana, Lee, Cross, Rivas-Drake, Schwartz, Syed, Yip, and Seaton 2014). Other works have illuminated the role of multiple contextual factors (e.g., racism) on the development of these identities for this population (Spencer 1995; Watts and Abdul-Adil 1998) for young African American men.

While research on racial and ethnic identity development has sought to explain behaviors and attitudes of adolescents and young adults of varying ethnicities and backgrounds (Cross 1991; Majors and Billson 1992; Phinney 1996), including African American women (Patton and Simmons 2008; Stevens 1997) and White men (Scott and Robinson 2001), a specific, multidimensional conceptual framework providing a simultaneous examination of the sexual, gender, racial, cultural, ethnic, socioeconomic, athletic, and academic identities of young African American men has not enjoyed like representation in the literature. Greater understanding of the thoughts, behaviors and outcomes of young African American men requires a fuller, more comprehensive understanding of the multiple identities they possess, how these are related to each other, how various contextual factors influence each of them uniquely and simultaneously (Bronfenbrenner 1986; Spencer 1995), and how each of these may precede various behavioral outcomes.

This book, then, seeks to answer one question: "What are the multiple identities that most young African American men possess?" To address this question, a conceptual model depicting the multiple identities of young African American men will be offered. The purpose of the model is to help education and social science researchers more fully understand the complexity and integrity of African American men's lived experiences and thus, their identities. Each form of identity (e.g., gender, racial, cultural, socioeconomic, cultural, sexual, athletic, and academic) contained in the model will be described throughout the text. Research supporting the existence of each identity characteristic will be used to justify its inclusion in the model.

There are at least two additional reasons for discussing the multiple identities of African American adolescent and young adult men. First, African American men remain a significantly understudied population in psychology and education (Bush and Bush 2013; Zimmerman, Ramirez-Valles, Zapert, and Maton 2000). While there are statistics highlighting the academic and behavioral challenges of this population, the theoretical and empirical research on the realities of young African American men—and the psychological and interpersonal antecedents of these realities, namely, their perceptions of self—are limited. As Bynum, Best, Barnes, and Burton (2008) state, research on African American men tends to focus largely on externalized problems such as poor academic performance rather than those internalized problems that often precede such behaviors.

In all, researchers and practitioners in the social sciences and education simply are not well informed of the multiple psychological, educational, and interpersonal issues and dynamics facing many young African American men. Instead, what we often examine are the behavioral outcomes of these dynamics and issues (i.e., poor academic performance, perceived sexual promiscuity, gang-related behavior, crime statistics). The development and examination of the conceptual framework articulating the presence of multiple identity components for African American men will facilitate a greater understanding of 1) their specific behaviors observed and studies by these scientific and lay communities and 2) their social identities that often precede these studied behaviors (Howard, Flennaugh, and Terry 2012).

Second, according to social identity theory (Tajfel and Turner 1979), identity development during the adolescent years involves 1) an individual's knowledge of membership in various social groups and 2) some exposure to contextual factors (i.e., popular media, peer, and family socialization) that will shape how members of these social groups perceive themselves (Hill, Bromell, Tyson, and Flint 2007). It is during the adolescent years that young African American men begin to grapple with messages inundated with racism, heterosexism, and monocultural ethnocentrism (Constantine and Sue 2006; Davis 2003; Noguera 2003; Nyborg and Curry 2003; Steele 1997). It is also during this period that most young African American men begin to receive greater messages regarding masculinity and their resulting place within the family and the larger society (Harris 1995). In addition, during this period of adolescence and young adulthood (ages 18–25), many young African American men will receive messages regarding sexuality and will begin to explore their own feelings regarding their own sexual identity (Corneille, Fife, Belgrave, and Sims 2012; Jamil, Harper, Fernandez, et al. 2009; Willis and Clark 2009). For example, in a study examining the sexual behaviors of African American male adolescents, Willis and Clark (2009) found that the odds of having a successful monogamous relationship were significantly increased by the presence of a father who was caring and warm. Thus, the messages received regarding sexual relationships were associated with the level of warmth and tenderness young African American males received from their own dads. Additionally, it is usually around adolescence where a young African American man will begin to actualize his development as an athlete and/or good student (Beamon 2012; Osborne 1999).

Many messages like these and others shape young African American men's perceptions of themselves as racial, cultural, sexual, and cognitive beings. These messages are also shaping the attitudes and opinions of those persons who are fearful or suspicious of young African American men (Mays et al. 2013). More importantly, some of these messages, specifically those informed by racist stereotypical beliefs about this population have the potential to negatively affect the self-perceptions of some African American men and as a result, lead to maladaptive academic and social behaviors (Tyler, Thompson, Burris, and Lloyd, under review). A recent study submitted for publication by my research team found that the more African American male high school students internalized or bought into negative stereotypes regarding African Americans, the more they engaged in activities that would sabotage their academic performance.

Indeed, identity development is occurring among young African American men. They are being exposed to positive and negative messages regarding masculinity, sex, race, achievement, culture, and status. Their processing of these messages will inform the types of activities they endorse, the preferences and attitudes they possess, and the behaviors they exhibit. For decades, social scientists and educators have investigated the incidence and corollaries of these behaviors and attitudes (e.g., home-based factors such as father absence). Yet, few have done so with a broad conceptualization of the multiple identities possessed by this population. That is, social scientists and educators have examined the outcomes to a problem that is not fully comprehended. The current understanding regarding the attitudes, dispositions, and behaviors of young African American men is limited by an insufficient comprehension and articulation of the multiple identities that actually precede these behaviors and attitudes. We are trying to solve the problem of a group of individuals we don't even know or understand.

I've been a part of this problem. Like many of my contemporaries in the social sciences, I've pursued a research agenda examining the schooling experiences of young African American middle and high school students without fully understanding the complexity of the identities that led to the decisions, attitudes, and/or behaviors that I sought to observe and analyze. I've asked myself "How can we expect individuals who may not have the best interests of young African American men at hand to appreciate the breadth and depth of their perspective if those who *have* the best interests of this population have not led in the development and articulation of the identities that influence this population?" Actually, the question in my head isn't that long or complex. The actual question is, "How come we [educational practitioners, researchers, and stakeholders] don't know more about "us"?" "Why is knowledge possessed by some of them limited to Black Entertainment Television, crime, sex, gang violence, fatherlessness, President Barack Obama, basketball, and now,

Trayvon Martin (may he rest in peace)?" "Why is it taking so long for the negative stereotypes about members of this population, about us, about me, and my own son to be countered?"

My reply (to my own question) is "because we haven't done enough." Seemingly, persons like me who have pursued careers exploring the lives and experiences of African Americans, namely African American men, have not done enough to eradicate the ubiquitous and dangerously marginalizing societal and racist stereotypes and images of this population. To be sure, as social science researchers, educational practitioners, professors, and social workers, many African American male scholars have become aware—through various research methodologies—of the varied and oftentimes, troubled realities of many young African American men. We've shared our personal and professional reflections with each other at conferences and have promoted interdisciplinary and interdepartmental and interinstitutional collaboration to facilitate the development and discussion of topics and ideas believed to enhance the lives of this population. Many of those African American male scholars whose research is groundbreaking will be cited throughout this text. For many of us, we've brought a particular sensitivity to the issue as a result of being members of the population that we research.

Resulting from an increasing presence of African American men in the academy and in public service, both of whom seek to enhance the lives of many young African American men, is the argument that the knowledge productivity regarding this population is perhaps the broadest and most comprehensive in the history of social science and educational research. In the twenty-first century, we know more about young African American men and know that there is more to being African American and male in this country than what the pervading images of this population convey. On this issue of young African American men and their realities, our talented tenth and its knowledge have expanded tenfold since the days of Dubois and Washington.

And yet, it is nearly irrefutable that many persons in the United States and abroad maintain perceptions of young African American men that reflect the same negative images that both Dubois and Washington battled against in the early twentieth century. Unfortunately, while this book is being written, tens, if not hundreds of young African American men will become incarcerated and thus, participants in a penal system that houses far too many members of this population. Also while this book is being written, hundreds or thousands more will graduate from eighth grade and high school and go onto college and graduate/professional schools. In both scenarios, many of these men will enter worlds where some will rely on negative stereotypes and myopic depictions to get an understanding of who these persons are and what their relationship to them should be.

A greater discourse on the identities of young African American men is needed to not only inform individuals—from those in the ivory tower to those in the general public—of the multidimensionality of this population, but also to shore up ideas for research studies which could generate greater efforts to enhance and facilitate the lives of young African American men vis-à-vis informing those persons with whom they interact about who they are. As Brown (2011) correctly pointed out, education and social scientists are well aware of the social forces which aid in the construction of young African American men's lives, but little is known regarding the "varied ways in which African American males conceptualize their own experiences." It is my hope that this book is at the table when that important discourse occurs.

Contextualizing this sentiment, I return to the Trayvon Martin tragedy. Here, I wondered what resources his shooter could have used to counter the negative and racist beliefs he may have channeled prior to his initiation of a confrontation with this young man. What alternative information did television, books and periodicals, movies, and other media and venues provide that could have given pause to and perhaps, redirected the shooter's idea that "those guys" always get away (with crime)? At the time of this writing, along with other writings (see Dixon-Roman 2012), the first website to emerge from a quick Google search on "young Black males" provided a link to an article entitled "The Plight of Young Black Males Is Worse Than You Think" (Coy 2012). Directly above the article is a picture of several African American male inmates at a New York correctional facility. It is entirely plausible that, at the time the shooter pursued Trayvon Martin, similar links and websites were offered. Even more plausible is the notion that the shooter did not need to rely on such publicized negative perceptions of this population, as most of these images and depictions are already known and internalized by members of different races and gender (Dale and Daniel 2013).

What additional resources, then, were available to the shooter prior to the incident? Could these resources have provided the shooter with a broader understanding of African American men, of Trayvon Martin, an understanding that could have saved the young man's life? Could the shooter, in having assessed Trayvon on the basis of physical characteristics (i.e., tall, black, athletic, hoodie, "looking suspicious"), have concluded, like millions of individuals across the country, that this young man was simply walking down the street and thus, should not be looked at as a criminal, but, as a young man? Did the way Trayvon Martin walked or talked or even looked from a distance have meaning that actually went beyond typical, negative, characterizations (Neal, McCray, Webb-Johnson, and Bridgest 2003)? Even with a sitting United States president who is an African American male, one who, in fact claimed that if he had a son, he would look like Trayvon Martin, it is likely that Trayvon Martin, and countless other young African American men are portrayed and thus, believed to be, criminals and therefore, unfit to participate in American society and its institutions (Brown 2011; Brown and Donnor 2011; Page 1997).

There was more to know about Trayvon Martin and those of his "kind" (i.e., young, Black, male). But, where were the resources? Where is this information that apprises the general public of who young African American men are, the identities we possess, and the resulting behaviors we exhibit? Where were the academicians with all this knowledge regarding African American culture and worldviews? Where were we? Our research findings? Our forums? Our guest contributions on MSNBC with Reverend Al Sharpton and Dr. Melissa Harris-Perry to discuss this terrible occurrence and the psychology not only behind the pursuit and the shooting itself, but the research-based conceptualizations of who young African American men are and what they experience and are exposed to within the U.S. context? With such discussions, where were our recommendations for educational stakeholders, lawmakers, and politicians?

We were scattered. Our research lay dormant in scholarly journals with a readership far fewer in number than the consumers of a media inundated with stereotypical images about young African American men. Without question, there has typically been a scientific focus on the experiences of young African American men. In 2013, for example, the *American Journal of Orthopsychiatry* published a special issue on young African American men. Studies found in that special issue ranged from correlates of hypermasculine attitudes (Cunningham, Swanson, and Hayes 2013) to racial socialization (Howard, Rose, and Barbarin 2013) to risky sexual practices and substance abuse (Murry, Simons, Simons, and Gibbons 2013) to gender roles (Santos, Galligan, Pahlke, and Fabes 2013), and depression (Ward and Mengesha 2013).

In that same year, one year after the shooting of Trayvon Martin, the *Journal of Social Action on Counseling and Psychology* (JSACP) produced a special issue on the tragedy. Two authors in the special issue, Dale and Daniel (2013) make certain that there is no equivocation about how, in the United States, "*most* of us [italics added] (both White persons and individuals who belong to ethnic minority groups) were socialized to view Black male adolescents and adults as inferior and dangerous, stereotypes that have negative and in some cases, deadly consequences for Black male adolescents and adults" (39–40). To combat this, they and other authors in the special issue agree that there is a need to promote cultural competency, share the research concerning racial bias and its impact on decision making, and have more frank conversations about race (Bell, Jones, Roane, Square, and Chung 2013; Pope 2013; Williams 2013).

Another author in the JSACP special issue even cited the suggestions made by members of the American Psychological Association Division 45 (Society for the Psychological Study of Ethnic Minority Issues) regarding next steps to emerge from the Trayvon Martin shooting (Pope 2013). These included, but were not limited to 1) sending a letter of support to Trayvon Martin's family and providing free mental health services, 2) writing and publishing of opinion articles that summarize psychological research on racism and racial stereotyping, 3) working with APA to keep the case in the spotlight and in particular, having psychologists to discuss racial profiling and stereotyping, and 4) offering forums to discuss the state of African American children in general and the Trayvon Martin tragedy in particular.

Still, another professor wrote an article in the JSACP special issue where he reported that he was able to hold a university-wide forum on the Trayvon Martin tragedy, although he initially sought to hold a much safer' event such as a candlelight vigil, which, in his opinion, would not have taken away from his professional responsibilities (Williams 2013, 81). It is important to know that several conversations with the author's wife and other senior faculty members led to his pursuit of a larger, more effective event that would better serve those interested in discussing and comprehending the specifics and science behind the Trayvon Martin tragedy (a classic case of behind every great man is a greater woman).

Indeed, in that special issue of JSACP, there was significant focus on how the Trayvon Martin tragedy should be addressed. The courageous authors in that special issue took a stand, on behalf of Trayvon Martin and his family, to discuss the need to combat the deleterious effects of racism and the equal influence that remaining silent on such an issue and related issues (e.g., lack of cultural competency) has on the lives of many young African American men. Yet, for all the recommendations suggested in the special issue of JSACP, none of these actually indicated some investigation of the identities of young African American men in an attempt to dispel and thus reduce the gross overreliance on negative stereotypes about this population. All of the authors seem to support increasing the dialogue on the impact of such stereotypes on the lives and psyche of both African American men. Some of the authors go as far as to discuss the impact and costs of racism on White persons (Dale and Daniel 2013).

However, the authors in the special issue seem to address cultural competency and racism effects without at all mentioning the specific lived experiences of young African American men. One courageous author, an African American graduate student, wife, and mother of a four-year-old son, came closest to the position I am advocating, particularly that of knowing more about young African American men. She writes "I wonder how Trayvon's parents cope knowing that he is permanently absent. Have they washed his linens since his death or do they go in at night and stretch across his bed, hoping to catch a lingering whiff of his scent, only to end up weeping for *all* that was lost [italics added]? Do they recall the funny things he said that *made him so unique and so remarkable*?"

[italics added] (Bell, Jones, Roane, Square, and Chung 2013, 91). This is one of the few times in the special issue where an author is vested in knowing who the victim was, and in doing so, asserting that academicians and laypersons alike could stand to know more about who Trayvon actually was, and thus, knowing more about young African American men in general.

How do we increase cultural competency about young African American men if we have not even discussed who they are, from a positive, agentic, integrity-based frame of reference? If we are not discussing the fact that many young African American men do not fit the racist stereotypes much of society holds about them, then how do academics begin to dispel and ultimately reduce these stereotypes and their influence on the thoughts and behaviors of those who may not have their best interests at hand? In all of the discussion of what needs to occur so that another Trayvon Martin tragedy doesn't happen again, what is lost on many researchers is the fact that our recommendations and courses of action seemingly omit the most important factor: who Trayvon Martin actually was. It is not likely that we can eliminate racial stereotypes and the fatal behavioral consequences of these if researchers are not beginning to actively discuss ways in which young African American men simply don't fit the stereotypes in the first place.

In my opinion, it is a disservice to Trayvon and his family to seek to ensure that "something like this never happens again" without articulating who this young man was in the first place. He had preferences. He had opinions. He has goals and dreams. He was more than the stereotypes present in the minds of not only his shooter, but perhaps hundreds of others who may have seen him. His parents knew this. His brother knew. His female companion on the phone with him the night his life was stolen knew. This information about Trayvon could have, at the very least, imparted newer images and ideas about him and other young African American men particularly to his shooter and would-be shooters of others like Trayvon Martin. This information, however, is almost systematically omitted from much of the discourse regarding this tragedy, particularly by the academic community. In some ways, young African American men are victimized even further by not only their would-be shooters and others who do not have their best interests at heart, but also by those who actually do have their best interests at heart.

Specifically, many academicians, like me, in our efforts to combat individual, institutional, and cultural racism (Jones 1997) have precluded critical discussions of its most prevalent victims: young African American men's identities, particularly their attitudes, their worldviews, and their experiences that could foreseeably counter many of the racist stereotypes that fuel the minds of many. While seeking to end their adverse experiences in the United States by promoting cultural competency, reducing racial bias, and dispelling myths about this population, many of us are doing so without an explicit articulation of who young African American's truly are. Our policy recommendations for educators in the classroom, our forums and classroom discussion with college students, our publications in research journals and book chapters to be consumed by other academicians are all seeking to prevent another tragedy while tragically overlooking a comprehensive articulation of the identities of young African American men. Young African American men, however, are literally dying trying to figure out who they are, how they should be treated, how to treat others like them, and how to live in the United States in the midst of such misunderstanding and strife resulting from their status as racism's most susceptible prey.

The academic and political communities needed to do more. We all needed to do more. For Trayvon. For Jordan. For Oscar. Most recently, for Ricardo. We still need to do more.

This call to better address the behavioral outcomes of young African American men vis-à-vis an understanding of the complexity of African American behavior and the identity components that precede it does not originate with this writing (Gordon and Gordon 1994; Howard, 2014; Howard, Flennaugh, and Terry 2012). As Stewart (2008) recently noted, "there is still a need for more empirical studies that document the experiences of students of color as they attempt to blend the multiple facets of their identities . . . and theoretical frameworks that explicitly consider multiple identities when projecting the development of students of color" (186). A more recent example of research adhering to this call for a more synthesized examination of the multiple identities of African American men is that of Watkins and colleagues (2010).

In their meta-analytic review of qualitative research on African American male mental health and well-being, the authors concluded that many of the studies included in their meta-analysis examined only one aspect of African American men's identities. The authors concluded that, throughout their study, they were unable to discern whether mental health outcomes for the African American male participants included in previous studies were due to the participants being "Black" or "male." These findings resulted in Watkins and colleagues calling for "research that simultaneously addresses the intersection of multiple aspects of socially constructed identity" (324). Also, Watkins, Walker, and Griffith (2010) suggested that some examination of the social and contextual factors that influence the identities of African American men accompany the exploration of these multiple identities.

An article by Schwartz (2008) provides an accurate synopsis of the state of identity research and thus, a literature-based rationale for the current article focusing on young African American men. Specifically, in his introduction of the *Journal of Early Adolescence* special issue, Schwartz (2008) suggested that the current examination of identity in psychological and educational literatures is limited. For example, one noted limitation is the observed fragmentation of identity, wherein certain components of identity have typically been studied in the absence of other identity components. Here, Schwartz (2008) argues that there is almost complete segregation between the literatures examining personal identity and racial/ethnic identity.

Another limitation Schwartz (2008) notes is the large concentration of White college student samples throughout the bulk of classic and contemporary identity studies. Here, the generalizability of identity processes, components, or outcomes cannot be determined for non-White school-age/adolescent populations whose socialization experiences leading up to the development of particular identities are believed to be distinct (Harris 1995; Myers 2004). Finally, Schwartz (2008) suggests a need to more fully examine contextual factors that shape or at least, co-vary with multiple identities. For young African American men, some of whom have had their lives stripped away from them due to issues regarding identity, shifting focus from behavioral outcomes to psychological, identity-based antecedents of such outcomes is of paramount importance.

This book seeks to address these issues brought forth by Watkins et al. (2010) Stewart (2008), Warikoo and Carter (2009), Schwartz (2008) and others (see Brown 2011; DeCuir-Gunby 2009; Howard, Flennaugh, and Terry 2012; Isom 2007; Narvaez, Meyer, Kertzner, Ouellette, and Gordon 2009; O'Connor 2001; White and Cones 1999) by offering an evidence-based conceptual model articulating not only the presence of multiple identities extant among young African American men—a population where much of the identity literature is not concentrated—but also some explanation of how these multiple identities are impacted by various contextual factors such as racism. The conceptual model can be used to provide opportunities for research seeking to enhance the lived experiences of young African American men.

Two frameworks, invisibility syndrome (Franklin 1999) and intersectionality via the Multiple Dimensions of Identity model (Jones and McEwan 2000; Meyers 2004; Silverstein 2006) will be referenced in constructing the conceptual model of African American male identity. A discussion of intersectionality as a theoretical framework, along with discussion of the Multiple Dimensions of Identity model will help to conceptualize the presence and interaction of the multiple identities young African American men have. In addition, invisibility syndrome will be used to offer a greater understanding of how racism—a salient contextual factor for young African American men—shapes the multiple identities of young African American men and most notably, what results when these identities are rendered invisible.

Before presenting the conceptual model of African American male identity, data on the behavioral outcomes of young African American men will be offered to provide further understanding of many young African American men. Next, an overview of identity development and influential contextual factors that shape such behavioral outcomes will be presented. Racism is the primary contextual factor discussed within the text and thus, the conceptual model of African American male identity. Additionally, invisibility and intersectionality will be discussed and followed by a presentation of the eight identity components (racial, cultural, ethnic, sexual, gender, athletic, socioeconomic, and academic) of young African American men. Finally, this book will conclude with a presentation of the conceptual model and suggestions to aid in its quantitative investigation. My personal thought and suggestions for parents, adults, media, and others regarding more immediate steps will be offered prior to the close of the book.

While the purpose of the book is to offer greater insight into the multiple identities which often precede the observed behaviors of young African American men, this book is written on behalf of young African American men like Trayvon Martin whose realities, freedoms, and lives were taken or truncated as a result of individuals simply not knowing or not caring about who these men truly are. The book is written to encourage dialogue and promote the development of research among social science researchers and educational practitioners on the lives of young African American men, particularly research that moves beyond status characteristics (i.e., race, gender) found among this population to a research agenda that investigates rather than ignores the complexity of African American male identity.

Most importantly, this book is written for those seeking to improve the lives of young African American men by gaining a better understanding of their varied social characteristics and the feelings and attitudes (i.e., identities) that accompany these. Young African American men are more than what you see in the movies; are more than the stereotypes about them. The social science and education literatures have begun to provide important research findings articulating the presence and purpose of several identity components of this population. The goal of this book is to unpack the content of those characterizations in an effort to broaden the conceptualization of this population while simultaneously diminishing an overreliance on one-dimensional racist stereotypes and inflammatory rhetoric which has, for centuries, wrongfully projected and maintained a blinkered and despicable image of who we are.

TWO

"Why We Can't Wait?"

Data on the Psychological and Behavioral Outcomes of Young African American Men

ACADEMIC OUTCOMES

It is well known that in academic arenas, young African American men have fared poorly (Davis 2003; Joe and Davis 2009; Roderick 2003). For instance, 61 percent of African American students perform below basic levels on eighth grade math achievement exams (Schmader, Major, and Gramzow 2001). It is plausible that the majority of these students are young African American men (Davis 2003; Roderick 2003; Schmader et al. 2001). Young African American male students are also significantly underrepresented in school-based gifted and talented tracking programs (Anderson, Howard, and Graham 2007; Grantham 2004; Kim and Hargrove, 2013; Thompson and Davis, 2013).

This underrepresentation, coupled with academic difficulties faced throughout their schooling, has been linked to later behavioral concerns both in and out of school. For example, Anderson and colleagues (2007) uncovered a statistically significant predictive association between African American male middle grade students' school suspensions and their reading achievement,with more suspensions being associated with reading performance outcomes. Also, 52 percent of young African American men who leave high school prematurely are reported to have prison records by their thirties (Hoytt, Schiraldi, Smith, and Ziedenberg 2002; Pettit and Western 2004). Further, African American students make up 16 percent of the K–12 population in the U.S. and 30 percent of all special education students in these grades (Artiles, Harry, Reschly, and

Chinn 2002; Davis 2003). Moreover, unlike other students, young African American men have been reported to hold beliefs that standardized tests are systematically designed to promote their failure (Schmader, Major, and Gramzow 2001).

Inside both traditional and special education classrooms, young African American men are more prone to nonverbal and verbal criticism than their African American female and European American female and male counterparts (Irvine 1985). In addition, when young African American men report their teachers' perceptions of them as "good students," such perceptions typically reflect appropriate classroom behaviors rather than academic achievement (Honora 2003). This perceivably inadequate attention to their academic performance may result in many young African American men in the elementary and secondary grades experiencing significant decline in academic achievement. For example, Swanson and colleagues found that, for many African American male students, it is around second grade that academic performance tends to decline and such a decline is fully entrenched by fourth grade (Swanson, Cunningham, and Spencer 2003).

In addition, Tatum (2003) cites that African American male students are often viewed as culpable for their academic failures and that this perception permeates the subconscious of many public school teachers in the United States Artiles, Harry, Reschly, and Chinn (2002) reported that African American boys are disproportionately referred to special education services. A qualitative study by Moore (2002) also showed that classroom teachers tend to refer African American male students to specified social and educational services. Additionally, African American male students have been shown to have fewer in-school academic support systems (e.g., benign neglect), higher in-school suspension and expulsion rates (Raffaele, Mendez, and Knoff 2003) and more dramatic declines in quality of schooling experiences, particularly as they make the transition from junior to high school (Roderick 2003).

Also, young African American men 1) are held to the lowest academic and behavioral expectations (Ferguson 2003; Roderick 2003), 2) have the highest school suspension rates of all students, 3) report lower average hours of homework per week than any other ethnic or gender group (Swann 2001), 4) are punished by classroom teachers more harshly than girls (Webb-Johnson 2002), 5) are perceived as having the lowest occupational goals (e.g., postal employee, cafeteria worker) (Terrell, Terrell, and Miller 1993), 6) are perceived as more likely to be characterized as violent, disrespectful, lazy, unintelligent, hypersexualized, aggressive, and threatening (Bryson 1998; Davis 2003; Epstein, March, Conners, and Jackson 1998; Franklin 1999; Harrison and Esqueda 2000; Hunter and Davis 1994; Isom 2007; Neal, McCray, Webb-Johnson, and Bridgest 2003), 7) strongly believe that their classroom teachers don't care about them (Noguera 2003; Payne 2008), 8) have more clinical depression symptoms than other children in school and are overrepresented for emotional and psychological services at school (Kistner, David and White 2003; Thomas, Coard, Stevenson, Bentley, and Zamel 2009), and 9) are less likely to see the connection between school and employment opportunities (Miller-Cribbs, Cronen, Davis, and Johnson 2002).

In fact, other studies support the findings provided by Miller-Cribbs et al. (2002) by showing that over 90 percent of African American male adolescents and young adults overwhelmingly reported athletes and entertainers as their role models more so than educators and/or academics (i.e., professors) (Assibey-Mensah 1997; Whiting 2006). Another study examining African American men in advertising reinforces the idea that African American male roles are linked to sports and/or entertainment. Specifically, Bailey (2006) showed that the majority of African American men in various advertisements in several magazines and periodicals were depicted as athletes and entertainers. Thus, given the overreliance on depicting African American men in these marginalized roles, coupled with the fact that many young African American men have significant disparaging experiences in school, it is hardly surprising to find that 1) some African American male students do not see educational attainment as a pathway to success and 2) believe entertainment and building a solid physical and athletic prowess will be such a pathway to success.

Though many statistics on African American male student achievement often describe the various and multiple difficulties many African American male students have at school, there is growing evidence suggesting that many young African American men are faring well in educational contexts. Specifically, several studies have shown that many young African American men not only highly endorse the role and purpose that education has in their lives, but also look to maximize their educational attainment by pursuing higher education and/or graduate and professional degrees (Frazier 2012; McGee and Martin 2011; Thompson and Lewis 2005). For example, Dr. Shaun Harper (2005 2009) has published several qualitative articles examining the experiences of several high-achieving African American male college students. In each of these studies, there is often an explicit dismissal of the notion that strong academic performance is exclusively relegated to White people. Additionally, more recent research by Dr. Harper has shown that African American male college students believe that education, particularly that beyond secondary education (high school) was an important path leading to economic viability and opportunities not only for themselves, but for the next generations of African American college students, especially family members (Harper and Davis 2012).

Similarly, throughout his quantitative research, Dr. Angel Harris has shown that many African American high school students not only believe that schooling is important to their abilities to become upwardly mobile in the United States, but such beliefs were actually higher than those of their White counterparts (Harris 2006 2008; Harris and Marsh 2010). Specifically, Dr. Harris' research findings show that a strong attitude and perception of being African American was associated with greater valuing of school and increased attachment with school (Harris and Marsh 2010). Thus, the authors demonstrate that many African American students are not only doing well in school, but their achievement is rooted in their affirmative ideas and beliefs about their racial group. Additional studies have demonstrated that many African American male students possess affirmative attitudes associated with educational attainment and, as a result, are strong academic achievers (Frazier 2012; Hines and Holcomb-McCoy 2013; Robinson and Werblow 2012).

In addition to these findings, some evidence of young African American men performing at exceptional academic levels has emerged in recent literature. For example, in 2010, the Chicago Tribune newspaper provided an article reporting on the success of 107 African American male high schools students (Eldeib 2010). In particular, at Urban Prep Academy for Young Men in Chicago, Illinois, 100 percent of its senior class—all young African American men—had been accepted to four-year colleges and universities. Other stories of African American men's academic successes are evident in the popular and academic literatures (Davis, Jenkins, and Hunt 2002; Franklin and Mizell 1995). While these findings from Drs. Harper and Harris are encouraging, what remains and thus, why we can't wait for significant action to be taken on behalf of our young African American men is the fact that many of them still experience schooling difficulties at the elementary, secondary, and postsecondary levels.

PSYCHOLOGICAL AND HEALTH-RELATED OUTCOMES

In addition to undesirable academically related outcomes for many African American men, the research literature is replete with data showing that psychological and health-based behavioral outcomes for this population are also of significant concern. For example, African American men make up 6 percent of the national population and between 44 percent and 49 percent of the prison population (Boyd and Watson 2004; Ogbar and Prashad 2000). Dixon (2009) reported that the incarceration rates of African American men quadrupled between 1980 and 2003. African American men also constitute 41 percent of death-row inmates (Gaines 2007; Wood and May 2003) and are three to four times more likely to be arrested than their Caucasian counterparts (Gaines 2007; Little 1995). Along with a limited perception of African American men among some of those who enforce the law, some research clearly articulated the fact that, overall, African American men are generally mistreated, held in low social regard, and/or discriminated against (Seaton, Caldwell, Sellers, and Jackson 2008).

The findings of Rodriguez (2008) further illustrate this point. Using a national dataset of over 1900 African American and White male and female adults, Rodriguez (2008) examined the intersection of race and gender by determining the degree to which these adults reported perceptions of discrimination and its correlates (i.e., perceived mistrust, verbal harassment). In the study, African American men were found to be four times as likely as African American women, 14 times as likely as White men, and 24 times as likely as White women to perceive that others mistrust them. Additionally, African American men were 16 times as likely as African American women, 63 times as likely as White women, and 77 times as likely as White men to report receiving inferior treatment (Rodriguez 2008).

In addition to the findings from the above study, African American men are also 1) viewed as having bad attitudes toward work (Littrell and Beck 2000) and 2) unemployed at two to three times the national average (King and Allen 2009; Task Force 2006). These statistics on the rates of unemployment and incarceration have led some authors to believe that a large percentage of African American men are not considered by many African American women to be 'marriageable' (King and Allen 2009).

An additional reason for the perceived lack of 'marriageable' African American men is the so-called "shortage" of African American men, which is attributed to heightened incarceration and death rates among this population (Felson, and Painter-Davis 2012; Stevens-Watkins and Graves 2011). Statistics on homicide among African American men reveal that, at 6 percent of the national population, this population makes up 47 percent of the homicide victims each year (Arias 2007; Harvey 2004; Hoytt, Schiradil, Smith, and Ziedenberg, 2002), making homicide the number one cause of death of African American men (Payne 2008; U.S. Bureau of Justice Statistics 2007). According to recent national statistics (see King and Allen 2009 for a review), African American men are twice as likely to become victims of homicide than their African American female counterparts. Other studies report that African American men are five times more likely to be a victim of homicide than African American women, ten times more likely than European American men and twenty times more likely than European American women (Hall, Cassidy, and Stevenson, 2008; Hoytt, et. al. 2002; Payne 2008; Phillips 1997; Stewart 2000).

In my hometown of Chicago, Illinois, the Chicago Tribune reported that in the first six months of 2012, 201 of 259 homicide victims were African American, with 145 of these persons being African American men between the ages of 15 and 35 (Heinzmann 2012). Equally staggering is the fact that an overwhelming majority of homicides among African American men are the result of their altercations with other African

American men (Hall and Pizarro 2010 2011; Phillips 1997). Cubbin and colleagues (2000) also noted that homicide rates for African American men are highest in regional areas with a large number of female-headed households. Given these statistics and more recent losses of life among African American men, even at the time of this writing, Bryant (1998) is certainly correct in his graphic, but accurate assessment: "prisons, emergency hospital-rooms on weekends, cemeteries, and street corners are overflowing with the bodies of African American males" (Bryant 1998).

Some empirical explanations for the homicide rates among young African American men have been provided in the social science literature. For example, Stevens-Watkins and Graves (2011) cite a recent report from the United States Department of Justice (2010) that indicates that African American men comprise close to two-thirds or 62 percent of all incarcerated males. Using a national dataset, the authors' longitudinal study found that peer substance abuse and low academic achievement were significant predictors of involvement in the criminal justice system among young African American men (ages 18–27 at the last wave of data collection).

Hall and Pizarro (2010) draw a link between unemployment rates and Black male–on–Black male homicide. Specifically, their quantitative study examined 461 homicide reports where both the victim and the assailant were men. Of these incidents, nearly 81 percent of these included both an African American male victim and an African American male assailant. The authors' most telling finding was that 1) Black male–on–Black male homicides are 2.5 times more likely to have involved unemployed victims and unemployed assailants at the time of the homicide incident. Thus, the perception of diminished economic opportunity and thus, the perception of limited contextual resources may have resulted in young African American men (the average age of assailants in the study was 25 years) seeking status through alternative manhood definitions, which, for some, have included violent interactions with other African American men (Bennett and Fraser 2000; Hall and Pizarro 2010 2011).

In addition to homicide statistics among African American men, in the past 30 years, suicide has increased in African American communities and is occurring most frequently among African American men ages 15–34 (Compton, Thompson, and Kaslow 2005; Joe and Marcus 2003; Joe, Marcus, and Kaplan 2007; Walker 2007). The Centers for Disease Control and Prevention (2005) reported that suicide is the third leading cause of death among African Americans, following homicide and unintentional injury (Griffin-Fennell and Williams 2006; Kubrin, Wadsworth, and DiPietro 2006). According to Wingate and colleagues (2005), there has been an increase in the numbers of completed suicide attempts among African American men. Among this population, firearm usage is the predominant method of suicide, accounting for 64 percent of suicide-related deaths (Wingate et al. 2005).

Along with these figures, reports on the physical health status of many African American men are staggering. For example, African American male children have the highest probability of stillbirth and death within the first year of life (Auerbach, Krimgold, and Lefkowits 2000). African American men also have the lowest life expectancy among all ethnic groups (Phillips 1997), averaging seven years less than their White counterparts (Ornelas, Arnell, Tran, Royster, Armstrong-Brown, and Eng 2009). Two reasons why the life expectancy of African American men is significantly lower than their White counterparts include 1) African American men succumbing to various physical illnesses and diseases at significantly higher rates than their White male counterparts and 2) African American receiving less preventive health care services (Ornelas et al. 2009).

In addition, statistics on transmission and prevalence of sexually transmitted infections (STIs) among African American men are equally alarming. Much of these data are relevant to young African American men, as they have been shown to have a longer history of engagement in sexual behavior. For example, a study by Lindberg, Lewis-Spruill, and Crownover (2006) found that, among a sample of heterosexual African American male adolescents (ages ranging from 15–18 years), the average age of first sexual experience was 13. Additional research by Kennedy and colleagues (2007) showed that, by age 13, 32 percent of an African American male sample had reported their first sexual experience and by age 17, 99 percent of the total sample reported engaging in sexual activity (Kennedy et al. 2007).

The results of this sexual behavior for some African American men are devastating. For example, in a longitudinal study examining predictors of African American male adolescent (age range 14–19) paternity, Miller-Johnson and colleagues (2004) found that 44 percent of their sample reported impregnating a woman. Beyond teenage pregnancy, the results of risky sexual practices for African American men extend to sexual transmitted infections (STIs). For example, Buseh, Kelber, Hewitt, Stevens, and Park (2006) reported that 37 percent of men living with HIV/AIDS were African American. According to Wilton (2008), a study of the Centers for Disease Control and Prevention conducted with over 1700 gay and bisexual African American men showed that 46 percent of the sample was HIV-positive and 67 percent were unaware of their HIV status. In addition, other studies have noted that African American men are eight times more likely to receive HIV diagnoses than Caucasian men and three times more likely than Hispanic men (Buseh et al. 2006). Also, African American men are reported to have the lowest AIDS survival rate (Buseh et al. 2006). Evidence of this is shown in the 2005 report where AIDS-related deaths statistics are a stifling one in three for African American men (Centers for Disease Control and Prevention (CDC 2005; Grinstead, Peterson, Faigeles, and Catania 1997). With these statistics, it is not surprising that AIDS is one of the top three causes of death among African American men between the ages of 25 and 54 (Thompson-Robinson et al. 2007).

The heightened incidence of STI transmission among African Americans has been linked to drug abuse and poor safe sex practices (Feist-Price, Logan, Leukefeld, Moore, and Ebreo 2003; Thompson-Robinson et al. 2007). For example, in a qualitative study examining the sources of high-risk sex behaviors among 57 African American men, Thompson-Robinson and colleagues (2007) found that engaging in risky sexual activity was reportedly due to impaired judgment resulting from alcohol or drug use. Several studies have noted that, in spite of the reported prevalence of HIV and other STIs among African Americans, there remains a relatively low concern for STI transmission among African American men (Grimley, Hook, DiClemente, and Lee 2004; Grinstead et al. 1997; Thompson-Robinson et al. 2007). For example, Grimley and colleagues (2004) found that although 65 percent of the African American male sample (N = 225, average age = 26) had been diagnosed with one or more STIs in the past, 66 percent reported that they were not motivated to use condoms during sexual intercourse. Moreover, Grinstead et al. (1997) reported that HIV testing and prevention strategies were being underutilized by a large sample of African American men who reported risky sexual practices. Feist-Price et al. (2003) reported similar findings.

Regarding drug abuse, Brown and Smith (2006) write that African American men are disproportionately incarcerated for drug use or drug-related crimes. Additionally, Brown and Smith (2006) cite that drug-related emergency room visits, drug overdose–induced deaths and HIV infections stemming from intravenous drug use are higher among African Americans than all other ethnic groups. Further, crack cocaine usage along with persistent alcohol abuse and smoking have become more prevalent among African American male populations (Brown and Smith 2006; Feist-Price et al. 2003), particularly among young African American men growing up in fatherless homes (Mandara and Murray 2006). Also, elevated alcohol and drug abuse has been linked with risky sexual behavior among some African American men (Dilorio, Hartwell, and Hansen; 2002; Wilton 2008).

PSYCHOLOGICAL EXPLANATIONS

According to social cognitive theory (Bandura 1986), the ability to carry out specific tasks is often preceded by a set of cognitive beliefs that guide the decisions to carry out such tasks. For many African American men, then, it is plausible that the choice to engage in risky sexual behavior, to commit suicide, to abuse drugs, or drop out of school is often the result of psychological, cognitive, interpersonal, and emotional processes. Similarly, it is often those same processes that precede the choice to remain in school and pursue higher education, stay out of jail, practice safe sex, and refrain from alcohol and/or drug use.

Given psychology's early discussion of the role of cognitive and affective factors that precede behavior, it is important to note that, at the core of these processes—leading to either adaptive or maladaptive behaviors—is some understanding of who the African American man believes himself to be, who he thinks he is, and what worth he thinks he has in the larger social context. That is, the questions of "Who am I?" "What are my core values?" and "How am I perceived by others?" often precede these behavioral outcomes. Responses to these questions reflect how the African American man identifies himself personally and socially.

It is plausible that these questions and their responses reflect what Erikson (1968) referred to as ego and/or personal identity. Similarly, preceding the behaviors of many young African American men is some evaluation of their social identity (i.e., "How am I viewed by others?"). Therefore, in seeking explanation of these behaviors, it is important for social scientists and education practitioners to more fully understand responses many African American men may have to these and other questions regarding identity. How African American men think of or identify themselves (i.e., "Who am I?" "Am I a good student?" "Am I a good person?") can provide explanation for many behavioral outcomes exhibited by them.

While the purpose of this text is to discuss research articulating the presence of multiple identity components for young African American men, it is important to provide a brief overview of identity in the social science literatures, particularly the definitions of the term identity and how it has been conceptualized and operationalized since the early days of classic psychoanalytical and social psychologists (i.e., William James, Sigmund Freud, Erik Erikson, George Mead, Henri Tajfel). The next chapter provides such a discussion.

THREE

"Living in America"

Identity, Context, and African American Men's Identity

African American. Biracial. Tall. Former high school basketball player. Harvard Law School graduate. Former U.S. senator (IL). Man. Father. United States president.

 Did you have someone in mind when you read the first word? Perhaps the first thoughts regarding the first word above conjure the names of hundreds of people in the United States. Some may be celebrities, others, close family members, maybe even yourself? Of course, there are millions of African Americans in this country and thousands more who have transitioned or are being born at the time of this writing. Thus, it is unlikely that one can know who you may have considered when you read the word "African American." Similarly, many African Americans are biracial and thus, the likelihood of pinpointing a specific person is small. Likewise, I'm certain that some, if not many would be above average height for either a man or a woman. Thus, the word "tall" does not provide some identification of the individual I am referring to. In all, these words, when read, may trigger the readers' thoughts of hundreds of individuals who may fit the characteristics being presented, including former U.S. Senator for the state of Illinois. It's the last words, however, that bring but one person to mind. President Barack Obama.

 When thinking about identity, it is typical for individuals to begin with a description of social locations, which entail characteristics spanning from race and gender to socioeconomic status, and sexual orientation. In answering the "Who am I?" question, I've often described myself as an African American man or a man of African descent first. Thus, for me, race and gender are more salient than other identities, typically those that I've acquired and/or earned (e.g., professor, father) rather than being born with (race and gender). While these specific social locations provide some description of the types of identities I possess and may indicate which identities are important to me, they do not adequately define what identity is.

The social science literatures, however, contain several theories articulating definitions and descriptions of various forms of identity (Owens, Robinson, and Smith-Lovin 2010). Owens and colleagues (2010) describe identity as a significant set of attributes that aid in the development of self-concept, which itself is defined as cognitive structures which allow the individual to make sense of the world and protect his or her self-worth (Oyserman et al. 2012). Most recently, Oyserman and colleagues (2012) describe identity as being those traits and characteristics, social relations, roles, and social group memberships that inform one's self-concept or past, present, and future thoughts and feelings about him or herself (Owens et al. 2010; Oyserman, Elmore, and Smith 2012, 69). Oyserman et al. (2012) provide a pragmatic description of identity by stating that the traits and characteristics, social relations, etc. that make up identity help individuals to better understand themselves, particularly by focusing on "what was true of oneself in the past, what is currently true of one's self, and what one hopes, wishes, or perhaps fears what he or she will become in the future" (Oyserman et al. 2012, 69).

Within the social sciences, particularly psychology and sociology, there has been a significant reliance on the early works of Drs. William James, George Mead, Erik Erikson, and Henri Tajfel to derive richer operational definitions of identity (Eccles 2009; Kashima et al. 2007; Nario-Redmond, Biernat, Eidelman, and Palensky 2004; Stirratt, Meyer, Ouellette, and Gara 2008). The conceptualization of identity was initiated by Dr. William James' (1892) and expanded by social psychologist Dr. George Mead. For both individuals, the idea of the "Me" self referred to that aspect of the individual that one comes to know through observation of his or her behaviors and characteristics (Eccles 2009; Harter 2012). The concept of the "I" self-discussed the role of the individual serving as his or her own agent in the development and acquisition of self-knowledge (Harter 2012; Kashima et al. 2007).

Specifically, James and Mead distinguished between the concepts of "I" and "Me," with the former discussing the individual being actively involved in the process (e.g., cognitive and behavioral processes) of acquiring knowledge of self and the world and the latter being the development of self-knowledge or self-concept (i.e., "the totality of a complex, organized, and dynamic system of learned beliefs, attitudes, and opinions that each person holds to be true about his or her personal existence (Purkey 1988). In other words, the "Me" concept speaks to what is actually known about an individual, whereas the "I" focuses on the processes involved in the development of such knowledge.

Returning to the President Barack Obama example, it is likely that President Barack Obama holds a "Me" self-concept that is, at least partially captured by most of the adjectives offered at the beginning of this chapter. We can see that he is of African descent (although it must be noted that skin complexion should not be equated with racial and/or ethnic background and lineage). Also clear to most individuals is the fact that he is a man, he is tall, he is a former U.S. Senator and he is currently serving a second term as president of the United States.

What may not be known to most of us, however, is the thinking and behavioral processes that went into the forging of these and additional identity components possessed by the current president of the United States. Even among those who know him personally and intimately, there may always be a degree of unfamiliarity with the processes that make the President Barack Obama who he is to others. For every individual, there is certainly more than just demographic information that defines who he or she is.

In other words, from his early days as a young child up to his second inauguration as president of the United States, it is not difficult for persons to "track" his development and progress toward and within the Presidency. We can know about the current president of the United States, his social identity, his "Me." However, what may always be unbeknownst to political consumers, fellow politicians, and perhaps to even those closest to him, including his wife and children, are those intricately personal internal dialogues, assessments, and decisions Barack Obama has, his "I." In furthering this concept of "I" versus "Me," President Obama's (and our) understanding of himself as 44th president of the United States, as an African American man, as a Christian, a husband and father, would be considered evidence of the "Me" self, the known self. This is his self-concept and the one he shares with the world.

Every thought that informs this self-concept (e.g., "Should I run for a second term?" "Are my children getting the best education possible?" "Is there more I need to do as a husband and father?" "As president, am I doing all I can and should?"), however, can be considered his "I" self, the self that is in a perpetual state of exploration and discovery, typically for the purposes of maintaining and/or changing the observed social selves which contain his social locations and thus, multiple identities .

In identifying the "Me" self, James and Mead articulate the presence of multiple social identities or what James called the multiplicity of social selves (Harter 2012: Kashima et al. 2007). James (1892) wrote: "A man has as many social selves as there are individuals who recognize him and carry an image of him in their mind." (Harter 2012, 190). Indeed, most individuals, including President Barack Obama, purposefully adopt several activities and perspectives that duly reflect an orientation toward a particular identity or several identities. Just as there are a set of roles and responsibilities associated with the earned title of *President*, so too are there roles and responsibilities associated with being a husband or of being a man of Christian faith. These multiple social selves or identities help construct not only perceptions of the individual by social others, but the individual's beliefs about himself or herself.

Along with the work of James and Mead, the research of Drs. Henri Tajfel and John Turner has also been widely referenced in the social science literature on identity. Specifically, Tajfel and Turner (1979) extend the initial identity conceptualization of James and Mead by arguing that identity is part of an individual's self-concept derived from 1) "knowledge of his or her membership in the social group" and 2) "emotional significance and overall value associated with such social group membership" (Azmitia, Syed, and Radmacher 2008, 4). From their perspective, identity is considered more social than personal. In Jamesian terms, for Tajfel and Turner, identity is considered more about the "Me"-self (social) than the "I"-self (personal).

For Tajfel and Turner, a focus on social identity rather than personal stems from the individual's recognition that he or she is a member of a social group. In recognizing this, the individual gathers knowledge or otherwise becomes informed about how that group compares to other social groups, particularly those within the same conceptual circle (i.e., boys and girls would share the gender concept, although they would be distinct social groups). Finally, the individual determines the degree of importance and value of being a member of that group is to him or her (Oyserman et al. 2012)

While much is owed to early psychologists such as James', Mead, and Tajfel and Turner for their initial articulations of identity, particularly the conceptualization of identity as having both personal and social aspects (e.g., "I" self and "Me" self), it is important to discuss the individual that the psychological literature identifies and credits with discussing identity formation among adolescents and young adults (Jones, Kim, and Skendall 2012; Schwartz 2001): Dr. Erik Erikson. One of Erikson's contributions to the discussion of identity was the contextualization of identity formation within a particular time period for humans (i.e., adolescence). While his most notable contribution to psychology is the development of the eight psychosocial stages in which an individual seeks to resolve identity crises throughout his or her lifetime, like James and Mead, Erikson also discusses multiple components of identity: ego identity, personal identity, and social identity (Erikson 1974 1980; Jones et al. 2012; Schwartz 2001).

Ego identity consists of an individual's most confidential perceptions and beliefs about him or herself and his or her past experiences (Erikson 1974). For Erikson, these beliefs—often referred to as "the self" lie at the very core of the individual and thus, perhaps unconsciously, inform his or her thoughts and prospective behaviors (Schwartz 2001). Personal identity is a second component of identity (Erikson 1974) and is comprised of idiosyncratic thoughts and behaviors that ultimately render the individual unique from others. That is, personal identity serves to distinguish the individual from others by showcasing specific patterns of thought (i.e., preferences, desires, and goals) and behavior (Schwartz 2001). In a Jamesian or Meadian view, these two types of identity would be referred to as the "I" or phenomenal self. Finally, social identity or group identity (Schwartz 2001) refers to the collection of roles and ideals specific to an individual's membership in and across multiple groups. Social identity is perhaps the most widely recognized category of identity as it includes such factors as racial background and ethnicity (Schwartz 2001). Social identity within Erikson's view is synonymous with that of James and Mead.

Additional articulations of identity have emerged since the initial conceptualizations put forth by classic psychologists such as James, Tajfel, and Erikson (Azmitia et al. 2008; Ashmore, Deaux, and McLaughlin-Volpe 2004; Eccles 2009; Owens et al. 2010; Oyserman et al. 2012). For example, Owens and colleagues (2010) discuss four sources of identity. The first is personal or individual identity, which is described as a basic form of identity which envelopes multiple self-descriptions derived from lived experiences and overall biographical details (Owens et al. 2010, 479). An example of personal identity would be "My name is Barack Obama and I am the husband of Michelle Obama and the father of Malia and Sasha Obama." Role identity is the second type of identity listed by Owens et al. (2010). Here, role identity is associated with the social position that one has in relation to others within a given institution and context (Owens et al. 2010). That is, role identity often captures the identity of the individual who holds a certain occupational or otherwise social status, particularly in relation to social others (Oyserman et al. 2012). This social status does not have to be permanent like those factors identified in personal or individual identity. "My name is Barack Obama and I am president of the United States" is an example of role identity as it identifies the title he possesses and to some degree, the rank, role, and responsibilities carried out in this position (e.g., commander in chief). Unlike the personal identity status of father, which holds more permanence, President of the United States is a finite role (maximum of eight years) and thus, the responsibilities and social interactions incurred with such a role are equally temporary.

The third and fourth forms of identity, according to Owens and colleagues (2010) include category-based identity and group membership–based identity. The authors note that the distinction between these forms of identity is often blurred. Category-based identity, is based on perceived membership in a meaningful social category, while group membership is contingent on an actual membership in an interconnected social group (Owens et al. 2010). For example, given his skin complexion and his birth certificate (both short and long form), President Barack

Obama can be perceived as a person of African descent born in the United States. Provided that the category in question is ethnicity, Barack Obama's categorical identity can be considered African American. Thus, category-based identity is premised on the perception of shared salient characteristics and do not necessarily have to be the result of the individual's own actions, particularly the joining of a group. Barack Obama did not "join" African Americans per se, despite the fact that his biracial history could allow him to check "biracial" or "other" on various applications and/or census forms. Rather, based on his physical characteristics, it is not uncommon for persons seeing President Barack Obama to conclude that he is a person of African descent. His birth in the state of Hawaii, another aspect of his identity that he could not choose, also places him in the category of American.

Group membership is the final identity reported by Owens and colleagues. Here, a major distinction between group membership identity and category-based identity is the overall volition and subsequent actions of the individual. Specifically, with group membership–based identity, the individual chooses the group to which he or she seeks identification with. This is oftentimes predicated on a variety of personal values and competencies the individual possesses and whether he or she believes that a particular group actually shares and expresses his or her beliefs, usually for a common good. Returning to the Barack Obama example, it is clear that the current president did not choose to be African American. However, he did choose to be a Democrat. This choice may have been fueled by the legacy of preceding and current politicians and voters who share and buy-in to many of the ideas and philosophies espoused by the larger democratic rhetoric and agenda. This group membership (i.e., Democrat) reflects the personal values and beliefs of the 44th president and therefore, identifying as a Democrat, for the most part, gives insight into these values and beliefs.

Though the literature evidences an extension of initial identity conceptualization forwarded by William James and others (see Eccles 2009 and her discussion of the "ME" and "WE" self), it is fairly common for most researchers in the social sciences to discuss identity in the original classifications, namely personal and social selves (Harter 2012). Unlike personal identity, where the individual gathers information (i.e., traits, characteristics, past actions, and feelings) about his or her self and reflects upon this, additional forms of identity such as role identity, as discussed by Oyserman and colleagues (2012) and category and group membership identity as discussed by Owens and colleagues seem to incorporate a social interaction. Under the social identity theme, answers to the "Who am I?" question are linked to his or her knowledge regarding group membership and the role that he or she maintains within this social group (i.e., role identity). It seems logical, then, that personal identity—where one's uniqueness is explored—and social identity—where one's ties to one or several social groups—are the major conceptualizations of identity most often explored by major theoreticians and social scientists, including Erikson.

SHORTCOMINGS OF CLASSIC IDENTITY RESEARCH

While many have deferred to Erik Erikson's (1974) seminal work and neo-Erikson identity research for greater understanding identity development (Schwartz 2001; van Hoof 1999), others have reported that Erikson and other classic identity psychologists (e.g., Freud) did not pay adequate attention to the multiple social identities many individuals have (Cass 1979; French et al. 2006; Jones et al. 2012; Sneed, Schwartz, and Cross 2006; Troiden 1979 1989; Whaley 2003). In fact, Jones and colleagues (2012) have recently argued that Erikson's conceptualization of identity development almost systematically excludes the impact of varied and multiple social identities that all humans have. Specifically, Jones and colleagues write "Although Erikson's conceptualization of identity nods to the role of external forces and social context (hence, the label of psychosocial given to his theory), his emphasis on a primarily internal and unconscious process silenced the influences of social identities such as race, class, and gender" (Jones et al. 2012, 699).

In essence, Jones and colleagues correctly assert that much of Erikson's work in psychology pinpoints the development and actualization of the personal self or "I" self. What are most often revealed from a review of Erikson's work in identity development are various psychosocial crises the individual contends with and some idea of how the individual's personal identity is emerging as a result of his or her attempts at resolving these psychosocial crises. Thus, despite the fact that Erikson follows an impressive line of psychologists and sociologists in championing the presence and complexity of both personal and social identities, much of his theoretical and empirical research seemed to focus on personal identity, the "I" self, rather than the "ME" self, which contains various social identities as a result of membership in several social groups and categories.

INCLUSION OF CONTEXT IN IDENTITY DEVELOPMENT

Along with the omitted discussion of the various social identities possessed by most individuals, but particularly, persons from racial, ethnic, and sexual minority backgrounds (French et al. 2006; Schwartz 2001; Sneed et al. 2006; Spencer 1995), a thorough discussion of the situational and/or contextual factors that shape these multiple identity components is not a salient feature of Erikson's work in identity. This observation is shared among an emerging chorus of interdisciplinary scholars who have persistently voiced concern about 1) their respective disciplines' inadequate delineation, recognition, and investigation of the multiple identity components that humans possess and 2) the various contextual factors that aid in the development of these multiple identities (Cole 2009; Deaux 1993; Jones, Kim, and Skendall 2012; Jones and McEwan 2000; Stirratt, Meyer, Ouellette, and Gara 2008; Yakushko, Davidson, and Williams 2009).

Despite these and other scholars (i.e., McLoyd 1990) who have increasingly called upon social scientists to develop conceptual frameworks which more closely examine the role that context/ecology has in the development, namely for persons of color or socioeconomically disadvantaged individuals, only a select few have heeded such a call (Bronfenbrenner 1979 1994; Garcia-Coll et al. 1996; Spencer 2000 2008). For example, Dr. Urie Bronfenbrenner's classic Ecological Systems Theory provides a framework that identifies the individual being shaped and influenced simultaneously by multiple ecologies, including the microsystem, mesosystem, exosystem, macrosystem, and chronosystem (Bronfenbrenner 1994; Spencer 2011).

The microsystem refers to those groups and institutions that directly influence an individual's cognitive, social, and physical development. Microsystem factors include, but are not limited to the individual's family, his or her primary context for formal schooling, his or her neighborhood and surrounding community, and his or her friends, peers, and fictive kinship (Bronfenbrenner 1994). An individual's mesosystem refers to the associations between different aspects of the microsystem. The degree to which there is two-way communication between a child's parents and his or her teacher would be an example of the mesosystem wherein two components of the microsystem are linked. The exosystem discusses the association between the individual's immediate social context (e.g., family, school) and another, more distal context where he or she does not have any direct involvement (Bronfenbrenner 1994). One example of the exosystem can be an African American parent whose work schedule does not allow him or her to interact frequently with his or her children, which may result in maladaptive behavioral expressions at school (e.g., poor grades, acting out, not attending school). The macrosystem can be defined as the overarching culture or value systems and beliefs that the individual, his or her community, and his or her mesosystem operate within (Bronfenbrenner 1994). Aspects of the macrosystem, Bronfenbrenner noted, can and often change over time, depending on the needs of the given society. It would be appropriate to argue, for example, that many individuals currently thrive within an increasingly technologically dependent macrosystem, wherein much of the culture's focus is on producing and retrieving information in a highly efficient manner. Finally, the chronosystem includes the multiple events that occur over the life course (Bronfenbrenner 1994) and have direct and indirect implications for a given macrosystem, but also persons within given mesosystems. A chronosystemic factor can include the United States foci on civil liberties over time. From the signing of the Emancipation Proclamation to women's suffrage to the Civil Rights movement in the 1960s, to the current civil liberties struggle for gay and lesbian persons, the United States has maintained a specific chronosystem focusing on the treatment of individuals from minority populations.

Extending Bronfenbrenner's theoretical framework examining the role of context on development are Drs. Cynthia Garcia-Coll (1996, 2004) and Margaret Beale Spencer (1995, 2000, 2008). Each of these scholars has provided theoretical and conceptual frameworks to articulate the experiences of children and adolescents, particularly young persons of color within specific contexts. In doing so, each has provided evidence to exemplify the notion that various contextual factors found across several ecological systems can be influential in how individuals come to think of themselves and the social groups and categories they have membership in.

In particular, Spencer has forwarded the Phenomenological Variant of the Ecological System Theory (PVEST) to illuminate various contextual factors that shape young African American men's ego, personal and social identities, and resulting behaviors. Much of Spencer's research has shown that several contextual factors such as the microlevel racism (e.g., racism experienced at the interpersonal level, typically within one's surrounding community) and macrolevel racism (e.g., racism experienced at the larger, institutional level; see Jones 1981, 2003, for further explanation) inform the racial identities and academic behaviors of young African American men (Dupree, Spencer, and Bell 1997; Spencer 2000, 2001).

Similarly, Garcia-Coll and Szalacha (2004) assert that contextual factors such as racism and segregation combine with social position factors such as an individual's ethnicity and social class to create a set of experiences that result in various maladaptive psychological outcomes (Patchen, Berstein, Szalacha, and Garcia-Coll 2010; Patcher, Szalacha, Bernstein, and Garcia-Coll 2010). For example, employing a sample of 277 ethnic minority children with an age range between 7 and 18 years old, Patchen et al. (2010) showed that 88 percent of them reported experiencing at least one racial discrimination situation, typically occurring within the childrens' microsystem or mesosystem (i.e., among peers or in a mall). In another study, the same authors showed that such experiences with racism were associated with increased anxiety, as determined by the Revised Child Manifest Anxiety Scale (RCMAS) (Patchen et al. 2010).

Along with the work of both Spencer and Garcia-Coll, others have identified additional micro- (i.e., father absence/presence) and macrolevel contextual factors (i.e., racism) that have been shown to influence how African American men think about themselves and their relationships with social others (i.e., self-concept, self-esteem, and their subsequent behaviors) (Bush 1999; Harris-Britt, Valrie, Kurtz-Coates, and Rowley 2007; Paschall, Ringwalt, and Flewelling 2003; Seaton, Caldwell, Sellers, and Jackson 2008; Thomas, Krampe, and Newton 2008; Watkins et al. 2007; Zimmerman, Ramrez-Valles, Zapert, and Maton 2000). For example, Thomas et al. (2008) found that, while African American nonresident fathers reported visiting their children more often than White, nonresident fathers, they were also constrained by the economic factors such as work-related responsibilities. Thus, aspects of Bronfenbrenner's exosystem seem to influence the degree to which African American fathers can influence the lives of their children.

This factor, father absence versus father presence, may have implications for the beliefs and values the child or children may come to develop for themselves, but of their fathers and their resulting behaviors. One study, for example, showed that young African American men in father-absent households were more likely to use drugs than their father-present counterparts (Mandara and Murray 2006). Thus, while work obligations may possibly hinder the abilities of African American to consistently interact with their offspring (context—exosystem), it should be noted that such a reality can and often does negatively impact the thoughts and beliefs that the young African American man has about himself. These thoughts and beliefs ultimately influence his decision to engage in damaging behaviors such as drug use.

Beyond the research literature, there is also anecdotal evidence supporting this notion that social interaction and context shape the young African American man's thoughts and beliefs about himself (i.e., his identities) and his observed behaviors. First Lady Michelle Obama supplies evidence of this in her statement "You can't really understand Barack until you understand Hawaii." In stating this, First Lady Obama is indicating that much of who she believes her husband to be, the values and belief systems he identifies with, and the social interactions and groups that President Obama believes are significant can be traced, in part, to his development in the ecological systems found in the 50th state.

Thus, given the classic (e.g., Bronfenbrenner) and contemporary (e.g., Spencer and Garcia-Coll) focus on contextual factors that influence identity development, it is plausible that the identity components of many young African American men are not only the result of various micro- (e.g., social interactions) and macrolevel factors (e.g., institutional racism), but also serve as psychological and/or cognitive antecedents of various behaviors and attitudes displayed by some young African American men. Returning to the Barack Obama example, from this perspective, it is likely that his experiences as a native Hawaiian have not only helped to shape his identities as a man, a father, a husband and a world leader, but these identities may equally inform many of his behaviors and attitudes in these roles.

Social interactions and social context, then, inform the behaviors and attitudes of African American persons as well. For example, some research has shown that participation in delinquent acts, poor identification with school, psychological distress or depression, and inappropriate sexual/gender-based attitudes and activities among young African Americans have been associated with perceptions of negative social interactions along with negative perceptions of their own communities (e.g., racial discrimination, limited community resources, peer substance abuse) (Cunningham 1999; Cunningham, Swanson, Spencer, and Dupree 2003; Paxton, Robinson, Shah, and Schoeny 2004; Stevens-Watkins and Graves 2011). This claim has been demonstrated for young African American men. One study in particular (Swanson, Cunningham, and Spencer 2005) found that the salience of bravado attitudes displayed by young African American men was predicted by low positive teacher expectations. This finding illustrates the link between the microsystemic context (i.e., school) of African American men and their gender-based identity development. That is, the more negatively a young African American person perceives aspects of his or her microsystem or mesosystem, the more likely he or she will engage in maladaptive behaviors. It is very likely that the perceptions of their respective contexts shape how the beliefs and values that the individuals holds about him or herself (i.e., "I" and "Me" identities).

With findings such as those listed above, to date, there is some research demonstrating the association between how young African American men think about themselves and their race-based social group, and how these thoughts are often derived from social interactions, perceptions of others, and contextual factors such as racism. While these findings are consistent with the early writings of classic psychologists such as James, Mead, Tajfel, and Erikson, wherein social identity was seen as a by-product of one's interaction with social others within one or several contexts, the classic and contemporary literature on identity has not thoroughly investigated the multiple identities of young African American men or the role that various contextual factors such as racism serves as a constant in the lives of this population. That is, within the social sciences, including psychology and sociology, there is little theoretical, conceptual, or empirical research capturing the synergistic totality of African American male identity or the contextual factors that inform them. To be sure, numerous research articles and book chapters in the last twenty years have proposed and conducted examinations of African American racial/ethnic, gender role/sexual, and academic/occupational identity correlates (French, Seidman, Allen, and Aber 2000, 2006; Isom 2007; Oyserman, Harrison, and Bybee 2001). Much of the identity research during this time period, however, has focused primarily on racial identity among African Americans (Cokley 2005; Ford-Harris and Harris 1997).

Beyond racial identity, however, researchers have only begun to examine the presence of additional identity components among African American men, such as gender, sexual, and academic identities (DeCuir-Gunby 2009). Given its link to the social category of race, it is plausible that racial identity reflects what Erikson would refer to as the social identity and therefore, is a worthy identity component for discussion in the educational, sociological, and psychological literatures. Indeed, among many African Americans, it is customary to acknowledge racial heritage, particularly when there is a palpable set of characteristics that speak specifically to such a heritage. Even President Barack Obama admits to omitting his biracial background and identifying almost exclusively as a "black American" as a result of his suspicion that other would believe that he was "ingratiating" himself to White persons (see *Dreams from my Father*, Obama 2004).

Thus, given that it is perhaps the most ostensible aspect of African American men's identity, it should be expected that racial identity is largely omnipresent within the identity development literature. However, other components of social identity are only beginning to be more fully articulated and discussed in these literatures for this population. As social identity is predicated on membership in specific social groups, it is important to consider that, for young African American men, there may be several social groups to which they belong and thus, several social identities and corresponding values and behaviors that require fuller consideration.

For example, as male adolescents and adults, young African American men have a gender identity. As individuals who bare aesthetic characteristics which may suggest an African lineage, along with various attitudes and feelings about being African American, young African American men have a racial identity. As heterosexual, homosexual, transgendered, bisexual, or asexual beings, young African American men have a sexual identity. As members of a specific group of individuals with distinguishable and multiple ethnic and cultural values and worldviews (Cohen 2009; Tyler, Uqdah, et al. 2008), young African American men have cultural and ethnic identities. As members of families that fall within a certain socioeconomic strata, young African American men have a socioeconomic identity. Finally, as students enrolled in academic institutions ranging from middle school to graduate school, young African American men acquire an academic identity or a sense of who they are as students and learners (DeCuir-Gunby 2009).

As previously mentioned, these multiple identities—stemming from memberships in various social groups (academic decathlon member, hip-hop dance troupe, etc.)—reflect what James, Erikson, and others referred to as social identity. However, the academic, cultural, gender, racial, ethnic, socioeconomic, and sexual identities of young African American men can also reflect the ego and personal identity components (i.e., the I-self), as articulated by Erikson. For instance, racial identity research has long suggested that many of the statuses inherent to the leading model of racial identity development are exhibited through an individual's behaviors (Cross 1991). Thus, racial identity—in accordance with Erikson's description—may be a reflection of personal identity or an individual's view of him or her "self" (i.e., his or her "I-self"). Similarly, academic identity could reflect a social identity wherein a young African American male student is identified as a student because he is at school. Yet, academic identity could also reflect Erikson's personal identity component wherein the young African American male student determines the type of student he is by comparing himself to other students or by simply assessing—through examination of past academic activities and experiences—the type of student he believes himself to be (DeCuir-Gunby 2009).

Clearly, the current literature provides some details into the multiple identities extant among young African American men. Yet, even among these works, there is little investigation of the possible associations among these multiple identities or whether these identities are corollaries of contextual factors such as racism or heterosexism. For instance, component four of Spencer's (1995) PVEST model (stable coping responses: emergent identities) highlights cultural, sex role or gender, and personal identities as the emergent identities that follow the negotiation of risk contributors and stress-inducing contextual factors such as racism. The model does not, however, articulate whether these multiple identities are or can be associated with each other. In a similar vein, some research has investigated the synergistic associations among these identities and how these combinations influence academic and psychological outcomes (Oyserman, Bybee, and Cokley 2005; Terry 2003; and Oyserman, Gant, and Ager 1995). However, the majority of the literature regarding African American male identity has often examined these multiple identities one at a time and independent of one another.

To review, this chapter focused on elucidating and unpacking the term identity and its various sources. Since its initial conceptualization by William James, identity has undergone several iterations and conceptualization by a variety of social scientists. Their works, past and present, have allowed researchers and laypersons to consider identity on at least two planes, the personal—which focuses on those cognitive, affective, and behavioral factors that make an individual unique and the social—which focuses on the characteristics an individual shares with and within a particular social group. In addition, the research on identity and identity development has been convincing in its discussion of various factors that shape identity, one of which is the context, including but not limited to interactions with social others.

These factors have certainly and rightfully set the tone for the types of discussions social scientists ought to have with the topic of identity and identity development. With all of the data highlighting the myriad social, academic, and health challenges of young African American men, it is surprising that only a few conceptual models have sought to investigate how various contextual factors such as racism and poverty can influence salient personal and social identities of this population (Spencer 2008; Garcia-Coll et al. 1996). Even among these frameworks, however, is minimal discussion of the multiple social identities that young African American men possess which are often impacted by the social and contextual conditions within their given microsystems. Along with the omission of how contextual factors influence these multiple identities (rather than just one or another), there is also a dearth of discussion that touches upon the possible associations among the multiple personal and social identities possessed by young African American men.

For example, it is widely known (and further discussed in the following chapter) that racism is a constant presence in the lives of African Americans. Hence, does racism impact solely the racial identity of young African American men or does it equally impact academic identity or athletic identity? In addition, is being poor associated with how young African American men think about how well they would do in college? Does racial identity have some influence on what young African American men believe it means to be a gay or heterosexual man? A scholar/student? An athlete? These questions and others have not been thoroughly addressed within the social science literature.

Part of the reason for this limitation is the absence of a conceptual framework that recognizes the presence of the multiple social identities, all of which may be linked to various social interaction and contextual factors such as racism. For example, experiences with racial discrimination can influence and alter the beliefs a young African American man holds about 1) being a man, 2) being an African American man, 3) being an educated African American man, 4) being an athletic African American man, 5) being a gay, heterosexual, or bisexual African American man, and 6) being a poor, middle-class, or wealthy African American man or 7) any combination of the above. These experiences with contextual factors such as racism can also influence that young man's feeling about what it means to be within the African American ethnic group and African American culture.

It is plausible that, without a conceptual model to uncover these multiple identities, greater misunderstanding of the impact of such racist experiences on young African American men's identities may result. At minimum, the social identities of young African American men need to be explored and articulated in a manner which 1) supports their simultaneous existence while 2) debating how racism and its corollaries may have confluence not only on these multiple social identities, but their resulting psychological and behavioral outcomes.

In closing, I return to the President Barack Obama example offered in the beginning. Mr. Obama is currently the 44th president of the United States. However, that is not all that he is. He is more than his experiences with racism from his adolescent years to his campaign for a second term as U.S. president. President Barack Obama is more than just an African American man. He is more than athletic. He is more than a democrat. There is so much more to his social identity, so many more social categories within his existence. It is easy, yet narrow-minded to think of him simply as an African American man who battles various forms of racism and their impact on his behaviors and ideas. However, a careful read of the social science research would demonstrate that this very perspective is often utilized when we consider the lives and identities of many young African American men. In psychology, we know and study how African American men cope with racism, disenfranchisement, etc. (with some research noting that our "adaptive" strategies aren't working so well). Yet, like Obama's characterization, there's simply more to who we are than our racial heritage and bouts with racism. There needs to be a conceptual model that explores this claim deeply. While greater discussion of the identities young African American men possess is offered later in the text, more immediately presented is an in-depth discussion of racism as a concept, as a process, and as a salient contextual factor in the lives of African Americans, particularly African American men.

FOUR

"Don't Call Me Nigger, Whitey!"

Racism and the Lives of African American Men

RACISM AS CONTEXT FOR IDENTITY DEVELOPMENT

Perhaps the strongest contribution to the discussion of racism as a concept and contextual factor in the lives of Americans, particularly African American men comes from the article "Racism, Mental Health, and Mental Health Practice" by Drs. Chalmer Thompson and Helen Neville (1999), published as a "Major Contribution" in *The Counseling Psychologist*. Though other works have certainly offered conceptual models and discussions of racism, its manifestation through overt and microaggressive behaviors, and its impact on the behaviors and well-being of different people of color in the United States (Clark, Anderson, Clark, and Williams 1999; Harrell 1997; Jones 1997; Sue et al. 2007), Thompson and Neville provide the most comprehensive discussion of the topic. They begin with the discussion of race and its varied interpretations from the first half of the twentieth century. Here, the authors recapitulate that race was initially viewed as a biological construct, specifically where one's aesthetic characteristics were brought about by genetics. Within the second half of the twentieth century, social scientists began to move beyond this belief as it was argued that the meaning of race and racial categories was determined largely by the sociohistorical relationships found among varying racial groups (Thompson and Neville 1999). The authors cite Cox (1970) who provided a reliable and broad definition of race. Cox (1970) writes "Race may be thought of as . . . any people who are distinguished . . . in social relations with other peoples, by their physical characteristics" (402).

Though many persons of color, particularly African Americans, had long been victims of violence and prejudicial treatment as a result of their physical characteristics, chiefly the color of their skin, according to Thompson and Neville (1999), race relations and the term racism itself did not appear in the scientific literature until the 1940s. In particular, the authors credit Cox (1948) for the initial articulation of what has come to be known as racism. Racism, according to Cox, focused on the existence of a social attitude that stigmatized a group of people for the purpose of exploiting both them and their resources (Thompson and Neville 1999). Since Cox's initial treatment, other social scientists have extended the definition of racism to include an institutional mechanism and an ideological belief that justifies its existence (Thompson and Neville 1999). For example, Clark and colleagues (1999) define racism as "the beliefs, attitudes, institutional arrangements, and acts that tend to denigrate individuals or groups because of phenotypic characteristics or ethnic group affiliation" (805).

To indoctrinate racism as just, its pioneers had to transform it from a set of social attitudes into a set of ideological beliefs and practices that were present across several U.S. institutions, including religion, government, commerce, health/medicine, and education. That is, to buy into the fact that hating and thus, enslaving, abusing, raping, or killing another human being is justified because he or she is perceived as dirty or inferior or lesser than or a detriment to the existence of your own people often required these messages to be disseminated beyond word of mouth and therefore, spread through messages put forth by these mainstream institutions. Moving beyond Cox's (1948) initial conceptualization of racism as a societal ideology that stigmatizes, marginalizes, and in many cases, kills those who are different, Thompson and Neville (1999) offer three assumptions about racism. Racism consists of four forms including individual, institutional, cultural, and environmental; racism has structural and ideological components; and racism has evolved over generations and across geographical regions. The first two assumptions will be reviewed here.

Thompson and Neville (1999) refer to Dr. James Jones' (1981) articulation of three forms of racism and discuss a fourth form. Though additional forms of racism have been identified (see Clark et al. 1999; Sue et al. 2007), James (1981) identifies three forms of racism, individual, institutional, and cultural racism. A fourth form, environmental, is offered in the work of Chavis (1993). Individual racism refers to personal situations where the distribution of goods and services are withheld from a person, based on his or her racial minority status and/or his or her physical characteristics, which are assumed to be part of a racial minority status (i.e., darker skin being equated with African lineage). An example of individual racism is the refusal of service to a person of color or the suspicion of wrongdoing projected onto a person of color as a result of racist, negative stereotypes that presume such behavior with this population. Another example of individual racism is physical abuse resulting from the hatred toward a person whose physical characteristics, most notably skin tone, are different from that of the would-be assailant. This form of individual racism seeks to degrade and/or humiliate the individual based on his or her racial group membership (Thompson and Neville 1999). Thompson and Neville also refer to this form of individual racism as "everyday racism," (Essed 1991) or racial microaggressions where the victims' exposure to mundane, but impactful and cumulative racist acts, are perceived as ordinary or even habitual occurrences.

Institutional racism refers to the policies, practices, and norms that aid in the marginalization of racial minority group members in an attempt to maintain inequality and therefore, White dominance (James 1981; Thompson and Neville 1999). Here, institutions such as government, education, and media create policies and practices that ultimately restrict life opportunities among persons of color, namely African Americans. These policies and practices are established and executed by individuals who believe they are justified in maintaining a social dominance hierarchy, with themselves at the top and racial minority group members well beneath their status. Institutions maintain the status quo of racial inequality through the promulgation of the biased, self-serving messages and practices of those seeking to remain in power.

For example, in education, racism has found its way into the classroom, namely by omitting important historical contributions by persons of color or lionizing the contributions of White Americans while not completely offering the larger pictures of their history, which for many, included mass murder (Loewen 2008). In psychology, the historical contributions of largely White social scientists are made paramount in comparison to those early psychologists who were also African American. Moreover, Guthrie (2003) writes that much of what is considered common knowledge in psychology, as far as theory and scientific knowledge and practice are concerned, are based primarily on the experiences of White psychologists, their White participants, and in some cases, their White lab rats and pigeons. Thus, the institution has long been an instrument in the conservation of White supremacy and dominance. In particular, institutions such as education have used social sciences and history to convey a message of the benevolent White travelers and the savage persons of color for centuries.

A third form of racism is cultural racism (James 1981; Thompson and Neville 1999). Cultural racism is defined as the conscious or unconscious belief that White cultural values are normative and thus, superior to those among racial minorities in the United States (Thompson and Neville 1999). Similar to the term ethnocentric monoculturalism, which is the belief that one's cultural heritage is superior to that of another individual's from another racial or ethnic group (Sue 2004), cultural racism focuses on delegitimizing or distorting the culture-based practices of one group and having those replaced by another set of practices, namely practices endorsed by those in power. Thus, within the institutions that promote the superiority of White persons is the agenda seeking to have those individuals who are discriminated against adopt the cultural practices and preceding worldviews of White persons. An example of cultural racism, according to the authors includes references to classical music and literature as "high culture" whereas other musical and literary genres are considered on a much lower level (Thompson and Neville 1999).

Lastly, environmental racism occurs when the health and well-being of ethnic minority populations are compromised as a result of policies and practices that endanger the communities to which these persons are predominant residents (i.e., low-income communities). Thompson and Neville (1999) use Chavis' (1993) definition where environmental racism is considered "racial discrimination in environmental policy-making [and] . . . in the official sanctioning of the life-threatening presence of poisons and pollutants in communities of color" (3). Evidence of this is provided in the following: in 1983, the United States Governing Accounting Office conducted a study where they found significant correlations between the presence of hazardous waste landfills and the percentage of African Americans residing in the communities where the landfills were located. Additional evidence in provided by Dr. Robert Bullard who has led the charge against environmental racism for well over two decades. One of his most recent cases involved an African American family in Dickson, Tn. who filed suit over the practices of local waste treatment facilities that claimed there were no carcinogens in the drinking and bathing water of the residents. The family claimed that the water well—which was 500 feet away from the waste treatment facilities and which supplied their bath and drinking water—was linked to their family members diagnoses of cancer (Bullard, Mohai, Saha, and Wright 2007).

The propagation of these various forms of racism in the United States—individual, institutional, and cultural racism in particular—were largely the result of structural and ideological components discussed by Thompson and Neville (1999). That is, the legality of one man to refuse service or to even assault another man as a result of his skin color (i.e., individual racism) occurred because of the social policies and practices (i.e., institutional racism) enacted by persons who justified such treatment as a result of the belief that they—as a racial group—were better and therefore, entitled to better treatment than those from different races (i.e., cultural racism). Similarly, the belief that African Americans do not deserve fair treatment and in fact, are better off as slaves or at least second-class citizens comes from an institutionalized ideology or set of beliefs that have maintained the inferiority of African Americans and the superiority of Whites.

Thus, for Thompson and Neville, the structural and ideological components of racism are central to the exhibition of the various forms of racism. That is, in order for these various forms of racism to work, there must be a central set of ideological beliefs affirming the superiority of Whites. Also, there must be the ability to execute plans that reflect such beliefs at both microsystemic (i.e., one-on-one interaction) and macrosystemic (i.e., media representation and reporting levels). Thompson and Neville (1999) delve further into this idea.

Specifically, Thompson and Neville dismiss earlier conceptualizations of racism (i.e., Cox 1948) because they omit the role that institutions have in the continued proliferation of hatred toward racially different others. The authors cite Smith (1995) who stated that the structural component of racism is necessary for its continuation. Smith (1995) writes that "One racial group must have the relative power—the *capacity* to impose its will in terms of policies. . . . Without this relative power relationship, racism is a mere sentiment because although group A may wish to subordinate group B, it lacks the effective power to do so" (143).

For Thompson and Neville (1999), such power comes from the laws, policies, and institutions which reinforce the political and economic domination of White persons and the privilege they receive as a result of being the racial group that predominates political, educational, and economic institutions. As individuals who have, as a racial group, amassed the highest amount of wealth (chiefly as a result of involvement in chattel slavery, which essentially provided a 200-year head start between White and African Americans in the race toward economic dominance), and have had an overwhelming majority representation throughout all institutions in this country, particularly in politics and economics, it is clear that White persons have had the money, the representation, and the policies necessary to maintain the subordination of persons of color in this country, particularly African Americans (Thompson and Neville 1999).

Thus, the structures that maintain racism include more than just persons who abhor African Americans, the color of their skin, their music, culture, or belief systems. Rather, this hatred for African Americans had to be institutionalized so that the widespread subjugation and annihilation of this racial group was more than just a "wish" or shared opinion by some White persons, but also a set of policy initiatives and eventually, a set of laws. When we consider much of the early Jim Crow laws during the 100 years between the Reconstruction era and the passing of the Civil Rights Act, it is clear that racism was not only alive and well among *most* White persons, but its enactment—through discriminatory policies and practices—was legal for *all* White persons. The political structures within institutions such as government, commerce, and education—and the wealthy White men in charge of them during the twentieth century—allowed racism to have such widespread impact, particularly among those poorer Whites who saw legal segregation from and discrimination toward African Americans as a means to help them achieve their idealized selves (Thompson and Neville 1999).

Today, a slightly different argument can be made. That is, while *most* White persons do not exhibit explicit forms of racism against African Americans, the system of privilege resulting from racist institutional practices that marginalize African Americans is still effective for and beneficial to *all* White persons. This is due, in large part, to the structural components of racism that pervade most institutions Americans participate in.

Along with a structural component, Thompson and Neville (1999) propose that racism also contains an ideological component. For Thompson and Neville, the ideological component of racism justifies the structural component of racism that is designed to keep victims of institutional racism at their perceived marginalized statuses. It does this by providing a rationale (if you can consider discrimination on the basis of skin color "rational") for the various forms of racism in the first place. Defined as a system of beliefs characteristic of a particular group (Williams 1977, as cited in Thompson and Neville 1999), ideology is the thinking that often precedes the creation of structures that allow racism to grow and flourish into the debauched and immoral system of oppression that it is.

Most racist ideologies include 1) negative and false representations about African Americans and other racial minority groups, particularly as culturally and intellectually inferior beings and 2) images and reflections of those in power (i.e., White persons) as superior and thus, the standard to which others from different racial groups ought to be compared. Perhaps the best articulation of how these racist ideologies have played out in the development of racism as a societal system of oppression comes from Thompson and Neville (1999):

> American racism began and continues to evolve as a means to subjugate its targets for the purpose of gratifying the economical, social, and psychological needs of mainly wealthy Whites. Racism accomplishes its objective of domination by relying on efforts to erase or deemphasize the malevolence of the perpetrator; consequently, many Whites in early America had to craft people of color as less human than themselves or merely deserving of mistreatment. Thus, for White American settlers to secure land in the New World from Native Americans, profit fiscally from the labor of enslaved Africans, and protect their prosperity from Asians and Mexicans, a host of measures were employed to sanction these actions. For example, stereotypical images of the savage Native American, the docile and childlike African, the dirty Mexican, and the conspiring or heathen Asian helped to portray the subjugated as inferior, and by implication, deserving of domination and exploitation. (180)

IMPACT OF RACISM ON AFRICAN AMERICANS

While Thompson and Neville (1999) dive even deeper into a discussion of racism, including how some Whites actually preserve racism through various defense mechanisms and other discussions, it is important to turn to the impact that racism can have on African Americans. Discussion of the impact of racism on the identity components of young African American men will be reserved for later chapters. However, prior to such a discussion, it is important to more fully understand the impact that racism—as a contextual factor (given its ubiquity within U.S. institutions and its "everyday" occurrence among African Americans)—has on the lives of many African Americans, particularly African American men.

Harrell (2000) discusses six forms of racism-related stress in her conceptual model of racism: *racism-related life events* (e.g., racial profiling leading to police harassment and/or following of suspected teenager Trayvon Martin), *vicarious racism experiences* (e.g., Trayvon Martin murder, where there was a collective understanding, at least among most persons of color, that racism was a central component to the initiation of that day's events), *daily racism microstressors*, which are similar to Jones' (1981) everyday racism and Sue et al. (2007) micro aggressions, where small, but damaging interactions and events remind African Americans of their marginalization in the United States (e.g., the following of Trayvon Martin on his way home as a result of one's racist suspicion of him), *chronic-contextual stress* (e.g., the belief that Trayvon Martin and those like him did not belong or live in the gated community in which he was murdered), *collective experiences of racism* (e.g., the sociopolitical statement made by many Americans, particularly African American to don "hoodies" in protest of the Trayvon Martin tragedy), and the *transgenerational transmission of group traumas* (e.g., the explanations offered to my son regarding racism and being an African American man; the same conversation I had with my own father as a teenager).

As Clark and colleagues (1999) point out in their conceptual model of racism effects, the perception of a given context (or an interaction or microaggression) as racist can lead to various coping responses, which either reduce or exacerbate the psychological and physiological stress responses, both of which are determined by what I consider "person-centered" factors such as one's skin tone (i.e., constitutional factors), socioeconomic status (i.e., sociodemographic factors), self-esteem (i.e., psychological factors), and anger suppression-expression (i.e., behavioral factors). These person-centered factors are automatically present upon having a racist encounter or even the perception of racism (Clark et al. 1999) because they are part of the individual experiencing the racism. They are who the individual is, even in the absence of an actual racist event or perception of racism.

Once the racist act or perception of racism occurs, Clark et al. (1999) posit in their model that it is how we cope with these racism-based stressors that determines likely psychological and physiological responses and subsequent behavioral outcomes. For Clark et al. (1999), adaptive (e.g., seeking social support) and maladaptive (e.g., lashing out, self-destructive behavior such as substance abuse) coping strategies aid in determining the type of psychological and physiological responses persons will have to the racist encounter or perception of racism. The authors list some psychological stress-related responses including anger, paranoia, anxiety, frustration, resentment, and fear (Clark et al. 1999). Physiological responses to racism-related stress are said to impact the immune system, cardiovascular functioning, and the neuroendocrine system (Clark et al. 1999). In both cases, how victims or observers of racist acts cope with racism-related stressors will inform the types of psychological responses they have, which will, in turn, inform their behavioral responses and resulting health outcomes (Clark et al. 1999; Harrell 2000).

Application of this conceptual model can be made with the Trayvon Martin tragedy. Here, the *environmental stimulus* could be the following of Trayvon by the shooter. Trayvon Martin's *person-centered factors* (i.e., African American, male, tall, dressed in manner consistent with African American youth culture, walking toward his home in a gated community, being perceived as "out-of-place") were factors that may have led to him being followed in the first place, despite the fact that there was nothing inappropriate or wrong with his own behaviors. While accounts regarding the confrontation between Trayvon Martin and the shooter are not fully known, it is likely that Trayvon perceived his pursuit by the shooter as evidence of being racially profiled or in his mind, according to eyewitness testimony, stalked by a sexual predator. Thus, this *perception of racism*—coupled with person-centered characteristics such as being a teenager, taller than the shooter, etc.—may have resulted in the confrontation *coping response*. That is, as a 6'3" 17-year-old young man, it is likely that Trayvon confronted the shooter as a result of being racially profiled by him. An 11-year-old African American boy would not likely have done the same thing because he would have likely been smaller than the shooter, not as strong as the shooter, and probably would not have been exposed to this degree of racism demonstrated by the shooter.

Explanations regarding Trayvon Martin's coping response of confrontation are speculative, but worthy of exploration. Trayvon Martin confronted the shooter possibly as a result of his perception of being racially profiled by the shooter. The pursuit may have led Trayvon to believe that his life was in danger. This belief may have emerged from Trayvon's own socialization, specifically with his parents, father Tracy Martin in particular, who had likely discussed with him the dangers of being an African American man in the United States. Thus, Trayvon may have been exposed to one of his dad's own stories of how young African American men tend to get followed because they are considered suspicious. Perhaps such a conversation included the idea that no man should ever be followed, and when he is, he has a right to confront his pursuant. Worse, however, is the possibility that this conversation may have never occurred between Trayvon and his dad and the only thing Trayvon knew was that someone who did not initially make his intentions explicit was following him. (As an African American father, I am certain the conversation did occur. However, I could never be sure from my vantage point of observed) Trayvon's coping response, as a result of *his* perception of racism, was to confront the shooter. It is important to note what Clark and colleagues, along with other (i.e., Harrell 2000; Sue et al. 2007) have argued in their respective works, namely that it is the personal perception of racism, not its verification through the observations and/or testimonies of others, that matter in the development of coping responses and subsequent behaviors. Also noteworthy is the fact that some research has shown that some behavioral responses African Americans have to racial discrimination include speaking up (Barksdale, Farrug, and Harkness 2009). In Trayvon eyes, his pursuit by the shooter could have been racially motivated and thus, his coping response of confrontation was culturally appropriate.

Thus, it is tenable to believe that Trayvon was likely exposed to this racism-related stressor because it was likely what *he* felt (i.e., everyday racism; being treated suspiciously), even before he confronted the shooter. Upon confronting the shooter, after the shooter followed Trayvon it is likely that another set of racism-related stressors emerged (i.e., the shooter may have called Trayvon a "nigger"—racism-related life events or been referred to as a "punk who always gets away"—daily racism microstressors; Harrell 2000). What happens subsequently only the shooter knows now. However, given Clark et al.'s (1999) model, it is likely that the Trayvon Martin tragedy followed, to some degree, the directions and hypotheses offered in their conceptualization of racism and its impact on African Americans.

Beyond the speculation and limited anecdotal evidence supplied in the Trayvon Martin tragedy, the research on perceptions of racism-related stressors (e.g., racial discrimination, perceived racism) has been ongoing in the psychological literature for several decades. The research program of Dr. Robert Sellers has sought to uncover the impact of perceived racism and racial discrimination on the well-being of African Americans. Specifically, research by Sellers and Shelton (2003) showed that more than half of the 267 African American college student sample had reported at least thirteen racial hassles in the past year, with the majority of these racism-related stressors categorized as "everyday racism" (e.g., being treated rudely or ignored), while the less frequently occurring racism-related factors being more explicit forms such as being called a name. Notably, African American male participants reported significantly more reports of everyday racism than their female counterparts. These reports were statistically associated with negative outcomes such as psychological distress. These findings were consistent with the conceptual model presented by Clark and colleagues (1999) and Harrell (2000).

Another study by Sellers, Caldwell, Schmeelk-Cone, and Zimmerman (2003) examining the associations among racial identity, racial discrimination reports, perceived stress, and psychological distress yielded findings consistent with the Clark et al. (1999) conceptual model of racism. In particular, their study with 555 young African American adults showed that perceptions of racial discrimination were linked to increased stress, and increased psychological responses such as heightened anxiety and depression reports (Sellers et al. 2003). Sellers and colleagues (2006) conducted a later study with 314 African American adolescents and found that not only were everyday racism stressors (e.g., being treated suspiciously or as if you were stupid) most frequently reported by the sample, but such reports were also associated with psychological distress and lower levels of psychological well-being. Findings such as these have been corroborated more recently in a longitudinal study by Seaton, Neblett, Upton, Hammond, and Sellers (2011). There, the authors examined the reports of 560 African American youth and showed that reports of racial discrimination perceptions were predictive of lower psychological well-being reports (Seaton et al. 2011).

Additional findings have provided evidence to support the association between contextual factors like racial discrimination and their corresponding behavioral outcomes. For example, Klonoff, Landrine, and Ullman (1999) found that, among a sample of African American adults, over 95 percent experienced some racial discrimination within the past year. In a study that actually employed the Clark et al. (1999) conceptual model as a framework to guide their own research, Swim and colleagues (2003) uncovered that experience of racism for over half of the fifty-one African American college student participants occur, on average twice a month. In both studies, such experiences with racism were linked to psychological distress and subsequent maladaptive behaviors (e.g., anger, increased perceptions of threat), many of which may have been the result of altered self-perceptions. That is, these negative contextual experiences may have negatively impacted their coping responses and the self-perceptions participants had of themselves.

Additional researchers have found similar associations between perceptions of racism and psychological and behavioral outcomes for African American populations (Brody et al. 2006; Caldwell, Kohn-Wood, Schmeelk-Cone, Chavous, and Zimmerman 2004; Kessler, Mickelson, and Williams 1999; Neblett, Philip, Cogburn, and Sellers 2006; Neville, Heppner, Ji, and Thye 2004; Scott and House 2005; Seaton and Yip 2009; Utsey, Chae, Brown, and Kelly 2002; Williams, Neighbors, and Jackson 2003). In brief, Neville et al. (2004) and Bynum, Burton, and Best (2007) found statistically significant associations between race-related stress and psychological distress among African American college students attending predominantly White institutions (PWIs) of higher learning; Caldwell et al. (2003) found that perceptions of racial discrimination were predictive of violent behavior reports among African American adolescents.

Similar findings have emerged among studies examining even younger African American students, namely those in middle and high school. Specifically, Harris-Britt, Valrie, Kurtz-Costes, and Rowley (2007) found that perceptions of racial discrimination were negatively associated with self-esteem among eighth grade African American adolescents, although the relationship between these two factors were contingent on the amount of racial pride socialization received by parents. Also, Patcher, Bernstein, Szalacha, and Garcia-Coll (2010) found that 88 percent of African American middle grade and high school level students (ages 8–16) had reported at least one experience with racial discrimination, one of which was being accused of wrongdoing, which left many students with the feeling that they were persecuted because of their race.

Regarding young African American men, a study by Nyborg and Curry (2003) found that experiences with racism were linked to lower self-concept and high levels of hopelessness. A later study of young African American men by Bynum and colleagues (2008) showed that African American men with more negative attitudes toward being Black reported greater psychological issues, namely anxiety symptoms. The authors in that study speculate that such attitudes and overall psychopathology may be linked to participants' exposure to racism (Bynum, Best, Barnes, and Burton 2008). Another study employing over 700 participants in the Black and African American Men's Health (BAAMH) dataset showed a positive association between experiences with racial discrimination and being the perpetrator of intimate partner violence with their current partner/spouse (Reed et al. 2010).

Two additional studies examined the impact of perceived racism in slightly different ways. The first study which examined African American male youth and their reports of violence propensity showed that internalized negative stereotypes or the belief to which African Americans actually endorse such stereotypes was positively associated with aggressive behavior, attitudes, and propensity toward violence (Bryant 2011). Additionally, DeGruy, Kjellstrand, Briggs, and Brennan (2012) employed a sample of 200 African American male adolescents and young adults in their study examining the role that African American racial respect or the degree to which participants felt respected as an individual and as an African American had in the exhibition of violent behaviors. The authors concluded that youth who were witnesses to violent acts and also had lower reports of African American/racial respect were more likely to engage in violent acts. That is, in an effort to maintain a strong sense of self-worth, especially in contexts where it is likely that one's identity may be marginalized as a result of racism, many African American men in the study and others (see Cox 2010) looked to adopting aggressive, hypermasculine attitudes and dispositions that underscored the importance of respect. What results from the adoption of these attitudes, particularly when the individual feels his membership in a specific social group (e.g., African American) is not being respected are heightened acts of violence (Degruy et al. 2012).

As discussed in the last chapter, for many African Americans, young African American men in particular, it is clear that racism—in its various forms—and racial discrimination influence their perceptions of who they are (i.e., ego and personal identity) and how others may perceive them (i.e., social identity). Yet, one major issue with the frameworks provided by Clark et al. (1999) and Harrell (2000), both of which discuss the role of racism and the development of maladaptive outcomes among African Americans, is the absence of limited articulation of those affect-based, person-centered factors that often precede the observed behaviors that follow the perceptions of racism and racist encounters. In this book, I argue that the coping strategies put forth by African Americans as a response to racism are argued to be a function of the self-perceptions (i.e., identities) that they have of themselves as individuals. Both personal and social identities of African Americans, namely young African American men, aid in the development of coping responses to racism. A more critical discussion of how this occurs and the roles that invisibility and intersectionality have in the process is provided in the next chapter.

FIVE
"Invisible Man"

Intersectionality and Invisibility as Conceptual Frameworks in the Study of African American Men's Identity

Many of my friends and colleagues from my doctoral studies days at Howard University may recall a particular interest I had in a then, relatively new Neo-Soul phenom. Miss Jill Scott. I remember first listening to *"A Long Walk"* and thinking that this is unlike anything I've heard on the radio in a while. Interestingly, I happen to remember the "arrival" of several new artists who may be considered part of the Neo-Soul movement. I remember hearing Maxwell's *Ascension (Don't Ever Wonder)* and thinking "Who the hell is this guy and why am I already thinking he's 'saved' Black music?" (I also remember thinking that "if my afro had done what his did, I'd likely still have it). I remember first hearing Erykah Badu and then seeing the video for *"On and On."* Somehow, that deep bass groove was not hip-hop, but also wasn't R and B. It was like it almost didn't fit the current scope of Black music, as my then abbreviated understanding of it would show. Musiq Soulchild, Bilal (*"Sometimes"* will never get old). India Arie. Kindred the Family Soul. I was and am very happy to state that, indirectly, I witnessed an explosion of multitalented artists that, in their inclusion within the unofficial "Black music" genre, literally had to be given a new category.

Yet, there was one who caught my eye. Jill Scott. More than just her beauty and talent, both of which are immeasurable in my eyes, I think I fell in love with the fact that she was in love then. How she sang *"Lyzel in E flat"* on "The Oprah Winfrey Show." That beautiful face singing beautiful words about a beautiful woman in love. I was hooked. I reluctantly but finally retired the Jill Scott 826+ Experience poster (yes, it was in a glass and wood frame for about 8 years or so). I also remember being at that concert where she recorded the aforementioned album. Constitution Hall, Washington D.C. Seats were ok, floor, near the aisle. I remember just watching and listening and just truly blessed to have experienced her concert and magnificent show she gave.

When she and the band performed "Lyzel in E flat" at that concert, it seemed like it was an ode to several genres of music, one of which was house music. Being a Chicagoan since birth, when that sound hits, it is instinctive to dance. So, I grabbed my son's mom and headed to the aisle. Most stayed in their seats to dance to the rhythmic tune. I needed aisle space. Needless to say, my son's mom and I were pretty much alone in those aisles as folks weren't as crazy as I to venture to the makeshift dance floor. I felt I had nothing to lose as it was the encore performance. To this day, one of my signature (and very few) bragging rights is that there's one part in that song on the live concert album where Jill Scott says "Get it, y'all." It was at that moment that I realized (or at least strongly believe) that Jill recognized my existence. She had to have recognized us, as we were the only standouts dancing in the aisle at the close of her concert.

Another recollection I have is the going away party my colleagues and friends had for me prior to taking an Assistant Professor position at the University of Kentucky in 2004. I distinctly remember one of my gifts being an *Essence* magazine with Jill Scott on the cover. I had also received Ms. Scott's book of poetry one year later from a close colleague and friend. I didn't realize that my appreciation of Jill Scott's artistry was so obvious. Apparently, however, some folks knew what I thought of her. In fact, if one of these former colleagues from Howard happened to enter my office at the time of this writing, he/she would find two *Ebony* magazines, both with Jill Scott on the cover.

I could assure him or her, along with the reader, that, while I still have a deep appreciation for Ms. Scott and her body of work, I purchased these two magazines (June 2011 and May 2013) for their additional content. No, seriously. In the June 2011 issue, *Ebony* published an article entitled "The State of Today's Black Men" (Johnson 2011). In the article, the author, Jeff Johnson, engages the reader by arguing that the presented articles will not be a continuation of the bleak statistics concerning African American men, but rather a unique concentration on those African American men who have personified "the legacy of Black intellects and servants from generations past" (Johnson 2011, 102). As part of an effort to "debunk the myths regarding the low-achieving Black man" (Johnson 2011), *Ebony* magazine presents several pages of stories illustrating the lives and work of many African American men in various fields and disciplines (e.g., media, education, politics) who have not only beaten the odds, but in their stories, share strategies and ideas that may enable others like them to achieve as they have. Included in the series are stories of Stephen Stafford, a child prodigy who, by age 13, was enrolled in Morehouse College studying mathematics and computer science. Also highlighted is the work of David Banks, Founder of the Eagle Academy, which, since its inception, has sent 90 percent of enrolled young African American men to college.

Throughout the series of articles, it is clear that Johnson's vision has been—with the assistance of additional contributors including Margena Christian and Kevin Chappell—achieved. From hip-hop stars to reverends to African American male high school students, the message *Ebony* magazine provides is a newer, fresher look at the African American man. What was curious in this edition of the *Ebony* magazine series, however, was the presentation of "The Black Man's Game of Life" on pages 106 and 107. While illustration credits are given, there is no explicit mention of the author of this "game." The premise is similar to that of a typical board game. There is a starting point, and with a roll of a die, you begin to advance through the path to the finish line, landing on one space at a time. These spaces, much like the board game Monopoly, provide some indication of the player's current fate. Some of these "space fates" included

- Growing up, you lived with your mom and dad = +10 spaces
- Misdiagnosed your creative energy—hello, special ed = −10 spaces
- As a tall, gifted middle schooler, teachers put a basketball in your hand = +5 spaces
- In high school, you were too focused to mess with drugs or alcohol = +10 spaces
- You and your girl had a baby named Lexis = −10 spaces
- You just got your driver's license. The cops stop you. You keep your hands visible. The cops let you go = +10 spaces
- You attended a four-year college but did not graduate = Lose a turn
- You're entering the workforce: You grow locs = +5 spaces
- You apply for a job for which you are obviously overqualified. They see the HBCU (historically Black college or university) on your resume. You don't get a call = Roll again
- You're offered the position and you negotiate a higher salary, a stronger benefits package, and a 6-month review for possible promotion = +10 spaces
- You and your wife are saving for retirement and to send your kids to college = +10 spaces
- You are scraping together bail money for Lexis = −10 spaces

I will admit to playing this game in the *Ebony* magazine. To examine my "fate," I recorded each roll of the die and outcome for one particular game. On the first roll with the die showing three, I landed on "You lived with your mom. +3 spaces." Second, with a die of 6, I landed on "In your neighborhood, kids were afraid of you. –5 spaces." Then, I roll a two "As a tall, gifted middle schooler, teachers put a basketball in your hand. +5 spaces." Then, it was "In high school, you were on a first-name basis with your counselor. +5 spaces." At that point, with the five-space advance, I landed on "It's bad business to smoke your own stash. –10 spaces. Next, I rolled a six and landed on "You were on a first name basis with the detention monitor. –5 spaces." When I rolled a three, I landed on "In your neighborhood, you settled the beefs. +5 spaces." Moving ahead 5 spaces, I land on "You went to a few parties, had a couple of drinks, smoked, but didn't inhale. Lose a turn." After I sat out a turn (although playing by myself), I rolled a four and landed on "You and your girl had a baby named Lexis. –10 spaces."

Out of sheer frustration, I ended this solo game of Black Man's Life. (Incidentally, with the regression, I landed back on "In your neighborhood, kids were afraid of you. –5 spaces"). After concluding the game in a bit of a huff, my initial thoughts were to trash the magazine altogether, but the Jill Scott cover and content allowed for more rational thinking. The problem was that the closer I got toward the finish line in the game, an event or incident would occur which would literally set me back. According to this "game" and my agitation resulting in my forfeiture, I never even made it out of my high school/late adolescent years.

It was then that I realized that this authorless "game," to some degree, began to reflect the lives of some young African American men. For some of them, there are events that occur during their late childhood and adolescent years that set the tone for the course of events that will soon follow. Of course, the exact sequence of events mirroring the actual lived experiences of a member of this population or anyone who has seen and played this *Ebony* magazine game is entirely coincidental. Yet, some of these "space fates" not only occur with young African American men, but can also have implications for the next steps and opportunities afforded to them.

For example, there are data to suggest that living in a two-parent household or at least in scenarios where the fathers of young African American men are present in their lives enhance psychological, behavioral, and academic outcomes more so than single-parent, father-absent, scenarios (Harris 2002, Mandara, Rogers, and Zinbarg 2011; Rodney and Mupier 1999; Paschall, Ringwalt, and Flewelling 2003; Thomas, Krampe, and Newton 2008). For example, one study employing a sample of over 1000 African American participants found that being raised by both parents was associated with less reported marijuana use among African American male adolescents (Mandara et al. 2011). There's also evidence to suggest that a misread of a young African American man's "creative energy" and expressiveness can be interpreted as aggressive and/or deficient and thus, he is relegated to special education services (Brown 2011; Neal, McCray, Webb-Johnson, and Bridgest 2003; Howard, Flennaugh, and Terry 2012). Specifically, one study by Neal and colleagues (2003) showed that the simple behaviors of many young African American male students (e.g., walking in the hallways) were often grossly misinterpreted to the point where many of the middle school teachers—who were the primary participants in the study—reported that those African American male students who displayed such behaviors were aggressive, low-achieving, and likely in need of special education.

Neighborhood safety and school attachment (as the *Ebony* magazine game presented "In your neighborhood, kids would jump on you" and "In high school, you were on a first-name basis with your counselor," respectively) have also been discussed as significant factors in the overall outcomes of African American youth in general and young African American men in particular (Busby, Lambert, and Ialongo 2013; Riina, Martin, Gardner, and Brooks-Gunn 2013; Walsemann, Bell, and Maitra 2011). Most recently, several studies have shown that community-based stressors (e.g., reported community crime rate and violence, overt and subtle forms of discrimination) are associated with African American adolescents' reports of negative views of interpersonal relationships (Kogan et al. 2013) and their reports of aggressive behaviors and depressive symptoms. In the latter study, it was shown that reports of community violence among African American students in the sixth grade were associated with reports of aggressive behaviors displayed at the seventh grade level, which were, in turn, predictive of lower academic performance at eighth grade (Busby et al. 2013).

Like much of the literature reporting the statistics on the much believed ill-fated African American man, the *Ebony* magazine "Black Man's Game of Life" also does not provide any insight into the identity-based factors that precede most of the behaviors exhibited and activities engaged in by this population. Of course, it is intended to be a game or, at best, a statement of what the trajectory of young African American men is or can be. Yet, a major problem with this game and its satirical representation of African American men's lives is that each "space fate" or event or activity that the young African American man playing this game is subjected to is the result of the roll of a die. According to this game, chance and probability have a significant impact on the specific behaviors and overall, lives of young African American men. Having chance determine my fate, as it did when I played the game, eliminated any opportunity I had to use what I felt and knew about myself (i.e., personal identity) to make better decisions, even in spite of what negative "space fate" I landed on. In fact, in the game, there is no decision making or any evidence to suggest that how the African American man feels about himself can lead to the behaviors exhibited (or landed upon). You simply roll the die, you see what happens, and you act in accordance with what appears on the "space fate."

While there are instances where the context did actually shape the current experiences of young African American men (e.g., "You lived with your dad." "Teachers ignored you when you raised your hand."), the "game" does not allow current and subsequent actions to be linked to feelings about who the young African American man believes himself to be. What happens to him is almost exclusively behavioristic, where something happens in a given environment (i.e., environmental stimulus) and there's an immediate behavioral reaction (i.e., behavioral response) to that event. In much the same fashion that chance determines what happens next in your proverbial race to the finish line, choice, and more importantly, feelings of who you believe yourself to be and what you deem yourself capable of (i.e., personal and social identity) are never offered or viewed as an antecedent to subsequent behaviors and activities. Of course, in the field of psychology, this behavioristic mode of thinking—where the environment has complete control over the actions of the individual—has been duly replaced with theories that actively acknowledge and investigate the role of cognitive and affective factors which mediate the association between a given context and an individual's behaviors (e.g., Piaget and Inhelder 1969). The *Ebony* "Black Man's Game of Life" does not reflect what we know about the lived experiences of humans: That how we think about ourselves and others and our context can actually influence our behaviors as much if not more than the environment itself.

Ok, yes, it is clear that I took this *Ebony* magazine "game" much too seriously. However, I'd make clear to the reader that, as an African American man, I guess I took the fictitious game of Black Man's Game of Life a little serious because, as the statistics presented in this and numerous other texts show, African American men, perhaps more than any other population in the U.S., do not fare as well at this so-called game of life. At the time of this writing, the other *Ebony* magazine—with Jill Scott and her son, Jett on the cover—makes this argument abundantly clear. The article in this issue, which is the first in a slated four-part series on young African American men, grips readers with its opening statement in the article "The State of Black Boys" by Nick Chiles. It reads "Over the past couple of decades, Black boys and their problems seem to have been studied, dissected, think tanked, and pilot programmed more than any other issue involving the conditions of African Americans" (Chiles 2013, 123). The article goes on to present startling statistics including one reporting that, in the nation's capital, Washington, D.C., three out of four African American men can expect to serve time in prison. Another statistic showed that African American male high school students who drop out of school are thirty-eight times more likely to be incarcerated than those with a college degree.

As an educational psychologist, one who is moderately versed in the literature on young African American men and their school-based dilemmas in particular and their adverse life experiences in general, these statistics certainly resonate with me. Unfortunately, my budding research in this area renders me familiar with these and like statistics on this population. I am, however, taken aback by the initial claim made in the *Ebony* magazine article. Specifically, the statement by Chiles indicating that young African American men have been researched perhaps more than any other U.S. population. As I look back over the development of this book, I nod my head in full agreement with this claim.

While I am very far from an expert on the African American male experience in the U.S. or any of its correlates and corollaries, in developing this text, to prepare this work, I read dozens of books, conceptual papers, empirical journal articles, and, of course, popular media such as *Ebony* magazine. I've read more books discussing young African American men than books on educational psychology theories of learning. Some of the earliest work I cite on African American men dates back to the 1970s and 1980s. In addition to a comprehensive review of the literature, the conceptual model proposed in this book and the research aiding in its development have been consistently reviewed and revised since 2005.

Beyond my own limited research in this area, in the social sciences such as psychology, sociology, and education, it is accurate to state that many researchers have long examined the contextual, social/interpersonal, psychological (i.e., cognitive, affective), and behavioral factors which precede and result from African American men's actions and attitudes. In recent years, there's been a proliferation of scholars who, as African American men themselves, have sought to investigate the realities of this population in an attempt to change them for the better. To this end, numerous research articles and journal issues, along with the development of scholarly journal outlets (e.g., *Journal of African American Men in Education*) have been dedicated to the pursuit and presentation of research that provides greater insight into and direction for enhancing the lives of young African American men. Some school systems have created special offices and departments to better understand the schooling and overall realities of young African American men. Others have adopted charters to pursue exclusive male-adolescent schooling models, including the Carter G. Woodson Academy in Lexington, Kentucky, which is modeled after the Black Men Working program (Warren 2012). Along with these efforts, millions of dollars have been generated to fund research on this population, as well as millions in additional funds stemming from multiple philanthropic efforts (Shah and Sato 2012). In each of these cases, the purpose has been to further understand and ultimately support the betterment of African American men's lives.

Indeed, the statement made by Chiles in his article concerning how much time, effort, and resources have gone into examining and bettering the lives of African American men is definitely a stark and necessary realization. What's interesting, however, is, within the *Ebony* magazine (Chiles 2013) article, the author concludes that the plight of many young African American men can be linked to a single word: love. Specifically, the section of the article is presented here, verbatim and in the same order as presented in the article:

> *Ebony*'s investigation into the plight of our boys reveals that, to a remarkable degree, what plagues them comes down to a single word: love. Not getting it, not knowing how to ask for it, presenting a pose to the world that makes it appears [sic] as if they don't need it or want it, making the world afraid to give it. It all comes down to love.
>
> In both sifting through the reports and talking to the experts, much of the commentary points to the challenge of giving Black boys the attention, affection, care, and concern they desperately require but rarely get. Our boys suffer in silence, unable to get the thing they most wanted and need. Without love, they more easily succumb to the destructive forces that swirl around them—bad schools, poor parenting, the lure of the violent streets, the corrosive desperation of poverty and the danger and hopelessness of too many Black communities. (Chiles 2013, 123)

Initially, I am a little baffled by the overall simplicity of the theme. Over half a century, millions, if not billions of dollars, hundreds of social scientists, social workers, graduate students, school administrators, teachers, and parents and each of their countless hours of interaction, observation, and data interpretations on the experiences of young African American men and the conclusion reached is that they are not loved enough? My cynicism, however, clouds my ability to really examine the statement and possibly extend the meaning behind it. My kneejerk reaction to reading this is "yeah, it will take a lot more than *love* to truly enhance the lives of this population of which I am a member."

I, then, begin to think back onto my own development. In looking back, I notice a pattern of interactions between social others, namely my parents, my former teachers and professors, and myself. It seemed like, throughout these interactions, I felt recognized. Though I was part of a relatively big family (mother, father, two brothers and a sister) and knew I was part of something much bigger than myself, I always felt recognized and wanted, never ignored or forsaken. My parents would always listen and support, even when my ideas were plain stupid or grandiose or irrational. I still find that their living room, in front of both of them, is still the best and only place I can reveal my truest self and my strongest feelings and ideas.

A long standing story that most folks in my family know and remind me of is the time where I received a "B" grade on some assignment back in the third or fourth grade, which upset me to the point where I publicly declared "revenge" on the classroom teacher. The world has, indeed, come a long way from publicly threatening teachers with no consequences other than talking about the grade. Yet, with that teacher in particular—who did talk with me about the grade—and within my family, I felt like I was known, that aspects of my identity, including my personal and social self (i.e., my 'I' and 'Me' selves) were recognized. To start, they knew I didn't know how to handle failure well. They knew that I had some physical limitations as a child and adolescent (e.g., overweight and asthmatic) and therefore, wasn't great in any sports at the time. They knew that I was very social and friendly because I knew that nobody likes nerds and sometimes, being too smart resulted in catching beatdowns. So, I learned how to be funny and smart and yes, occasionally, allow someone to cheat off my schoolwork.

Throughout my matriculation from grade school through graduate school, I think it is fair to say that my parents and many of my teachers and a few of my college professors knew me pretty well. For my parents, I knew they loved me by their recognition of me and in their nurturance of those multiple characteristics and behaviors I would exhibit, which would soon solidify into stable identity characteristics. The old cliché, "To know me is to love me," seemed to finally make sense to me.

Yet, in pondering the veracity of the *Ebony* magazine claim that many of our African American male youth are 'unable to get the thing they most want and need' (i.e., love), I wondered whether this issue of loving being equal to recognition had any merit. Are we truly seeing and recognizing our young African American male youth? Are their shared and unique characteristics and identities recognized by the individuals who seek to assist them? Do we embrace their personal and social identities as they are or do we simply use stereotype and/or preexisting knowledge to determine how we will interact with them? Do we really even know about young African American men, at least, beyond the stereotypes that exist about them? Are psychologists and sociologists and social workers, along with teachers and school administrators truly recognizing the individual worth and idiosyncratic nature of each and every African American male adolescent and young adult they come across? As Chiles (2013) alluded to, are our young men suffering in silence because many of them did not have mentors and parents and teachers and professionals who often recognized their inherent personal and culture-based values and preferences?

With these questions, I actually find myself in agreement with *Ebony* magazine author. It is likely the case that many young African American men are not 'loved,' in the sense that they are duly acknowledged by social others as individuals whom are provided sufficient attention and whose voices and concerns are heard and addressed. To paraphrase Ralph Ellison, many young African American men are made invisible, where the knowledge of them and those within their social group are relegated almost exclusively to what is portrayed in the media and/or existing stereotypes about them. Critically portraying African American men's experiences with and stresses associated with feelings of invalidation, Ellison (1952) wrote: "I am an invisible man. . . . I am invisible, understand, simply because people refuse to see me. . . . When they approach me, they see only my surroundings, themselves, or figments of their imagination—indeed, everything and anything except me" (Ellison 1952, as cited in Franklin and Boyd-Franklin 2004).

We cannot love these individuals if we do not know them and do not allow them to inform us of who and what they think they are. In order to love someone, to care about his or her overall well-being, it is important to begin the process of truly knowing that individual. Without such knowledge, without that level of love provided to them, it is more than likely that the lives of young African American men, as the Black Man's Game of Life clearly showed me, may be left to chance.

In essence, those interested in enhancing the lives of young African American men should begin by enhancing their efforts to become truly informed about them. That is, in addition to focusing efforts and resources on reducing and eventually eliminating what have always been disheartening achievement or incarceration statistics of young African American men, educational stakeholders and social scientists should develop greater understanding of the complexities associated with being a male African American adolescent and young adult. Much like Ellison believed in the 1950s, it is very likely that many educational stakeholders and researchers including myself—an African American man—possess a very myopic and perhaps, inaccurate or incomplete perception of the young African American man.

For example, in the middle and high school years, many individuals will come across young African American men and observe how they dress (cultural identity) and assess their overall behavioral expressions and demeanor (cultural identity). A few of these observers may even assess their own level of comfort and safety based on this information (Tovar-Murray and Tovar-Murray 2012). Some may also look at these factors and surmise how well this young man does in school. This same African American male middle school or high school student, unbeknownst to the observers, may be a gifted student (academic identity) who is wrestling against societal expectations to be heterosexual (sexual identity and gender identity). He may be from a low-income family (socioeconomic identity) and have limited athletic ability (athletic identity), both of which may impact his degree of attachment with school. Finally and resulting from his peer interactions regarding his perceived sexuality, his family's socioeconomic status, and awkwardness in sports, he may also dislike being "Black" (racial identity and ethnic identity). This student—who, despite his appearance, is more than just Black and male—would not only need individuals for whom he could talk with about these issues, but would also need these individuals to have sufficient knowledge regarding these identities and their potential influence on how he comes to think of himself. *If we are to show this young African American love and support, we must first recognize all of the characteristics and factors that he possesses and are in need of that love and support.*

A framework pinpointing the multiple identities of young African American men can be a step in the right direction on this issue. Two concepts found in the psychological literature will serve as theoretical frameworks to guide the development of a conceptual model of African American male identity which articulates the presence of multiple, intersecting identities for this population. In particular, the invisibility syndrome offered by Franklin (1999) will be used to demonstrate how the multiple identities of young African American men are shaped by various contextual factors such as racism. The other concept, intersectionality, will further the understanding of the synergistic nature of these multiple identities that have, by and large, been studied independently of one another.

INVISIBILITY AND THE IDENTITIES OF YOUNG AFRICAN AMERICAN MEN

From an ecological perspective (Bronfenbrenner 1986; Spencer 1995), many of the academic, social, physical, and psychological dilemmas African American men face are the result of their exposure to and interactions with racism and oppression. This exposure to and negotiation of interpersonal and institutional experiences of racism typically result in a compromised sense of identity for African Americans (Allen-Meares and Burman 1995; Bigler, Averhart, and Liben 2003; Franklin 1999; Thompson and Neville 1999). This compromised identity has been referred to as invisibility syndrome (Franklin 1999).

Invisibility syndrome is the first conceptual framework used in the development of the proposed conceptual model of African American male identity. Invisibility "seeks to explain the intrapsychic struggle for personal identity by African American men as they confront specific, stress-inducing encounters with racism (Franklin 1999). Invisibility, according to Franklin (1999), is defined as an inner struggle with the feeling that one's talents, abilities, personality, and worth are not valued or even recognized because of the prevalence of racism in its multiple forms (Jones 2003). Invisibility is believed to emerge from overall negative attitudes and perceptions of African Americans (Franklin and Boyd-Franklin 2004). As Ellison wrote, those "figments of others' imagination" are the lenses under which many African Americans are viewed.

Franklin (1999) writes that repeated encounters with microaggressive forms of racism results in African American men feeling a) a lack of recognition or appropriate acknowledgement, b) self-doubt about legitimacy (e.g., "Should I be here?"), c) little validation from the experience (e.g., "Am I a person of worth?"), d) disrespected, e) that one's sense of dignity is compromised and challenged and f) that one's basic identity has been shaken and uprooted or at the very least, compromised (Franklin 1999). According to Franklin, African American men react to invisibility or feelings of being disrespected, unrecognized, invalidated, and dissatisfied by constantly searching for contexts and interactions where they feel accepted (Franklin 1999). When such contexts are not available or are limited in number, the development of maladaptive behaviors and/or a lowered sense of self-worth result. It is at this point that behavioral manifestations of invisibility syndrome are said to develop (Franklin and Boyd-Franklin 2004). Franklin and Boyd-Franklin (2004) write that consistent attempts in dealing with active (e.g., being called a "nigger") and more tacit forms (e.g., being told "I don't think of you as Black") of racism may result in many African Americans, particularly young African American men, developing maladaptive coping strategies and often, self-destructive behaviors such as homicide and substance abuse.

For example, it is likely that homicidal and suicidal tendencies among some African American men are the result of an identity development process saturated with feelings of being disrespected, invalidated, dissatisfied, and humiliated as an African American man. He may not feel that his personal identity has been respected (e.g., disrespect toward his decisions, thoughts, and/or beliefs) and/or he may feel that his social identities are invalidated (e.g., his capabilities as a learner or as an athlete or as a man are not being respected or recognized). These feelings, according to Franklin, are brought about by interactions with social others and are typically the result of racism. This belief regarding the role of context and interpersonal interaction in the shaping of identities and corresponding attitudes and behaviors of young African American men in particular has recently gained traction in the educational literature (Bush, and Bush 2013). Specifically, Bush and Bush (2013) employ and extend Bronfenbrenner's Ecological Systems Theory to illustrate how each of the ecological systems (microsystem, mesosystem, exosystem, macrosystem and chronosystem) influences the cognitive and social development of the young African American man. Consider the following description below.

If, for example, a young African American man feels that much of society views him as a liability rather than an asset, as an animal rather than a civilized human being, as intellectually inferior rather than cognitively stimulating and stimulated, as dependent rather than responsible, as docile rather than complex and uneducable rather than learned (Bryson 1998), it is likely that a positive sense of self (both personal and social) will not emerge. That is, those positive aspects of his personal self are rendered invisible. Thus, there is a unique and unequivocal role played by not only members of a given context (i.e., microsystem), but also by the larger cultural attitudes socialized within and beyond microsystemic circles. That is, it is likely that these feelings of inadequacy, despair, and ultimately, invisibility may emerge from actual social interactions with persons in a given context as well as from messages socialized indirectly within the more robust ecological systems (i.e,. mesosystem, exosystem, macrosystem, and chronosystem).

In addition, if that same young man does not possess identity components that are favored within society (e.g., athletic prowess, upper middle class, heterosexual, highly intelligent), then it is likely that those identities—and therefore, he—will be rendered invisible as well. With the earlier example of the young middle school student/high school student, it is likely that his emerging sexual identity (i.e., homosexual) is rendered invisible, at least largely among many African American communities (Hunter 2010), and is not, therefore, an accepted sexual identity, particularly because it is not believed to reflect positive perceptions of manhood (Harris, Palmer, and Struve 2011; Hunter 2010). Similarly, a young African American man who is tall and/or stocky may have his athletic identity focused on almost at the expense of the development of and concentration on his academic identity. Thus, his academic identity may be invisible to others and instead of seeing a tall and/or stocky scholar, most would likely assume they are observing a tall and/or stocky basketball or football player.

The absence of effective coping mechanisms resulting from these feelings of invisibility can bring about depression, disillusionment, and psychological disengagement. Soon, negative thoughts concerning his own viability, integrity, and overall, identity will emerge. Finally, most identity development theories (Erikson 1968; Freud 1949; Marcia 1966) contend that behaviors aligned with such damaging perceptions would soon follow.

While Franklin (1999) makes it clear that invisibility syndrome is largely the result of African Americans' exposure to and interaction with a racist environment, it is likely that the syndrome stems from additional contextual factors, including social others. For instance, academic performance difficulties and decisions to disengage from the schooling process—either by physically dropping out or psychologically disengaging from school—may be due to a compromised sense of identity resulting from individual, institutional, and cultural racism (Jones 1981). However, these behaviors could also likely result from students' exposure to heterosexism, monocultural ethnocentrism (Constantine and Sue 2006), or even those factors indirectly related to schooling outcomes such as activities within the classroom, community, and the home.

For example, the literature supports the idea that African American students, male students, in particular, are exposed to behaviors that reflect the lowest of teacher expectations for academic success (Ferguson 2003; Noguera 2003). These findings, coupled with overrepresentation in special education programs (Chang and Sue 2003), heightened expulsion and in-school suspension rates (Epstein, March, Conners, and Jackson 1998), and overall, frequent exposure to racial discrimination (Seaton, Caldwell, Sellers, and Jackson 2008) may result in African American male students' psychological disengagement from schooling in general and achievement-related behaviors in particular (Honora 2003). As these students are typically portrayed and even viewed by some as problematic rather than complex, unruly rather than dissatisfied, unmotivated rather than unchallenged, and feared rather than misunderstood (Irvine 1985; Isom 2007; Price 1998; Osborne 1999), it is likely that 1) some teachers will begin to interact with young African American male students with these beliefs guiding their behaviors and 2) the young African American male student may also internalize these images and messages,, and accordingly, begin to display those maladaptive coping mechanisms.

Thus, it is plausible that the negative images of young African American men may be explicit and assumed by classroom teachers, thus rendering invisible the actual feelings and attitudes held by many members of this population. That is, the academic identities of many of these students are, for Franklin (1999), invisible or otherwise, unseen by social others (i.e., some teachers) who are relevant to the students' matriculation throughout school. While racism may lie at the root of these images and beliefs held for this student population, endorsement of these beliefs is, nonetheless, expressed inadvertently or purposefully through the actions and attitudes of social others.

Invisibility stems from negative attitudes about and negative perceptions of African Americans (Franklin and Boyd-Franklin 2004). These attitudes and perceptions can lead to dangerous interactions. Such was the case with Trayvon Martin. Regardless of what happened at the time of the altercation between the shooter and Trayvon, what was clear in that scenario was the shooter's characterization of Martin, which ultimately led to Trayvon being followed by the shooter, along with the phone calls to the local police which preceded his pursuit of Trayvon. Given our race categorization as African Americans, it is likely that shared feelings of invisibility may have emerged among other African American men as a result of the perception that this young man, Trayvon Martin, was suspected of criminal activity based on his physical appearance. Many African American men, including my son, and myself, felt that "it could have been us." That no matter who we are and what we are to different people or what we do, we can be viewed as or drastically reduced to criminal, based on no incriminating evidence whatsoever. This is what happened to Trayvon Martin. This is what Ralph Ellison and Dr. Anderson Franklin were talking about. This is how invisibility manifested itself.

Perhaps Trayvon felt a reduction in his identity as a result of the shooter's pursuit and interrogation prior to the altercation that led to his tragic death. In his mind, Trayvon had no reason to be followed, and there was no reason for him to be considered a criminal, suspected of malicious and illegal activity. Perhaps, the reduction of his identity to criminal suspect and his challenge of such a reduction can serve as evidence of Martin not allowing him to be minimized to such a caricature. In fact, his question to the suspect which preceded the altercation may have been an attempt by Martin to become more than he had been reduced to in the eyes of the shooter. Based on police evidence and witness testimony, Trayvon Martin asked the shooter "Why are you following me?" which can indicate that he wanted an explanation from the shooter's regarding his reduction of his of Trayvon's character from "young man" to "suspect." That is, Trayvon's question to the suspect was his fighting chance to determine why the shooter did not see what was actually in front of him: a tall, lanky teenager with a fruit drink and a bag of candy.

As the previous chapter already discussed, for Trayvon, his question to his shooter was not only a likely coping response to probable racial profiling, but likely his quest to remain visible, to challenge those who believe he fits the stereotypical profile of young African American male criminals, rather than a decent kid with aspirations. This question and this response to an obvious racist encounter, unfortunately, cost Trayvon his life. With this hypothetical scenario, it is at least tenable that, prior to Trayvon Martin's sudden and tragic transition from the world, he sought to remove the shackles of invisibility imposed upon him by someone he didn't know, had never met, or possibly even seen before. Prior to his death, Trayvon asked a question that many, if not most, young African American men want to ask of those who treat them or think of them differently based on the actions of a select few and on prevailing stereotypes about this population: Why is what I am and who I am invisible to you?

Actual evidence to support invisibility throughout the lived experiences of African American men has been found by Drs. Darrick and Maria Tovar-Murray (2012). The authors used qualitative research to investigate perceptions of invisibility among ten African American men between the ages of 18 to 31. For the majority of the study participants, invisibility was described as a struggle of "not being seen by members of the majority culture" (Tovar-Murray and Tovar-Murray 2012). For participants, this struggle became a significant and undesired burden in their lives, particularly when their efforts to move beyond the pervasive images of Black men that rendered them invisible were not effective. Several of the participants indicated that the manifestation of their own invisibility was through the "angry Black man" image, wherein many perceived this stereotypical image as being imposed upon them by White persons. Specifically, one participant stated "Unfortunately, some Whites will always view me as an angry Black man. No matter what I do or say, they will cross the street to avoid passing by me" (Tovar-Murray and Tovar-Murray 2012, 29).

Feelings of disconnection and marginalization resulting from perceptions of invisibility were the second theme to emerge from Tovar-Murray and Tovar-Murray's research. Here, as a result of being perceived as invisible or not perceived beyond negative, stereotypical images, participants reported feelings such as helplessness and anger. One participant stated "I was mad at myself for allowing others to make me feel as if I was not as good as them" (Tovar-Murray and Tovar-Murray 2012, 29). Another stated "I walked around thinking that the world was out to get me because of the color of my skin. So, I used to live life thinking to myself, 'Why even try to make a difference in this world?'" (Tovar-Murray and Tovar-Murray 2012, 29). In all, perceptions of invisibility made many of the participants believe that they were outsiders who kept their distance from White persons while simultaneously feeling that neither they nor their work were respected (Tovar-Murray and Tovar-Murray 2012).

Given these recent findings, invisibility, then, is viewed in this text as the feelings of alienation, illegitimacy, invalidation, disrespect, humiliation, and overall indignation brought about by various social and contextual factors including, but not limited to racism and race-based prejudice. Invisibility emanates from preconceived racist notions and images of African Americans, which are often more heavily relied upon to garner information about this population than actual intimate social interaction (Franklin and Boyd-Franklin 2000). These images are often used to determine the degree of interaction one would have with an African American man. These decisions are often manifested behaviorally, typically in the form of avoidance, ignoring, or acting under presumption. Reactions to these "racial slights" include feelings of alienation and disrespect and can be followed by maladaptive coping mechanisms (Franklin 1999; Franklin and Boyd-Franklin 2000; Tovar-Murray and Tovar-Murray 2012).

The major contribution made by the invisibility framework to the overall literature on African American men and the proposed conceptual model of African American male identity in particular is its elucidation of the cognitive and affective processes endured by African Americans when they are exposed to contexts and/or social others who do not view them in positive manners. Specifically, the introduction and critique by Franklin and his contemporaries (see Parham 1999; Wyatt 1999; Yeh 1999) make clear that the exhibited attitudes and behaviors (e.g., cool posing, anger, nihilism) of some African American male students and young men are linked to maladaptive coping strategies that result from their interactions with social others and contexts where 1) negative, often racist images and beliefs inform individuals about this population and 2) the actual behaviors and attitudes of this population—particularly those which may counter the racist beliefs—are not sought or known.

Aligned with the sentiment expressed in the recent *Ebony* magazine article, much of the love that many young African American men do not receive may result from the lack of recognition and acknowledgement of their personal and social identities, even among those seeking to enhance their lives. With Franklin's work on invisibility, it is clear that, when it comes to knowledge about this population, there is often more assumption than inquiry, more ignoring than listening, and much lower expectations for excellence and upstanding than higher ones. As a result of not seeing what may be present and instead, assuming and adhering to many distorted images of this population, those actual characteristics reflective of young African American men's personal and social identities often remain invisible. As the *Ebony* magazine article inferred, they are not loved, because they are not seen or heard or truly understood. That article underscored a well known but understudied reality African American men face: We are invisible.

INTERSECTIONALITY AND THE IDENTITIES OF YOUNG AFRICAN AMERICAN MEN

Given Franklin's conceptual work on invisibility, along with some evidence articulating African American men's perceptions of invisibility and their behavioral and emotional reactions to them (Tovar-Murray and Tovar-Murray 2012), it is clear that various social and contextual factors (e.g., racism) can negatively impact how young African American men feel about themselves. Additional evidence highlights young African American men's feelings of discontent as a result of being exposed to a social system that questions his motives and actions. Specifically, in an autoethnographic analysis of a two-man performance entitled "A Man," Waymer (2008) and an African American male colleague discuss what it meant to be an African American man. In one scene, Waymer (2008) noted that many African American men grow increasing disenchanted and angered by the perceptions of being linked—almost instantaneously—to failure and negativity. Waymer (2008) cites, "I hate how you make me feel. . . . I hate how you look at me like a visitor, a foreigner, a local, an annoyance" (Waymer 2008, 971).

These feelings of invisibility result from the slighting of his status as an African American man by social others. While it is important to acknowledge that many African American men may be disaffected by the negative images associated with their race and gender, it is plausible to consider that such negative images often adversely impact additional identity components of these individuals. That is, when a young African American man is exposed to racism, the impact of this experience may and often does take a toll not only on his beliefs about himself as a man and as an African American man, but also his beliefs about himself as a student or intellect, as a member of a given ethnic group and subculture, as a sexual being, as an athlete, and as a member of a given socioeconomic class.

Keep in mind that many of the racist images of African American men have depicted them as intellectually inept, hypersexualized (albeit, heterosexual), dull, but often chiefly athletic, often poor and/or disenfranchised, and emerging from what can be considered broken homes and communities where the value systems salient within these are deficient, particularly when compared with mainstream American values (Brown 2011; Howard, Flennaugh, and Terry 2012). For example, research by Brown (2011) showed that the social narrative on African American men has gone from "absent and footloose" in the 1930s to "impotent and powerless" in the 1960s to "soulful and adaptive" in the 1970s to "endangered species" and "in crisis" from the 1980s until the current day.

To address this issue regarding the impact that racism has on multiple identity components, this work in creating a comprehensive model of African American male identity will refer to the conceptual framework of intersectionality. Intersectionality is considered a theory where race, gender, class, and sexuality are interconnected, social categories whose meanings are historically premised (Steinbugler, Press, and Dias 2006). Under the intersectionality framework, varying components of one's identity, including a person's race, gender, social class, sexual orientation (Frable 1997; Robinson 1993), and several additional identity factors (e.g., student) are believed to coexist and to some degree, are impacted simultaneously by different contextual factors (Collins 2001; Howard 2000; Yakushko, Davidson, and Williams 2009). Additionally, these multiple identity factors help shape the person's self-image or social and personal identities (Robinson 1993).

Intersectionality, as a concept, emerges from Pastrana's concept of postmodernity and that of simultaneity offered by the late Gloria Anzaldua (Anzaldua 2003). In each of these concepts, the lines of identity distinction are blurred "in order to arrive at multifaceted definitions or understandings of identity" (Pastrana 2004, 75). Collins (2001) and Reid (2002) write that intersectionality explores how race, gender, and sexuality mutually construct one another rather than examining issues of race, gender, class, and sexuality as separate identity systems. Thus, a commitment to the simultaneous examination of all salient features of personal identity, including, but not limited to issues of race, gender, ethnicity, culture, and sexuality, is made within an intersectionality framework.

Leslie McCall (2005) and Elizabeth Cole (2009) comment that interest in the intersectionality framework emerged in the 1980s and stemmed from a failure of race and gender-based research to examine multiple identities and roles of research participants, namely women of color. For them and many of the pioneers of the intersectionality framework, including the work of Kimberle Crenshaw, who coined the term intersectionality, (Torres, Jones, and Renn 2009), much of the research in the social sciences sought to separate and investigate isolated identities or social locations (i.e., race, gender, social class) rather than examine the interactive aspects of identity. That is, a major impetus for the emergence of intersectionality was a reaction to the dangers of limiting the expression and/or understanding of the individual vis-à-vis, examining only a singular aspect of his or her social locations or identities. Several claim that much social science research literature has often taken into consideration how phenomena are either predictive of or predicted by a singular identity component (e.g., race, gender, socioeconomic status) (Cole 2009; Purdie-Vaughns and Eibach 2008; Yakushko, Davidson, and Williams 2009). However, under an intersectionality framework, there is a push to provide greater understanding of how multiple identity components possessed by the individual are associated with one another, how they are simultaneously impacted by varying contextual factors such as racism, and their confluence on various outcome variables.

As a conceptual framework, several have called for the use of intersectionality to guide examination of identity development among sexual, racial, and gender minorities in the United States (Cole 2009; Steinbugler et al. 2006; Zinn and Dill 1996). For example, Pastrana (2004) argued that a standard practice within social science is omitting issues of gender and sexuality when exploring issues of race. Pastrana (2004) suggests that researchers must resist placing emphasis on one particular identity over another and instead, seek ways to explore how such factors intersect one another. Regarding African Americans, Pastrana (2004) notes that any examination of African Americans must seek to uncover the depth of their experiences, particularly as stigmatized, oppressed, multi-identified individuals. For example, under Pastrana's articulation of intersectionality, it would be important to understand how racism impacts African American men and women of varying socioeconomic statuses. Thus, a simultaneous examination of the salience of race, gender, and socioeconomic status would occur with a central focus on the role of contextual and/or interpersonal experiences with racism. Examining identities in this manner and thereby, employing intersectionality as a theoretical framework to guide identity research, would eventually eliminate what Pastrana (2004) calls fragmented and lopsided articulations and analyses of what it means to be African American in particular and a member of a given social group in general (Steinbugler et al. 2006).

One example of intersectionality within the social science literature is the work of Meyers (2004). In her study, Meyers (2004) observed that young African American women were victims of racist stereotypes promulgated by media. The stereotypes concerned the women's perceived sexuality. She notes, in particular, that by focusing on the scantily clad and physical posturing of some of the women at the 1996 Freaknik—an informal, albeit heavily attended street party in Atlanta during spring break—news reporters often blamed sexual assaults on the women themselves.

That is, the objectification of African American women by African American men was not only a reflection of the women's socialization within a sexist context such as the United States, but was exacerbated by a mainstream media purporting that such women—due to their behaviors and physical appearances—invited the behaviors that sexually objectified them (Meyers 2004). With this example, Meyers (2004) simultaneously explores the racial, gender, and sexual identities of African American women in an attempt to uncover how each of these identities may have led to their sexual objectification. Also in the article, African American men were considered victimized as they were socialized in a sexist and heterosexist environment where being a man is oftentimes synonymous with the aggressive pursuit of sexual conquests of women. Among African American men, Meyers (2004) underscores the use of intersectionality by examining how their gender, racial, and sexual identities have been represented in the mainstream media. Along with this work, several additional works have sought to simultaneously examine the multiple identities among members of various populations (Deaux 1993; Reynolds and Pope 1991; Stewart 2008).

Perhaps the strongest model of intersectionality as a conceptual framework comes from the research of Dr. Susan Jones (Abes, Jones, and McEwen 2007; Jones 2009; Jones and McEwan 2000; Jones, Kim, and Skendall; Torres, Jones, and Renn 2009). Jones and colleagues refer to previous limitations in the literature, specifically those often examining one identity component while ignoring others, along with previous models which discussed multiple identities (see Atkinson, Morten, and Sue 1993; Deaux 1993; Reynolds and Pope 1991) to create the conceptual Model of Multiple Dimensions of Identity (MMDI).

Initially based on qualitative research examining the experiences of female college students from varying ethnic backgrounds, Jones and McEwan (2000) constructed the model of multiple dimensions of identity containing several social identities (or "me-selves") which revolve around a core identity, which houses the individual's personal identity (or I-self). Based on their initial research, Jones and McEwan (2000) identified six identity components which served as the research participants' social identities, although many of the participants suggested that such identities held much less significance than their inner identity or their core feelings and beliefs about themselves. These social identities offered by the study participants were premised on the participants' race, culture, sexual orientation, gender, religion, and class. Jones and colleagues portray these identity components as intersecting rings around a core identity.

Similar to the planet Saturn, the atmospheric, ice and rock-based ring system (me-self) surround a much larger, physically dense mass of rock and gas (I-self). Yet, it is highly unusual to identify the planet as either the larger mass or the distinctive rings. That is, you don't describe Saturn by its rings *or* its globe. Appropriate descriptions and references to the planet will often include a reference to, and thus, acknowledgement of both the larger insulated mass as well as the rings surrounding it. Similarly, for persons espousing an intersectional approach to the investigation of lived experience, Jones and colleagues argue that it is inappropriate to considered an individual by one of his or her singular identity components (e.g., race, gender). Instead, the individual should be consider by all of them; the personal identity components which outline the individual's feelings about him or herself and the social identity components, which help to construct information about him or herself in relation to other persons.

The use of intersectionality, particularly through Jones and McEwan's Model of Multiple Dimensions of Identity, promotes adherence to recognizing the whole person, inclusive of his or her multiple identities. Jones and colleagues have extended the model by incorporating contextual factors believed to influence the multiple identity components individually and simultaneously. That is, contextual factors such as racism can now be considered a more systematic aspect of an individual's environment which impacts how he or she views him or herself and his or her resulting behaviors (Bush and Bush 2013; Garcia-Coll et al. 1996; Spencer, Noll, Cunningham, Harpalani, and Munoz-Miller 2003). More recent research by the authors have allowed for their model to incorporate meaning making, thereby allowing the model to provide "a richer portrayal of not only what relationships students perceive among their personal and social identities, but also how they come to perceive them" (Abes, Jones, and McEwan, 2007, 13).

Much like Jones and colleagues assert throughout their research, the use of an intersectionality framework aids in the articulation of the multiple identities that individuals have and the salience each possesses in their lives. Intersectionality, as a conceptual framework, then, makes the case that more than salient characteristics of the individual (e.g., race and gender) ought to be considered in the discussion of the whole person as it argues that limiting his or her voice to more ostensible characteristics is another way in which he or she can be oppressed (Reynolds and Pope 1991). This is especially important among persons of color, namely African Americans. Only seeing race—and the stereotypes and stigmas associated with it—limits the ability to observe additional behavioral expressions of an individual's identities.

As Williams (2005) points out in her discussion of counseling African American women, many members of this population feel pressure to choose a singular aspect of their identity (race or gender) as central to their being and thereby, are forced to minimize other aspects of self (279). For Williams (2005), promoting one aspect of identity results in the silencing of a central component of an African American woman's identity and therefore, adds to her oppression. For women in general, and African

American women in particular, this notion of uncovering the multiple aspects of identity has been championed in the research literature (Collins 2000; Pastrana 2004). In fact, using an intersectionality framework, Stevens (1997) developed a model of African American female adolescent identity.

Yet, despite the call for more research to focus on the intersection of multiple identities among African American male youth and young adults (Harper 2010; Howard 2013), a framework to identify and investigate the multiple dimensions of identity for this population has not been developed. As a result, much of the research on this population is only slowly beginning to focus on the simultaneous examination of multiple identity components. Without such a framework, it is likely that research in this area will continue to examine this population from the same singular lens that does not allow for a more fruitful analysis of young African American men's lived experiences. What we know about this population is oftentimes the result of what we have seen or currently view in the media. Thus, gaining a more comprehensive understanding of this population will require researchers to acknowledge that 1) this population has a set of identity components that are part of their decision-making processes and subsequent behavioral outcomes, 2) these identities exist simultaneously, and 3) these identities can be impacted simultaneously by a variety of contextual factors, namely racism.

The Trayvon Martin tragedy also fits with a discussion of intersectionality or at least the identification of the multiple identities possessed by young African American men. Earlier, it was posited that Trayvon Martin reacted to his racism-related stress event (i.e., being pursued by the shooter) with a coping response typical of many African Americans. In this response, Trayvon may have sought to make himself visible, that is, have his pursuant and assailant perceive more than just a stereotypical image of himself. In addition, it is plausible that Trayvon Martin, in confronting his shooter, sought to protect the multiple identities he did possess. Trayvon was a beloved sibling (one who cared enough about his younger sibling to purchase him candy and a soft drink that rainy night), a student, a consumer of American and hip hop culture, a friend, and an athlete, was interested in young women, and lived in a gated community with his father.

In other words, there was value to Trayvon's life, simply in his existence. Before he became a symbol, he was a son, a young African American man making sense of his young 17 years of life. These identities were not likely observed or understood by his shooter, but they were there and they were simultaneous and they were certainly beyond the unidimensional and stereotypical images that the shooter maintained of the young man and communicated to police dispatch the night he killed him. Trayvon Martin was a lot of things to a lot of people. A lot of good things. He likely knew this and decided that those identities, the ones he possessed and the ones the shooter could not see, were worth protecting, because they were valuable; because they meant something to someone; because *he knew* he meant something to someone.

LINKING INVISIBILITY AND INTERSECTIONALITY

A careful read of the literature on invisibility syndrome and intersectionality allows for some consideration of their complimentary nature. In particular, it appears that invisibility underscores the effects of contextual factors on the African American men's perceptions of self as racial beings. Intersectionality, however, argues that because such self-perceptions are reflective of cultural, gender, sexual, and academic identities, various contextual factors such as racism may equally affect more than just perceptions of self as racial beings. That is, if we consider that cultural, sexual, gender, and academic identity all intersect with racial identity, then it is plausible that factors such as racism may also invalidate thoughts, feelings, and behaviors associated with each of these identities.

For instance, several studies have shown that many African American male students are exposed to negative and/or lower teacher and school-based expectations for their academic progress (Ferguson 2001; Noguera 2000). One explanation for why these expectations are maintained for this population is racism. Thus, if a young African American male student has teachers who do not challenge him or he observes that teachers may challenge non–African American male students in a manner grossly distinct from him, it is possible that 1) these expectations are rooted in racist beliefs about the academic capabilities of young African American men and 2) his academic or intellectual identity will be compromised. Given these expectations, he may believe that he is not cut out for schooling. Similarly, that same set of behaviors which allow the student to conclude that his teachers do not hold him to high expectations may result in the young African American male student focusing on the development of additional identities such as cultural identity. Receiving a message that he is not expected to perform well in school, the young African American male student may engage in hypermasculine activities and/or cool posing behaviors because, at that school, the young African American male student will desire to feel that he is good at something, that he has control over some aspects of his life.

It could be that the observation of the teachers' low expectations and attitudes—which may be rooted in racism—towards young African American male students may propel him to focus more on the development of socioeconomic identity by way of athletic and/or cultural identity. That is, this student may believe that his chances to pursue a good life by way of academic excellence are limited (e.g., "these teachers don't believe I can make it . . . why should I?"). Thus, this young African

American male student may begin to think of other ways in which he may eventually seek a path to bettering himself. Racism-based teacher expectations for young African American men may determine the extent to which they focus on developing a jump shot or rhyme skills, both of which have been shown to provide plausible avenues for young African American men to pursue in order achieve economic prosperity (i.e., a change in socioeconomic identity).

Those same teachers with those same attitudes toward and expectations for this population may also impact racial and/or gender identities as well. Those challenged in the literature by several research studies, it is likely that many young African American male students who do not fare well in the classroom may adopt the belief that doing well in school is relegated to be White and/or female (Fordham and Ogbu 1996; Harris, Palmer, and Struve 2011; Ogbu 2001; Spencer 2001; Whiting 2006). In adopting such a deleterious belief, it is likely that the young African American male student—though still enrolled in school—may not develop a strong sense of academic or intellectual identity. That is, if exposed to racist beliefs regarding his academic capabilities, he may look at school as the place where he has to be, but not necessarily a context where he wants to be or believes he can thrive in. Such exposure to racist beliefs may also result in the development of resilience and grit attitudes, which will promote positive academic outcomes (Howard 2008, 2013; Noguera 2001)

Though the above examples are merely speculative and anecdotal (i.e., based on my own experiences and that of others I'm familiar with), the theoretical frameworks of invisibility and intersectionality offer an opportunity for researchers and education stakeholders to consider how feelings associated with invisibility syndrome—which are brought on by negative contextual influences such as racism—can simultaneously impact several identities of young African American men. With these frameworks, persons interested in enhancing the lived experiences of this population will be able to garner a more comprehensive understanding of how different social interactions and experiences within a given context may influence young African American men's attitudes regarding race and gender, along with other identity components not typically discussed (Gullan, College, Hoffman, The Children's Hospital of Philadelphia, and Leff 2011). Such a set of frameworks will be imperative to more critically engaging young African American men as they will not only help invested persons to more closely identify those identity components young African American men possess, but can also aid in the identification of the sociocontextual and sociohistorical factors that help shape such identities.

Part II

SIX
"Guess Who's Coming to Dinner?"

Identities of Young African American Men

> Little of the African American male image is his own or defined by his values of humanness or maleness; his maleness remains externally defined, practically eliminating him from his own picture.
> —Isom (2007)

With invisibility syndrome and intersectionality as conceptual guides, the following sections explore the current literature on the various identities of young African American men and will offer examples of how these may intersect and are simultaneously influenced by racism. The premise for the current work lies in a belief that, in order to better understand experiences of young African American men, it is important to go beyond issues of race (Harper 2011). The identities found in the literature and reviewed in the next section include gender identity, sexual identity, racial identity, ethnic identity, cultural identity, socioeconomic identity, athletic identity, and academic identity. Each identity will be defined and/or described and when available, a discussion of the development of the particular identity will be presented. Following this will be reviews of the literature supporting the existence and/or impact of each specific identity component possessed by many young African American men. Also, an articulation of how each identity may be rendered "invisible" (Franklin 1999) by various contextual factors and experiences will be offered. Finally, in each section of identity, the intersection of the particular identity with other identity components and how both identities can be influenced by various contextual factors will be discussed. Research studies and conceptual papers have been reviewed to promote the existence of the multiple identity components and their possible intersections with one another. Research studies demonstrating an association between racism and these identities will also be offered.

The review of the multiple identities of African American men reveals that the racial, cultural, ethnic, sexual, gender, socioeconomic, athletic, and academic identities of young African American men are, indeed, simultaneous in nature. Also, aligned with Franklin's invisibility syndrome, each identity component is rendered invisible at some point by various contextual factors such as racism. To better understand the synergistic, interactional nature of African American male identities, I offer a conceptual model of African American male identity.

CONCEPTUAL DESCRIPTION OF AFRICAN AMERICAN MEN'S IDENTITY MODEL

This conceptual model of African American male identity may complement other models that have identified the contextual factors that shape the identity development of ethnic minority children and young adults (Garcia-Coll et al. 1996; Spencer 1995). In particular, Spencer's PVEST model provides a comprehensive articulation of the various contextual factors that influence the identity of African American youth. Missing from this account, however, is a description of the multiple identities that such contextual factors impact simultaneously. Similarly, the conceptual model of the effects of racism does not fully discuss how the multiple identities of African Americans, particularly African American men, can be simultaneously impacted by racism or how these multiple identities can influence the development of coping responses to perceived racism and/or racist events.

The conceptual model of African American male identity displays the interactional nature of the different identity components for young African American men. The arrows provide the reader with an idea of how each identity is associated—theoretically and empirically—with other identities. That is, arrows between identity components within the model suggest that the two factors are associated, according to some empirical research. The reader will also note that the racial, ethnic, cultural, sexual, gender, socioeconomic, athletic, and academic identities of African American men are considered synergistic and therefore, do not necessarily follow a temporal or developmental sequence. Rather, following an intersectionality perspective, the multiple identities are simultaneously present and influence each other, particularly as the young African American man enters those stages of identity development, as outlined by Erikson and other psychologists (i.e., adolescence and young adulthood). For example, for African American men, racial identity is likely to develop simultaneously with cultural, sexual, gender, socioeconomic, ethnic, athletic, and academic identities as encounters that shape each of these occur early and often during adolescence (Corby et al. 2007; Dube and Savin-Williams 1999; Hill 1999; Hughes et al. 2006; Worthington, Savoy, Dillon, and Vernaglia 2002).

The proposed model (see figure 6.1) offers researchers an opportunity to empirically examine how identities are affected by contextual factors (i.e., racism, teacher-school relationships). The model also allows for some examination of whether these identities are associated with one another (i.e., visual arrows between identity components). With a fuller description of the racial, cultural, sexual, socioeconomic, gender, ethnic, athletic, and academic identities that young African American men possess, researchers can retrieve and/or construct instrumentation to capture reports of each identity component and whether one is statistically linked to another. The dotted lines in the model highlight the current research underscoring the established relationships between various identities for African Americans.

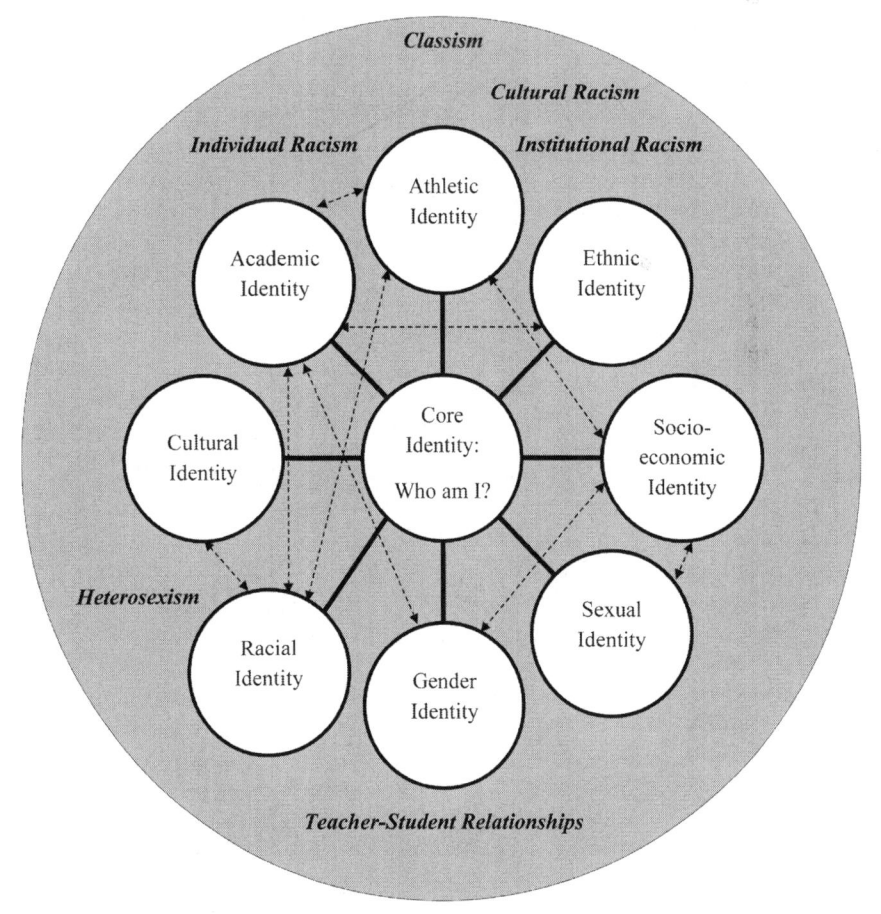

Figure 6.1. Conceptual Model of African American Men's Identity

As alluded to throughout this text, the identities of young African American men are simultaneously present and are likely to develop, manifest, and change as a result of their interactions and encounters within a racist environment. Within figure 6.1, each of the identity components discussed are presented along with the various forms of racism and other contextual factors that have been said or shown to impact various identities of young African American men. In particular, the model illustrates the fact that 1) each identity component is linked to a core identity or central sense of self, 2) there are some additional associations—most of which have evidence provided by the social science and educational literature—between different identity components (e.g., athletic and academic identities are associated in the literature as some studies have shown that many African American men forego development of their academic identity (i.e., low academic identity) in lieu of athletic identity development (i.e., high athletic identity), and 3) all identity components develop within the larger microsystemic and macrosystemic ecologies where social ills such as racism, heterosexism, and classism exist.

To close the introduction of the conceptual model, readers should note that, in figure 6.1, there is a representation of the identity components that most African American men have, along with the presence of several negative contextual factors such as racism. In figure 6.1, the context of racism and related 'isms' are noted by the actual words, along with the dark charcoal gray color filling the larger circle. This color represents the heightened impact of racism, usually resulting from a racist encounter or event—and related on the identity components. Following is a discussion of each identity component and how contextual factors can and often do adversely impact their development and behavioral expression. Following this discussion of each identity component, how it is deemed invisible, and how it intersects with other identity components for young African American men, a figure depicting the invisibility of each identity component will be presented. The reader will note that the figures in each following chapter represent the impact of contextual factors on one identity component. The circle containing the compromised or invisible identity component will be the same dark charcoal grey color as the larger circle it is encompassed in. Also noteworthy is the slight greying of all other identity components, which represents the impact of various contextual factors on those identity components as well. In summary, dark charcoal grey identity components are rendered invisible in each figure and because of their inter sectional nature, other identity components are also impacted.

SEVEN

African American Men's Gender Identity

Gender Socialization and Identity Development

Gender identity refers to the beliefs about one's masculinity and femininity and the feelings associated with those attributes (Mandara, Murray, and Joyner 2005; Stewart and McDermott 2004). Early research on gender identity development reflects the thinking of Dr. Lawrence Kohlberg (Martin, Ruble, and Szkrybalo 2002). Kohlberg (1966) proposed three stages of gender development. Stage one of Kohlberg's identity development theory is gender labeling, where children are able to identify themselves and others as either girls or boys. Such labeling is based on physical appearance. The second stage, gender stability, is where children begin to recognize the stability of gender, particularly by noting the more biologically derived activities associated with being a boy or girl (i.e., giving birth). The final stage, gender consistency, is characterized by the recognized constancy of gender across time and situation (Martin et al. 2002).

Resulting from gender identity development is gender identity. Gender identity has been conceptualized as a multidimensional construct (Egan and Perry 2001). It includes an individual's a) knowledge of membership in a gender category, b) perceived compatibility with his or her gender group, c) perceived pressure to conform to gender-appropriate roles and behaviors, and d) gender contentedness, which is one's degree of satisfaction with his or her gender (Egan and Perry 2001). Wilson and colleagues (2010) aptly summarize some of these specific roles relegated to men within the United States. These roles include 1) man as breadwinner and responsible head of household, 2) man as antifeminine, including emotion concealment, 3) man as heterosexual, with heterosexuality being considered the "normal" sexual orientation, 4) man as homophobic and 5) man as physically strong.

For young African American men and men living in the United States overall, fulfillment of these roles is considered a major step toward achieving manhood. For African American men in particular, it is widely held that they will grow up to become the primary providers for their families (Collins 2001; Diemer 2002; Martin and Harris 2006). It is also believed that men—upon reaching adulthood—will display greater competitive tendencies and more aggressive behaviors, along with fewer displays of sensitivity and vulnerability (Chesebro and Fuse 2001; Mahalik et al. 2003). These beliefs regarding men's gender identity are considered an outcome of a gender socialization process during early childrearing (Bem 1974; Harper 2004; Hopkins 2002).

Conformity to traditional gender roles is especially important for young African American men. Corby and associates (2007) found that, though gender contentedness was positively linked to self-esteem for both African American and White fifth graders, African American students reported greater pressure to conform to gender-appropriate roles from parents and significant others than did White students. Moreover, for African American boys, there was a positive correlation between reports of gender typicality (i.e., the degree to which a child feels that he or she is a typical member of his or her gender) and reported pressure to conform to gender-appropriate roles. This study suggests that young African American men are socialized toward gender-appropriate roles early and often. Also, their understanding of what a young man is supposed to be and do is largely a reflection of their socialization toward gender-appropriate activities (Hill 1999; Hill and Sprague 1999; Watkins et al. 2010).

Manhood characteristics deemed by the larger society and within the African American communities were investigated in two studies (Hammond and Mattis 2005; Hunter and Davis 1994). Specifically, Hunter and Davis (1994) sought to determine the degree of salience many maladaptive considerations of masculinity and manhood had among thirty-two African American male participants. Among the themes found in their study were perseverance or maintaining the will to move on in spite of significant challenges, economic viability, directedness or having the resources and capability to take care of oneself, and self-betterment.

Using content analysis for the written responses of 152 African American men ranging in age from 17 to 79, Hammond and Mattis (2005) found that nearly 50 percent of the men reported that an appropriate manhood characteristic was responsibility/accountability, which was defined as the "taking, handling, or being aware of one's responsibility to oneself, family, and others, while being accountable for one's actions, thoughts, and behaviors" (119). This theme, it should be noted, has some similarity to the "directedness" theme that emerged in the study by Hunter and Davis (1994). In all, fifteen themes were generated and recorded among the responses of African American men to the question of 'What does manhood mean to you?" including autonomy (having control over individual choices), being a provider for oneself and family, having a spiritual and moral base for decisions and behaviors, and keeping family at the center of one's life (Hammond and Mattis 2005).

Supporting the work of Hammond and Mattis (2005) is a set of qualitative studies examining gender identity among African American men. Specifically, research by Harper (2004) and Martin and Harris (2006) found that many African American men often adhere to traditional gender-specific roles, as well as some factors that move beyond what is considered normative male characteristics (Harris, Palmer, and Struve 2011). For example, Harper's (2004) qualitative study examined perceptions of manhood among thirty-two high-achieving African American college-age men. The author found that most of these individuals considered many of the characteristics named in Hammond and Mattis' (2005) study to be important qualities of manhood, but noted that academic excellence and demonstration of leadership are also important aspects of manhood. Similar findings with African American male college students emerged in Martin and Harris (2006), Dancy (2011) and Harris, Palmer, and Struve (2011). In each of these studies, doing well academically was seen as an important component of manhood.

Additionally, a study by Isom (2007) examined the perceptions of African American male middle grade students toward manhood and found similar themes to those studies examining manhood perceptions with African American male college-age students. Specifically, Isom (2007) noted that many of the young men in her study reported a form of masculinity that went beyond the stereotypical perception of manhood specific to young African American men, one which ostensibly includes sexualizing women and focusing on material acquisition (Majors and Billson 1992). Young African American men in her study also reported feeling that being a man consisted of helping those who need help and being calm and respectful and working harder at education.

INVISIBILITY AND AFRICAN AMERICAN MEN'S GENDER IDENTITY

While it is clear from the previously cited works that many young African American men espouse values and behaviors which are aligned with traditional and adaptive expressions of manhood, there is evidence in the literature to suggest that many other African American men espouse a set of alternative and potentially pathological masculinity characteristics (Hunter and Davis 1994), many of which are linked to poor academic performance, and are also reflective of feelings of powerlessness and an overall perception of an inability to enact traditional manhood roles and behaviors (Czopp, Lasane, Sweigard, Bradshaw, and Hammer 1998; Harris 1995; Pfeifer and Sedlacek 1974; Silverman and Dinitz 1974). To address this socialization toward those masculinity characteristics that seemingly do more harm than good, it is feasible to employ the invisibility framework.

Under an invisibility framework, for example, it is tenable that many young African American men are frequently socialized toward traditional gender roles because of the reigning societal perceptions of this population, which often include racist images of intellectual inferiority, docility, irresponsibility, and aggression (Gilmore, DeLamater, and Wagstaff 1996; Page 2004; Rodriguez 2008; Rushton and Jensen 2005). That is, many parents and community members may socialize young African American men toward more functional and proactive manhood roles and beliefs. Doing so, it is believed, would deter them from adopting behaviors and beliefs that reflect racist, stereotypical images of African American men perpetuated by media in particular and society in general. As previously noted, many scholars write that the leading perception of young African American men include unpredictability, untrustworthy, volatile, emotionally unavailable, and physically intimidating while simultaneously lacking intelligence, thoughtfulness, and the ability to take care of one's self or others (Harris 1995; Hopkins 2002; Johnson 2010).

To ward off the psychological effects of such racist perceptions, it is plausible that most African American parents will socialize their young men toward those behaviors and preferences deemed more consistent with the White, middle class standard of gender appropriateness, including feelings of competitiveness, financial independence, responsibility for one's own actions and beliefs, and aggression (Bush 2004; Hammond and Mattis 2005; Hill 1999; Hopkins 2002; Myers 2004; Peters 1997).

Supporting this claim that African American men are socialized towards specific gender roles is a comprehensive literature review by Hughes and colleagues (2006). Here, the authors cite some empirical studies that found that many African American young men receive messages regarding racial barriers throughout their gender socialization (Bowman and Howard 1985; Thomas and Speight 1999). That is, while parents of young African American men are consistent with instilling the values and behaviors patterns associated with manhood, much of these messages are juxtaposed with discussions of racism, usually as a rationale for why these young men must act in specific ways.

Though the authors also cite several studies which found no significant differences in the types of socialization messages received by young African American male and adolescent females (see Hughes et al. 2006 for greater detail on these studies), some social science literature suggests that, for young African American men, gender socialization (i.e., learning what it means to become a man, particularly an African American man) typically includes messages regarding the presence of racism and how to cope with it in order to become successful later on in life. For many young African American men, achieving this success in life typically requires the neutralization of feelings of invisibility and resulting maladaptive attitudes and behaviors (Franklin 1999; Franklin and Boyd-Franklin 2000). That is, parents of young African American men often tell their young men about how to become and be men not only because it is their responsibility, but also because they recognized the limitations (e.g., feelings of invisibility) and dangers (e.g., development of unfavorable behaviors) that living in the U.S. has for their male children.

Given the pervasiveness of racist images and beliefs about African American men in the U.S. (Hunter and Davis 1994; Hopkins 2002), it is not surprising that African American parents stress that their young men conform quickly and often display those characteristics deemed acceptable by mainstream society (Hughes, et al. 2006). For these parents, such socialization wards off feelings and behaviors consistent with the idea that African American men are lazy, intellectually inferior, financially unstable, and irresponsible. This socialization also protects the young African American man from feelings associated with invisibility syndrome by promoting notions of hard work, resilience, and strength amidst adversity.

However, when young African American men begin to internalize the racist societal images of themselves, feelings of invisibility may eventually transform into hypermasculinity. Hypermasculinity is the degree to which a man is perceived as being overly aggressive, and having an excessive emphasis on the acquisition of wealth and sexual conquests (Hunter and Davis 1994). It is characterized by the presence of misogynistic, sexist, and violent attitudes (Burk, Burkhart, and Sikorski 2004; Jamison 2006) and has been said to be a prevalent ideology among many African American male adolescents and young adult men (Majors and Billson 1992). This image, also termed "cool pose" (Adams and Fuller 2006; Majors and Billson 1992; Osborne 1999), is viewed as a physical and psychological stance taken on by African American men to defend against their media characterization as irresponsible, financially unstable, intellectually inferior, docile, and sexually aggressive/exotic beings.

Behavioral outcomes resulting from the development of hypermasculinity among some African American men include working diligently to maintain a rather composed outward social appearance. Such an appearance may include, but is not limited to accumulating high numbers of sexual conquests with women and the possession of several expensive material goods (Majors and Billson 1992). In the popular culture, this is referred to as "flossing" or "hustling." In all, feelings of hypermasculinity emerged from a need to compensate for feelings of powerlessness, guilt, and shame resulting from a perceived inability to endorse and realize traditional manhood-based roles (Harris 1995, 280). The outcome of such perceptions is the adoption of alternative masculinity roles that underscores violence, risky sexual behavior, and present rather than future time orientation (Harris 1995; Majors and Billson 1992).

Each of these psychological and behavioral factors is part of the invisibility syndrome, according to Franklin. For Franklin, these young African American men with hypermasculine gender identities endure the denial of their own frailty resulting from exposure to a racist environment where they are systematically devalued. For many, hypermasculine behaviors and attitudes are coping mechanisms used to evade feelings associated with invisibility put forth largely by racist stereotypes emanating from early historical and racism-laden perceptions of the African American man (Bush 1999; Harris 1995).

Many young African American men are socialized to work diligently to become good students, responsible leaders and overall, upstanding citizens. Many of them internalize messages (e.g., doing well in school) in an effort to fulfill the goal of becoming "good" men. Yet, for some, the persistent exposure to and even accusations and perceptions of being lazy rather than responsible, athletic rather than academic, and criminal rather than civil leads to an adoption and manifestation of the hypermasculine characteristics. As Roy and Dyson (2010) noted, "Men disadvantaged by racial, ethnic, or class inequalities may reject . . . avenues to manhood and instead, craft different ways to 'be a man'" (141).

Consonant with Frankin's perspective on invisibility, Wester, Vogel, Wei, and McLain (2006) contend that institutional racism does not often allow African American men to fully meet traditional gender roles. When they do, it is often at the expense of maintaining more culturally aligned gender roles, including respecting women and espousing more collectivistic orientations (Hill and Sprague 1999; Oyserman, Coon, and Kemmelmeier 2002). A similar argument is presented by Harris (1995) who stated that "Although most African American men have internalized and accepted [European] standards of manhood, inequities in earning potential and employment and limited access to educational opportunities prevent the expression of these behaviors" (279). Harris (1995) goes on to write "For those who are unable to meet traditional standards of masculinity, manhood has been redefined to be consistent with their alienation from mainstream values and institutions" (279). What results from this compromised gender identity are hypermasculine ideologies and attitudes (Gilmore, DeLamater, and Wagstaff 1995). As Watkins, Walker, and Griffith (2010) noted, "Because [African American men] are an economically and socially marginalized population and do not have access to the White male power and economic structure, Black men are reportedly more likely to exhibit forms of masculinity detrimental to their health" (305). Thus, even though many African American men, regardless of age or socioeconomic status, are socialized toward traditional manhood themes (Harris, Palmer, and Struve 2011), their exposure to individual and institutional racism may facilitate the development of feelings of invisibility, particularly those associated with manhood.

Unfortunately, there has not been a significant amount of research examining associations between hypermasculinity and behavioral and academic outcomes (Brown, McGregor, and Gary 1997; Diemer 2002; Watts, Abdul-Adil, and Pratt 2002). Among the few extant studies, a major finding among them has been that less hypermasculine attitudes and behaviors are associated with more positive academic and psychological outcomes for African American men. Still, more in-depth examination of the source and rationale behind hypermasculinity and "cool pose" awaits further research. Given the literature, it can be surmised that expressions of hypermasculinity are attempts by young African American men to redefine how they are perceived by society (i.e., redefining their social identity). In doing so, however, there is often an adverse impact on their academic outcomes and perceptions of intellectual aptitude (Czopp et al. 1998; Pfeifer and Sedlacek 1974; Silverman and Dinitz 1974). For example, using vignettes with college undergraduates, Czopp and colleagues (1998) found that many participants believe that the vignette character displaying a hypermasculine style of interaction was more emotionally detached from school and had a lower GPA than the vignette control character (i.e., one not displaying hypermasculine characteristics). Thus, one irony is that the adoption of hypermasculinity attitudes and behaviors, as a result of feeling invisible, actually affirms the invisibility of this population, particularly by manifesting behaviors deemed consistent with the racist stereotypes about them in the first place.

INTERSECTIONALITY AND AFRICAN AMERICAN MEN'S GENDER IDENTITY

Given the findings from some studies, it is tenable that some variance in the gender identity development of this population is linked to issues of race and racism. The young African American man has to successfully negotiate both gender- and race-based socialization messages in order to establish a healthy gender identity. Unsuccessful reconciliation of race and gender identity can result in the development of hypermasculine attitudes and behavioral expressions.

Based on the literature, it is clear that gender socialization for young African American men often includes some discussion of race and racism (Hughes et al. 2006). Some aforementioned work (see Brown, Linver, Evans, and DeGennaro 2009; Isom 2007; Rodriguez 2008) suggests that there is an intersection between race and gender in the gender identity development of this population. Perhaps the strongest research emerged from the review by Hughes and colleagues (2006) in which the authors noted that much of the gender socialization of young African American men dutifully includes discussions of race and racism.

In addition to the intersection of race and gender, it is important to explore issues of gender as they are related to academic identity (McMillian, Frierson, and Campbell 2010; Niemi 2005; Whiting 2006). Enrollment and achievement statistics in higher education reveal that African American women outnumber African American men with respect to graduation and entry into graduate and professional schools. Similarly, young African American women are typically more successful academically during the elementary and secondary school years than their male counterparts (Brown et al. 2009; Gay 2000; Lee 2001; Ladson-Billings 2005; McMillian et al. 2010). Such poor performance and overall academic and social experiences at school may be linked to what Whiting (2006) refers to as the development of scholar identities or what McMillian and colleagues (2010) refer to as academic identification. In particular, Whiting (2006) writes that young African American men who have an underdeveloped or negative academic identity are 1) less likely to remain persistent in school and 2) more likely to be tracked into special education. Those African American students with strong or positive academic identities, however, will view themselves as academically self-efficacious and overall, capable of maintaining significant performance in academic contexts.

Simultaneously, Whiting (2006) argues that African American men with positive scholar or academic identities would not associate intelligence with a lacking sense of masculinity or "acting White," but a characteristic that enhances manhood. Some previous studies showed that some African American male students believed that doing well in school is or should be associated with perceptions of manhood (Harris, Palmer, and Struve 2011; Martin and Harris 2006). It is likely that much of the poor academic performance and overall negative attitudes toward schooling said to be displayed among many young African American men are the results of academic disidentification (McMillian et al. 2010) or inadequate scholar identity development. Given the relatively negative expectations, perceptions, interactions, and feedback young African American men are exposed to in school (Ferguson 2003; Neal et al. 2003; Noguera 2003), it is likely that feelings of invisibility precede academic disidentification or inadequate scholar identities. What may result is a psychological disengagement from schooling (Gay 2000; Parsons 2003) and a simultaneous adoption of hypermasculine attitudes and behavioral expressions, many of which may reflect a rejection of academic achievement (Ogbu 2003). Majors and Billson (1992) have noted that "cool pose" is seemingly incompatible with academic success in most public schools. However, these claims regarding adoption of hypermasculine attitudes and concurrent psychological disengagement from school—which results from feelings of invisibility—have not been supported by research. Nonetheless, it will be important for future research to determine the degree of intersection extant between African American men's gender identity and their academic identity.

ILLUSTRATION OF AFRICAN AMERICAN MEN'S IDENTITY INVISIBILITY—GENDER IDENTITY

In figure 7.1, the reader will note that gender identity of young African American men has been compromised. Here, its adoption of the same color as the racist and heterosexist context shows that it has melded with these social ills and the result is a diminished or invisible gender identity

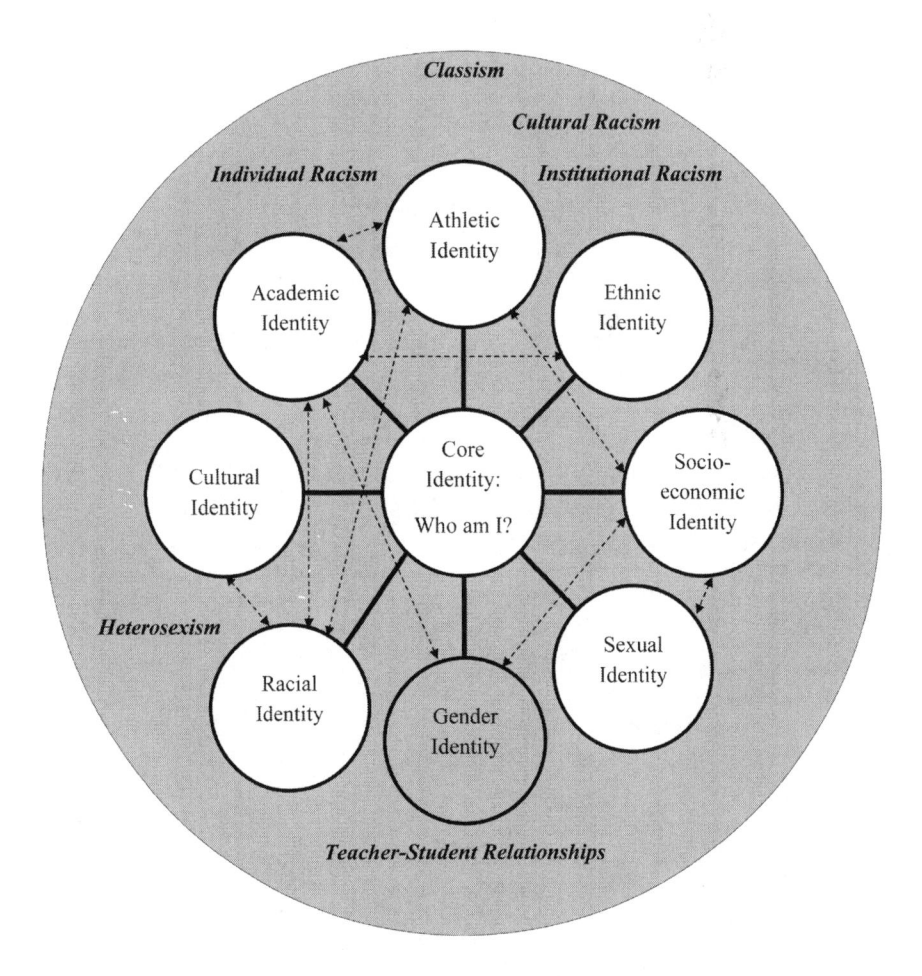

Figure 7.1. Conceptual Model of African American Men's Identity: Compromised Gender Identity

(i.e., what it means to be a man in the United States) Historically, this compromise of gender identity made sense as, during the time of chattel slavery, the African American man was unable to take care of his family or his children. In most cases, these individuals were stripped away from him, sold, physically and sexually assaulted, and or killed. Any revenge sought as a result of these actions typically resulted in his own death. Thus, if a central tenet of manhood was the ability to take care of one's self and his loved ones, then it is clear that, during that period in time, African American men would have had a significant compromised gender identity; one rendered invisible.

Yet, in more contemporary times, it is plausible that many African American men experience a similar feat to those who were slaves in the nineteenth and early twentieth centuries. With persistently lower numbers of African American men pursuing higher education, in comparison to their White and female counterparts, coupled with higher levels of incarceration rates, homicide, and joblessness, the attempts to demonstrate manhood in ways consistent with more traditional conceptualizations of manhood have been less effective for this population. A large contributor to the compromised gender identity of young African American men today is the role that mainstream society has in maintaining the damaging images of this population as lazy, unintelligent, and irresponsible. That is, racism has contributed to the invisibility of African American men's gender identity because it has, historically and contemporarily, offered very limited images of and opportunities to this population. It is arguable that no other male ethnic group has been bastardized as much as African American men, especially when compared to the traditional standard of manhood, the White male. In fact, most of the images found in the media support this claim, particularly with the majority of news and television coverage about African American men being linked to either crime (30 percent) or sports (43 percent) (Meyers Communications, LLC 2010).

Recognizing that their abilities to achieve traditional manhood status in the United States have been, to some degree, disrupted as a result of racism, some African American men have pursued alternative, albeit, more damaging expressions of manhood (e.g., cool pose and capital identity projection). These alternative, hypermasculine expressions include, but are not limited to focusing on sexual conquests with women, acquiring alternative means of making ends meet (i.e., street economy), explicit display of extravagant material goods, and even being incarcerated. What has been made invisible, perhaps to young African American men themselves, is their ability to pursue manhood vis-à-vis more traditional means. These alternative behavioral manifestations are how some of them cope.

EIGHT
African American Men's Sexual Identity

The gender identity development and socialization of gender roles of African American men are said to be, at least, somewhat consistent with the gender appropriate behaviors of men in the United States, namely White, Anglo-Saxon Protestant men from middle class communities (Hammond and Mattis 2005; Hill 1999; Martin, Ruble, and Szkrybalo 2002). One feature of this standard image of masculinity—as determined in the United States—includes socialization toward heterosexual relationships (Burk, Burkhart, and Sikorski 2004; Johnson 2003; Mohr 2009; Thompson, Pleck, and Ferrera 1992; Worthington, Savoy, Dillon, and Vernaglia 2002). Given this focus on heterosexual relationships, it can be discerned that the work delineating the gender identity processes of young African American men is rooted in the belief that these men have sexual interests in members of the opposite sex. That is, most African American men are presumed heterosexual (Wise 2004)

Yet, a fairly recent social phenomenon referred to as the "down-low" has called into question the belief that most young African American men are heterosexual or have sexual interests in members of the opposite sex. The down-low describes African American men who lead ostensibly heterosexual lives while covertly engaging in homosexual behavior (King 2004). Thus, there are many African American men who "fit the bill" concerning gender identity roles, including exhibitions of physical strength and competitiveness (Burlew and Serface 2006; Mahalik et al. 2003), but also engage in homosexual practices. Given this, it is erroneous to assume that young African American men—based on perceptions of race and gender—are heterosexual.

Though actual numbers of homosexual men in the United States have been difficult to obtain (Hughes and Saxton 2006), the proliferation of several initiatives geared toward mainstream and global acceptance of gay, lesbian, bisexual and transgendered individuals (i.e., Gay Pride Parades) has made it clear that there are significant numbers of homosexual men and women in the United States. At the time of this writing, the United States Supreme Court had struck down a legislative act that disallowed persons in same-sex marriages from being recognized by the federal government as a married couple. For persons in same-sex marriages who were wed in states that allowed same sex marriage, any lack of recognition by the U.S. government concerning the legitimacy of the union and/or its benefits and corollaries (e.g., tax filings) would be considered unconstitutional. Federal law now protects many individuals choosing to marry a same-sex person in an allowing state. Many of these individuals choosing to do so are men. Many are young African American adult men and many of them exhibit behaviors and characteristics that may typify conventional conceptualizations of manhood, including competitiveness, aggression, physical strength, and even sexual conquest.

Providing anecdotal support of the claim that sexual minority men continue to maintain gender identities consonant with manhood are the national headlines made by current National Basketball Association player Jason Collins. In April of 2013, Mr. Collins, an African American man and center for the Boston Celtics, announced in the magazine Sports Illustrated that he is gay. For many young African American men, the process of coming out as gay can be difficult at best and often does not include national media coverage and/or an article in a major periodical. For Jason Collins, however, coming out as gay marked the first time in history that an active player in one of the four major U.S. sports associations (Major League Baseball, National Basketball Association, National Football League, and the National Hockey League) announced that he is gay. In the self-written article, Mr. Collins' first statement is "I'm a 34 year old NBA center. I'm black. And I'm gay." While much of the article is penned with intricate and comforting discussion of Collins' coming-out process, including the timing of his announcement, those persons he came out to, and their reactions, his writing of his role and activities as an NBA center are relevant to the issue of sexual orientation and manhood. Specifically, what Collins writes makes clear that, in the NBA, he went against the "gay stereotype" and notes that he has always been an "aggressive" player, to the point where he, at one time, led the NBA in personal fouls.

It is clear from Collins' article that who he is as a man and as an NBA center could be discerned from his sexual identity. His article may have inspired other African American male athletes to come out as gay. Most recently, University of Missouri standout Michael Sam, a 6'2" 260-lb defensive lineman, publicly declared his homosexuality and is currently the first known gay athlete in the National Football League (NFL). Collins' article and the degree of openness Sam shared during his interview indicate that gay, lesbian, bisexual and transgendered individuals can exhibit traditional gender role identities, particularly within the public eye while maintaining homosexual preferences and practices in their private lives.

Thus, it can be gleaned that gender and sexual identities are two different constructs and thus, each construct should be examined independently. Wise (2004), for instance, discusses the distinction between gender and sexual identity, with the former referring to roles associated with being a man or a woman and the latter focusing on one's identified, displayed, or reported sexual preference. Similar distinctions are found in Blumenfeld (1995). In particular, Wise's (2004) distinction between gender and sexual identity emerges from an ethnography study of gay African American men where her findings concluded that manhood characteristics (i.e., possessing strength of character, responsibility) were not tantamount to whether the participants were attracted to men or women. In fact, Wise (2004) makes the argument that, perhaps, gay African American men tend to exhibit expanded forms of manhood as a result of having to deal with 1) being African American man in White dominated society, 2) being an African American man within the Black community and 3) being an African American man with a homosexual identity in both contexts. Her research with successful African American men who were gay evidenced that manhood, for these participants, meant being able to thrive and show resolve and strength in each context, not only as an African American man, but also as a gay African American man. Thus, for Wise (2004), she makes clear that her research argues for a new conceptualization of African American manhood and masculinity, one that does not equate homosexuality as a weakness of manhood or being African American, but an extension of them. In making this argument, it is also ostensibly clear that Wise (2004) advocates for a demarcation of gender and sexual identities.

By more fully discerning these constructs, researchers lessen the chances that sexual identity will be subsumed under gender identity. Moreover, by partitioning sexual and gender identity, researchers examining identity issues among sexual minorities will be able to better illuminate the integrity of gay, lesbian, bisexual, or transgendered persons' lived experiences. Thus, some discussion of the lived experiences of African American gay men is warranted, as their lives as sexual minorities have been far less visible in the literature than members of the sexual majority. Prior to this, discussion of the sexual identity development for heterosexual as well as a general discussion of homosexual identity development is provided below to couch the discussion of sexual identity among African American men.

Given that predominance of sexual minorities and the impact their movement for civil liberties and equal protection under the law has had on the economic, political, and legal climate within the United States, it is important to examine the processes by which heterosexual, homosexual, and bisexual identities develop. This is especially important for young African American men whose experiences within the U.S. have not been favorable. Having a sexual orientation perceived as equally unfavorable may exacerbate their experiences. Thus, it is vital to explore sexual identity in order to gain a more comprehensive view of this population.

In research examining correlates and associations related to masculinity and male gender identity, however, the development of heterosexual identity is often assumed as normative and therefore, sexual minority status (i.e., gay/homosexual, bisexual) has been, at best, commonly overlooked in the research literature on identity (Hoffman 2004; Mohr 2008; Worthington et al. 2002). To address this, below is a brief description of heterosexual identity development, followed by a discussion of homosexual identity development.

HETEROSEXUAL IDENTITY DEVELOPMENT

Worthington, Savoy, Dillon, and Vernaglia (2002) describe heterosexual identity development as the process by which individuals recognize, define, and accept their needs, values, orientation, activities, and expressions of sexuality. For these authors, heterosexual identity development includes either a conscious or unconscious understanding of membership in a privileged group. Throughout these processes, sexual identity development is influenced by various social, biological, and psychological factors.

Using this framework of both individual and social influences on the development of heterosexual identities, the model of heterosexual identity development proposed by Worthington and colleagues establishes a unique set of five statuses through which an individual's sexual identity ebbs and flows. For Worthington et al. (2002), these statuses include 1) *Unexplored Commitment*, 2) *Active Exploration*, 3) *Diffusion*, 4) *Deepening and Commitment*, and 5) *Synthesis*. These five statuses are fluid and therefore individuals are able to transition between them with minimal restraint.

Unexplored commitment describes strict alignment to socially mandated gender roles and sexual behavior. Active exploration is a period where individuals intentionally and purposefully examine their sexual attitudes, behaviors, and preferences. In order to be considered active in exploration, an individual must question the socially mandated ideals featured in unexplored commitment (i.e., heterosexual relationships/dating). Diffusion is discussed as the absence of exploration or commitment (Worthington et al, 2002). Individuals with this status often unintentionally experience a variety of sexual situations because they are primarily concerned with nonconformity and the rejection of social norms. Worthington et al. (2002) argue that many individuals enter this status as a result of being traumatized (i.e., sexual abuse and/or exploitation). Once in diffusion, the only way to progress is through active exploration (Worthington et al, 2002).

The deepening and commitment status consists of various markers indicating an individual's certainty regarding sexual values, needs, preferences, and orientation. Deepening and commitment also relate to more defined attitudes toward sexual minorities and perceptions of privilege in regards to sexual identity (Worthington et al, 2002). The last stage, synthesis, suggests that individuals arrive at an understanding and acceptance of their sexual values, needs, preferences, and orientation. For Worthington and colleagues, synthesis requires a congruent self-concept, inclusive of individual sexual identity, awareness of group membership, and attitudes about sexual minorities.

HOMOSEXUAL IDENTITY DEVELOPMENT

Blumenfeld (1995) defines sexual identity as the label persons give themselves to describe their sexual preferences and practices. In noting the various labels that individuals give themselves to demarcate their sexual identities (i.e., lesbian, gay, transgendered, bisexual, queer, heterosexual, straight, and asexual), Blumenfeld also notes the distinctions between sexual identity and sexual orientation. The latter is determined by whom the individual is sexually attracted to, while the former focuses on the label and various colloquialisms describing such attractions (Blumenfeld, 1995). Generally, these sexual orientation categories include homosexuals or individuals attracted to members of the same sex, bisexuals or individuals attracted to members of both sexes, heterosexuals or individuals attracted to members of the opposite sex, and asexuals, individuals attracted to neither sex (Blumenfeld 1995; Storm 1980; Worthington, Savoy, Dillon, and Vernaglia 2002).

For Blumenfeld (1995) and others, sexual identity development is a multistage developmental process that, depending on the individual, varies in duration and intensity (Cass 1979 1984; Cox and Gallois 1996; Halpin and Allen 2004; Troiden 1989). While Cass's theoretical model of homosexual identity development has guided research on this topic for almost four decades (Cass 1979), other conceptualizations have been offered in the literature on sexual minority identity development (Dube and Savin-Williams 1999; Kulkin, Chauvin, Percle 2000). Specifically, Troiden's (1989) homosexual identity development model offered four stages of identity development for sexual minorities. While some have cautioned against the supposed universality of sexual minority identity development (Dube and Savin-Williams 1999), the literature finds that Troiden's work is considered a leading model of sexual minority identity development (Cox and Gallois 1996; Halpin and Allen 2004). A review and comparison between these two leading homosexual identity development theories will be offered below.

Dr. Vivienne Cass (1979 1984) first offered a description of homosexual identity formation or development in response to little research being offered to articulate the experiences of gay men and their identity development. Much of what was known about homosexual identity was uncovered in clinical and personal settings among either therapists or family (or both), but little in the way of theory and/or research was present to aid either the individuals immersed in the "coming-out" process (Halpin and Allen 2004). Moreover, the stigmatization of being gay or lesbian often lead to perceptions of pathology among this population and thus, deserving of second-class citizenship.

To address these issues, Cass (1979 1984) created a stage model of homosexual identity development, which allowed persons within the coming-out process and members of their support network to better conceptualize and operationalize the issues faced by persons with a homosexual orientation. For Cass, there is an underlying cognitive component associated with movement from one stage of homosexual identity development to the next. Cass (1979) views homosexual identity development as the interaction between individuals and their sociocultural contexts, such that the development of a homosexual identity is contingent on the degree to which an individual 1) perceives his/her sexuality (i.e., "am I straight or gay"), 2) perceives his/her own sexual behaviors (i.e., "do I act on my sexual attractions toward members of the same-sex or opposite sex?") and 3) how others perceive the individual's sexual identity (i.e., "do others think I am/act gay or straight?").

The first stage in Cass' homosexual identity development is Identity Confusion. Here, the individual begins to question his/her imposed heterosexual orientation, particularly as he or she begins to develop attractions or intimate feelings for members of the same sex. At this stage, there is confusion because the individual has a self-perception regarding his sexual identity that may be different from his past and current behaviors and also different from the social perception others might have. This leads to the second stage, Identity Comparison, where the sexual questioning individual begins to feel that he or she is not part of the initial social group to which he/she belonged. This is the result of his or her knowledge that he or she does not act in the manner that the group perceives. That is, the feeling that the individual is hiding the possibility that he or she is attracted to members of the same sex results in increased self-imposed social isolation from the larger social group (Cass 1984; Halpin, and Allen 2004).

The third stage of Cass' model is Identity Tolerance, wherein the individual begins to explore his or her sexual orientation as a gay person or lesbian vis-à-vis engaging in what is considered a homosexual subculture (Cass 1979, 1984). At this stage, the individual begins to accept or at least tolerate the likelihood that he/she is gay and therefore, delves into the culture to determine, most likely to explore his or her feelings as well as to determine the degree to which such feelings are accepted and support by other members of this population. The fourth stage is Identity Acceptance, where individuals begin to significantly increase their contact with others who identify as homosexual. Cass (1984) points out that with this acceptance of a homosexual identity and the behavioral exhibitions of such (e.g., living in and/or exploring gay communities), comes the difficulty of "passing," particularly within the larger heterosexual society (Halpin and Allen 2004). Here, the individual is preoccupied with whether and how his or her new sexual identity will be accepted in the larger mainstream society.

In the fifth stage, Identity Pride, the individual, in gaining a more positive sense of self as a gay person, begins to condemn heterosexual society itself. This may have resulted from the negative images and stereotypes and the overall difficulties faced by gay individuals at the hands of many members of heterosexist society. In the sixth and final stage, Identity Synthesis, the individual may begin to have richer discussions and overall experiences with heterosexuals, which results in a mitigating belief that all or most members of heterosexist society are against persons with homosexual orientations. That is, gay persons in this stage, as a result of their interactions with heterosexual persons who support their sexual orientation, will arrive at the belief that they can coexist. What is important in this stage is the idea that homosexual is but one of several identities that the individual possesses and thus, it become synthesized with all other existing identities. Thus, for Cass, the final stage of Identity Synthesis seems to focus on both social and personal integration of the homosexual self. First, the gay person views him or herself as belonging in contexts where heterosexism predominates and among heterosexual persons as well. Also, personal integration of homosexual identity emerges when the gay person realizes that his or her homosexual identity is but one component of his or her comprehensive identity.

Building on Cass' work is that of Dr. Richard Troiden. Troiden's stage theory of homosexual identity development emerges from data provided by 150 gay men. Emerging from these data are four stages of homosexual identity development. The first stage of Troiden's homosexual identity model is the sensitization stage where the person begins to experience feelings of marginality and differentiation from same-sex peers as a result of his or her budding homosexual interests. The second stage is identity confusion, where during early adolescence, there is psychological instability and uncertainty surrounding issues of sexual identity. It is during this stage that the individual begins to examine more closely his or her feelings regarding sexual preferences and interests. The third stage of Troiden's (1989) model is identity assumption. During late adolescence, there are greater feelings of identity tolerance and acceptance along with increased immersion into gay culture. The last stage, commitment, is characterized as a sense of self-acceptance and comfort with a homosexual identity. It is at this stage that many homosexual individuals exhibit pride in being gay or lesbian while concomitantly working to educate and inform others about homosexuality (Troiden 1989).

While both models of homosexual identity development provide readers with a much more detailed understanding of the experiences of gay individuals, there are some distinctions between the two theories. To begin, Troiden's theory is premised on research with gay men, while Cass' work is largely conceptual. Cass's theory, however, provides a much richer articulation of such experiences. For example, in Troiden's last stage, identity commitment, there seems to be a focus on self-acceptance regarding one's sexual orientation while simultaneously working to enhance the lived experiences of others who have similar initial experiences with "coming out." Cass' model, which is not sociological in scope, focuses more on the integration of the homosexual identity model into the larger spectrum of identities possessed by gay persons. While there is some discussion of the gay person's ability to coexist with heterosexuals and thereby, integrate him/herself into the larger social world, Cass' last stage seems to focus on how the individual deals with an integrated homosexual identity internally or psychologically while Troiden seems to focus on how the individual deals with such an identity externally or socially.

For the purpose presented in this book, the conceptualization and comprehensiveness of homosexual identity as a personal issue (i.e., Cass model) has greater relevance to a discussion of young African American men because it explicitly details how some members of this population make sense of their experiences as gay men without undermining the presence of additional identity components. Specifically, in examining Cass' last stage, Identity Synthesis, for persons with additional marginalized social locations (e.g., being African American, poor), there is a greater emphasis on how homosexual identity fits with the rest of these identity components in order to allow the individual to have the most cohesive identity possible. With this theory articulating the development of homosexual identity, a focus on how such an identity can be and is often rendered invisible among young African American men is provided below.

INVISIBILITY AND AFRICAN AMERICAN MEN'S SEXUAL IDENTITY

Despite the fact that the American Psychiatric Association and the American Psychological Association removed homosexuality from their lists of mental disorders well over thirty years ago, a careful read of the psychological research on sexual identity reveals a curious loyalty to heterosexuality (American Psychological Association 2012; Mohr 2009; Savin-Williams 2001; Wilson et al. 2010). While some are beginning to include sexual orientation in the data collected (ADDHealth 2007), it is not uncommon practice for researchers to neglect query of the sexual preferences and practices of young African American men, as they are typically assumed to be heterosexual (Carver, Egan, and Perry 2004; Gibbs 1997; Howard, Davis, Evans-Ray, Mitchell, and Apomah 2004; Mohr 2009; So 2003; Wise 2004). In fact, it is rare for the issue of sexual identity to emerge in psychological research unless there is a comparative focus between gay and straight study participants (Savin-Williams 2001; So 2003). Assumptions of heterosexuality in psychological research along with omissions of sexual identity queries in research on adolescent and adult populations—what Mohr (2009) refers to as "scientific heterosexism"—contribute to the stigmatization of sexual minorities or persons with nonheterosexual identities in this country (Burlew and Serface 2006; Crawford, Allison, Zamboni and Soto 2002; Mohr 2009).

Assumptions regarding heterosexuality emerge in research on African American men. For example, Gilmore et al. (1996) report that by age nienteen, 96 percent of African American adolescent males report an average of eleven sexual partners. However, there is no discernment of the partners' gender or sexual identity (i.e., homosexual or heterosexual), let alone that of the research participants. It is not uncommon for many to assume that sexual intercourse was between two heterosexuals (one man and one woman). However, it is likely that it could have occurred between two homosexual men.

In addition to homosexuality being rendered invisible throughout the majority of psychological research, the invisibility of homosexual identity is especially prevalent in African American communities. In particular, research by Peterson (1992) and Savin-Williams (1996 2001) has concluded that most African American sexual minorities are urged to withhold disclosure of their sexual identity or even deny it. So (2003) and others have concluded that African American gay men are the least likely of all ethnic groups to disclose their sexual orientation to others or have a protracted period of time where they are questioning their sexual identity (see Cass' theory of homosexual identity development) (Dube and Savin-Williams 1999; Green 2007; May, Chatters, Cochran, and Mackness 1998). Consequences of disclosing homosexual orientation include physically and psychologically ostracizing from the African American community (Herek and Capitiano 1995; King 2004).

For example, in a 2007 qualitative study of thirty African American gay men, Green (2007) found that close to 80 percent of the sample reported that many of the same individuals and institutions that provide a strong racial self-concept among the men were also critical and unsupportive of their emerging homosexual identities. Additionally, Waldner and Magruder (1999) found that African American college students had significantly more negative attitudes toward gay men than did Hispanic and White college students. Further, Johnson (2003) writes that famous African American actors and comedians such as Eddie Murphy (the author references Murphy's gratuitous and frequent use of the term "faggot" during one of his recorded comedy shows, "Delirious"), have transmitted perhaps unknowingly, have transmitted the negative attitudes towards homosexuality. Further, Lemell and Battle (2004) noted a trend suggesting that African American female churchgoers held unfavorable attitudes towards African American homosexual men. Finally, Burlew and Serface (2006) and Miller (2007) observed that many African American homosexual men have to deal with being ostracized by members of their race.

Based on these works, it can be concluded that the social experiences of African American men identifying as homosexual are, at times, adverse and may result in feelings of invisibility. A study by Wilson and Miller (2002) uniquely characterizes these feelings of invisibility felt among gay African American men and the resulting behaviors exhibited by them. Specifically, Wilson and Miller (2002) examined the strategies used to cope with homosexual identity among thirty-seven gay African American men. In the study, it was found that the majority of the participants engaged in what the authors called role flexing or the alteration of their behaviors, dress/appearance and overall mannerism in what the authors referred to as "non-gay-friendly" (NGF) contexts.

One example of role flexing reported among the participants included the adoption of an extreme masculinity, which included engaging in violent and disrespectful acts towards homosexuals (homoantagonism) and avoiding public affection and intimacy with men. Another form of role flexing was referred to by the authors as "being sanctimonious," wherein gay African American men sought to make their sexual identity invisible via a focused intent on adhering to religious and/or spiritual teachings, particularly those transmitted in church. Still another, more blatant form of role flexing was referred to as "the cover-up," where participants reported lying about their sexual identity or associated activities (e.g., frequenting gay clubs), identifying as heterosexual, and being on the downlow or establishing sexual relationships with women while concealing their homosexual identity and resulting sexual practices with men. A final strategy reported by the participants in the study was avoidance or changing of homosexual activities (Wilson and Miller 2002). Some men in the study reported that, at earlier points in their lives, they sought to avoid sexual activity with same-sex partners in order to avoid the negative consequences of being identified as homosexual (Wilson and Miller 2002).

In this and other studies (Brown 2005; McCready 2004; Ward 2005), it has been shown that many African American men who maintain a homosexual identity are often relegated to second-class citizen status at best, and at worse, are victimized vis-à-vis, self-imposed or others' behaviors resulting from the perception that these men are not men. This limited conceptualization of what manhood is, particularly within African American communities has often resulted in gay African American men feeling inferior or needing to hide their true sexual identities and thereby, avoid any negative encounters with those who feel that manhood is tantamount to sexual attraction to and conquest of women (Miller 2007; Wilson et al. 2010). Supporting this claim are two studies which found that among ten gay African American churchgoing men living with HIV/AIDS (Miller 2007) and among thirty-nine gay African American male adolescents (Wilson et al. 2010), there were frequent reports of being marginalized and/or ostracized by members of their communities (i.e., clergymen/churchgoers and peers, respectively). Such was also the case in a study examining the lived experiences of older African American gay men (Burlew and Serface 2006).

INTERSECTIONALITY AND AFRICAN AMERICAN MEN'S SEXUAL IDENTITY

Discrimination, ostracizing, and their psychological and physical consequences are not unique to African American male members of sexual minority groups (Dube and Savin-Williams 1999; Green 2007; Huebner and Davis 2007). Overall, adolescents and young adults with homosexual identities or gender nonconforming behavioral characteristics and exhibitions often have to cope with marginalization in a largely heterosexual, but increasingly homosexual tolerant context such as the United States (Dressler 1985; Herek and Glunt 1993; Morrison and Morrison 2002; Worthington et al. 2002).

In all, the psychological effects of heterosexism on homosexual persons have resulted in attempted and completed suicide (Kulkin, Chauvin, and Percle 2000; Savin-Williams and Ream 2003), high risk sexual behavior (Folkman, Chesney, Pollack, and Phillips 1992), delinquent and criminal behavior, poor academic performance, drug abuse, running away from home, and prostitution (Rotherman-Borus et al. 1995; Savin-Williams 1994).The effects of heterosexism for sexual minority group members are exacerbated by issues of race (Crawford, Allison, Zamboni, and Soto 2002; Icard 1986). As previously noted, Wise (2004) and others (Ward 2005) explain that African American homosexual men must negotiate the psychological realms of being 1) an African American man within a racist society, 2) an African American homosexual man in a heterosexist society, and 3) an African American man ostracized by his own community.

What results for these men coping with racism, homophobia, and heterosexism are often a disaffiliation with predominantly heterosexual

African American communities and a simultaneous disaffiliation with predominantly homosexual White communities (Green 2007; Loiacano 1989; Ward 2005; Wilson and Miller 2002; Wilson et al. 2010). Evidence to support these claims is found in the literature (Burlew and Serface 2006; McCready 2004). These reports suggest that gay African American men are not only rendered invisible by racist, homophobic, and heterosexist communities, but much of this invisibility is a reflection of the intersection between race and sexual identity. That is, being an African American gay man has kept many members of this population from being accepted in and supported by their own African American communities as well as gay communities predominated by White, homosexual men.

From an intersectionality framework, homosexual identity for African American men also intersects with racial identity and gender identity. Paraphrasing Wise (2004), it is necessary to examine issues of race as they relate to gender and sexuality, particularly for African American men because much of the conceptualization of masculinity for this population has been linked to institutional racism. That is, given the unique experiences of African American men in the United States (e.g., during chattel slavery they were removed from households and families, unable to protect loved ones), it had become expected that African American men, no longer slaves, would demonstrate manhood by pursuing sexual relationships with women and supporting their families. Thus, for many gay African American men, not adhering to this traditional concept of manhood is exacerbated by the fact that, for decades, African American men—because of institutional racism—were not always capable of pursuing sexual associations with women and/or protecting their female counterparts and their offspring (Wise 2004). Thus, members of the African American community likely frowned upon homosexuality because, for a very long time, African American men had been stripped of their ability to be "traditional" men.

In addition to the intersection between race and sexual identity for African American men, there is evidence to suggest that sexual identity, particularly homosexual identity intersects with ideas about one's racial identity. Specifically, one study has investigated the role of both sexual identity and racial identity in various behavioral and psychological outcomes for young African American homosexual men. Crawford, Allison, Zamboni, and Soto (2002) created a typology to account for African American gay and bisexual men's (AAGBM) experiences with racism and heterosexism. The categories reflected the current racial and sexual identification status of the participants based on their daily life experiences.

The first category was assimilation (low sexual identification/high racial-ethnic identification), where the AAGBM denies his existence as a gay man, but acknowledges his existence as an African American man. The second category was integration (high sexual identification/high ethnic-racial identification), where an AAGBM acknowledges his homosexuality publicly while doing the same for his African American status. Given his proclamation of his homosexual identity, along with the obvious race category, it appears that NBA player Jason Collins would have been in the integration category with strong orientation toward both racial and sexual minority identities. The third category, separation (high sexual identification/low ethnic-racial identification), characterized the AAGBM that acknowledged his homosexuality publicly while not acknowledging or participating fully in the social and political agenda of the larger African American community. The final category was marginalization (low sexual identification/low ethnic-racial identification) where there is little association or acknowledgement of either homosexual or African American identity identities.

Crawford et al. (2002) found that AAGBM reporting adherence to the integration category reported higher self-esteem, HIV prevention efficacy, stronger social support networks, greater levels of life satisfaction, and lower levels of male gender role and psychosocial distress. Those participants in the marginalization status, however, reported the greatest amount of psychological distress and the lowest levels of self-esteem and life satisfaction (Crawford et al. 2002). The authors concluded that, to better understand the complexities of African American homosexual men, it is necessary to examine how sexual identity is integrated and accepted within one's racial-ethnic identity. Extending these conclusions, it is important to recognize the intersection of racial and sexual identities for both homosexual and heterosexual African American men (Hoffman 2004; Worthington, Savoy, Dillon, and Vernaglia 2002). More recent findings by Wilson and colleagues (2010) support these claims that many African American sexual minority men must negotiate the dominant masculinity/traditional male gender role, while simultaneously addressing their own issues with sexual identity.

In another study, Hunter (2010) investigated which identity (racial or sexual) was more salient among a sample of fifty self-identified African American gay men. Using qualitative research methods, including one-on-one interviews, three themes emerged from participant data: interlocking, up-down, and public-private (Hunter 2010). Within the interlocking theme, race and sexual identity were deemed inextricably linked. One participant offered his refusal to choose between the two (in terms of importance and salience) "because they work together in a way that's different." In particular, the respondent argues that "Because I am not White, my gay experience is different and because I am gay, my Black experience is more complex . . . [and] in order for me to understand myself, I've had to place my understanding of myself in a way that helps me consider both gay and Black at the same time" (Hunter 2010, 85). Among the participants, Hunter (2010) noted that the interlocking conceptualization emerged as a primary way of identifying for 24 percent of the sample.

In the up-down conceptualization of race and sexuality, there is clear evidence among the participants that one identity is privileged over the other, such that the self-identification is viewed as either "Black then gay" or "gay then Black" (Hunter 2010). Here, another respondent argued his stance on the issue of race being more salient than sexual identity in claiming "I am Black first and always. That's what people see, and that's what I deal with. The gay thing is something else. . . . Gay is an action and Black is a way of life. When I go out . . . people still see me as a Black man" (Hunter 2010, 87). In providing support for this up-down conceptualization of race and sexual identity, another study participant noted that race is much more salient than his homosexual identity as it is the former that is often used as a rationale for his exposure to and experiences with negative social interactions. Specifically, the participant stated "Not to take away from . . . being gay, but I truly feel that people do not see that. When I'm being followed in the store, it's because I'm black, not because I'm gay; folks don't even see that" (Hunter 2010, 87). The reverse of this stance was a "gay then Black" concept among participants where there was openness about their sexual identity, along with explicit indicators that would allow others to conclude that they were gay (e.g., public displays of affectionation with same sex partners). One participant noted,

> I think before people even realize that I am Black they think I am gay. Because it's in the way I act, walk, speak, and relate to other people. I truly only feel Black when I am in an all Black community, or an all Black function. Otherwise, I always feel gay first. I hold my boyfriend's hand and everything. I don't hide it from anybody. (Hunter 2010, 92)

Among the study participants, Hunter (2010) noted that up-down conceptualization of race-sexual identity intersection emerged for 50 percent of the sample.

Finally, Hunter (2010) found that public-private identities, which accounted for 26 percent of the sample's responses about how they identify themselves, were specific to context or what the author referred to as "space." Here, participants' aesthetic characteristics (i.e., skin color) were considered self-evident and thus, the race-based identity was largely viewed as a public identity, whereas the homosexual identity was viewed as being more private as participants often decide when, where, and to whom they would disclose such an identity. One participant eloquently stated,

> When I come in, the people I work with and work for see a Black employee, not necessarily a gay one. . . . When I am out on a date with another man . . . that space makes my sexuality work like how my race works when I am at the office. By being on that date . . . my sexuality is visible. [Thus], I recognize that both my identities matter, but I think

are best captured if you are aware of the spaces in which they are made to matter. (Hunter 2010, 92)

Given this literature articulating the influence of racism in particular and race-based issues in general on the development of both heterosexual and homosexual orientations for African American men, researchers must begin to follow the path of authors like Hunter and Crawford and colleagues to more fully explore the intersection of race, gender role, and sexual identity for African American men. Some gaps in the literature include an exclusion of the coming out process for African American male adolescents, particularly those who may have initially adhered to a heterosexual identity that may have resulted from feelings of invisibility (Wilson and Miller 2002). Given that identity development typically occurs during adolescence, it would be important to provide a better understanding of the experiences of young African American male adolescents who 1) may be at different stages of the homosexual identity development process, 2) are simultaneously balancing the pressure of adhering to traditional and acceptable standards of Black masculinity and 3) do so within a racist context that undermine their efforts toward becoming a man. Though some studies have provided some rationale for a reconsideration of leading conceptualizations of manhood, particularly when it comes to perceiving the essence of Black manhood as a heterosexual male (Oware 2011; Wise 2004), much of the literature exposing new conceptualizations of African American masculinity ideals, which preclude the assumption of heterosexuality, has limited representation in the educational and psychological literature.

Along with these issues, it would be important and timely to explore the race and sexual identity intersection with young African American men today as several social media, support groups, along with the presence of young, gay African American men who have been successful in the entertainment industry (e.g., Frank Ocean—hip hop artist, Jason Collins—professional basketball player, E. Lynn Harris—author, Don Lemon—cable news anchorman; Rahsaan Patterson, R & B singer; Shaun Thompson—fitness celebrity; Darren Young—World Wrestling Entertainment superstar) may have, to some degree, relaxed the social stigma associated with being an African American man with a homosexual identity (Wise 2004).

112   *Chapter 8*

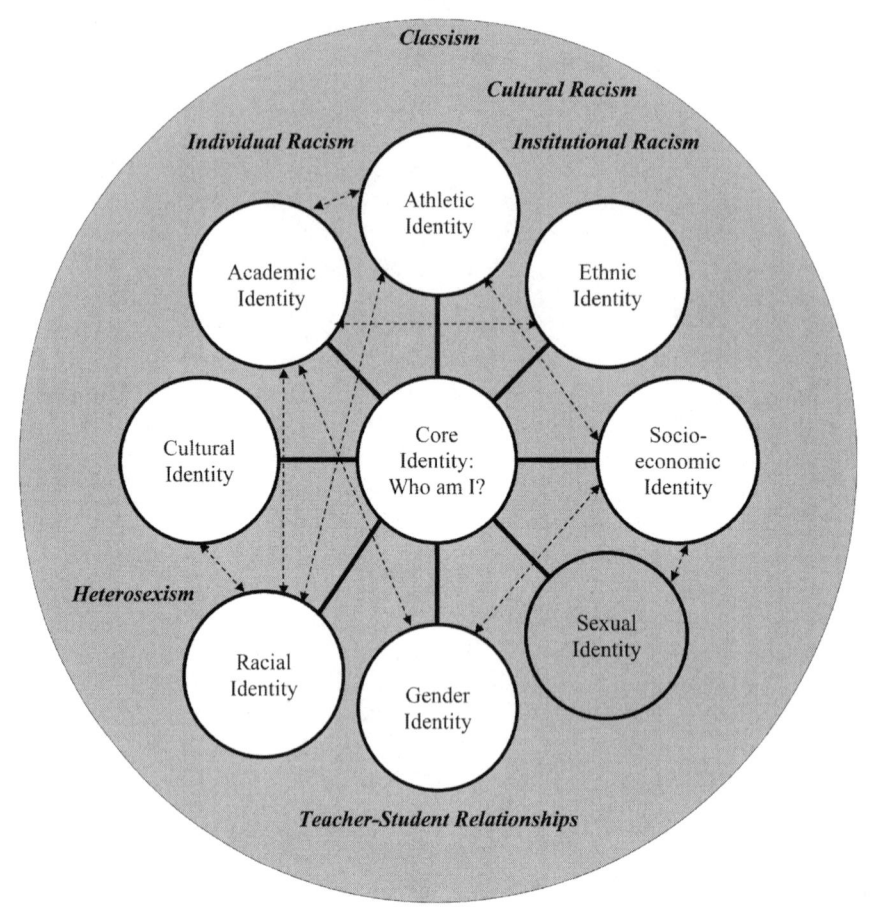

Figure 8.1. Conceptual Model of African American Men's Identity: Compromised Sexual Identity

ILLUSTRATION OF AFRICAN AMERICAN MEN'S IDENTITY INVISIBILITY—SEXUAL IDENTITY

In figure 8.1, the darker charcoal circle of racism and related social ills begin to compromise sexual identity. While it is more appropriate to consider the role of heterosexism as the primary reason for a compromised and/or invisible sexual identity, it is also important to consider the role that racism plays in this regard as well. The role of gender identity seems to have some association here. Specifically, long ago, racist acts, events, and perceptions of this population had stripped African American men of their manhood, especially when we consider the manhood definition to be the ability to take care of one's self and one's loved ones. Thus, a major theme within African American communities had been to ensure that African American men would be able to take care of their wives and children. The assumption was that African American men, because they, for so long, had been unable to prove themselves as men, would always seek to be men, heterosexual men, in particular.

For many, African American men, homosexuality counters the social and community-based emphasis and definition of what it means to be a man. That is, homosexuality likely became invisible within the African American community because that community's historical and contemporary experiences with racism resulted in a unidimensional conceptualization of manhood, one that reflected more traditional themes of manhood, even when mainstream society kept some African American men from achieving such status. For some African American community members, to be a man meant you had to have heterosexual relationships and thus, take care of women; something that many African American male slaves were unable to do.

Racism not only indirectly linked itself to sexual identity by way of its association with feelings about manhood within the African American community, but it also impacts the experiences of African American sexual minority men as well. Some research has already shown that African American gay men have different and more antagonistic experiences both within their own African American communities and within the larger gay communities predominated by White men, to the point where they often have to hide or refrain from disclosing their true sexual identities (Green 2007; King 2004; So 2003). With these examples, it is clear that sexual identity has been impacted by racism, and thus, is often rendered invisible for some African American men, notably African American gay men. The sexual identity of heterosexual African American men are not necessarily considered invisible as their actions are consistent with the expectation of men in a predominantly heterosexual context such as the United States. However, the expectation that they will engage in such relationships to the point of perceived pathology (i.e., hypermasculinity) does reflect a racist belief and thus, this identity can be, to some degree considered invisible as well.

NINE
African American Men's Racial Identity

Of all forms of identity investigated among African Americans, racial identity research is arguably the most prominent in the psychological literature (Sellers et al. 1997; Trimble, Helms, and Root 2002). Ford and Harris (1997) reported that, in 1997, more than 400 empirical studies had explored the correlates and corollaries of racial identity among African Americans. Nearly 20 years since that publication, it is likely that that number of studies has, at least, doubled. Indeed, racial identity has been considered a significant factor in human development (Burrow, Tubman, and Montgomery 2006).

Helms (1990) and Cokley (2007) define racial identity as a sense of group or collective identity that is premised on one's perception of a common racial heritage or legacy shared with a particular racial group. Unlike the social construct of race itself, which is a categorization premised chiefly on physical and phenotypic characteristics such as skin color, racial identity focuses on feelings about being a member of a group that possesses such physical and phenotypic characteristics, along with additional ethnic and cultural characteristics specific to that given group. Distinctions between race and ethnicity have been made elsewhere (Cokley 2005, 2007; Helms, Jernigan, and Mascher 2005; Helms 2007; Phinney 1996; Trimble 2007; Trimble et al. 2002). While some have sought to combine the two constructs (Umana-Taylor et al, 2014) it is not the position in this text that these two identity components (i.e., racial identity and ethnic identity) are considered the same. Thus, ethnic identity will not be discussed as a proxy to racial identity in this paper. Rather, ethnic identity will be discussed as a separate identity component that is distinguishable from racial identity within the psychological and educational literature in particular and the social science literature in general.

In the past thirty years, the research on racial identity with African Americans has enjoyed theoretical, conceptual, and empirical advances (Cokley 2002; Helms 1990, 2007; Pierre and Mahalik 2005; Sellers et al. 1997). Since the advent of the highly heralded Nigrescence model (Cross 1971, 1995), revisions and new conceptualizations of African American racial identity (Helms 1997; Parham and Helms 1985; Oyserman and Harrison 2002; Sellers et al. 1997) and corresponding instrumentation (Altschul, Oyserman, and Bybee 2006; Oyserman, Bybee, and Terry 2003; Oyserman, Gant, and Ager 1995; Oyserman, Harrison, and Bybee 2003; Resnicow, Soler, Braithwaite, Selassie, and Smith 1999) have been advanced to empirically investigate the accuracy of Black racial identity theories (Helms 1997; Sellers et al. 1997; Vandiver et al. 2002). To date, there are at least four models of racial identity that have been forwarded to describe the racial identity development of African Americans. The three presented here are those of Drs. William Cross, Janet Helms, and Robert Sellers.

AFRICAN AMERICAN RACIAL IDENTITY MODELS

While the origins of Black racial identity development can be traced to the work of Thomas (1971), it is the work of Dr. William Cross that has catapulted racial identity into current psychological discourse. In response to Thomas' initial model of Black racial identity development, Cross (1971) forwarded the model of Nigrescence, or the psychology of becoming Black (Pope-Davis, Liu, Ledesma-Jones, and Nevitt 2000). A major impetus for the model was Cross' belief that an overidentification with mainstream or White culture could be psychologically damaging to African Americans (Kohatsu and Richardson 1996).

Initially, Cross proposed a five-stage model where each stage was characterized by African Americans' feelings, thoughts, and corresponding behaviors about being Black or African American. The first stage was *preencounter*, which was characterized by African Americans' preference for White culture and a simultaneous denigration of themselves and their respective culture. The second stage was *encounter*, where a particular racial/racist event challenges the rationale behind White preference found in the preencounter stage. *Immersion/emersion* is the third stage of the Nigrescence model where African Americans, after having the racist/racial encounter, begin to immerse themselves in the "Black experience," primarily by adopting "pro-Black" attitudes. Accompanying immersion was emersion, where African Americans begin to develop a balance between such pro-Black attitudes and those less ethnocentric. The fifth and final stage is *internalization/commitment*, which focuses on African Americans' commitment to eradicate racism and oppression (Cross, 1971).

Psychologists have since revised the Nigrescence model. To begin, Cross (1995) reconceptualized the encounter stage, wherein attitudes at this stage not only reflect a focus on espousing anti-Black attitudes, but also the insignificance of being African American. Dr. Janet Helms offered a newer conceptualization of racial identity as Cross' initial Nigrescence model entered the psychological discourse. Helms (1990), in particular, noted that the Nigrescence stages reflected one's current attitudes and interactions with social others and thus, were not fixed or specific to different age or developmental levels. Helms (1990) argued that these attitudes were better characterized as statuses and not stages. Thus, one set of Black racial identity attitudes could be dominant at any time (Helms 1989, 1990, 1997). Helms' reconfiguration of Cross's original Nigrescence model led to the development of the first instrument used to assess the presence and effects of revised racial identity statuses (Helms 1989, 1997). In particular, Helms' work with colleague, Dr. Thomas Parham, led to the development of the Racial Identity Attitudes Scale (RIAS), which measures Nigrescence stage model components with some variations, based on their reconceptualization (Marks, Settles, Cooke, Morgan, and Sellers 1997).

Parham and Helms (1981) forwarded two ideas that advanced discussions of Black racial identity development. First, Parham and Helms (1981) argued that one major limitation of the initial Cross' model of Nigrescence was its sample homogeneity. That is, most of the studies used in creating and validating the Nigrescence model emerged from data provided by African American college students. The implication, according to Parham and Helms (1981), was that much of Black racial identity development occurs during young adulthood. To this end, Parham and Helms (1981) proposed three phases of adulthood in which they believed racial identity occurred: Early adulthood, where there is an emphasis on overt behavioral manifestation toward "Blackness" (e.g., having African American friends and supporting African American initiatives and causes); middle adulthood, where there is an emphasis on one's role within a given institution (e.g., increasing the number of African American applicants and/or employees at a given institution/job); and late adulthood, where the emphasis is on reflection, particularly about being African American and what remaining contributions can be made to facilitate the lives of younger African American generations (Marks et al. 1996). Parham and Helms (1981) also did not believe the stage model structure to the Nigrescence model was appropriate as it was likely that individuals, in progressing through the model could either remain stagnant within a given racial identity stage or recycle/regress back to a previous stage.

Adding to the various conceptualizations of Black racial identity and building on the work of both Cross and Helms is the Multidimensional Inventory of Black Identity (MIBI) by Dr. Robert Sellers and colleagues

(Neblett, Philip, Cogburn, and Sellers 2006; Rowley, Sellers, Chavous, and Smith 1998; Sellers et al. 1997; Sellers, Caldwell, Schmeelk-Cone, and Zimmerman 2003; Sellers and Shelton 2003). The MIBI contains four dimensions: racial identity salience, racial identity centrality, racial identity ideology, and racial identity regard. Salience and centrality refer to the significance of race (i.e., "how important are race and race-based issues to you?"), while ideology and regard focus on the qualitative meaning that individuals ascribe to their membership in the African American race (i.e., "what does it mean to you to be a member of this particular race?") (Sellers et al. 1997).

In particular, salience is defined as the extent to which a person's race is a relevant part of her or his self-concept at a given moment. Centrality refers to the extent to which one views race as a central and integral part of his or her self-concept. It asks the question "How important is being Black/African American to me and my overall sense of self?" Ideology focuses on how one feels members of a given race should act, and it contains four conceptual components: nationalist, oppressed minority, assimilationist, and humanist (see Sellers et al. 1997 for a review of these components). A sample item from the nationalist subscale of the MIBI is "It is important for Black people to surround their children with Black art, music, and literature." A sample item for the oppressed minority subscale includes "Black people should treat other oppressed groups as allies." A sample item from the assimilationist subscale of the MIBI is "Blacks should try to work within the system to achieve their political and economic goals." Finally, a sample item from the humanist subscale of the MIBI includes "Blacks and Whites have more commonalities than differences." (Sellers et al. 1997).

Finally, the last major subscale of the MIBI, regard, reflects one's positive or negative feelings toward African Americans and his or her membership in that group (i.e., I am proud to be Black/African American). The regard dimension contains two components, private and public regard. The former focuses on how the individual perceives African Americans (i.e., "What do I think about other African American/Black people?"), while public regard examines the individual's perceptions of how social others think and feel about African Americans (i.e., "What do other people—most likely non–African Americans—think about African Americans?")

Each model of Black racial identity has led to several quantitative measures, including the MIBI, the Cross Racial Identity Scale (CRIS) and Helm's Black Racial Identity Attitudes Scale (BRIAS). While some debate exists regarding the best instrument to use in measuring Cross' Nigrescence model (Cokley 2007; Helms 2007), some validation work has been performed on each scale (Cokley 2002; Helms 1990; Sellers et al. 1997; Scottham and Sellers 2008; Vandiver, Cross, Worrell, and Fhagen-Smith 2002; Worrell, Vandiver, Cross, and Fhagen-Smith 2004; Yanico, Swanson, and Tokar 1994). More importantly, each scale has been used to examine the associations between racial identity and various psychological and academic outcomes for African American children and young adults and college students including academic achievement/GPA (Altschul, Oyserman, and Bybee 2006; Byrd and Chavous 2009; Chavous et al. 2003; Harper and Tuckman 2006; Witherspoon, Speight, and Thomas 1997), academic self-efficacy (Oyserman, Harrison, and Bybee 2001; Witherspoon, Speight, and Thomas 1997), adjustment to college and overall psychological health at college (Anglin and Wade 2007; Pillay 2005; Thomas, Townsend, and Belgrave 2003), risky sexual behaviors (Oparanozie, Sales, DiClemente, and Braxton 2013), psychological distress (Sellers, Copeland-Linder, Martin, and Lewis 2006; Sellers, Caldwell, Schmeelk-Cone, and Zimmerman 2003), religious orientation (Sanchez and Carter 2005), school involvement (Oyserman, Bybee, and Terry 2003), African American childrearing beliefs and practices (Thomas 2000; Thomas and Speight 1999), negative stereotypes about African Americans (Cokley 2002; Okeke, Howard, Kurtz-Costes, and Rowley 2009), perceptions of and coping with racial discrimination (Scott 2003; Sellers et al. 2006; Sellers and Shelton 2003), and self-esteem (Goodstein and Ponterotto 1997; Rowley, Sellers, Chavous, and Smith 1998).

Given its omnipresence within the psychological and educational literature (Burrow, Tubman, and Montgomery 2006), it is not surprising that racial identity and its impact on a variety of psychological and behavioral outcomes has been well established for African American populations. For example, an earlier study by Jackson and Neville (1998) examined the racial identity attitudes of 122 African American college students and found a significant association between these reports and their perception of hope, particularly toward academic and career-based goals. A study by Pillay (2005) examined the association between racial identity reports of 136 African American undergraduates and their reports of psychological health. Results revealed that earlier racial identity stages, namely, preencounter and encounter stages (sample item: "I believe that Black people should learn to think and experience life in ways which are similar to White people.") were related to lower scores on psychological health reports. In that study, the RIAS was used as the racial identity measure (Parham and Helms 1985) later, a 2007 study by Anglin and Wade (2007) found that an internalized multicultural racial identity—as measured by the CRIS internalization subscale—was significantly predictive of better adjustment to college for African American college-age participants.

Regarding young African American men, a handful of studies have shown that racial identity components have significant associations with various academic and psychological outcomes. For example, Whaley, Allen, and Dana (2003) found that immersion-emersion scores significantly predicted Minnesota Multiphasic Personality Inventory (MMPI) subscales four (psychopathic deviation) and nine (hypomania) scores in African American men. Internalization scores were predictive of MMPI scale six (paranoia) scores for this population. Pierre and Mahalik (2005) found that internalization scores were associated with greater self-esteem for young African American men. Preencounter and immersion racial identity attitudes were associated with greater psychological distress and lower self-esteem for this population. Using an African American male college sample, Campbell and Fleming (2001) found that fear of success was positively correlated with preencounter and encounter attitudes and negatively correlated with internalization attitudes.

More recently, Bynum and colleagues (2008) used the private regard subscale of the MIBI to examine associations between racial identity—as conceptualized by Sellers et al. (1997)—and various indices of psychological well-being. Findings showed that African American men who reported a greater sense of private regard (i.e., identification with racial group) were less likely to report depressive symptoms. A fairly recent study by Fhagen-Smith and colleagues (2010) used the CRIS to determine the association between gender and racial identity reports among African American college students. Findings revealed that many African American male college students endorse racial identity attitudes that reflect an immersion into all things African American, while limiting exposure to/interaction with White persons and culture. The authors concluded, that African American male college students may not endorse racial identity attitudes that focus on building relationships with non–African Americans because of their frequent and sometimes, deleterious experiences with racial discrimination and prejudice (Fhagen-Smith, Vandiver, Worrell, and Cross 2010). These results find support in a more recent qualitative study where Bridges (2011) found that many African American male undergraduates attending predominantly White universities (PWIs) adopt an emersion/immersion racial identity wherein participants discussed both psychological and physical distancing from other White students and the student body overall.

In all, the psychological literature has demonstrated the relevance of racial identity to the lives of African Americans overall and young African American men in particular. For the most part, how African American men feel about being African American and how they perceive others think about African Americans have an impact on their self-perceptions and their psychological health and well-being. While the current literature would likely benefit from a set of studies that examined the associations between multiple forms of racial identity (i.e., Cross and Helms and Sellers' models), it is clear that racial identity research literature, particularly that including African American male participants, has demonstrated the influence racial identity has in the attitudes, feelings, and behaviors of many young African American men.

INVISIBILITY AND AFRICAN AMERICAN MEN'S RACIAL IDENTITY

Conceptually, invisibility syndrome is intricately woven into African American racial identity development. For the leading African American racial identity theory, Nigrescence, progression through its various identity statuses begins with the perception of a racist encounter. However, progression toward the various identity statuses following the racist encounter can be viewed as attempts by African Americans to ward off its stressful psychological effects. These effects include the feelings and attitudes associated with Franklin's invisibility syndrome.

As noted earlier, invisibility "seeks to explain the intra-psychic struggle for personal identity by African American men as the individual confronts specific encounters with racism and how these experiences obscure genuine identity and promote inherent stress related to their management" (Franklin 1999, 763). Inherent to invisibility syndrome is the racist encounter that African American men will have at some point in their lifetime. It is this racist encounter that typifies the commencement of movement throughout Cross' Nigrescence model (1995). That is, it is the perception of a racist encounter that renders the young African American man invisible. It is this feeling of invisibility that serves as a catalyst toward movement throughout the racial identity statuses.

To thwart the negative psychological effects of the perceived racist encounter (i.e., invisibility), the young African American man will likely progress through a series of identity conflicts to resolve and manage feelings of invalidation, dissatisfaction, and illegitimacy brought about by the racist encounter. According to Cross' model, exposure to racism will propel young African American men toward the immersion/emersion status in order to gain a sense of validation and satisfaction with one's racial identity. Invisibility, then, is a vital, albeit unarticulated characteristic to the Nigrescence model, as progression through its various identity statuses—particularly from preencounter to immersion/emersion—is contingent on the African American man or woman's feelings of invisibility brought about by a racist encounter. That is, progression through the racial identity stage model (i.e., Cross and Helms, respectively) is largely premised on how the African American man deals with feelings of invisibility resulting from his encounter with individual and/or institutional racism (Jones 1991).

In being discriminated against or being called a racial slur or additional behaviors which may exemplify some racist undertones (e.g., being followed at a retail store or home from a convenience store by a person suspicious of your activity in a given neighborhood), young African American men will likely begin to immerse themselves, perhaps even moreso, in African American culture and activities in an attempt to impede feelings of helplessness, invalidation, and derision. They will likely begin to display attitudes that proclaim not only a grounded masculinity, one characterized by strength of resolve, but also a set of attitudes that demonstrate a pride in being Black, a pride that cannot be made invisible by the words or actions of others.

Thus, upon experiencing a racist encounter, invisibility syndrome plays a significant role in the progression from encounter to immersion-emersion and other stages of racial identity, because it is this set of invisibility feelings and attitudes that are being fought against in an effort to maintain a stable sense of self-worth, not only as a man, but as an African American man. In seeking to move beyond these feelings of invisibility, it is likely that current and future attitudes and activities displayed by young African American men who experience a racist encounter will be qualitatively distinct from the preencounter stage of racial identity.

Similar to its relevance with the racial identity stage models of William Cross and Janet Helms, invisibility syndrome can also be associated with the racial identity conceptualization forwarded by Dr. Robert Sellers and colleagues. As mentioned earlier, the four components of Sellers et al. (1997) conceptualization of racial identity can be partitioned into two areas: Racial identity salience and racial identity centrality speak to how the degree of importance or significance race has, while racial identity ideology and racial identity regard focus on what being African American actually means to the individual. Each of these racial identity components can be impacted significantly by a specific racist event/encounter.

For example, it is likely that the Trayvon Martin tragedy discussed previously made issues of race much more salient for young African American men. These feelings regarding the importance of race may have emerged from the need to combat feelings of invisibility following the fatal incident. These young men, many of whom may have dressed like Trayvon, walked and talked like Trayvon, and pursued the same activities as Trayvon on that fateful Sunday night, may have come to believe that who they are and what they are considered to be in this United States context is not fully seen or appreciated. That is, following (and most likely, prior to) Trayvon Martin's murder, this population of young men may have felt invisible in certain situations and scenarios within the U.S. Certainly after the incident, these possible feelings of invisibility may have shaped these young men's feelings about the importance and meaning of being African American (racial identity centrality and salience) and also how they and others think and feel about them as a group (racial identity ideology and regard).

For example, in order to combat feelings of invisibility and promote a positive sense of self-worth, especially after the Trayvon Martin tragedy, many young African American men likely concluded at best and at worst, were coerced toward accepting the fact that being African American is central to their experiences, primarily because it is what everyone can see first (racial identity centrality). In Trayvon Martin's case, this characteristic is likely the central factor that cost him his life. Thus, this factor likely gained a significant degree of primacy for many young African American men. Similarly, some of these same young men may have adopted the attitude that many, if not most persons, may not trust or are afraid of young African American men (racial identity public regard), while others themselves may have developed the belief that had Trayvon Martin dressed differently, talked differently, and walked differently, he would not have been suspected and thus, he would still be alive today (racial identity private regard).

Despite the logical underpinnings of invisibility 1) as a psychological catalyst for movement from preencounter to immersion/emersion and 2) its possible presence in the attitudes and perceptions African Americans have about being African American and African Americans as a collective, there is no empirical support for the idea that feelings of invisibility a) follow a perceived microaggressive racist act or b) precede behaviors and attitudes indicative of movement beyond the preencounter racial identity status. Also, there is no evidence in the research literature to support the claims that feelings of invisibility can shape 1) African Americans' attitudes about being African American or 2) their and others' perceptions of the racial group to which they belong. While these hypotheses can be more thoroughly developed and tested in future research, they, nonetheless, imply that invisibility certainly can play a role in the development and manifestation of various racial identities possessed by young African American men.

INTERSECTIONALITY AND AFRICAN AMERICAN MEN'S RACIAL IDENTITY

This section begins with the fact that racial identity research has been well represented in the literature. As previously noted, much of the psychological literature continues to investigate the associations between racial identity—in its varied forms—and a multiple of psychological, academic, and behavioral outcomes (Rivas-Drake, Syed, Umana-Taylor, Markstorm, French, Schwartz, and Lee, 2014). From an intersectionality framework, however, the empirical literature is only beginning to examine the relationships between racial identity and other aspects of identity, such as gender, culture, and sexual identity (Akbar, Chambers, and Sanders Thompson 2001; Allen and Bagozzi 2001; Carter, Williams, Juby, and Buckley 2005; Crawford et al. 2002; Thomas et al. 2003; Pope-Davis, Liu, Ledesma-Jones, and Nevitt 2000; Sanchez and Carter 2005).

For example, Pope-Davis et al. (2000) examined the associations between measures of racial identity and measures of acculturation, which served to assess the degree of identification to African American culture study participants reported. Specifically, the authors used the African

American Acculturation Scale (Landrine and Klonoff 1995) and the Black Racial Identity Attitude Scale (BRIAS: Helms and Parham 1996) and found that among the 187 African American college student participants sampled, high preencounter scores were related to lower African American acculturation scores, which assessed the degree of endorsement African Americans have for specific cultural customs, beliefs, and practices. Also, high immersion scores were related to higher African American acculturation scores. In another study, Carter and colleagues (2005) examined the data provided by fifty-two African American male participants who reported their attitudes regarding traditional gender roles—as measured by the Gender Role Conflict Scale (O'Neil, Helms, Gable, David, and Wrightsman 1986), racial identity—as measured by the Black Racial Identity Attitude Scale (Helms, and Parham 1996), and a psychological symptoms checklist—as measured by the Global Severity Index (Derogatis 1983). The study showed that the racial identity subscale, immersion-emersion, mediated the association between reports of traditional gender roles and severe psychological symptoms.

Thus, the degree to which African American men's endorsement of traditional gender roles (e.g., breadwinner, restricted emotional expression) covaried with their reports of negative psychological symptoms (e.g., depression) was largely determined by their beliefs and actions that demonstrated a strong immersion into African American culture and ways of life. That is, as African American male participants endorsed a strong, pro-Black attitude (almost to the exclusion of White persons), their reports of traditional gender roles became less predictive of adverse psychological symptoms. In essence, if African American men are already dismissing traditional, mainstream (i.e., White) standards, then it is likely that these same standards won't be used to determine whether or not they feel they are fulfilling their roles as men. Wade (1996) reported a similar finding.

Another study showed that positive racial identity statuses were significantly associated with academic performance, thereby reinforcing the idea that how African American students think of themselves personally and socially has implications for how well they do in school (Harper and Tuckman 2006), thereby implying some association between racial identity and academic identity, which will be described later in this chapter.

Some additional studies examining racial identity with other identities for African Americans are presented in the literature. One study examining the intersection between racial and sexual identities is that offered by Crawford, Allison, Zamboni, and Soto (2002) described earlier. Another study (Oyserman et al. 2003) examined the confluence of racial and ethnic identities REI—feelings about the self and the group participants belong to—and school involvement among African American middle grade students. Specifically, the authors found that racial-ethnic identity (REI) components predicted different schooling outcomes for African

American middle school boys and girls. In particular, the REI connectedness component—which assessed a positive sense of belongingness to the racial in-group— predicted improved grades, increased study time, and better attendance for boys, while the REI embedded achievement component—which assessed the belief that school achievement is a significant part of being a member of the racial in-group—predicted improvement in grades for girls. Additional interactions between race, racial identity, and culture have been shown in other work (Gaines et al. 1997).

Along with Oyserman et al's (2003) study that combined racial and ethnic identities and operationalized the constructs as an amalgam rather than separate factors, other studies have sought to investigate the independent contribution of racial and ethnic identity. For example, Phelps, Taylor, and Gerard (2001) employed a sample of African American, African, and West Indian/Caribbean college students in their examination of the associations between ethnic identity and racial identity on reported self-esteem. Regression analyses showed that the internalization status subscale scores—as reported on the Racial Identity Attitude Scale (RIAS: Helms 1990), along with the other-group orientation subscale scores—as reported by the Multi-group Ethnic Identity Measure (MEIM: Phinney 1992) were the only statistically significant predictors of self-esteem (Phelps et al. 2001). The authors noted that these subscale predicted self-esteem emerged statistically significant only for the African American college students.

In all, it is certain that beliefs about one's racial group membership, along with beliefs regarding the race-based issues will remain a significant aspect of the lives of many African Americans and thus, a significant factor examined within the educational and social science literatures. It is important, however, to note that, while racial identity has been shown to be predictive of several behavioral and psychological outcomes for African Americans, it should not be investigated independent of additional identity components and contextual factors. As some research reviewed above has shown, variation in racial identity reports for many young African American men is often times associated with how they feel about being a man, their sexuality, and even their academic performance. That is, there is some degree of intersection between one's racial identity and additional identity components. One of these components that has shared some degree of intersection and perhaps, overlap with racial identity is ethnic identity, which will be discussed in the next chapter.

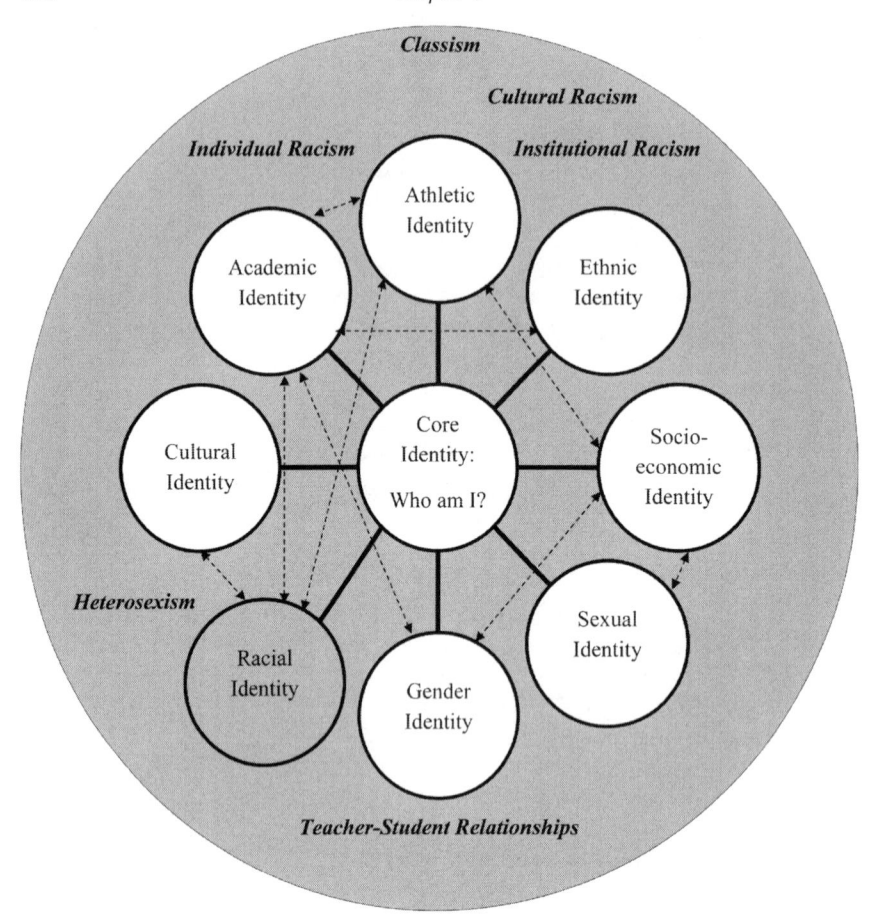

Figure 9.1. Conceptual Model of African American Men's Identity: Compromised Racial Identity

ILLUSTRATION OF AFRICAN AMERICAN MEN'S IDENTITY INVISIBILITY—RACIAL IDENTITY

In figure 9.1, readers will note the darker charcoal grey and the melding of the racial identity component with this color. Here, the impact of racism has modified the racial identity so that the invisibility of the racial identity component is illustrated. As noted in this chapter, when racist encounters or perceptions of racism make young African American men wish that they were members of other races or allow them to hold negative and damaging perceptions of not only themselves, but other members of their community and of their own race, it is very likely that they will have a compromised or invisible racial identity. It is likely that the omnipresence of racism—in its various forms—in most, if not all facets of life for young African American men, including schooling, sports, hip-hop culture, and in mainstream society in general, can negatively impact one's perception of being Black or African American specifically by forcing them to think negatively of themselves and those who look like them. With such a negative public and private regard (Sellers et al. 2003), it is more likely that the lives of these individuals and those within their community become less valuable, almost to the point where some are willing to kill others because the value in being African American or in being an African American man is diminished.

In my hometown of Chicago, Illinois, a place where the first African American president will likely reside after his second term, there seems to be endless reports of senseless murders within African American communities. These crimes are typically carried out by young African American men, many of whom do not see the value of life in others, likely because the value associated with their own lives have been grossly tapered as a result of perceptions of racism and its larger, generational impact. Their racial identity within a racist environment that already views them as a threat and criminal becomes compromised and likely results in one of the strongest examples of a self-fulfilling prophecy that exist within this population. That is, some African American men, as a result of living within a racist environment that compromises the integrity of being African American (i.e., racial identity), live up to the lowered expectations that mainstream society generally has of them.

TEN
African American Men's Ethnic Identity

The research of Dr. Jean Phinney has provided the psychological literature with the most comprehensive conceptualization of ethnic identity (Phinney 1990, 1996; Phinney and Ong 2007). Though early social psychology theorists such as Lewin (1948) and Tajfel (1979) provided some initial understanding of the role of social identification and membership within a particular social group, Phinney's work has pioneered critical discourse as well as empirical inquiry into ethnic identity.

By definition, ethnic identity is considered a sense of belonging to a particular social group. In Phinney's conceptualization, that social group is comprised of members who share ethnicity. For Phinney, the term ethnicity goes beyond an understanding of race. Specifically, Phinney (1996) points out that "the psychological importance of race is derived largely from 1) the way in which one is responded to by others... and 2) the implications of such responses for one's life chances and sense of identity" (918). Phinney argues that race can be subsumed under the term ethnicity.

For Phinney, there are at least three aspects of ethnicity. These include 1) the cultural values, attitudes, and behaviors that distinguish among various ethnic groups, 2) ethnic group membership or a feeling of belonging to a particular ethnic group, and 3) minority status experiences, which, for most, include instances of powerlessness, prejudice, and discrimination (Phinney 1996). Discussion of the specific cultural values of African Americans will be presented in the next section. Also, the previous section on racial identity among African Americans articulates the minority status experiences Phinney mentions in her discussion of ethnicity components. Thus, the following section will be limited to the ethnic group membership or ethnic identity.

Several authors have viewed ethnic identity as a component of self-concept and social and personal identity that is present in rudimentary forms during childhood. It is said to become a more fully developed component of social identity during adolescence (Phinney 1996; Phinney and Ong 2007). It is argued, however, that the prevalence and negotiation of ethnic identity from childhood through adolescence is experienced more among adolescents of color, including African American young adult men and women (Holmes and Lochman 2009; Phinney 1996; Phinney and Ong 2007; Street, Harris-Britt, and Walker-Barnes 2009).

While Marcia's theory of identity development has typically been used to articulate ethnic identity formation (Phinney and Ong 2007), Phinney (1990) and Banks (1994) offer a detailed account of the ethnic identification process experienced by many adolescents of color. Specifically, Phinney discusses three stages of ethnic identity development, while Banks (1994) discusses six. The first stage in Phinney's model of identity development is *unexamined ethnic identity*, where adolescents of color or ethnic minority children and teenagers have a significant preference for the dominant culture and/or have not begun to explore issues of ethnic identity for themselves. The second stage is referred to as *exploration*, where the individual begins to immerse him or herself into his or her own ethnicity, typically as a result of an experience which may have called into question his or her "preference" for the dominant culture. Similar to the racial identity models that have articulated the encounter phenomenon as a predecessor to immersion/exploration (Cross 1991; Helms 1997), the encounter experience in ethnic identity often results in the individual seeking to learn more of his or her own ethnicity and culture vis-à-vis reading, discussing, and participating in cultural issues and events. In some cases, Phinney (1990) notes that such activities result in an overall rejection of the dominant culture. *Ethnic identity achievement*, the third stage, describes individuals contending with two major psychological issues. The first is acknowledgment of the distinct cultural differences between their own ethnic group and the dominant group. The second is acknowledging and addressing the lower social status of their ethnic group in comparison with others. In addressing these issues, the individual in the third stage of ethnic identity development is able to "come to a deeper understanding and appreciation of their ethnicity" (Phinney 1990, 504).

Banks (1994) offers a slightly more detailed account of ethnic identity development, though there are some similarities between his model and Phinney's model. Specifically, Banks (1994) proposes six stages of ethnic identity development. The first stage is *ethnic psychological captivity*. Here, an individual feels he or she—as a member of a specific ethnic group—has been excluded from mainstream society and possesses feelings of ethnic self-rejection. Similar to the immersion status in racial identity development models (Cross 1991; Parham 1980), the second stage of ethnic identity development is *ethnic encapsulation*. Here, an individual immerses him or herself deeply into his or her ethnic group, its artifacts, belief systems, customs, and traditions in an effort to develop and sustain a belief that his or her ethnic group is superior to those groups with negative beliefs about/interactions with the respective ethnic group. The third stage, *ethnic identity clarification*, describes the individual developing the ability to accept both the positive and negative facets of his or her ethnic group (Branch and Young 2006). Specifically, the individual begins to clarify his or her own beliefs and attitudes regarding the ethnic group to which he or she belongs.

Following this is the fourth stage, *biethnicity*, in which the individual acknowledges the need to proactively and positively exist in the cultural realm specific to his or her ethnic group as well as that within mainstream society. Thus, in the biethnicity stage, individuals are beginning to adopt what Banks (1994) refers to as a healthy sense of ethnic identity. In stages five and six, there is evidence of explicit manifestation and extension of the attitudes and beliefs found in stage four, biethnicity. Specifically, stage five, *multiethncity and reflective nationalism* captures the self-actualization of the individual, where he or she—after critical examination of his or her own ethnicity and culture—develops positive attitudes regarding their own as well as other ethnic groups. Stage six, *globalism and global competency*, extends the development of multiethnic attitudes and awareness by focusing on the recognition and exploration of multiple ethnic groups around the world and their respective cultures.

Both Banks' and Phinney's models of ethnic identity development have at their core some in-depth discussion of the individual's attitudes and ideas about his or her ethnic group and the dominant ethnic group within a given society. Thus, issues of acculturation are central to both ethnic identity models. Acculturation—as a process—focuses on how an individual relates both to his or her own ethnic group and his or her perceptions of how that particular ethnic group relates to the larger, dominant societal group (Phinney 1990). More specifically, acculturation is considered the process of change in specific cultural values, attitudes, and behaviors as a result of interacting within two distinct cultures (Phinney 1990).

The stage components evidenced in both Phinney and Banks' ethnic identity development models reflect four possible acculturation statuses articulated by Phinney (1990). For example, both models discuss some adherence to the dominant culture or at least an absence of consideration of an individual's own ethnic group membership. This acculturation status is referred to as assimilation and is described in the first stage of both Banks' and Phinney's ethnic identity development models. Exclusive and purposeful identification with the individual's own ethnic group—typically following an encounter experience—is referred to as separation. Here, the individual behaviorally immerses himself or herself in the learning and edification of his or her own ethnic group, while simultaneously seeking to distance himself or herself from being psychologically and affectively associated with the dominant culture. Strong identification with multiple ethnic groups, particularly to which the individual belongs and the dominant group, is referred to as integration and/or biculturalism and is characterized in the last stages (Banks' fifth and sixth stages and Phinney's third) of both ethnic identity development models. Though not unpacked within either model, Phinney (1990) describes a fourth acculturation status, marginality, where the individual does not identify with either his or her own ethnic group or the dominant ethnic group.

Throughout ethnic identity development, Phinney (1990; Phinney and Ong 2007) and others (see Ashmore, Deaux, and McLaughlin-Volpe 2004) have described several components that demarcate the multiple acculturation/ethnic identity statuses. Some of these components include self-categorization, commitment and attachment, exploration, in-group attitudes or what Sellers et al. (1998) refer to as private regard, ethnic values and beliefs, and ethnic and national identity. The first component, *self-categorization,* is the simplest of the components as it focuses on how one identifies him or herself as a member of a particular social/ethnic group (Ashmore et al. 2004; Phinney and Ong 2007). Here, the ethnic categories (i.e., African American) an individual uses to describe himself or herself are captured. The second component is *commitment and attachment* (Phinney and Ong 2007). Phinney and Ong (2007) consider commitment and attachment the most important component of ethnic identity as it is what researchers and laypersons invariably refer to when discussing ethnic identity. Here, commitment and attachment refer to an individual's sense of belonging to a particular ethnic group. Exclusive commitment to one's own ethnic group would, for example, illustrate a separatist acculturation status, which would be present in Phinney's exploration stage and/or Banks' encapsulation stage.

A third component is *exploration* and it entails the seeking of information and experiences relevant to one's ethnicity (Phinney and Ong 2007). As previously noted, exploration is characterized in both Banks' and Phinney's ethnic identity development models as it often determines the level of commitment an individual will have to his or her own ethnic group or to the dominant ethnic group. A fourth component, which can result from an unexplored/foreclosed ethnic identity or from an explored and consequently, achieved identity is *in-group attitudes or private regard* (Sellers et al. 1998). Here, Phinney and Ong (2007) discuss the perceptions of the ethnic group to which an individual belongs, particularly whether he or she possesses positive or negative attitudes toward the group. The development of these attitudes typically follows an encounter where ideas, attitudes, and behaviors of the particular ethnic group are challenged or otherwise condemned or ridiculed and one has to, subsequently, decide how to effectively deal with these beliefs about his or her ethnic group (i.e., similar to the invisibility syndrome that can precede racial identity progression toward immersion/emersion stages and/or feelings of invisibility that can inform how one feels about his or her ethnic group).

INVISIBILITY AND AFRICAN AMERICAN MEN'S ETHNIC IDENTITY

Perhaps the best example of the invisibility of ethnic identity can be found in the empirical literature examining the construct known as "stereotype threat" (Steele and Aronson 1995). According to Steele and Aronson (1995; Aronson 2002), stereotype threat is defined as a "socially premised psychological threat that arises when one is in a situation or doing something for which a negative stereotype about one's group applies" (Steele 1997, 614). Another description of stereotype threat suggests that an individual is at risk of confirming a negative stereotype about his or her group (Steele and Aronson 1995). Ethnic identity is inherent to stereotype threat as the stereotype is typically reflective of and specific to a particular ethnic or otherwise, social group, namely one that has historically received and/or experienced stigmatization and ill treatment (i.e., African Americans).

Here, a person who experiences stereotype threat is 1) acknowledging that a negative stereotype exists about the capabilities of his or her social group (i.e., race/ethnicity, gender, age, socioeconomic status) and 2) demonstrating apprehension about confirming the negative stereotype by engaging in or refraining from certain activities. For Steele, it is unnecessary for the group member to believe the stereotype to be true for stereotype threat to produce negative psychological consequences for him or her. For Steele and colleagues, the emotional reactions to stereotype threat are enough to alter the attitudes and behaviors of individual group members and produce maladaptive psychological and cognitive functioning.

Specifically, as a result of being exposed to contexts and messages that convey such negative stereotypes, African American students are more likely to exhibit attitudes and behaviors that are not always conducive to success. In particular, Aronson notes several ways in which perceptions of negative stereotypes lead many individuals to engage in activities such as self-handicapping (Midgley, Arunkumar, and Urdan 1996; Salinas and Aronson 1997), challenge avoidance (Good and Aronson 2001), self-suppression (Pronin, Steele and Ross 2001; Steele 1997) and disidentification or disengagement with the task or the context where the task is to be performed (Aronson 2002; Major, Spencer, Schmader, Wolfe and Crocker 1998; Stone 2002; Steele 1997). For Steele and colleagues, each of these may disrupt optimal performance, especially on academic tasks (Aronson 2002).

In their seminal research on stereotype threat among ethnic groups, Steele and Aronson (1995) produced an experimental design to test stereotype threat with African American college students. In this work, Steele and Aronson (1995) gave a 30-minute Graduate Records Exam (GRE) verbal subtest to 114 undergraduates, all of whom were matched in academic scoring ability on the exam. Using a two (race) x three (threat condition) factorial design, Steele and Aronson (1995) created and analyzed the effects of race (African American and White) and testing condition on students' performance on the GRE subtest.

In the first testing condition, African American and White students were exposed to the stereotype threat condition, where the researchers described the GRE subtest as a test to determine diagnostic ability on verbal competence. The second condition, nonstereotype threat, consisted of communication by the researchers that the students' test taking and performance were not diagnostic of ability and were only considered to be a routine laboratory task. Finally, the third condition consisted of communication by researchers indicating that the nondiagnostic task should be considered a "challenge," but not indicative of their fixed intelligence. Results from the first study indicated that, after controlling for differences in GRE scores, African American students in the diagnostic (stereotype threat) condition fared worse on the GRE verbal examination than their White counterparts in the same condition and also African American students in the nondiagnostic and challenge conditions (Steele and Aronson 1995).

In a second study, forty undergraduates were recruited to participate in the study where the same experimental conditions and procedures were employed. Here, a significant interaction emerged, with African American students in the diagnostic (stereotype threat) condition performing significantly worse than all other students in the remaining experimental conditions. Also noted were the findings that African American students in the stereotype threat condition yielded lower response accuracy and had more incomplete responses than their African American counterparts in the nondiagnostic condition. White students in both conditions also had higher response accuracy than African American students in the diagnostic, stereotype threat condition.

In each of these and several other experimental studies examining the impact of stereotype threat, African American students did not fare well in academic settings and/or with academic tasks when they were primed to think about negative stereotypes about their ethnic group. Specifically, in the previously described studies, Steele and colleagues manipulate the threat condition (i.e., whether the test is explicitly mentioned to diagnose academic ability) so that the pervasive image of African American students underperforming on academically diagnostic examinations is invoked. Thus, being a member of a historically stigmatized group is factored into the experiment. Those who are not members of this stigmatized group are not hypothesized to do poorly as a result of exposure to the stereotype threat experimental condition (i.e., diagnostic test of academic ability). As mentioned, the presence of the negative stereotype associated with the academic task resulted in lower academic performance for African American students.

Steele (1997) later explains that the deliberate manipulation of the stereotype threat does not have to occur in order for the effects of stereotype threat to be felt by many African American students. Specifically, for Steele (1997), stereotype "threat" is in the air or more concretely, present throughout the contexts and situations where historically, African Americans have been given examinations and have not always performed well on them (i.e., public schools). Consistent with the description of invisibility forwarded by Franklin (1999), for African Americans—students in particular—ethnic identity is rendered invisible vis-à-vis a historical and societal concentration on the negative stereotypes associating their ethnic group with academic difficulty and/or failure. That is, African American students have been and continue to be viewed—almost exclusively—as persons who face significant academic challenges in educational settings. Alternative conceptualizations of African Americans as good students and/or learners are not as prevalent in mainstream context, and thus, are invisible, even to some African American students themselves.

For many African American male students who have been viewed as and placed at risk for academic failure more often than their White or female counterparts (Graham, Taylor, and Hudley 1998), it is plausible that the threat of confirming the stereotype of bad student or "dumb" is especially prevalent for them. Moreover, some recent research has shown that many young African American male high school aged students not only internalize such negative beliefs about themselves and their ethnic group, but reports of such beliefs were shown to be statistically associated with academically self-handicapping behaviors (i.e., procrastination; Tyler, Thompson, Burris, and Lloyd, revise and resubmit).

Additional writings in the psychological and educational literatures support these and similar claims. Specifically, several researchers have shown that the ethnic group membership of African American students must oftentimes be minimized, downplayed, and/or made invisible in order for them to flourish academically. In classic works by late anthropologist Dr. John Ogbu (1986), it has been argued that many African American students, in an attempt to achieve academically, must forego any and all association with the salient preferences, proclivities, and behaviors of their ethnic group. Often referred to as "acting White," Ogbu (1986 2000) and others (see Fordham 2000) have shown through qualitative research that many African American students believe that, in order to achieve in school, they must dismiss tangible aspects of their ethnic identity (i.e., dress, culture-specific activities, talk) and adopt aspects of other ethnic groups, particularly those associated with students who typically demonstrate academic excellence (i.e., White persons). By dissociating themselves from various aspects endemic to their ethnic group, many African Americans are said to feel that they are giving themselves an opportunity to disprove the stereotype which states that they are part of a group that does not fare well academically (Davidson 1996; Ogbu 2000).

In addition, by arguing that some African American youth and communities hold beliefs that academic success is relegated to members of a particular racial group (i.e., Whites), Ogbu—through his research—has been perceived as a researcher who, for the most part, offered a pathological and self-loathing view of African American youth, family, and cultural values (Foley 2005; Foster 2005). Specifically, Ogbu's published book in 2003 and his posthumous publication sought to address the issue of "acting White" within academic and other social contexts. Ogbu (2004), however, concludes in both works that there are very few students who actually believe that earning good grades or getting As in school is associated with acting like or being like a White person. In fact, Ogbu (2003) ethnographic study with African American students in a middle-class neighborhood in Ohio showed that many students who earn good grades are, in fact, supported by their members of their social network, many of whom are African American.

Rather, Ogbu (2004) summarized his most recent work with the argument that what most of the African American students have rejected was the adoption of ways of speaking and activities that reflect less of their own ethnic background and is associated with many White persons in the United States. Specifically, student participants in the research undertaking in Shaker Heights, Ohio reported a rejection of speaking standard English and having too many White friends (Ogbu 2004). Similarly, students interviewed in Oakland, California indicated a rejection of those students who talked proper and having mostly white friends. For many of them, it was believed that obtaining good grades did not have to occur in a manner that exhibited some initial rebuff of their own ethnic background and identity. These students saw academic achievement as independent of White or mainstream culture and thus, saw little need to adopt elements for this culture in order to perform well in school.

While several works have challenged the idea that ethnic and academic identities cannot coexist (Adelabu 2008; Foster 2005; Gordon 2012; Graham and Anderson 2008), the fact remains that some data have supported the idea that the ethnic identity of many African Americans is often times viewed negatively. Whether in public school classrooms where African American male students are either personally (i.e., believing that they have to forego their ethnic identity—act White—in order to achieve) or inadvertently reminded of the academic difficulties they face as a group (i.e., stereotype threat, coupled with the low representation of African American in academic arenas as students or instructors), some literature makes clear that other identities of African Americans, including and perhaps, especially African American men, are often times rendered invisible as a result of ethnic identity. Grantham (2011) notes that the negative stereotyping of Black males, coupled with the expectations for their underperformance often results with this population being overlooked in academic settings, particularly in gifted and talented programs. Indeed, that continued inability to view members of this ethnic group, male members in particular, as academically capable often results in feelings of invisibility.

INTERSECTIONALITY AND AFRICAN AMERICAN MEN'S ETHNIC IDENTITY

The previous section on ethnic identity has noted some literature evidencing the intersectionality between ethnic identity and other identity components (e.g., Bergin and Cooks 2002; Grantham 2006; Osborne 1997). The following section will further illuminate the concept of intersectionality between ethnic and other identity components. To begin, a qualitative study conducted by Graham and Anderson (2008) sought to address the question of "How do academically gifted African American male adolescents at a predominantly African American urban high school negotiate the tension between their academic identity and ethnic identity?" Through interviews with several high-achieving African American male high school students, the authors found that ethnic identity is viewed as central to participants' academic endeavors and achievement-related practices. Specifically, Graham and Anderson (2008) concluded that the young African American men in the study were able and willing to pursue academic success while maintaining a strong ethnic identity. For all of the study participants, having a positive attitude toward being African American and a strong regard for African Americans in general was a significant part of their desire to achieve academically (Graham and Anderson 2008).

A major factor that facilitated such coexistence between ethnic and academic identity was the degree of exposure to racial/ethnic socialization, primarily carried out by the participants' parents. In particular, Graham and Anderson (2008) recorded that each participant's parents were instrumental in providing a strong sense of pride in being African American. For the participants, achieving at high levels was one manner in which such pride in being African American was displayed. Additional studies have also highlighted the idea that, for many African Americans, students in particular, academic achievement rather than academic underperformance was a unique way to demonstrate a positive sense of ethnic identity (Adelabu 2008; Bergin and Cooks 2002; Grantham 2004). For example, Bergin and Cooks (2002), in their qualitative study examining attitudes toward academic achievement among African American and Mexican American high school students, showed that the majority of participants not only heavily favored an orientation toward high academic achievement, but also vehemently disregarded accusations that maintaining such an orientation was evidence of "acting White." A more recent study by Ford, Grantham, and Whiting (2008), however, showed that some African American middle school and high school students equate intelligence and getting good grades in school with "acting White," while "acting Black," for a much smaller subset of the sample, was equated with lacking intelligence and placing low priority on academic achievement and strong school performance.

Still, a positive ethnic identity or feeling good about being part of the African American community, particularly among African Americans, has been linked to various academic and psychological outcomes including high achievement (Adelabu 2008), positive perceptions of self-esteem (Goodstein and Ponterotto 1997; Street, Harris-Britt, and Walker-Barnes 2009; Tovar-Murray and Munley 2007), life quality (Tovar-Murray and Munley 2007), interpersonal relationships (Street, et al. 2009) life satisfaction (Tovar-Murray and Munley 2007), and a negative association with depressive symptoms (Street et al. 2009). Most interesting of these findings is that several of these psychological outcomes have also been statistically associated with racial identity (Rowley, Sellers, Chavous, and Smith 1998; Sellers, Caldwell, Schmeelk-Cone, and Zimmerman 2003), suggesting that there may be an association between racial and ethnic identities. However, research examining the intersection between these two identity components is limited (Cokley 2005; Goodstein, and Ponterotto 1997; Phelps et al. 2001).

Still, some research examining the interaction between racial and ethnic identity among African American populations does exist. For example, Cokley (2005) examined the associations between ethnic identity and racial identity through the use of Phinney's Multigroup Ethnic Identity Measure (MEIM) and subscales on the Cross Racial Identity Scale. With 201 African American college students, Cokley (2005) found that ethnic identity scores were significantly correlated with the multiculturalist inclusive and Afrocentricity components of the CRIS Internalization subscale. Specifically, the findings show that ethnic identity scores were positively correlated with attitudes displaying appreciation for and acceptance of a multicultural society along with attitudes in favor with the central beliefs of Afrocentrism (Grills and Longshore 1996). Using the Black Racial Identity Scale (BRIS) (Parham and Helms 1981) as a measure of African American racial identity, Johnson and Arbona (2005) showed that among African American college undergraduates, scores on the Multigroup Ethnic Identity Measure were positively associated with internalization scores while negatively associated with preencounter scores. Similar findings were produced in previous research (Goodstein and Ponterotto 1997; Phelps, Taylor, and Gerard 2001).

While there is some evidence to support the intersection between ethnic identity and racial identity and ethnic identity and academic identity, along with a push to combine these constructs, the empirical data supporting or at least underscoring the presence of intersections among ethnic identity and gender and sexual identity or socioeconomic identity have not been shown in the literature. There is, however, some encouraging work on this intersection among these specific identity components. In particular, Wilson (2008) offers a brilliant dynamic-ecological model of identity formation that displays the intersections between ethnic identity, sexual identity, and gender (masculine) identity among African American men. Wilson (2008) discusses how various contextual/ecological factors (i.e., church, parental socialization) inform not only ethnic identity of African American men, but also how this ethnic identity formation has implications for their sexual and gender identity development as well. Still, much more research is necessary if greater understanding of the confluence of ethnic identity with other African American identity components is to be known.

ILLUSTRATION OF AFRICAN AMERICAN MEN'S IDENTITY INVISIBILITY—ETHNIC IDENTITY

In figure 10.1, ethnic identity begins to meld with the darker grey charcoal circle, indicative of a compromise of this identity component in such a way that it is made invisible. The priming of racial stereotypes of African American men can compromise ethnic identity in the same fashion that racial identity is compromised. Many of these racist perceptions can pervade the minds of some young African Americans and thus, impede their progress as well as diminish their motivation to do well. The best examples of these were found in the stereotype threat literature and the research on "acting White" by Ogbu. In these cases, the fact that African American students were members of an ethnic group historically stereotyped as the group that does not perform well on standardized exams was associated with these persons actually not performing well on academically related experimental tasks. Similarly, some African American students, African American men in particular, may believe that academic performance is something that White persons are to excel at while members of their population are likely to excel in athletics.

Thus, racism rears its head in these examples by reducing ethnic minority classification to a set of stereotypes and destructive beliefs about African Americans, which inform the future behaviors of this population. More importantly, racism is the reason why such perception of this population exists. As Thompson and Neville (1999) pointed out, racist pre-

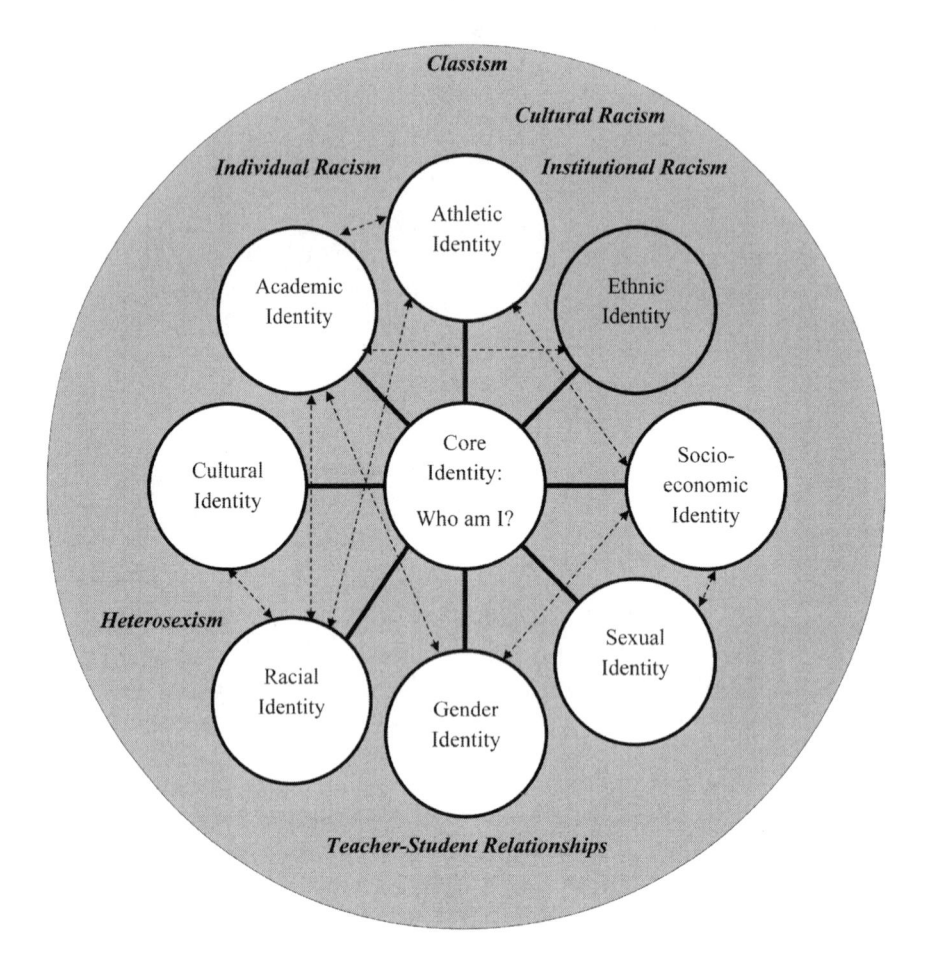

Figure 10.1. Conceptual Model of African American Men's Identity: Compromised Ethnic Identity

scriptions of African Americans were used to maintain and institutionalize their oppression. Stereotypes such as African Americans being docile, intellectually inferior, hypersexualized, and criminal/threatening had been conjured up and institutionalized across various U.S. mainstream media and outlets, including religion, education, commerce, and science. Thus, for well over two centuries, the stigma attached to being a member of this ethnic minority group is something that many African Americans have had to fight against. Unfortunately, there have been far too many young African American men who have bought into these stereotypes and thereby, have a compromised identity or a limited perspective regarding African Americans as an ethnic group. For these individuals, ethnic identity—as a result of its invisibility in the racist mainstream context—would be compromised.

ELEVEN

African American Men's Cultural Identity

As Phinney (1996) has written, culture is considered a unique aspect of an individual's ethnicity. By definition, culture is considered the conventional patterns of thought, activity, and artifacts passed on from generation to generation in a manner generally assumed to involve learning and socialization (Boykin 1986). Cultural identity, then, focuses on how an individual espouses and/or manifests the particular values and behavioral patterns he or she is socialized towards. Unlike other conceptualizations of cultural identity that suggest that it is essentially an amalgam of both racial and ethnic identities (Cokley and Chapman 2008), the focus of cultural identity in the current work seeks to explicitly identify those cultural values and beliefs said to reflect African Americans' lineage with West Africa (Boykin 1986; Boykin and Toms 1985).

While it is clear that, in the U.S. context, it is difficult to fully discern and compartmentalize the racial and cultural experiences of African Americans, the scientific literature reflects an understanding that several explicit cultural values and worldviews 1) were present before and throughout the transport of slaves from Africa to what is now the United States and 2) persisted from generation to generation. These cultural values and beliefs survive in the present day, despite the presence and ongoing impact of race-based institutions like chattel slavery and then federally sanctioned discrimination practices. Several writings articulate various cultural values among African American populations (Cokley and Williams 2005; Johnson 2003; Jones 2003; Klonoff and Landrine 1999; Mbiti 1980; Moemeka 1998; Oyserman, Coon, and Kemmelmeier 2002).

With an understanding that being African American constituted more than just daily grapples with issues of race and racism within the United States, Dr. Wade Boykin put forth perhaps the most comprehensive articulation of the cultural values present among African American populations. In his Triple Quandary framework, Boykin (1986) argues that African Americans negotiate three realms of psychosocial experience: 1) mainstream society and culture, 2) racism, prejudice, and discrimination, and oppression—which has been discussed in a previous chapter—and 3) specific cultural values reflective of an indigenous African worldview. Similar to the characterization of African Americans in DuBois' "The Souls of Black Folks," Boykin's discussion of the first two realms, mainstream realm and minority realm (e.g., racism-based psychosocial experiences) captures the negotiation of African Americans' participation in two worlds, one where they are outright participants in mainstream society and the other where they are often victimized by such participation. The mainstream realm is believed to contain many cultural themes that are rooted in European worldviews and are omnipresent within U.S. institutions and behavioral patterns and preferences (Boykin 1983; Tyler, Boykin, Boelter, and Dillihunt 2005).

Two cultural themes considered to be mainstream are individualism and competition. Individualism refers to a person's orientation or disposition toward autonomy and the premium placed upon solo or individual accomplishments (Boykin, 1983). An example of individualism would be the belief that an individual can do a better job when he or she does it alone. Another mainstream cultural theme that has been evidenced within U.S. mainstream institutions, particularly public schools, is competition (Boykin, Miller, and Tyler 2005; Boykin, Tyler, Watkins-Lewis, and Kizzie 2006; Tyler, Boykin, and Walton 2006). Competition refers to the individual's desire to surpass the performance of other so that he or she can be viewed as the best in a given domain, academics, athletics, or otherwise (Boykin, 1983). An example of the competition mainstream cultural theme is an individual preferring to do better than others at a given task and receive public recognition of such, including awards (Boykin et al. 2005; Marryshow, Hurley, Allen, Tyler, and Boykin 2005; Tyler et al. 2005). The minority realm, refers to racial discrimination and prejudiced-based experiences of African Americans as a result of their marginalized status in the United States. Many of these experiences are captured in the chapters examining invisibility of both racial and ethnic identities, and therefore, will not be detailed here.

Boykin's major contribution to the discourse on the experiences of African Americans is the articulation of a "third world" or realm of psychosocial experience. As the third component of his Triple Quandary framework (Boykin 1983, Boykin 1986), this third realm of psychosocial experience is often referred to as the Afro-cultural realm. Here, the worldviews and corresponding cultural values of African Americans are presented. These cultural values—which are believed to have survived U.S. chattel slavery—include 1) spirituality—an acknowledgment of a nonmaterial entity that is salient in all human affairs, 2) harmony—an implication that how one behaves or otherwise functions, is fundamentally linked to nature and the universal elements, 3) movement—an implication for the salience of percussiveness, rhythm, and physical motion in all endeavors; personified by a musical beat, 4) verve—a connotation of particular receptiveness to high levels of "sensate stimulation," 5) affect—an implication for the "centrality of affective information and emotional expressiveness linked to the coimportance of feelings and thoughts," 6) expressive individualism—which connotes the prevalence of uniqueness of personal or idiosyncratic expression, style, and their authenticity, 7) communalism—which denotes a supreme commitment to the "fundamental interdependence of people" manifested in social relationships and interactions, 8) orality—which connotes the salience of oral/aural modes of communication for dissemination of information and the cultivation of speech as a performance rather than just an interaction, and 9) social time perspective—which denotes a "commitment to time as a social construction such that there is an event orientation towards time" (Boykin 1983).

For Boykin, these cultural values add a unique layer of complexity to the negotiation of lived experience within the United States context. In particular, in addition to seeking to achieve mainstream participation status in the U.S., many African Americans are simultaneously dealing with the impact of racism and race-based prejudice and discrimination. Coupled with these experiences is the significant process of upholding one's sense of integrity through the maintenance of and socialization toward esteemed cultural values that are intricately woven into the behaviors of African Americans (Boykin 1986; Boykin and Toms 1985).

Many have supported the notion that these values are salient within African American households and communities in general and are less salient in mainstream context such as public schools, particularly those serving low-income African American students (Boykin, Albury, et al. 2005; Boykin, Tyler, and Miller 2005; Gay 2000, 2002; Sankofa, Hurley, Allen, and Boykin 2005; Tyler, Boykin, Boelter, and Dillihunt 2005; Tyler, Boykin, Miller, and Hurley 2006; Webb-Johnson 2002). Boykin has also argued that because these Afro-cultural factors are salient during the development of cognitive abilities and skills for many young African American students and children, these cultural values and their behavioral expressions will become preferred modes of learning for these individuals.

Boykin and his team of graduate students and post doctoral research associates spearheaded a set of experimental and correlational designed research studies to examine the presence and impact of these cultural values in the home and school lives of many African American students and their parents. A major thesis considered at the time when much of this research was being conducted was that examining low-income African Americans would likely evidence the strongest source of Afro-cultural values as their income status may limit, to some degree, the amount of exposure to mainstream cultural themes they may have and thus, Afro-cultural themes may prove to be more prominent throughout the behaviors and socialization experiences within African American households.

One study examined the perceptions of eighty-one fourth grade African American students regarding their preferences for communal, vervistic, individualistic, and competitive value-based behaviors (Tyler, Boykin, Miller, and Hurley 2006). Also assessed was whether the students believed that their own parents and teachers would endorse these cultural themes, with perceptions of parents' endorsements being based at home and teachers' endorsements being based at school. Using vignette-based research, where a hypothetical scenario based on each cultural theme was developed by researchers and read by students, results showed that students believed that they and their parents endorsed the communal and vervistic behaviors significantly more than the individualistic and competitive behaviors.

Two additional studies corroborated these findings with the actual parents of African American middle grade students (Tyler, Boykin, Boelter, and Dillihunt 2005; Tyler, Dillihunt, et al. 2007). African American parents of school-age children in both studies reported preferences for learning and working in ways consistent with Afrocultural themes (e.g., communal, verve) than more mainstream oriented cultural themes (e.g., individualistic, competitive). These preferences for culturally aligned learning contexts and activities are salient in the households of African American families is consistent with Boykin's theoretical claims regarding 1) the survival of culturally thematic behaviors stemming from a West African lineage and 2) the salience of these cultural themes during the development of cognitive skills for African American children.

Not only would Boykin and colleagues set out to prove that the culturally aligned behaviors and preferences brought to the classroom by young African American are integral to their socialization experiences, they would also seek to disprove the hypothesis that an embrace and preference of African American culture will result in low preference for high academic achievement. Specifically, some studies authored by Boykin and colleagues sought to determine whether African American students reject academic achievement as initially claimed by anthropologist John Ogbu, who according to "acting White" hypothesis, suggested that many African American adolescents equate strong school performance with a rejection of one's ethnic background and related identities and behaviors (Boykin, Albury, et al. 2005; Marryshow, Hurley, Allen, Tyler, and Boykin 2005; Sankofa, Hurley, Allen, and Boykin 2005).

The first study by Boykin and colleagues (2005) examined the preferences for high-achievement behaviors between sixty-six African American and seventy-two White fifth grade students. Students read vignettes of high-achieving students whose behaviors and activities that led to strong achievement outcomes were reflective of one of four cultural themes (communalism, verve, individualism, and competition). African American students reported significantly higher endorsement for the hypothetical high achiever that employed communal and vervistic-based behaviors. White students reported a stronger endorsement for those hypothetical high achievers who exhibited individual and competitive-based classroom and studying behaviors. This study, along with others (Marryshow et al. 2005; Sankofa et al. 2005) was important in countering the argument that African American students often reject strong academic performance. What was rejected in this study was not academic achievement, but rather, the manner in which such achievement was attained, chiefly with behaviors that reflected a mainstream cultural orientation.

Sankofa et al. (2005) extended this initial study by examining African American elementary grade students' perceptions and their reports of their parents' perceptions of high achievers exhibiting strong academic performance in one of four culturally aligned ways (i.e., communal, vervistic, individual, and competitive). Findings showed that students endorsed and reported parental endorsement of achievers who exhibited Afrocultural ways of achieving. Similarly, Marryshow et al. (2005) examined the perceptions of ninety African American middle grade students regarding vignette-based high achievers who performed in ways consistent with one of the four aforementioned cultural themes. In addition, Marryshow et al. (2005) captured the students' perceptions of their teachers' preferences for the culturally aligned high-achievement behaviors. Results showed that while African American students endorsed communal and vervistic high achievers, they reported that their teachers would endorse the individualistic and competitive high achievers.

This last finding—that classroom teachers are believed to endorse mainstream cultural themes when it comes to learning—is consistent with the findings that emerged in several other studies by Boykin and colleagues. For example, Tyler et al. (2006) showed that African American students believed that their classroom teachers would prefer students who behaved and carried out tasks in manners reflective of both individualistic and competitive mainstream cultural values. The student participants in that study also reported that they would likely get in trouble at school if they used communal or vervistic-based behaviors. A later study actually corroborates the findings of Tyler et al. (2006) with actual teachers' reports of their use of cultural aligned learning practices.

Specifically, Boykin, Tyler, Watkins-Lewis, and Kizzie (2006) asked eighty-one teachers about their actual classroom practices and results showed that the teachers report classroom practices which are aligned more with mainstream cultural practices of individualism and competition than the Afro-cultural values of communalism and verve. A qualitative study observing twenty-one first through fifth grade classrooms corroborate the finding that teachers employ more mainstream cultural themes than Afro-cultural themes. Here, Boykin, Tyler, and Miller (2005) found that among the 429 observations conducted across twenty-one classrooms, 381 of them were reflective of mainstream cultural values, while only forty-eight were reflective of Afro-cultural values. Finally, Tyler, Boykin, and Walton (2006) found that teachers rated hypothetical students who employed individualistic and competitive learning behaviors higher in academic motivation and overall achievement than those hypothetical students who employed communal and vervistic learning behaviors in class.

Despite teachers overall low endorsement of Afro-cultural learning behaviors and the belief that students who employ them will not be motivated to perform well or demonstrate an achievement orientation, the incorporation of the African American student-preferred Afro-cultural values into formal and experimental learning contexts has been shown to facilitate academic performance (Bohn 2003; Boykin and Allen 1998; Boykin and Cunningham 2001; Boykin, Lilja, and Tyler 2004; Day-Vines and Day-Hairston 2005; Dill and Boykin 2000; Hollins and Spencer 1990; Hurley, Boykin, and Allen 2005; Lee 2001; Neal, McCray, Webb-Johnson, and Bridgest 2003; Rodriguez, Jones, Pang, and Park 2004; Serpell, Boykin, Madhere, and Nasim 2006; Tucker and Herman 2001; Tucker, Herman, Pedersen, Vogel, and Reinke 2000). For example, in a longitudinal experimental research design, Boykin and colleagues (2004) found that exposing African American middle grade students to communal settings versus more traditional or mainstream academic settings such as an individualistic or competitive classroom context enhanced students' academic performance.

Similar findings were yielded in an experimentally designed study that incorporated aspects of movement expressiveness, another cultural value said to permeate the experiences of many African Americans (Serpell, Boykin, Madhere, and Nasim 2006). Here, ninety African American and seventy-two White fourth grade students were randomly assigned to either a computer simulation or a context where they used physical tools to work on a motion acceleration task. A separate control group was also part of the research design to examine simple pre-post effects without the intervening experimental conditions. The groups, which were ethnically homogeneous to examine the effect of ethnicity as well as the experimental conditions, had students working in a communal setting (groups of three, one set of materials) while the control group did not complete the task. Results from the study showed that while African American and White students yielded similar results for learning outcomes than students in the control group, African American students in the communal groups were able to transfer the lessons from the communal learning contexts significantly more than their White counterparts in the communal learning contexts.

Dill and Boykin's (2000) research yielded similar results with a communal learning experimental design. Here, seventy-two African American fifth graders read and completed a language arts task in one of three learning conditions they were randomly assigned to: communal group (two persons per one set of learning materials, focus on helping one another), peer tutoring (two persons per one set of materials, with each participant writing questions to ask the other), and individual (one person and one set of materials to study). Result showed that participants in the communal learning context had significantly higher recall on the language arts than students in the peer tutoring and the individual learning context. More recently, Hurley, Boykin, and Allen (2005) found similar results among African American fifth graders completing math estimation tasks in a communal oriented learning condition. Still, other works have determined that these cultural values help many African Americans to cope with racial discrimination and are predictors of various psychological and behavioral outcomes such as self-esteem and moral reasoning (Bowen-Reid and Smalls 2004; Mattis, Hearn, and Jagers 2002; Moore, Madison-Colmore, and Moore 2003; Mutisya and Ross 2005; Okech and Harrington 2002; Scott 2003; Stevenson 2002; Wallace and Constantine 2005; Walker and Dixon 2002; Walker and Satterwhite 2002; Woods and Jagers 2003).

In each of these works, it is suggested that many African American students are purposefully socialized toward many of these specific cultural values. In being raised and socialized within contexts where such values and activities abound (Boykin 2001, 2002; Boykin and Ellison 1995; Gay 2000), these values tend to inform these students' behaviors and preferences. In essence, young African American men become communally oriented, movement expressive, vervistic, spiritually grounded, expressively individualistic, orally expressive, and affective (Boykin 1986; Jones 2003). These values, for Boykin and his colleagues, are part of the collective cultural experiences of young African American men. With such experiences, these cultural factors are likely to inform their cultural identity.

HIP-HOP CULTURE

Just like communalism and orality (e.g., call and response) have a significant place within African American culture, there is another important element of African American culture that is typically embraced by most young African American men: hip-hop culture. As Prier and Beacham (2009) have noted, hip-hop culture represents a significant portion of African American culture within the twenty-first century. Some writers believe that hip-hop has now become a forerunner in socialization images of young African American male youth (Prier and Beachum 2008). Thus, it becomes important to consider the role that hip-hop has in the cultural identity formation of this population.

Sealey-Ruiz and Greene (2011) write that the origin of hip-hop can be traced back to the early 1970s in the Bronx, New York. Believed to be the original efforts of Afrika Bambaataa, hip-hop began as a set of block parties in response to local gang violence that took the lives of many young people. It has often included the lives and voices of urban youth, primarily African American and Latino men, who were among the first to fashion the parameters of hip-hop vis-à-vis, music, style, artistry, and most importantly, social message. As Emdin and Lee (2012, 5) have noted, hip hop has become "the chief mechanism through which populations that are not accepted in mainstream society, and who do not ascribe to distinct 'Western' cultural norms such as 'appropriate' ways of dress or talk, find solidarity."

While rap music is considered the most common expression of hip hop within African American culture (Edmin and Lee 2012; Wessel and Wallaert 2011), there has been continuous expansion in the elements that help to shape any current understanding of hip-hop. Initially, hip-hop encompassed deejaying, rapping, dancing, specifically breakdancing, and graffiti (Brunson 2011). Baggy jeans, work boots, and brimmed baseball caps were also adopted by hip-hop participants and artists. Though these elements remain steadfast in the twenty-first century, additional components of hip hop now include art forms such as poetry/spoken word, acting/theater, R and B sampling/inclusion in rap tracks, complex communication patterns (e.g., elaborate handshakes), and activism (Baszile 2009; Brunson 2011; Emdin and Lee 2012). At the time of this writing, elite hip-hop artist Jay-Z created a video wherein he raps the lyrics to his track "Picasso, Baby" while several noted spoken word artists, poets, actors and actresses, dancers, film producers and the like provide visual displays of their work and their presence. The point Jay-Z makes in the video is that rap in particular and hip-hop in general is a major art form that can be meshed with, "traditional" forms of art and human expression in an effort to make something much bigger and better than what they would be by themselves.

Hip-hop, overall, seems to align itself with the Triple Quandary framework outlined by Boykin and colleagues. Specifically, it appears that the initial purpose and growth of hip-hop emerged from a message articulating individuals' experiences within the minority realm of the Triple Quandary framework. Within the minority realm of the Triple Quandary framework, there is significant discussion surrounding the lives of African Americans, who, as a result of their race, are disenfranchised, neglected, and discriminated against. Much like the invisibility syndrome articulated by Franklin (1999), Boykin makes the case that

African Americans' experiences with such factors (e.g., discrimination, second-class-citizen status, limited economic mobility) are part of the minority experience.

One coping mechanism used to cope with such experiences was the advent of hip-hop, which for many, gave voice to the experiences and issues among those within the Triple Quandary minority realm. Hip-hop also gave visibility to these individuals. As the art itself grew, so too did the manner in which it was showcased, along with the complexity of the rhymes produced by hip-hop emcees. While the Sugarhill Gang was one of the first to put hip-hop on the map, many others used the burgeoning art form to forward opinions and ideas on matters much more germane to urban life and survival than what was presented in *"Rapper's Delight."* Indeed, hip-hop became a platform for those whose voices and statements regarding urban life were not being heard by the larger mainstream society (Baszile 2009). As Baszile (2009) brilliantly stated, "hip-hop emerges, in part, as a counter-story . . . that works sometimes to 'repair' [progressive hip-hop] and other times to act out [gangsta rap] the oppression of marginalized identities" (Baszile 2009, 13). Hip-hop seemingly became the cultural expression of those individuals experiencing the adversity within the Triple Quandary minority realm.

In addition to reflecting aspects of the minority realm of psychosocial experience, hip-hop maintains a good degree of alignment with the Afro-cultural realm of psychosocial experience, as outlined by Boykin and colleagues. For example, certainly most hip-hop artists, including emcees, deejays, and graffiti artists desire to have their identities stand out among the rest. Among these hip-hop artists and producers, there are instances where one's ability to express his or herself become a central aspect of his or her lyrics, artwork, or dancing style. Thus, hip-hop contains the expressive individualism cultural factor identified by Boykin.

Another Afro-cultural factor identified by Boykin that can be found within hip-hop is the notion of communalism. Rare is the emcee that does not take into consideration aspects of family and fictive kinfolks. In fact, it is much more common within hip-hop culture to have an entourage of individuals who the artist feels is close to him or her and thus, can serve as a fictive kin (Emdin 2009; Emdin and Lee 2012). Also, within hip-hop are the notions of verve and movement expressiveness, and orality, which, all of which, for many hip-hop artists, provide the necessary atmosphere to deliver freestyle lyrics.

Specifically, with verve, the hip-hop artists, most notably, the rapper/emcee, must often develop a rhythm and cadence of a beat in order to allow the flow to be consistent and timely (i.e., on beat). Within the freestyle rap, he or she typically pays attention to his or her surroundings, particularly social others who, to their knowledge or lack thereof, may end up being a significant part of the freestyle lyrics delivered. In both of these instances, there is some example of an adherence to operating within an environment where one engages in more than one task. Similarly, with movement expressiveness, the delivery of freestyle, unrehearsed lyrics, which is where most emcees earn their credibility as true rappers/hip hop artists, comes the physical movements and gestures that facilitate the delivery of the verses. Some artists may jump, point, and bob their heads side to side, while others use specific hand and facial gestures for emphasis. Also contained within the freestyle rap session or cypher or freestyle rap battle is the cultural factor of orality. Here, there is an emphasis placed on primacy of oral skills or "speaking from the dome" (i.e., off the top of one's head). Much like the majority of African and African American culture has been passed down from generation to generation by way of specific stories told from memory, hip-hop emcees who are revered are those who are clever and intentional in their delivery of lyrics, but are also able to do so without the use of written or prerecorded/prescribed materials (Callahan and Grantham 2012). Rap artist Jay-Z has been said to have never written down any of his lyrics, which is one of the reasons why his lyrical flow, coupled with his complex and intricate rhyming style and his rap topics, make him one of the best in the game, along with Chicago's own rap artist Common and Kanye West, both of whom have demonstrated superior freestyle rap abilities and a showcasing of at least three of Boykin's cultural themes (i.e., verve, movement expressiveness, and orality). Still another major aspect of Boykin's cultural themes that can be found in much of hip-hop, at least amongst the artists themselves is spirituality. Though mostly shown during award shows or on the CD booklet, it is common for most hip-hop artists, emcees in particular, to thank God for much of their success.

Indeed, hip-hop has been and will likely always be a part of African American and American culture that I, and millions of others had the opportunity to witness since its inception in the late 1970s. Unlike painting or theatre or various musical forms like classical or jazz, many readers of this text will remember the first time they heard the musical expression of hip-hop, particularly through rap music. The first song that I really paid attention to and wanted to commit to memory was *I Go to Work* by Kool Moe Dee. It's fast-paced delivery and cadence in the music, coupled with the message of excellence in execution of whatever the task at hand was (e.g., doctor, architect, boxer) spoke to the type of person I wanted to be at 15 years old, when the song first dropped in 1990.

More than just a way to capture the mindsets and educate the youth, hip-hop, as a cultural artifact of African Americans and as a globally recognized art form, has also found its way into the hallways of public school classrooms and higher education. Already considered an intellectual art form in its own right (Jenkins 2013), hip-hop verbal expression and communication is believed to create among African American and other youth the ability and desire to write, think, and critique their experiences within the United States while using wit, cleverness, and creativity. It is likely because of this intellectual capacity and complex and creative expression demonstrated among many hip-hop artists that hip-hop culture has found its way into the classrooms and hallways of leading U.S. institutions of higher learning. According to Walker (2006) and Wessel and Wallaert (2011), more than eighty-five courses about hip-hop were taught across America's colleges and universities in 2005–2006. At the time of this writing, Harvard University's Hip-Hop Archive coupled with the W.E.B. DuBois Institute—also housed at the institution—to create the Nasir Jones Hip-Hop Fellowship, named after hip-hop superstar "Nas."

Along with these activities at the institutional level, educational and social science literature and research are beginning to more closely examine the role that hip-hop plays in the lives of students. For example, several research papers have been presented in recent years at the National Association for Gifted Children conferences to discuss the role that hip-hop has among African American gifted students who are college bound or are already enrolled at a four-year institution (Callahan 2008, 2009; Callahan, Grantham, and Harris 2010). Additionally, Kelly (2013) argued that hip-hop has often been used as a pedagogical tool; particularly to aid in students' development of literary analysis. The effectiveness of hip-hop as an instructional tool has been demonstrated in a study by Stovall (2006), who used rap as a method of enhancing critical thinking among high school social studies students (Kelly 2013).

Another study by Emdin and Lee (2012) also showed the impact that hip-hop can have in the classroom. Specifically, the authors observed that using science-related events during President Obama's first term and incorporating these events in the science classroom resulted in African American students becoming more engaged in discussion about science. Specifically, President Obama's appointment of Harvard University physicists Drs. John Holdren and Jane Lubchenco resulted in discussions pertaining to science as a career field and its impact on students' daily lives. This "Obama effect"—where the president is viewed as an influential African American who also happens to listen to and understand hip-hop—resulted in an observed increase in students' motivation to learn about and become better in science. For the authors, science was made much more relevant because the president of the United States, who is an African American man who listens to hip-hop, talked about the importance of science. For many of the students in the study, their love for and identification with hip-hop culture was juxtaposed with science and science education when President Obama—who, according to them, "has Jay-Z on his iPod"—affirmed the importance of science, which also affirmed the students' identities as cultural beings who can love science and hip-hop simultaneously.

SPIRITUAL/RELIGIOUS IDENTITY

Throughout Boykin's articulation of the cultural value-based behaviors and orientations among African Americans, perhaps none is more salient than the role of spirituality. Spirituality has been defined in several ways, with a leading definition as "the degree to which individuals endorse a relationship with God or a transcendent force that brings meaning and purpose to their existence" (Berkel, Armstrong, and Cokley 2004; Lewis 2008). Jacqueline Mattis, a leading researcher on spirituality and religiosity among African American populations, offered a critical description and analysis of spirituality, with respect to its definition, how it is viewed among African Americans, and various outcomes stemming from maintaining a spiritual identity. In particular, a study by Mattis (2000) posited that much of what social science researchers know about spirituality stem from their "intellectual formulations . . . rather than out of the direct experiences and articulations of lay people (103). To this end, Mattis (2000) interviewed 128 African American female college students to gather their conceptualizations of spirituality. Four leading themes emerged among the sample. Over half of the sample described spirituality as a belief in the existence of a sacred, divine, and powerful force that is external to the individual (109). Another leading definition was that spirituality denotes an awareness of forces that show that life is not confined to physical existence and otherwise, defy scientific explanation (109). Thus, for much of the sample, spirituality was conceptualized as an intimate relationship between God and the individual, which is reflected in a journey characterized by self-reflection, self-criticism, and self-awareness.

It is argued that understanding of the spiritual relationship between God and the individual is, for many African Americans, promoted through the development of a religious identity or set of religious practices and activities typically associated with an institution (Herndon 2003; Letiecq 2007; Mattis 2000). In demarcating the two concepts, spirituality and religion, Lewis (2008) suggests that spirituality is seen as more subjective, less formal, and often times, less visible whereas religion and religious practices are viewed as having more of a community focus, more formal and observable and also, more objective. Most recently, for some authors, religion is considered to be the specific, concrete expression or tool used in being spiritual (Berkel, Armstrong, and Cokley 2004; Weddle-West, Hagan, and Norwood 2013). Many of these practices include 1) organizational religious involvement (e.g., church membership and church service attendance), 2) nonorganizational religious involvement (e.g., individual, subjective, and private behaviors such as prayer), and 3) subjective religiosity (e.g., religious attitudes and beliefs) (Mattis et al. 2001). Additional religious behaviors include but are not limited to seeking help and/or advice from clergy and church officials such as ministers (Chatters et al. 2011; Mattis et al. 2007) and reading the Bible (or other religion-based text) (Hamilton, Moore, Johnson, and Koenig 2013).

While the concepts of spirituality and religiosity have been used interchangeably (Berkel, Armstrong, and Cokley 2004; Letiecq 2007; Lewis 2008), the research literature on these important cultural factors has shown that both are significantly associated with various psychological and behavioral outcomes including helping behaviors and satisfication with such behaviors (Grayman-Simpson and Mattis 2013), volunteerism (Mattis et al. 2004), health-promotive behaviors (Debman, Holt, Clark, Roth, Southward 2012), friendship and peer support (Mattis et al. 2001), resilience (Coates, Phares, and Dedrick 2013; Cook 2000; Teti et al. 2012), and academic success (Dancy 2010; Herndon 2003; Jett 2010). Additionally, maintaining a spiritual foundation and some religious practices have been shown to enhance coping among African Americans with coping with significant health problems such as HIV/AIDS diagnosis and maintenance (Foster, Arnold, Rebchook, and Kegeles 2011; Hill and McNeely 2013; Miller 2005), cancer (Holt et al. 2009; Holt et al. 2011; Maliski, Connor, Williams, and Litwin 2010), diabetes (Polzer and Miles 2007), and other chronic illnesses (Harvey and Silverman 2007).

Regarding spirituality and religious practices among African American men, the theoretical literature suggests that spirituality and religious participation are central components to conceptualizations of African American manhood (Dancy 2010; Hunter and Davis 1992). The research literature is beginning to evidence some focus on this population and their spiritual and/or religious practices. For example, a study by Mattis and colleagues sought to investigate the church attendance practices of 217 African American men. The sample was separated by church attendance, with 118 African American reporting attending church/religious services and ninety-nine participants reporting nonattendance. Nonattendees reported that religion was less important to their families and thus, had not attended church regularly during childhood (Mattis et al. 2004). Interestingly, African American nonattendees also reported significantly less father church attendance during childhood than their African American counterparts attending church. Twenty-nine percent of the nonattendees reported barriers to attendance such as schedule conflicts and lack of time.

Despite the finding that some African American men have difficulties in regularly attendance religious services, other research has shown that many African American men not only attend church and religious services, but also have a spiritual basis that guides their presence and practices during and beyond such services. Such a basis and the practices guided by it have been linked to African American men's persistence and resilience in college (Dancy 2010; Herndon 2003; Jett 2010; Riggins, McNeal, and Herndon 2008; Teti et al. 2012). For example, an earlier qualitative study by Herndon (2003) interviewed thirteen African

American male college students regarding their beliefs about spirituality and its link to their ability to stay in school. Herndon (2003) reported three themes based on sample responses, including 1) spirituality strengthening resilience, 2) spirituality providing purpose in their lives, and 3) spiritual support demonstrated by African American churches. In all, the author concluded that the majority of participants saw spirituality as a source of comfort and support and that such spirituality—when exhibited through prayer, religious service participation, and private devotions—was associated with participants' desire to remain in college and excel (Herndon 2003). Similar findings were provided in other qualitative and quantitative studies (Riggins, McNeal, and Herndon 2008; Teti et al. 2012) with a larger sample of African American male college students and with a quantitative study of African American male college students (Watson 2006).

Though the literature examining spirituality is chiefly conducted among African American adults, there is some literature that has explored the role of spirituality in the lives of young African Americans. For example, using critical narrative inquiry, Norton (2008) showed that the spiritual practices of an African American male student (i.e., walking around and singing songs such as "What a Mighty God We Serve") were accommodated by his first grade instructor. When the instructor took the opportunity to understand the intricacies of the first grader's spiritual expression while in class, it showed him that such expressions were prominent aspects of the student's cultural identity.

INVISIBILITY AND AFRICAN AMERICAN MEN'S CULTURAL IDENTITY

Despite the salience of the cultural values found specifically in hip-hop and within African American culture in general, these cultural values—which are exhibited and endorsed by a broad range of young African American men, from academicians (Milner 2006) and athletes and entertainers (Simons 2002) are oftentimes, misunderstood and reprimanded in mainstream institutions. In many public schools, African American students are forced to "check" their cultural identities at the school door. As some reviewed research has already shown, teachers may hold preferences for mainstream cultural value-based behaviors in their classroom and thus, admonish students for exhibiting behaviors reflective of the students' indigenous home culture and not those behaviors which reflect mainstream culture (Boykin, Tyler, and Miller 2005; Boykin, Tyler, Watkins-Lewis, and Kizzie 2005; Tyler, Boykin, Miller, and Hurley 2006; Tyler, Boykin, and Walton 2005; Tyler, Uqdah, et al. 2008).

Many teachers in predominantly African American public schools often view the cultural values and corresponding behavioral exhibitions of this population to be aberrant or deficient and therefore, in need of correction (Delpit 1995; Gay 2000; Neal et al. 2003). Others report that teachers believe themselves to be ill-equipped to effectively incorporate aspects of African Americans' home culture into the classroom (Bennett 2001; Cochran-Smith 2005; Ladson-Billings 2005). For most African American students, then, particularly African American male students, aspects of their cultural identity are rendered invisible in school contexts.

For example, many school boards across the country have rejected prayer and spirituality in the classroom, although it is considered a salient feature of out-of-school socialization for African American children (Constantine et al. 2006; Klonoff and Landrine 1999; Mattis 2000; Milner 2006). Also, there is a push by many public school systems serving predominately African American populations to maintain individualistic and competitive classrooms (Parsons 2003; Tyler, Boykin, Miller, and Hurley 2006). Such classrooms are believed to restrict opportunities for African American students to express preferred cultural modes of learning such as communal learning, which reflects cultural socialization that occurs in out-of-school contexts (Boykin 1986; Parsons 2003; Tyler et al. 2005).

The integrity inherent in the African American cultural values often goes unrecognized, unacknowledged, or worse, suppressed by public school teachers and administrators (Parsons 2003; Rogoff 2003). For example, Boykin and colleagues have shown, that most often, African American middle grade and high school students perceive their classrooms as inundated with sanctioned behaviors and activities which reflect a Eurocentric or mainstream cultural value system more so than an African cultural worldview (Boykin, Tyler, and Miller 2005; Boykin, Tyler, Watkins-Lewis and Kizzie 2005; Tyler, Boykin, Miller, and Hurley 2006; Tyler, Boykin, and Walton 2005). Although the actual quantitative assessment of the cultural discontinuity between home and school has not adequately been addressed (see Tyler et al. 2008 for further discussion on measurement of cultural discontinuity), such discontinuity of these cultural value-based exhibitions from home to the classroom is still said to exist within the schooling experiences of most African American students. This process renders the cultural values of these students and thus, their cultural identity invisible in mainstream contexts such as the public school (Tyler et al. 2008).

The cultural values and expressions of young African American men are oftentimes prohibited in recreational and entertainment setting as well. Simons (2003), for example, notes that the "trash talking," excessive celebrating, spiking, dancing, dunking, and inciting opponents are part of the cultural identity for African American athletes (i.e., expressive individualism). Support for this has been garnered in the literature (Boykin and Ellison 1995; Lee 2001). Yet, the expressive individualism of African American men is often prohibited and in some cases, outlawed in the professional sports industry (Simons 2003). The discontinuing of the cultural value-based exhibitions from home to work renders some components of cultural identity invisible in the mainstream workplace.

With hip-hop culture, which reflects many of these cultural factors identified by Boykin and colleagues, there is often the same result: dismissal and rejection of the culture and its utility in students' cognitive and personal growth. For many schoolteachers, administrators, and related personnel, hip-hop is hardly viewed as a viable and relevant aspect of students' culture that can be utilized in a formal learning context. Rather, many of these individuals maintain that hip-hop is antithetical to the cognitive development and academic growth of youth, particularly African American youth (Bridges 2011; Callahan and Grantham 2012; Prier and Beachum 2008). Thus, among many education stakeholders, the perception is that hip-hop is rightfully marginalized and typically excluded from any academically related tasks (Bridges 2011; Emdin and Lee 2012; Evelyn 2000: Sealey-Ruiz and Greene 2011).

This adds to the invisibility already felt among young African American men as they feel a rejection of their preferred cultural form of expression and communication and thus, a possible rejection of self. The irony with hip-hop, however, is that the invisibility endured by many young African American men as a result of their affinity for hip-hop culture stands in sharp contrast with the fact that hip-hop is a global phenomenon that is seen and heard and appreciated from persons in other countries and cultures (Sealey-Ruiz and Greene 2011). It is used in television and radio commercials, in television programming, and through various forms of commerce. At the time of this writing, rap, and therefore, hip-hop was even used to explain the aircraft passengers procedures and emergency guidelines. Specifically, an Internet video shows an African American male airline flight attendant having the majority White audience clap to a beat while he provided the instructions for the aircraft and flight crew hip-hop style.

Rap and therefore, hip-hop is and will likely always be a significant component of American culture. Yet, many educators and other mainstream social agents consider such a cultural expression useless (Collins 2006; Sealey-Ruiz 2011). Those young African American men who adhere to such a cultural form, whether it is expressed verbally (i.e., rap) or aesthetically (i.e., clothing, appearance) are more often than not, deemed invisible.

INTERSECTIONALITY AND AFRICAN AMERICAN MEN'S CULTURAL IDENTITY

Aspects of African Americans' racial and cultural identities have been linked to academic performance for African American students (Gaines et al. 1997; Walker and Dixon 2003; Walker and Satterwhite 2002). For example, Gaines et al. (1997) used several multiethnic samples across five separate empirical studies to investigate the associations between ethnic background, ethnic identity, and three cultural value orientations, including collectivism, individualism, and familism. Overall, Gaines and colleagues concluded that the association between ethnic background and the three cultural value orientations was mediated by varying levels of ethnic identity. That is, participants' endorsement of either collectivism, individualism, and familism was indirectly linked to their perceptions of their ethnic identity (see Phinney 1992 for further discussion of the Multigroup Ethnic Identity Measure MEIM used to assess ethnic identity) (It should be noted that Gaines' et al. (1997) referred to their ethnic identity construct as a racial/ethnic identity rather than racial or ethnic identity.)

Additional research has noted the association between racial and cultural identity components (Carter et al. 2005; Pope-Davis et al. 2000). For example, Brookins (1994) found that maintaining an Afrocentric belief system was positively correlated with internalization attitudes. Ewing and colleagues (1996) showed that such a belief system was negatively associated with preencounter attitudes. Finally, Akbar, Chambers, and Sanders-Thompson (2001) showed that Afrocentric values were positively related to Black identity.

Additionally, Cokley (2002, 2005) examined the associations between Afrocentric values and racial identity. In his first study, Cokley (2002) found that Afrocentric attitudes, as measured by a subscale on a widely used racial identity scale (Cross Racial Identity Scale, CRIS: Vandiver et al. 2000) was related to negative attitudes toward White persons. In 2005, Cokley found that another measure, the Afro-centrism scale (Grills and Longshore 1996) was statistically associated with anti-White attitudes, which is a component of the Black racial identity models forwarded by Helms (1990) and Cross (1995).

These findings demonstrate some association between racial and cultural identity. From an intersectionality framework, however, the interaction between various racial identity statuses and cultural identity components and their prediction of psychological and behavioral outcomes has yet to be established. One possible reason for the lag in investigating the interaction between these two constructs is the limited measures for cultural identity.

For instance, Cokley and others have reported some reservations with the current instrumentation assessing cultural identity for African American populations. For instance, the internalization Afro-centricity (IA) subscale of the CRIS (Vandiver et al. 2000) measures the degree to which African Americans believe that holding an Afrocentric worldview can empower African Americans. A major conclusion reached by Cokley (2002, 2005) was that the Internalization Afro-centricity subscale was not derived from theory and thus, an inadequate measure of Afro-centricity.

Furthermore, the AFRI scale (Grills and Longshore 1996) used in some of his additional work (Cokley 2005; Cokley and Williams 2005), while based on theory which specifies several Afrocentric worldviews (Karenga 1998), resulted in a single factor solution which does not fully capture the multiple cultural values and ideologies said to govern the behaviors and preferences of most African Americans (Boykin 1986; Jones 2003). In fact, closer inspection of the theory informing the AFRI (Nguzo Saba; Karenga 1998) find that the definitions and themes present are not conceptually discernible and in most cases, display considerable overlap. Thus, an empirical measure of African American cultural values would be unidemensional and therefore, incorrect.

Boykin's (1986) Triple Quandary theory does a much better job of identifying the African American cultural values and some preliminary work has sought to empirically discern the presence of these values in the lives of African American children and their parents (Tyler, Boykin, Boelter, and Dillihunt 2005; Tyler, Boykin, Miller, and Hurley 2006; Tyler, Dillihunt, et al. 2008). To date, however, no instruments have been developed or rigorously validated for these cultural values. Tyler (forthcoming) has created and begun investigating the psychometric properties—particularly factor validity and internal consistency—of a set of measures designed to assess the presence of several cultural value-based activities said to permeate the lives of many African Americans. Instrumentation for Afro-cultural values would shed light on the utility and accuracy of the Triple Quandary theory and allow it to be examined with additional identity measures. Specifically, researchers could a) investigate the relationship between racial identity and cultural values of African American men and b) examine the intersection between these two identities; particularly by creating and assessing the impact of the interaction term between these two measures.

African American male identity research could also be significantly enhanced by examining the intersection between gender, sexual, and cultural identities (Cokley and Moore 2007). Returning to the "cool pose" phenomenon (Majors and Billson 1992; Oliver 1984; Osborne 1999), it is believed that such a hypermasculine gender role is evidenced in much of the current rap music listened to by 98 percent of African American young adult men (Jamison 2006; Rebollo-Gil and Moras 2012; Tyree 2009). According to Jamison, the themes found in rap music typify a broad range of both racial and cultural identities.

In particular, Jamison (2006) notes that "conscious" rap reflects self-awareness and a strong commitment to African Americans and the global African community. In contrast, the "reality and recreational" rap category represents racial and cultural negation as well as misogyny and related categories that typify the "cool pose" forwarded by Major and Billson (1992). Her examination of the association between scores on the African Self-Consciousness Scale (ASC; Kambon 1996), the Cultural Mis-orientation Scale (Kambon 1997) and the Hyper-masculinity Inventory (Mosher and Sirkin 1984) revealed that African American male undergraduates with higher ASC scores listened to more conscious rap music. Those with lower ASC scores listened to more recreational or reality rap music.

Jamison's work underscores the intersection among cultural and gender identities for African American men, primarily by examining the relationship between cultural affiliation and proxies of gender identity (i.e., masculinity represented in rap music). Yet, how these interrelationships are linked to African American men's behavioral and perhaps, even academic outcomes, is still unclear.

Similarly, the interrelationships among gender, sexual, racial, ethnic, and cultural identities and their association with academic identity are not fully known. With regards to academic performance, some research has countered the hypothesis stating that academic success is perceived as an "acting White" phenomenon and instead, has suggested that positive racial identity attitudes are associated with academic achievement and school persistence (Bergin and Cook 2001; Cokley and Chapman 2008; Harper and Tuckman 2006; Horvat and Lewis 2003; Oyserman, Gant, and Ager 1995; Oyserman, Harrison, and Bybee 2001; Roderick 2003; Sellers et al. 1998; Shelton and Sellers 2003; Whaley 2003). Though some research has argued that the association between racial identity and academic performance is trivial (Lockett and Harrell 2003) or even zero (Awad 2007), other studies have been successful in uncovering statistically significant associations between racial identity and academic performance reports. Few studies, however, have examined the association between cultural identity and other identity components. In fact, some studies examining racial identity may actually assess culturally aligned factors.

For example, a relatively recent study by Nasir, McLaughlin, and Jones (2009) employed a mixed-methodology research design to examine racial identity meanings among African American high school students. In their work, the authors were able to discern the presence of two African American racial identities. The first was the "street savvy" African American identity and included "wearing popular clothing . . . speaking Ebonics, and not seeing one's African American identity as being connected to school." The second identity to emerge in Nasir et al.'s (2009) work was "school-oriented and socially conscious," which "involved being connected to school, community, and a cultural and historical legacy, and seeing oneself as a change agent . . . in the community" (86). The authors note the similarities between the two identities, including shared language (i.e., 'Ebonics') and clothing. Though Nasir et al. have produced important findings regarding the intersection of racial and academic identity, it can be argues that what may have been uncovered are cultural values and therefore, evidence of cultural identity.

Two studies examined a more specific form of African American culture. In particular, Jett (2010) examined the spiritual beliefs and practices of four African American male college students enrolled in mathematics graduate programs. For each African American male participant, spirituality was reported as central to their mission of achieving their goals since their undergraduate days and through their tenure in their graduate program in mathematics. For example, one participant indicated that mathematics was what he was called to do and therefore, his commitment to doing well in his mathematics program was considered "ordained" (Jett 2010).

Another study placed spirituality and spiritual identity as a central identity component for African American college students (Dancy 2010). Similar to the findings of Jett (2010), participants in this qualitative study also discussed how their spiritual beliefs and religious practices were influential in their academic and professional outcomes. In particular, most of the African American male participants indicated how important it is to thank God for what they have and believe that God plays a central role in their lives. Most also believe that maintaining a strong, spiritual relationship with God was an important characteristic of manhood, particularly for African Americans. One participant stated "I . . . feel like a man should have, you know, God in his life. Whatever religion you believe in is fine, but . . . you definitely need to have God in your life." (Dancy 2010, 425). For many of the participants, having a spiritual identity was viewed as more important than church or religious participation (Dancy 2010).

In addition to these reports, Dancy (2010) noted that some participants actually experience some tension between merging their spiritual identities with others. For example, one participant indicated a somewhat distinct experience when considering the role of spirituality in his life. In particular, Dancy (2010) noted that when it comes to the experiences of gay African American men, the intersection between their sexual identity and their religious orientation and practices, tension is often the result. One participant stated that "when you have a good, strong, Christian foundation [being gay] is a battle that you deal with." (Dancy 2010, 426). Dancy (2010) would report that the scrutiny associated with the participant's sexual identity often led to reports of low self-esteem and stress disorders. Other studies have also shown the difficulties of negotiating racial, sexual, and religious identity among African American men (Yarbouse, Nowacki-Butzen, and Brooks 2009). In all, these studies show that many young African American men not only hold spiritual identities as central to their core beliefs regarding manhood and achievement, but several maintain such beliefs despite risking ostracization due to their marginalized sexual identity.

Concerning hip-hop culture, the research is only beginning to more fully explore the association between students with an affinity or orientation toward hip-hop and other identity components. One previously mentioned study (Jamison 2006) examined the association between different types of hip-hop consumption and racial and gender identities. Other previously mentioned studies have underscored a link between hip-hop culture and student motivation in science (Emdin and Lee 2012). Another recent study by Wessel and Wallaert (2011) examined the qualitative data of eleven college students who self-identified as consumers of hip-hop, particularly rap music. Researchers were interested in examining how hip-hop music had influenced their experiences as college students. The college students, four African American, four White, two biracial, and one Samoan, reported that hip-hop culture and music aided in their socialization on campus (i.e., making new friends), and gave them the motivation needed to achieve academic and career goals, particularly through the emphasis of education in some hip-hop lyrics. Thus, there appears to be some evidence for an association between cultural identity, with an emphasis on hip-hop culture, and components of what can be considered an academic identity, which will be more thoroughly defined later.

Though it is accurate to conclude that a significant portion of rap music consumed and produced by many young African American men contain messages of misogyny and violence (Oliver 2006; Rebollo-Gil and Moras 2012; Tyree 2009), others, like those rap songs listened to by the college students in the Wessel and Wallaert (2011) study found more positive socialization messages. Other research has shown that some hip-hop music does contain more positive images of African Americans, particularly the mothers of male hip-hop artists (Oware 2011). In Oware's study of nearly 400 rap songs over a five-year period, it was shown that many rap artists displayed contempt for the mothers of their children, but love and respect for their own biological mothers or female guardians.

It is important to note, nonetheless, that the messages in the lyrics of these rap songs must be more fully understood by those individuals seeking to enhance the lives of young African American men. Regardless of our comprehension of the message, the language used to communicate the message, or our preference for the music and its messages, hip-hop culture has and will always use the medium of music to illuminate various and multiple contextual and societal issues happening with the communities where scores of young African American men call home. As several authors in this area have already noted, it remains important that we discontinue the process of making young African American men invisible because of their hip-hop cultural adherence and exhibition. Doing so not only diminishes any opportunity for significant change and betterment for this population, but also dismisses the very message of disenfranchisement and discrimination that many of them are discussing— sometimes vehemently—through rap music in the first place. In this sce-

164   *Chapter 11*

nario, dismissing the medium of the message devalues the message as well as the messenger, keeping them both invisible.

ILLUSTRATION OF AFRICAN AMERICAN MEN'S IDENTITY INVISIBILITY—CULTURAL IDENTITY

In figure 11.1, the identity component of cultural identity begins to meld with the larger circle of racism, thereby indicating a compromised cultural identity. The invisibility of cultural identity begins to make sense when the reader considers a specific kind of racism, most notably cultural racism (Jones 1981) or what Sue (2004) referred to as ethnocentric monoculturalism. Here, there is a belief that builds off of the initial sentiment

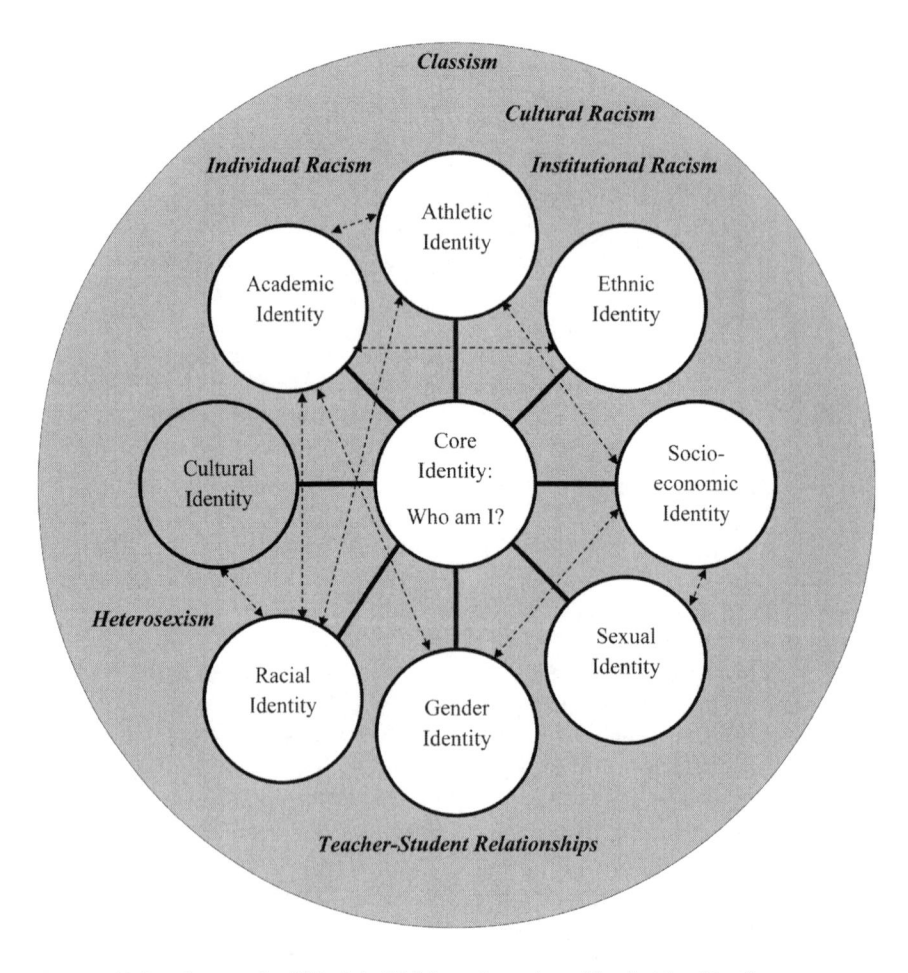

Figure 11.1. Conceptual Model of African American Men's Identity: Compromised Cultural Identity

that Whites are superior to all persons of color. By design, this is the foundation of racism: an acknowledgement of one group's superiority and domination over another group. Many agents of mainstream culture, including but not limited to some White persons, believe that their cultural values are not only preferable, but should be adopted by persons of color as the standard or ideal mode of living and interacting.

For many young African American men, they realize that in order to make it in life, they must check their cultural selves at the mainstream door. For example, the research of Boykin and associates has shown that teachers prefer and think more highly of students who achieve in ways consistent with a mainstream culture. Similar research has found that even culturally appropriate ways of acting and operating at school have implications for how teachers may view their African American male students (Neal et al. 2003). Teachers, in these instances, won't view the integrity attached to that particular style of walking or a culturally aligned way of learning and achieving. For many of them, according to some research, achieving in ways that promote African American culture rather than mainstream culture is tantamount to an unwillingness to learn (Boykin, Tyler, and Walton 2005). Thus, many classroom teachers render these cultural value-based behaviors, despite their preferences by African American parents and students and their salience within African American households, invisible.

Hip-hop culture seems to take a similar compromise. There are many teachers who seemingly reject hip-hop culture, primarily its communication medium of rap music, despite the fact that it captures the essence and realities of some African Americans and its development and delivery is considered an intellectual exercise in its own right (Jenkins 2013). Rejection of that hip-hop culture, a cultural artifact that resonates greatly among African American men, is, to some degree, rejection of the African American male students who listen to and learn from it. When these students don't feel like they are accepted by agents of mainstream institutions, namely school officials and teachers, it is likely that they, in turn, will develop negative perceptions of school and mainstream culture-based achievement. This is a coping response to feeling invisible.

TWELVE

African American Men's Socioeconomic Identity

Much like racial and gender identities, socioeconomic status also plays a major role in the development and understanding of self (Frable 1997; Howard 2000; Thompson and Subich 2011). It has been viewed as one of the central identity components in the intersectionality literature, particularly with discussions regarding class status (Jones 2009; Jones and McEwan 2000). The current literature is replete with empirical support for the impact of socioeconomic status in the physical and psychological well-being of African Americans, particularly economically disadvantaged youth and college-aged students (McLoyd 1998; Nuru-Jeter, Sarsour, Jutte, and Boyee 2010) and low-income African American male adolescents (Hardaway and McLoyd 2009; Slaney and Brown 1983). For example, Walpole (2003) used a longitudinal database to show that many low-SES African American students report having lower grades and lesser college-campus activity involvement than their upper-SES African American counterparts. Differences in hours worked were also statistically significant between these two student groups (Walpole 2003). Follow-up data reporting student status and experience nine years later showed that many low-SES African American students reported lower aspirations for graduate and/or professional postbaccalaureate degrees, along with lower household incomes.

Regarding the impact of SES on psychological outcomes, an older study by Slaney and Brown (1983) showed that many low-income African American male students expected higher levels of interpersonal conflict than their upper-income African American male counterparts. Regarding African Americans from more affluent backgrounds, some research has shown that socioeconomic status (SES) has a positive impact on educational outcomes and mixed effects for more psychologically based outcomes. Specifically, Hurtado, Inkelas, Briggs, and Rhee (1997) used a longitudinal dataset and uncovered that low-income African American students submitted significantly smaller numbers of college applications than did their upper-income counterparts. Similarly, Perna (2000) used a longitudinal dataset and found that, among African American college students, postsecondary enrollment at four-year institutions was statistically associated with higher parental education levels. In addition, a fairly recent review by Hardaway and McLoyd (2009) cited that while some African American students from higher income families experience greater discrimination—most likely the result of their interactions within a more racially integrated schooling context—many low-income African Americans remain the victims of both racial and social class stereotypes (Woods, Kurtz-Costes, and Rowley 2004, cited in Hardaway and McLoyd 2009).

Within this literature exist some select studies examining the association between socioeconomic status and academic performance among African American male students. Recently, data analyzed across seven years showed that eighth grade African American male students on free and reduced lunch (a standard index of family income and thus, socioeconomic status) living in large cities (where poverty is much more highly concentrated) consistently produced lower reading and math National Assessment of Educational Progress test scores than their non–free lunch African American and White male counterparts (Lewis et al. 2010). In another study employing a sample of low-income African American adolescents, Wood and colleagues (2007) found that both parents and teachers reported lower expectations for future educational attainment for African American boys than their African American female counterparts. Though not compared to students from more affluent backgrounds, this study argues that even among those sharing a similar socioeconomic status, there may be distinctions between how young African American male and female students are perceived, thereby implying some intersection between gender and socioeconomic status. Similarly, Griffin and colleagues (2010) found that most African American men enrolling in college for the first time had come from affluent socioeconomic backgrounds (i.e., high parental income and college degree attainment). From these studies, it can be gleaned that socioeconomic status and the resources and opportunities associated with it have predictive utility in the academic lives of young African American men.

Although the literature has long demonstrated the associations between socioeconomic status, as determined by various economic and numeric indices (e.g., parental income) and educational and psychological outcomes, discussion of socioeconomic status as an actual identity component and its subsequent inclusion in empirical studies as a predictor of such outcomes has only recently been acknowledged in the psychological, educational, and sociological literature (Liu et al. 2004; Ostrove and Cole 2003; Thompson and Subich 2007).

One major reason why the social science and educational literatures have not largely discussed a more psychological role of socioeconomic status is the relative unavailability of measures that actually assess internalized messages and ideas regarding the factors that comprise socioeconomic status (Thompson and Subich 2007). Despite the call by several researchers over the years to conduct research examining more social and psychological aspects of socioeconomic status (American Psychological Association 2006; Day-Vines, Patton, and Baytops 2003; Hardaway and McLoyd 2009), socioeconomic status has only recently begun to be investigated beyond its more conventional assessments such as parental or self-reported education, income, and occupation (Liu et al. 2004; Thompson and Subich 2007).

While the impact of these factors has been shown among young African American men (Lewis et al. 2010; Sanchez, Liu, Leathers, Goins, and Vilain 2011), researchers and education stakeholders are not fully informed of the psychological toll that being from a given socioeconomic status may have. That is, while it is important to understand the role that socioeconomic status has in the academic and social lives of young African American men, perhaps more significant is the meaning that such status has to members of this population. Also, the meaning others assign to this status would likely be taken into consideration and thus, prove influential in the development of their own feelings and attitudes about this socioeconomic status. Thus, it is tenable to consider that how young African American men identify with and respond to living within a given socioeconomic status may inform the types of attitudes they develop about themselves and others, along with the behaviors that correspond to such attitudes. As Ostrove and Cole (2003) point out, it is important to understand the values and attitudes associated with the classed location an individual is in.

To this end, several researchers have recently begun to distinguish between social class and socioeconomic status as a way to articulate how the objective measures of socioeconomic status shape individuals' values, attitudes, and behaviors (Liu et al. 2004; Thompson and Subich 2011). For example, Liu and colleagues (2004) define social class as an individual's position within an economic hierarchy determined by known objective measures such as income, education, and occupation. Their definition of socioeconomic status is "a person's perceived place in an economic hierarchy based on subjective indices such as prestige, lifestyle, and control of resources" (Liu et al. 2004, 8). Similarly, Saegert and colleagues (2007) discuss socioeconomic status as a psychological feeling and comparison of self to others in the neighborhood, work, or larger community, while social class is largely considered a more objective, stratification variable (Saegert et al. 2007).

Much of the distinction between socioeconomic status and social class emerges from the seminal research of Fouad and Brown (2000). In their conceptualization of differential status identity, the authors promote an intersectionality perspective by arguing that one's social status is intricately related to his or her race/ethnicity, gender, and social class, which was initially defined as an individual's occupation and annual income (e.g., Duncan's Socioeconomic Index) (Thompson and Subich 2007). Their articulation of differential status identity focused less on the tangible indices of a given occupation (i.e., income) and more on the cognitive and psychological processes present during the internalization of these indices. Fouad and Brown (2000) also sought to understand the meaning individuals would ascribe to such indices. That is, Fouad and Brown (2000) sought to uncover the psychological and social consequences of occupying a specific social position in a given hierarchy-based context such as the United States. For the authors, rather than focusing on what position or role one has in a given environment (e.g., teacher versus politician versus sanitation worker), there was a specific focus on determining how individuals processed and internalized the roles they served and the meanings of these roles. Thus, social status became more about the attitudes and behaviors associated with possessing such a role.

Influencing the development of differential status identity was the research of Rossides (1997), who was one of the first social scientists to consider social status as being more than tangible economic indicators such as income or occupation. Specifically, Rossides' (1997) model identified three major components when considering social status: economic resources, social prestige, and social power. The first component, economic resources, included factors such as personal assets, education level, personal and/or family income stability and degree of control over others' resources (Rossides 1997; Thompson and Subich 2007). Next was social prestige that included the individual and social valuation of one's occupation. Finally, social power focused on one's perception of his or her social power or degree of influence on societal and/or political issues (Rossides 1997; Thompson and Subich 2007).

In all, Rossides' (1997) work set the course for the reconceptualization of social status, which would include a more multidimensional, psychological, identity-based perspective. The emerging conceptual distinctions between socioeconomic status and social class forwarded by Rossides (1997) and Fouad and Brown (2000) and others have provided an opportunity for researchers to investigate the psychological and affective/personal factors associated with social class indices such as income and occupation. That is, no longer is income, in its numerical sense, or occupation viewed as the primary indices of social class. Rather, a multidimensional view of socioeconomic status forwarded by these authors allows for the attitudes and values (i.e., social prestige and social power) associated with such social class indices to be assessed. Toward this end, some instrumentation assessing this multidimensional representation of socioeconomic status has emerged in the literature (Thompson and Subich 2007). For these researchers, the factors assessed with such instrumentation are considered identity components (Thompson and Subich 2007).

Specifically, based on the research of Rossides (1997) and Fouad and Brown (2000), Thompson and Subich (2007) developed and validated the Differential Status Identity Scale (DSIS) using the numerical responses of 454 undergraduates to a sixty-item scale. Factor analytic techniques showed a four-factor solution was the best interpretation for categorizing the distinct conceptual themes that emerged from the participant data. Consistent with Rossides' conceptualization of social status, the first theme was economic resources—amenities, followed by social power, economic resources—basic needs, and social prestige (Thompson, and Subich 2007).

The first factor, economic resources—amenities, assessed an individual's material possessions and leisure activities. The second factor, social power, assessed an individual's perception of his or her job responsibilities and resources, including access to legal assistance. The third factor, economic resources—basic needs, assessed an individual's ability to meet his or her basic needs, such as education, exercise, medical care, insurance, as well as personal possessions. The final factor, social prestige, assesses how the individual perceives him or herself in terms of being valued within his or her ethnic group and overall physical appearance and possessions (Thompson and Subich 2007). Within the same validation study, the authors hypothesized and examined mean differences across each subscale of the Differential Status Identity Scale between African American and White undergraduate participants. Results showed that scores for each status identity subscale for African American participants were lower than those for their White counterparts (Thompson and Subich 2007).

In keeping with the belief that the lives of many African Americans are hindered, to some degree, by racism and race-based institutional practices within the United States, the findings by Thompson and Subich (2007) underscore the fact that many members of this population—as a result of these factors—do not believe they have access to economic resources or significant social power or prestige within the United States. This finding emerging from the Thompson and Subich (2007) study is relevant to the current work on African American male identity because they detail the attitudes, beliefs about, and the values associated with more conventional indexes of socioeconomic status (e.g., personal/family income, occupation, educational level). That is, the work by Thompson and Subich (2007, 2011) allow socioeconomic status to move beyond these conventional indices of SES into those factors that may allow for socioeconomic identity—or feelings that one has about membership in a particular socioeconomic status—to emerge. Given this, the term socioeconomic identity will be used herein to describe the more subjective aspects of social class membership, which, for many, has more direct association with behavioral outcomes than do more objective measures of social class (Ostrove and Cole 2003; Thompson and Subich 2011).

INVISIBILITY AND AFRICAN AMERICAN MEN'S SOCIOECONOMIC IDENTITY

It is clear that most of the historical experiences of many African American men in the U.S. have been wrought with racism-based images and incidences that have negatively impacted their upward mobility, particularly through more traditional means such as education and entrepreneurship (Hardaway and McLoyd 2009). Such disparities in academic achievement and educational attainment have been shown to impact the economic earning potential of many African Americans (Olneck 2006). The diminished or reduced opportunities for economic well-being have resulted in what Drs. Luke Wood and Idara Essein-Wood refer to as the capital identity projection (Wood and Essien-Wood 2012). Capital identity projection is defined as a "harmful psychosocial disposition that occurs when an image of economic success is projected to the point of one's own detriment" (Wood and Essein-Wood 2012). For these authors, capital identity projection is demonstrated when individuals purchase goods and services (e.g., clothing, jewelry, entertainment) and in doing so, offer a deceptive image or representation of success (Wood and Essein-Wood 2012, 987). That is, individuals who engage in such behaviors do so to project a positive socioeconomic image and thus, make a statement regarding their socioeconomic identity.

For some African Americans, namely young African American men, it is plausible that their engagement in capital identity projection is their way of coping with a fragmented masculine identity. As most African American men believe that one defining characteristic of manhood is the ability to be self-sustaining or the ability to take care of one's self (Hammond and Mattis 2005; Hunter and Davis 1994), engagement in capital identity projection activities could be a manner in which these individuals are coping with the perceived inability to be self-sustaining within the U.S. context. If African American men have the highest unemployment rates among all Americans, have the lowest graduation rates and the highest incarceration rates, then it is likely that their earning potential will be compromised. That is, given these circumstances, it is likely that these men will project an image that they struggle to take care of themselves or their familial and financial responsibilities. Not having security with these factors may lead to a compromised gender identity. Here, the African American man may feel like less of a man if he is perceived as unable to take care of himself or his obligations.

To counter such a perception, even if it is his own the African American man will likely engage in capital identity projection to make his economic struggles less visible and to heighten his social perception and self-perception that he is able to take care of himself, almost to the point where he can afford luxuries and activities that may be difficult for others to enjoy. In their qualitative study of African American male community college students, Wood and Essein-Wood (2012), one participant stated "If they (other African American community college students) ain't got the new Jordans or if they ain't fresh, they gonna be considered a bum. They don't want people to think they a bum" (Wood and Essein-Wood 2012, 991). Unlike other ways in which invisibility manifests itself with other identity components, particularly for young African American men, here, the young men who engage in capital projection identity are, perhaps, looking to camouflage what is seemingly a disjointed socioeconomic identity. To protect themselves from this, they may engage in behaviors that display the opposite of a compromised sense of socioeconomic identity, namely one that showcases the African American men with an abundance of material goods. In doing so, young African American men are able to keep their true socioeconomic identity invisible.

Certainly, the invisibility of young African American men's socioeconomic identity cannot and should not be determined with the findings of a singular study. Indeed, much more research in this area is needed in order to draw conclusions regarding whether the socioeconomic identities of young African American men are linked to their acquisition of (or desire to acquire) material goods. Yet, such a hypothesis is plausible, especially when considering the stories of many young African American entertainers and athletes who, in achieving financial success and wealth as a result of their talents, displayed a capital identity projection.

Though many of these stories appear anecdotally among entertainers, capital identity projection was made explicit in the lyrics of prolific hip-hop artist Kanye West and his song, *All Falls Down*. Some authors have stated that some rap music has glamorized material acquisition in the United States, particularly among young African American men (Kitwana 2002; Oliver 2006). Thus, it is fitting that a description of capital identity projection occurs with a rap track that actually discusses material acquisition and more importantly, the rationale for such within the mind of a young African American man. At the time of this writing, clearance to publish the copyrighted lyrics was not obtained. Thus, the reader is strongly encouraged to find the lyrics to West's *All Falls Down* (2004) online.

In the first verse of West's *All Falls Down*, there is a discussion of a single black female who is "addicted to retail." Here, West discusses how the woman struggles with college enrollment, particularly with the selection of a college major. West's discussion of the woman's issues seems to center around the decisions she has to make regarding college (whether to drop out because her major "don't make no money") and her future. In this instance, the woman West discusses seems to be more concerned with the income she can have more immediately (with a job as a hairdresser/stylist) than as an individual who could possibly secure a career based on her major. Another instance of the character's struggles with socioeconomic identity is captured in West's lyric where the woman, in an attempt to identify with big ticket, luxury items, names her own daughter Alexis, a play on the luxury vehicle line, Lexus. Here, if this thesis is accurate, the woman projects a capital identity by naming her daughter Alexis or Alexus (A Lexus). The woman in West's lyrics seemingly 1) fights off the social/peer pressure of demonstrating an ability to take care of oneself *and* live extravagantly and 2) compensates for the fact that her current income does not allow her to actually purchase the luxury car Lexus.

More aligned with the topic of this book, West's second and third verses discuss the issues germane to capital identity projection from the perspective of a young African American man. In West's second verse to *All Falls Down*, he offers an inside look into his life and his identity issues pertaining to socioeconomic status or socioeconomic identity. For the reader, I would urge you to keep in mind that, though these arguments are largely conjecture and would take some expansion by the author/artist in order to validate the claims made, as an African American man who has felt very similar to what West raps about, I don't feel that my deductions are too far off the mark.

The first line in the second verse of *All Falls Down* is a testament to a compromised socioeconomic identity that is masked by the accessorizing with materials goods (i.e., his Rolex watches). In writing that he's so self-conscious in discussing the remedy to alleviate this feeling, West believes that the addition of an expensive piece of jewelry may assist him in overcoming the feelings of invisibility that may be associated with the self that once did not have these lavish items. This point is continued in the lyrics where he discusses his inability to go to the grocery store without looking like he's accumulated a specific income status.

At the time of this writing, one external reviewer brought to my attention the discrepancy between West's articulation of "ones." Initially, in his lyric where he talks about "ones" being clean, I thought he was referring to dollar bills, as in one dollar bills. The reviewer, a middle school teacher from Chicago, acknowledged that this could very well mean the name brand Nike Air Force Ones (1s), a popular sneaker among urban youth. In either case, his clean or crisp dollar bills or his Nike Air Force 1s that are clean allow him to feel "fresh." In keeping with the dollar bill application of "ones," the fact that the dollar bills are clean could also represent the notion that, crisp, new dollar bills have had limited transactional history and thus, are likely freshly printed and/or newly arrived at a bank. The acquisition of such bills can highlight West's caricature of the young African American man who is thrilled not only to have money, but newly printed money, money that no one else has likely had their hands on. This, for some reason, still excites me during banking transactions. Similarly, a fresh pair of shoes, particularly Nike sneakers that were popular and coveted also made me and perhaps, many other young African American men feel pretty fresh.

The reference to a team in West's lyrics can draw upon the socioeconomic status of superstar athletes on major sports team. By wearing the shirt, he, too, can identify, to some degree, with those individuals who have their names printed on shirts and therefore, those individuals who are wealthy and live extravagantly, like many professional sports athletes do. Furthermore, by owning and donning the shirt simply to go to the grocery store, he identifies with the socioeconomic identity that most superstar athletes are believed to have (i.e., wearing expensive clothing to do simple tasks).

In verse three, West (2004) speaks more to the outcomes of capital identity projection discussed by Wood and Essein-Wood (2012). A major component of the capital identity projection is the acquisition of material goods and services that often are detrimental to the person's overall livelihood and/or overall long-term security. That is, individuals who project a capital identity vis-à-vis, the acquisition of expensive items and services will often do so while not securing basic fundamental or more appropriate and necessary items. This is evidenced in West's lyric where he claims that, at one point, he traveled to Jacob (a famous diamond and gem jeweler who has a reputation for dealing with many wealthy customers, including sports athletes and entertainers) to spend twenty-five thousand dollars on jewelry. West reportedly engages in such behavior although he has not secured a place to live (i.e., a house). His desire to spend such an amount of money on luxury items despite not having a permanent address is his desire to be seen as a man who has 'made it.' This is evidence of a capital identity, according to Wood and Essein-Wood (2012).

In that same lyric, West (2004) discusses the fact that he engaged Jacob the Jeweler before he had a house and that he would likely do so a second time while driving a luxury vehicle (Mercedes-Benz) because he wanted to give the appearance of his financial well-being to the public for its consumption. This consumption of West's financial status would occur on Black Entertainment Television (BET), on a show entitled "106 and Park," which is known for highlighting top ten hip-hop and R and B videos to an audience of primarily African American teenagers and young adults. It is common for famous African American entertainers and artists to visit the show to discuss past and/or upcoming projects that most likely are of great interest to the audience members. Thus, for West, in that specific lyric, projecting an image of success (i.e., driving/showing up in a Mercedes-Benz luxury sedan/vehicle while wearing expensive jewelry despite not having a home of his own) to the 106 and Park audience is a testament to his own capital identity projection. What West wants visible is his image of financial success vis-à-vis, the acquisition of materials goods. What he may want invisible is the notion that he, at the time of the purchase of Jacob's jewelry and/or the Mercedes-Benz, did not have a home. The appearance of the expensive jewelry and the luxury vehicle would camouflage this fact for West and thus, project an image that he is doing exceedingly well in life.

While the veracity of the claims made by West in *All Falls Down* is not entirely known, especially since it has been ten years since the track was produced and its author has done exceptionally well during this time, it is likely that West's verses still represent the mindset of some young African American men, who deal with limited employment opportunities, significant school-based challenges, and an overall racist environment that cuts at the very core of what manhood means to this population (i.e., being able to take care of one's self and his loved ones). In West's second and third verses, along with some scholarly literature, it can be inferred that the socioeconomic identity of many African American men is seemingly associated with their gender identity. Studies that have discussed manhood being linked to financial responsibility, at the very least, to one's self, have indicated such (Wood and Essein-Wood 2012). Thus, in order to project an image of success, much like that captured in the "cool pose" phenomenon (Majors and Billson 1992), it is plausible that projecting an image of economic security in the face of those factors that may compromise this security (i.e., racial discrimination) allows some African American men to veil the adverse economic realities they face. That is, some African American men would rather look like they can afford nice things than live with the perception that they cannot afford these things. This "gross materialism" (Edmin and Lee 2012) is a phenomenon that occurs among those—particularly in low and working-class income communities—who seek to hide their own insecurities regarding financial stability, which, for them, may have implications for their self-perceptions of manhood. For some African American men, there is a need to replace a gender identity being made invisible by racism with an ostensibly visible socioeconomic identity, exhibited chiefly through the acquisition of material goods.

INTERSECTIONALITY AND AFRICAN AMERICAN MEN'S SOCIOECONOMIC IDENTITY

For many young African American men, perceptions of manhood are inclusive of economic stability or the ability to make ends meet and take care of one's self. Thus, for this population, it is not surprising that there is an automatic intersection between gender identity and socioeconomic identity. For some African American men, they may feel "more like a man" when they are able to afford items beyond basic necessities and in some cases, luxurious "big ticket" items (e.g., expensive clothing, car, jewelry). Not being able to do so may result in a compromised socioeconomic identity and thus, gender identity. In some extreme cases, capital identity projection forwarded by Wood and Essein-Wood (2012) discusses the result of a compromised socioeconomic identity wherein there is a tendency to acquire expensive and lavish items, at the expense of obtaining or maintaining basic necessities.

Though this line of research pursued by Wood and Essein-Wood (2012) illustrates a connection between two identity components, gender and socioeconomic identity, there is still a much greater need to emphasize the attitudes and behaviors associated with socioeconomic status, rather than just socioeconomic status being viewed simply as an income and/or educational level. Specifically, within the past ten years, the American Psychological Association Task Force on Socioeconomic Status (2007) reported the importance of investigating the intersection of socioeconomic identity with additional person-centered factors (i.e., race, gender) to gain a richer, more comprehensive portrait of individuals. Unfortunately, the relatively slow recognition of the need to examine socioeconomic identity—rather than social class indices such as annual income—through a more subjective lens has resulted in limited measures to assess this specific construct. Thus, very few studies, particularly those using quantitative assessments, have examined the role of socioeconomic identity and its intersection with other identities.

Regarding young, African American men, however, one qualitative study employing fourteen African American male graduate students captured the subjective experiences of socioeconomic identity (i.e., attitudes) rather than objective measures (i.e., income) and their intersection with race and gender. Using consensual qualitative research methodology, Sanchez and colleagues (2011) found that the study participants were made aware of their socioeconomic identity at earlier ages and such experiences led to their attitudes regarding manhood and what financial role a man plays when he has a family. Specifically, most participants believed that financial security and income were among the most important characteristics of manhood. One participant stated "You may be as real as a real man can get and be as manly as manliness can be, but you're diminished in the eyes of others if you can't [financially] support yourself" (Sanchez et al. 2011, 374). Study participants also noted that perceptions of race and stereotypes concerning race are viewed as negatively impacting upward mobility and thus, socioeconomic identity. Specifically, one participant noted that "No matter how much money I'm making and no matter how I operate as a professional . . . I will be seen as a Black male first and then I'll be seen as a father, a husband, a graduate student, and hopefully a professor. . . . Those will always be second" (Sanchez et al. 2011, 373). Here, the student argues that regardless of his social status or its accompanying socioeconomic identity, perceptions of him will always be linked to race and the societal images about African American men in general.

While the research of Sanchez et al and Wood and Essein-Wood (2012) have certainly provided greater insight into the role that socioeconomic identity plays in the lives of young African American men, much more research is necessary to more fully comprehend the influence of one's perceived socioeconomic identity and how it impacts additional identities and subsequent behaviors, particularly among African American male populations who are disproportionately impacted by issues of social class status.

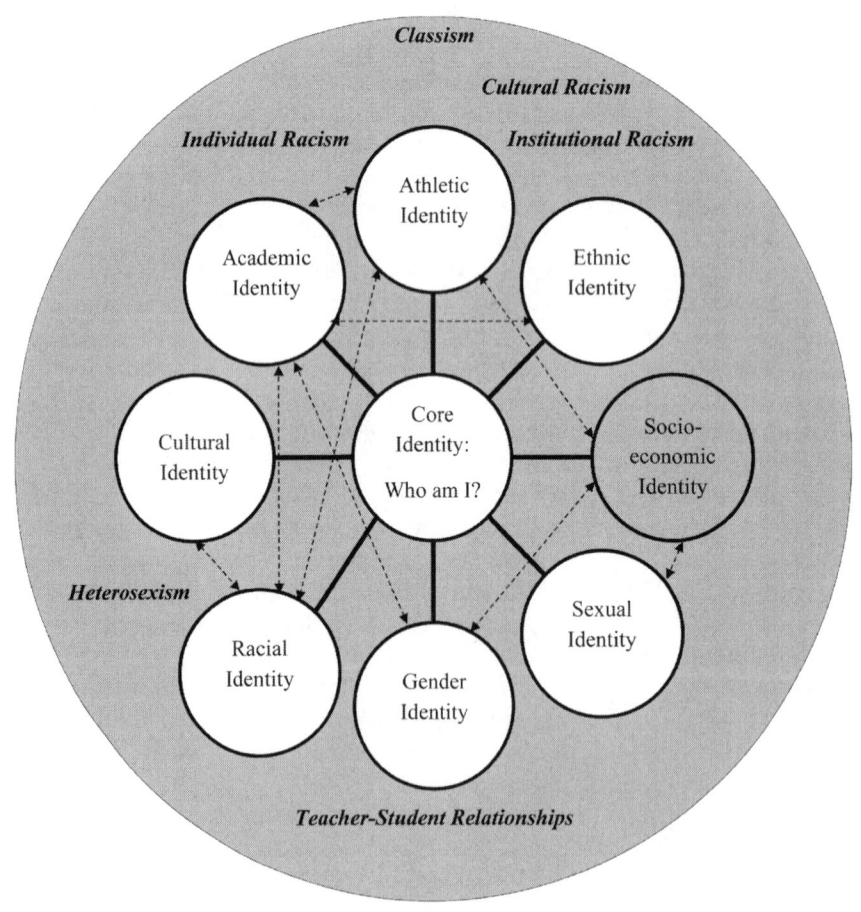

Figure 12.1. Conceptual Model of African American Men's Identity: Compromised Socioeconomic Identity

ILLUSTRATION OF AFRICAN AMERICAN MEN'S IDENTITY INVISIBILITY—SOCIOECONOMIC IDENTITY

In figure 12.1, socioeconomic identity melds with the contextual factor of racism. Here, socioeconomic identity is fused conceptually with gender identity, in that one's ability to sustain himself via access to economic resources is linked to his perception of himself as a man. Thus, it is likely that a compromised socioeconomic identity is, for many African American men, a reflection of a compromised gender identity or manhood. Racism enters the fray by putting in place mechanisms that often inhibit some African American men from idealizing and eventually actualizing themselves as men, particularly those able to take care of themselves and others financially. In trying to become men, it must be remembered that there are significant obstacles to this goal for some African American men. One of these includes racism and its manifestation among those who have the power to limit their opportunities to become financially stable. Lazy, irresponsible, criminal, stellar athlete, and physical prowess are just some of the racist themes that mainstream society employ to demotivate some African American men from seeking achievement within traditional mainstream institutions such as education and commerce.

Moreover, teachers and school officials hold these same expectations for many African American male youth. Thus, it is likely that the joblessness and high incarceration rates among African American men are the result of a racist schooling environment, which holds lower expectations for this population. Such expectations, in turn, force some African American male students to 1) adopt the belief that achieving mainstream success vis-à-vis traditional means (i.e., academic achievement and educational attainment) is unrealistic and therefore, 2) exhibit a sound socioeconomic identity and thus, a sound gender identity by replacing traditional means of success with alternative means (i.e., development of athletic identity, hip-hop/cultural identity or immersion into street culture such as drug trafficking). Here, in adopting these behaviors, some African American men are coping with the perception that they are not able to acquire success in life via traditional means. That is, they are dealing with feelings of invisibility resulting from a compromised socioeconomic identity.

This compromised socioeconomic identity and the resulting coping behaviors resulting from these feelings of invisibility is illustrated among some African American male youth who acquire luxurious material goods, which, to them, represent a positive, albeit temporary socioeconomic identity (Wood and Essein-Wood 2012). That is, for some African American men the acquisition of name-brand gear and jewelry can send an image of financial security and thus, secure manhood. However, such behaviors tend to only mask the fact that some of these young African

American men are—because of the effects of racism, either personal or vicariously—insecure about their financial stability and thus, their abilities to take care of themselves long-term. This compromised socioeconomic identity will likely lead to a compromised sense of manhood or gender identity for this population.

THIRTEEN
African American Athletic Identity

Some of the writing in this manuscript has occurred on a laptop in a car outside my son's football practice. At the time of this writing, Asa had earned the spot of starting running back for the citywide youth tackle football league. During tryouts, I watched him work tirelessly, pouring water over himself to battle the heat, only to run out of it and become somewhat dehydrated and fatigued. Not having ever been an athlete as a youth, I felt bad when I realized that I hadn't kept any water in my car so that he could replenish himself with liquids at the end of the day. (Driving off, I stop and asked a very gracious man if he could fill up my son's water bottle from his home. He politely acquiesced and made small talk about football. I thanked him and rushed to the car where my son swiftly glugged the water.)

I'm happy to report that, since that first practice, his two-hour practices have been filled with fun and sweat, a few scrapes, and mostly importantly, water. I love watching him play and become a serious student of the game, a game that I, now, am only starting to become familiar with. In 2012, it was flag football that his mom believed he should try out for. I was concerned with his overall desire to play, which he didn't initially indicate. He was "on the fence" about playing. Having already earned a "black belt" in Taekwondo at the age of nine, I understood (and partly condoned) his weariness about committing to another sport. Long practices, commutes to and from said practices, not to mention getting homework done and eating late lunch or dinner before practice starts. Keep in mind that all of this would happen at least three days a week during the school week, and after a full day of school.

Despite my initial misgivings and hesitation I shared with my son about this, his mother—who knew best—saw something in him that I hadn't seen. Perhaps she saw ahead of time the emerging of his athletic identity. We knew Asa was fast, and strong and stocky and solid and overall, had the makeup of something wonderful on somebody's field or court. I remained reserved but also yielded with the statement "He's your son, too; if you want him to play football, let him play." Those words were the last we ever discussed about our son's football career. More accurately, those were the last words that I spoke that contained a hint of reluctance about our son playing football.

He. Was. Brilliant! Being from Chicago, and his mom and her husband being die-hard Chicago Bears fans, no one took kindly to him being a member of the Lexington Packers, complete with the Green Bay Packers logo and all. Yet, one thing that could not be denied, quarter after quarter, game after game, was that this kid was impressively fast. He needed to work on his receiving skills for touchdowns, but as a running back that was often handed the ball behind the quarterback, Asa always took off and soared to the end zone. He scored at least twice every single game and I'm talking long yards, too. Once that hand tucked that ball away and the other came down from the sky like he was waving the checkered flag in Indianapolis, Asa became a machine.

Well, he became a running back, a strong and fast and successful running back. Through the playoff game, the championship game, and his selection as most valuable player for the Lexington Packers after they won the "Super Bowl," Asa had solidified his identity as a football player. It didn't stop at the end of the quarters or the seasons, though. Over the summer, he acquired this encyclopedic knowledge of the game and its players, past and present. He'd save his allowance for football cards and watch the NFL draft and the NFL network and he'd purchase rare cards of players online and he'd understand the X's and O's and pretty much everything that a budding football star would do. An uncle and cousin of mine played football in their high school and college careers and my son was aching to hear their gridiron stories. He even convinced me to drive him six hours away for an overnight stay in Canton, Ohio to visit the Pro Football Hall of Fame on *my* birthday.

While he became this four foot, six inch, 87lb connoisseur of the game, I would have my one or two quips about the Bears versus Packers rivalry and on a rare occasion, rap a couple of verses from the Chicago Bears' "*Superbowl Shuffle,*" where in 1985, the championship season the Chicago Bears had ended with a Super Bowl XX victory against the New England Patriots. These were seemingly my only contributions to any discussions about football. I occasionally enjoyed a good game, but could not likely tell you stats or colleges certain players emerged from. To be sure, I have loved ones who thoroughly enjoy the game of football—particularly the Chicago Bears—and I've probably attended three Super Bowl parties in my lifetime, including the 1985 game with my parents. However, I am proudly resigned to the fact that when, it comes to football, Asa is the far more knowledgeable and enthusiastic one in the home he and I share.

What I witnessed and realized then and now, as I type this section at one of Asa's practices, is that Asa is an athlete. I realized that becoming an athlete is something you are socialized toward, something you work passionately toward with the hopes of standing out amongst your teammates as an individual who can make plays consistently and contribute to the number of 'W's in the win-loss column. What's more important and one of the many things I am thankful for is Asa's mom recognizing his potential as an athlete, a potential and love for a sport that I may have thwarted by not emphasizing that he should at least give it a try. She saw an athlete. Of course, he's much more than that, having been inducted into the Lexington Young Achievers' Program, a church usher, a bit of a science whiz, and an overall great, great young African American man. Yet, Asa's mom saw more, much more than I did at the time.

Deep down, I struggled with the initial decision I had made regarding Asa's youth football career. Upon learning and witnessing how great he was/is on the football field, I felt ashamed that I hesitated in making an affirmative decision regarding football. Was it the fact that I had not been an athlete before and simply didn't understand what it took to play organized, contact sports? Certainly, Asa did exceptionally well in the martial arts, but it is arguable that progression in that sport is often linked to one's own volition, whereas team sports require the elimination of an individual perspective that focuses on the self. Did I unconsciously impose my own fear of failure or my own athletic shortcomings onto this young man? Did I fear he would be hurt? Did I unconsciously want to emphasize academic achievement in lieu of athletic development? Again, I was not an athlete as a kid. The closest I came to physical activity during my formative years was freestyle skateboarding and bicycling, sports you'd now find in ESPN's "X-Games," sports that are almost completely based on individual rather than team effort.

These questions ran through my head and continued to do so as I watch him on the football field while typing this paragraph. As I admire his form during sprints and tackle drills, I am reminded of his days as a toddler, between the ages of one and two. I remember frequenting a restaurant with Asa's mom and Asa, standing in line and awaiting a table for an early dinner. Asa, being his usually active self at age two, would begin to walk while holding my hand or finger, wanting to see and experiment with everything there. I recall an older White gentleman, in a trucker's hat and overalls, at the same establishment, with his own family, at least a wife and two much older children, a teenage boy and an adolescent girl. Watching Asa pull away from me to reach for the boxed candies, the gentleman smiles and says "Gotcha yourself a football player, there, I see!" At first, I am amused as Asa demonstrated this feat of strength in pulling his daddy toward him as he reaches for candy.

Yet, a part of me begins to feel awkward upon processing the statement. Was this the only thing the gentleman saw? In this two-year-old male child, did he really see the potential to be an athlete? Was it because of the color of his skin that he saw an athlete? I'm no athlete, although some people would have argued, both then and now, that I'm put together like one. I was a professor and I had never played a game of organized football in my life. Did the gentleman presume that because of my own stocky, defensive lineman build that my offspring would have what it takes to play ball as well? Why did he say that? Was I reading too much into his commentary? Or did I just experience some microaggression that exposed the marginalized status of African American men, which seemingly begins at a very young age.

The gentlemen and his family were seated while I was mulling clever, but purposeful responses in my head. I only remember saying "Yeah," pretending to chuckle a bit as I stepped toward my tugging son. Ten minutes later, the only thought in my head is telling that gentleman "Yeah, or he could be a professor like his daddy." It was too late, though. Asa, at the time of this writing, just sacked a carrier and caused a fumble play, and retrieved the ball for a first down for his team. So, the guy, like his mom, was correct. He is one heck of a football player. But, was that all he saw? Was Asa in danger of the world quite possibly only seeing him as an athlete, some superstar physical specimen who entertained crowds through his style of play and speed?

Perhaps this was the reason I wanted to shield him from playing the sport he immediately grew to love. I didn't want him to be viewed as simply some entertainer, as an athlete who solely trained his body to its maximum in lieu of training both his body and mind. Perhaps I was fearful that society would only see him as an athlete and thus, make certain assumptions about his capabilities and intellect, and as a result, continue to have disdain for him. My fear was that Asa would become invisible and that, at two years of age, he was already typecast into a specific margin: athlete.

Anecdotally speaking, this fear of my child being viewed as invisible was warranted. The gentleman's comment was the first and only comment—beyond how adorable he is—that was made about him as a toddler. This gentleman saw Asa, at two years of age, as a football player, as an athlete. His mom saw it too, but she nurtured that talent for the sport and saw everyday the raw skill Asa had to be competitive in any sport. She witnessed this over years of physical, physiological, cognitive, and emotional development. She's justified in her assumptions about Asa. Yet, I was curious still about how that gentleman knew about Asa's future as a football player. How did he know that Asa, at two years of age, had what it took to be a football player, an athlete? How did he know such from the first and only time he had laid eyes on my toddler son?

While some researchers have argued that there is a general connection between male youth and sports, particularly professional, organized sports, the connection is considered much more pronounced for young

African American men (Johnson and Migliaccio 2009). Though collegiate and professional sports were initially reserved for White men, African American male athletes have been the primary participants in a variety of sports, including basketball, football, boxing, and track and field. Sailes (1996) wrote that African American athletes accounted for 80 percent, 60 percent, and 25 percent of the athletes in professional basketball, football, and baseball, respectively. Coakley (1994), cited in Sailes 1996) stated that, during the 1990s, African American athletes accounted for 67 percent and 44 percent of the athletes participating in National Collegiate Athletics Association (NCAA) Division I basketball and football, respectively. In 2011, seventy-eight percent of NBA players were African American men, while 67 percent of NFL players were African American men (Lapchick 2011, 2012). In 2009–2010, African American male athletes constituted 61 percent in Division I basketball and 46 percent in Division I football (Zgonc 2010).

Indeed, African American men are seen as overrepresented in professional sports such as basketball and football (Oseguera 2010; Sellers, Chavous, and Brown 2002). Yet, there are several reasons why young African American men have become such a dominant presence in professional sports such as basketball and football. To begin, for many African American male athletes, athletic development is viewed as one significant way to arise out of poverty (Sailes 1996). Specifically, excelling in sports is often viewed as one of a limited set of opportunities that they will have to thrive and become successful (Edwards 1992, 2000; Eitle and Eitle 2002). In fact, many young African American men look up to African American male athletes as role models not only for their skill set, which has put them in a position to excel in their respective sports and thus, earn lots of money, but also for their personal stories of triumph and succeeding against the odds, particularly when growing up in tough neighborhoods, being poor, and like situations (Sailes 1996).

These images of African American male athletes, most of whom endured the same dire straits as many younger African American men, often inspire these young men to develop their athletic prowess and thus, a solid and formidable athletic identity (Johnson and Migliaccio 2009). It is not surprising then that many young African American men develop athletic identities—defined as self-perceptions as individuals who participate in exercise and/or sports (Anderson 2004)—early on and to the point where they seek to emulate, if not surpass their sport icon idols (Beamon 2012; Johnson and Migliaccio 2009; Richardson 2012). For many young African American men, developing a strong athletic identity— especially as a means to gain respect and ultimately (and hopefully) move toward a better, more lucrative future—is something *they want to do*.

This desire to develop athletic identities early among African American male youth is not only salient among the individuals themselves. Rather, there is evidence to support the fact that both immediate family and the African American community tend to socialize this population toward the development of a sound athletic identity with the purpose of attaining a better life. Specifically, Johnson and Migliaccio (2009) write that the family is one of the primary socializing agents for young African American men and the development of their athletic identities. Early research by Lapchick (1982) has shown that African American parents and family members are seven times more likely than White families to encourage their young African American male children into sports in particular and the development of an athletic identity in general. In a qualitative study examining the reports of twenty-seven African American male collegiate athletes, Martin, Harrison, and Bukstein (2010) found that African American parents of these athletes maintained high expectations for both athletic and academic success. In many cases, the athletes' participation in collegiate sports was contingent on how well they were doing in the college classroom. Finally, a qualitative study by Beamon (2012) showed that the majority of research participants (twenty African American former collegiate and professional athletes) believed that their formative years were replete with messages from parents and community members articulating the need to participate in organized sports as an adolescent and young adult.

In addition to this research indicating that family plays an important role in the development of athletic identities among young African American men, other qualitative research by Richardson (2012) showed that coaches of young African American male athletes play a significant role in socializing members of this population. In his study, coaches of young African American male athletes provided significant bonding and enrichment experiences with their athletes and their parents, thereby establishing a sense of trust and constancy in the lives of many of these young men. Coaches, according to Richardson (2012) provided supervision of athletes' activities, exposure to the dealings within the adult world, including negotiating and avoiding violent confrontations and the identification and selection of positive peers and adults to interact with. In addition, the coaches, in their desire to develop positive identities among these young African American men through sports participation, often created "safe zones" wherein African American male youth were able to come and play ball while being able to discuss the dealings in their everyday lives with a trusted adult (Richardson 2012). Though much more data—particularly with younger African American male adolescents and young adults and their parents—are needed to confirm the belief that many African American parents socialize their children toward the development of athletic identities through organized sports participation, there are some data to verify this claim (Martin et al. 2010; Richardson 2012).

More than just African American parents and coaches socializing young African American men toward sports participation, some authors are also convinced that the communities in which this population learns, lives, and grows also aids in the development of an athletic identity. From a historical standpoint, it is argued that African American communities have viewed sports participation as a way for young African American men to compete, thrive, and succeed against the odds (Anderson and South 2000; Johnson and Migliaccio 2009). Johnson and Migliaccio (2009) note that such a belief existed during the early years of the 20th century, specifically when African American heavyweight boxer Jack Johnson won the World Heavyweight Title. Such a triumph was perceived by many African Americans as a "way of making it to the 'Promised Land'" (Harris 1997; Harrison 1998; Johnson and Migliaccio 2009, 99).

Since that event and others (e.g., Jackie Robinson integrating major league baseball; Arthur Ashe and Tiger Woods becoming dominant champions in their respective sports of tennis and golf), sports have long been viewed as a means to elevate the status of African Americans in general and African American men in particular (Johnson and Migliaccio 2009). The claim regarding the viability of sports participation among African Americans has been particularly salient among those living in low-income and working-class communities (Martin et al. 2010; Sailes 1996). For many members of the African American community, including athletes, their parents, and their coaches, participating in sports and thus, developing an athletic identity is something they want their young African American men to experience in hopes of preparing for a better tomorrow. Participating in sports and developing an athletic identity is something *they should do*.

The role of media also plays a significant role in the development of athletic identities among young African American men (Coakley 1994, Sailes 1996). Sailes (1996), for example, argues that mass media, including radio, television, and more currently, internet reporting now give young African American men a glimpse into the lives of star African American athletes and in doing so, sensationalize their achievements and possessions. Similarly, Johnson and Migliaccio (2009) claim that much of the representation of African American men in the media are images of sport icons, particularly in television and internet advertising. Thus, it seems practical for young African American men, particularly those looking to achieve the so-called American dream, will emulate these African American professional athletes, especially when they are able to see their value not only in terms of material possession and wealth, but in terms of social interaction as well. In the eyes of many African American male youth, Michael Jordan, Lebron James, Kevin Durant, and Kobe Bryant, along with the late Walter Payton, Adrian Peterson, Robert Griffin III, and Cam Newton will always have the status of icon because, in society's eyes, they are visible. They were and are professional athletes who, through tireless practices and an indefatigable work ethic to hone their skills at the games they love, became warriors on the courts and the fields *and* members of the 1 percent of families in the United States earning millions of dollars in annual income.

Many African American male youth witness such a transformation by way of media outlets and, as a result, seek to achieve the same status; a status of visibility that emerges through the development of an athletic identity. In the media, most African American male athletes likely become heroes to younger African American men largely because they are the predominant image of success offered to this population (Hawkins 1992; Johnson and Migliaccio 2009). The irony of this scenario where many African American male athletes are considered successful is that, according to Smith and Hattery (2007, as cited in Martin et al. 2010), there are roughly "1,600 or so African American men making money playing professional sports, but there are 1,700 African Americans who earn a PhD every year . . . and there are more than 41,000 African American medical doctors—25 times the number playing professional sports" (Smith and Hattery 2007, 186). Couple with the fact that there are limited opportunities for young African American male athletes to "turn pro" (e.g., chances of becoming a professional football player is less than 1 percent; Czopp 2010), it is clear that media images of this population seem to maintain a singular perspective regarding their achievements, particularly by not illuminating the fact that African American achieve greatly in other, non-sports-related arenas.

For many African American male youth, it is conceivable that many of them seek to develop an athletic identity because they want to enjoy the life that many sports superstars and athletic entertainers have. Through their athletic identities they seek to become and will likely remain visible throughout their lifetimes. The message from the larger mass media to young African American male youth is that developing a strong athletic identity and following the paths of those who have achieved success by way of sports and sports entertainment is something that *they need to do*.

INVISIBILITY AND AFRICAN AMERICAN MEN'S ATHLETIC IDENTITY

The push for young African American men to develop positive athletic identities emerges from a variety of sources, including their own parents, their coaches, their communities, and even from various media sources. Based on the research reviewed in this section, it seems feasible to project that many young African American men—as a result of witnessing the success stories of other African American male sports players—*want* to develop athletic identities and participate in organized sports. Also tenable is the fact that many of their parents, coaches, and community members view their participation as a means to a better life, and thus, believe they *should* participate in organized sports and thus, develop an athletic identity. In addition, unidimensional images of African American men achieving success within the realm of sports and thus, achieving societal visibility carries the message that African American male youth *need* to participate in sports and develop a strong athletic identity if they want to be achieve notoriety and visibility.

Another unexamined facet in the development of athletic identity among young African American men are the messages communicated directly or indirectly to young African American men stating that, in order to achieve visibility as an African American man, they *have to* develop a strong athletic identity, particularly by participating in organized sports. This was the fear I had for my son when the gentleman referred to him, then, a two-year-old toddler, as a future football player. I was concerned that, at least one member of society had already marginalized my son into an identity status that he had no choice to adopt. He saw a very young African American man, a toddler, as a football player. He never said, "football player or teacher or scientist or musician or lawyer." One option (football player). One category (athlete). One role (to entertain). Some have argued that many African American male athletes are culturally connected to sports participation, most notably in sports requiring strength and explosiveness (i.e., football) (Anderson, and McCormack 2010). My fear was that my child, a two-year-old African American male toddler, was already stereotypically connected to and expected to participate in such a sport.

This perception that many African American men must play sports or at least be directed more often and more purposefully to sports participation is not unique to my experience or that of my son's experiences. Specifically, one exceptional experimentally designed study by Czopp (2010) investigated the perceptions of 274 White undergraduate research participants who were told to evaluate hypothetical high school student profiles and provide career-related advice. The hypothetical student profiles describe one of four high school students. The first profile was of a White male student interested in French and electronics. The second profile was of a White female student who achieved in her theater and business courses. A third profile, which had two versions, contained a description of a male student who maintained a C average throughout his high school coursework and a total SAT score of 910 (Czopp 2010). Despite such low-to-average academic performance, the narrative on the hypothetical student, named James, indicated that he maintained an interest in schoolwork. Specifically, one part of the description offers that James "tries very hard" but "struggles with understanding concepts" (Czopp 2010). Other components of the narrative stated that James was captain of the varsity football team and received a scholarship to a major

Division I university to play football. Description following this narrative indicated that he was "a gifted athlete with unlimited potential." (Czopp 2010). For half of the research participants, they received this description along with a picture of a White male student, while the other half received the same written description with a photograph of an African American male student. After reviewing these materials, study participants answered questions regarding the career and schooling advice they would offer to the hypothetical students. Students were prompted to provide advice that would offer each hypothetical student the best chance for success (Czopp 2010). In addition, the study participants had to indicate the amount of time they thought each student should spend on academic (e.g., studying) and athletically (e.g., team practices) related activities.

Interestingly, there were no significant differences found among the reports by female study participants regarding the African American and White students and their career advice and time management advice for each. Specifically, White female study participants reported virtually the same career advice for the White and African American hypothetical high school student athletes. Findings among White male study participants indicated a different phenomenon. Here, White male participants reported statistically significant differences in the career and time management advice provided to the hypothetical high school athletes, with African American athletes being advised to spend more time on athletic development and less time on academically-related tasks. White male hypothetical students, on the other hand, were advised to spend more time on academically-related tasks rather than on athletic development. (Czopp 2010). Czopp (2010) concluded that the White male study participants might have deemed the athletic training and development as more appropriate for the hypothetical African American male athlete than for the White male athlete. That is, White men in the study believed that athletic development is more appropriate for young African American men. In Czopp's study, what is invisible is the academic identity among African American male athletes. I limit my inference of what was invisible among the hypothetical African American male athletes to athletic and academic identities as these were the primary identity components present in the narratives written and provided to study participants. Nonetheless, it is clear from Czopp's work that athletic identity and the development of athletic prowess is considered central and important to young African American men, even at the expense of their academic development and other identity development.

Other authors write that African American male athletes in particular experience the overbearing salience of athletic identity at the expense of their academic identity development and strengthening. Sailes (1996) claimed that many universities earn millions of dollars off the labors of gifted African American male athletes and their "reward" is their exploitation resulting from a culture that does not require them to attend classes or earn an actual degree. While the NBA and the NFL have both addressed these by requiring all eligible draftees to have completed at least one or three years of NCAA competition, respectively, it is no secret that oftentimes, the scholastic development of many athletes, particularly young African American male athletes are not the primary reasons these individuals are recruited. The unfortunate aspect of this reality is that even when some African American male athletes get to campus, they will have experiences that further marginalize them academically and as a result, have them focus on the development of their athletic prowess at the expense of their academic identity (Beamon and Bell 2006; Benson 2000; Bimper, Harrison, and Clark 2013; Stone, Harrison, and Mottley 2012).

For example, relatively recent research by Melendez (2008) showed that many African American football players at major universities reported feeling isolation and a general lack of acceptance from their classmates and their professor. Singer (2005) also highlighted the adverse experienes of African American male athletes on college campuses, specifically reporting that these athletes felt they received harsher penalties for minor infractions than did their White counterparts. Some research has also cited that many African American male athletes have been viewed as less intelligent and less motivated to successfully carry out academic tasks, often referred to as "the dumb jock" stereotype (Stone, Harrison, and Mottley 2012).

Additional work by researchers such as C. Keith Harrison and Eddie Comeaux have shed more light on these adverse experiences of young African American male athletes on college campuses. Specifically, in their qualitative study, Comeaux and Harrison (2007) found that many African American male athletes who participated in the study have less personal interaction with their professors than their White peers. More recently, Martin, Harrison, Stone, and Lawrence (2010) conducted a qualitative study where the majority of African American male athletes reported feeling that their professors and academic advisors considered them "dumb jocks," which often resulted in harsher penalties for late assignment or unexcused missed classroom time.

Even beyond the classroom, some former African American male athletes believe that they were still largely referred to in terms of their athletic abilities and identities (Beamon 2012). One study by Beamon (2012) showed that seventeen of the twenty African American male participants who were also former athletes believed that most of the people who know them consider them from the vantage point of an athlete. From her study, many participants believed that not only were they socialized toward sports at an early age by parents, teachers, coaches, and significant others, but even once their participation in sports had ended, they felt they were still viewed as linked to their respective sports and thus, unable to move beyond their athletic identity or be perceived as someone other than a person who participated in a particular sport. Similar findings had been reported in other studies (Harrison, Sailes, Rotich, and Bimper 2011).

Thus, for many young African American men, particularly those looking to become athletes, there is often a premium placed on them by family members, teachers, coaches, and even the media to ensure their athletic excellence, even at the expense of the development of other identities and characteristics such as having a strong academic record (Czopp 2010). Though there are some studies which suggest that African American athletes have positive experiences with faculty and staff members at their respective universities and thus, feel supported in their pursuit to hone both their athletic and academic talents (Martin, Harrison, and Bukstein 2010; Oseguera 2010), by and large, research on this topic seem to also support the notion that most African American male athletes are marginalized and subjected to negative perceptions of their academic capabilities while being viewed only as a physical specimen designed to win games (Bimper et al 2013; Richardson 2012). Moreover, amongst these same athletes are reports of adverse, discriminatory, and prejudicial experiences resulting from their race and status as athletes (Beamon 2012; Czopp 2010; Engstrom, Sedlacek, and McEwen 1995; Hodge, Harrison, Burden, and Dixson 2008; Simons; Bosworth, Fujita, and Jensen 2007).

Though much more research is needed to support the claims of many authors, particularly regarding the notion that African American male youth are socialized at early ages toward sports participation in particular and athletic identity development in general, it is clear that when athletic identities do fully emerge among this population, these identities may be perceived by some as the only valuable identities and thus, visible characteristic these young men possess. Thus, athletic identity will likely be the identity component that remains visible while others are rendered invisible. A major problem here, however, is that this visibility afforded to young African American men as a result of their athletic identity is consistent with a racist ideology that expected African American men to demonstrate excellence in only physical activity such as sports entertainment.

INTERSECTIONALITY AND AFRICAN AMERICAN MEN'S ATHLETIC IDENTITY

One of the best-known examples of the intersection between racial identity and athletic identity occurred on October 16, 1968, where U.S. Olympic sprinters Tommie Smith and John Carlos finished first and third on the morning's 200-meter race. After the race, the athletes went over to receive their medals at the podium. It is said that the black socks they wore, sans shoes, represented the poverty experienced by an overwhelming and disproportionate number of African American during the 1960s (Spander 2006). First place winner Tommie Smith donned a black scarf, representing African American pride, which during the 1960s, had emerged as a significant clarion call to African Americans seeking solidarity and community in the face of continued racial discrimination and oppression (Smith and Steele 2007). Perhaps, the best known gesture at the podium was the sharing and raising of fisted hands by both Smith and Carlos to show solidarity with the Black Power movement of the 1960s, where African Americans sought to immerse themselves in their own culture while simultaneously protesting the practices and policies of mainstream society which had continued to deny basic human rights to this population, even long after the passage of the Civil Rights Act. The salute to Black Power was delivered during the playing of the "Star-Spangled Banner" and were subsequently booed by the spectators in the stands. Reacting to the crowd, Tommie Smith later stated, "If I win, I am American, not a black American. But if I did something bad, then they would say I am a Negro. We are black and we are proud of being black. Black America will understand what we did tonight." (BBC 1968; Smith and Steele 2007). Carlos would later state that "I didn't do what I did as an athlete; I raised my voice in protest as a man" (Spander 2006).

Placed on display after their Olympic win was the intersection between race, racial identity, and athletic identity for these two African American male athletes and Olympians. From a psychological research standpoint, it could be argued that their racial identity, most notably, their orientation toward immersion within African American culture and issues of justice, took the proverbial stage or podium at the same time their athletic identities did upon winning first and third in the 1968 Olympics.

Along with this example, there have been other examples in the research literature that have evidenced the presence of athletic identity and other identities, such as racial identity. For example, one study examined how racial and athletic identity affect college student adjustment for 163 African American male football players (Steinfeldt, Reed, and Steinfeldt 2010). Using the Multidimensional Inventory of Black Identity (Sellers et al. 1998) and the Athletic Identity Measurement Scale (AIMS; Brewer et al. 1993), the authors found that athletic identity reports were not predictive of college adjustment while racial identity, namely. Nationalist Ideology and Public Regard were significant predictors of social adjustment and institutional attachment. Specifically, lower levels of public regard (i.e., perceptions individuals believe others have about them) were predictive of higher levels of social adjustment and institutional attachment. Also, African American football players who had high endorsement regarding African American culture and people (i.e., high Nationalist Ideology) indicated less attachment with their host institution.

Another study by the same authors (Steinfeldt and Steinfeldt 2012) investigated the association between athletic identity (AIMS; Brewer et al. 1993) and conformity to traditional masculine norms, a proxy to gender identity that was assessed by the Conformity to Masculine Norms Inventory-46 (Parent and Moradi 2009). The CMNI had nine subscales, each measuring an attitude or activity associated with conventional masculinity norms within the United States, including "winning," emotional control, risk taking, violence, power over women, playboy, self-reliance, importance of work, and heterosexual self-presentation (Parent and Moradi 2009; Steinfeldt and Steinfeldt 2012). The authors hypothesized that higher levels of athletic identity would be linked to reports of masculinity norms. Also hypothesized was that football position play (e.g., defensive positions) would have higher levels of masculinity conformity. Steinfeldt and Steinfeldt (2012) found that higher levels of athletic identity were associated with seven of the nine masculinity norms reported by football players (athletic identity had no association with emotional control or the playboy persona). In addition, defensive position football players had higher reports of heterosexual self-presentation than their offensive position football player counterparts. Though this study found no differences in associations as a function of student-athlete race, it would be important to know if such attitudes regarding masculinity and athletic identity exist among African American male athletes in other sports such as basketball and boxing.

In some instances, the presence of an athletic identity has been detrimental to student athletes. Specifically, two studies, which borrowed from the similar methodology provided by the earlier stereotype threat work of Dr. Claude Steele and colleagues, showed that when college student-athletes are reminded of their athletic identities while in an academic performance scenario, they tend to perform less well than those who are not primed of their athletic identities (Stone, Harrison, and Mottley 2012;Yopyk, and Prentice 2005). In the first study, the authors asked football players, hockey players, and singing group members attending Princeton University to complete a questionnaire that primed their identities as students, athletes, or entertainers. Questionnaires were randomly assigned to student participants. Specifically, students in the extracurricular priming conditions were asked to write about their last athletic competition, particularly their feelings before, during, and after the game, while singers in the extracurricular priming condition were asked to do the same with reference to their last singing performance. In the student identity priming condition, all participants were asked to to write about their last academic success at the university, particularly their preparation and their feeling before, during, and after the performance (Yopyk and Prentice 2005). In the no prime condition, all students wrote out directions from their dorm to the university main library. After exposure to the conditions, student participants completed a general self-esteem scale and ten math test items found on standardized tests such as the SAT and GRE. The authors found that athletes who were primed in the athletic identity, extracurricular activity condition performed less well than those athletes who were primed in the student condition and athletes in the no priming condition. In addition, athletes primed in the athletic identity extracurricular activity condition reported significantly lower academic self-regard than athletes who were primed in the student condition. Here, being reminded of being an athlete—and the priming of the possible negative stereotypes regarding athletes—impacted student performance.

In a similar study, Stone and colleagues examined the effects of academic engagement and identity priming on the exam performance of African American and White college athletes (Stone et al. 2012). Specifically, the authors found that when African American athletes were primed for their athletic identities and their scholar-athlete identities (in much the same way shown by Yopyk and Prentice (2005), they performed much worse on verbal analogy standardized test items than their White counterparts. Thus, even among those athletes who placed a premium on their desire and abilities to do well in their studies, when the prime "scholar-athlete" was provided to them prior to their performance on a verbal analogies exam, they actually performed worse than academically engaged White athletes and athletes who were rated as not having high academic engagement (as reported by scores on a preexperimental survey assessing intellectual disengagement). Thus, many of the African American student athletes, in seeking to disconfirm the stereotype that they were "dumb jocks," actually performed worse on standardized exam items than those who were not exposed to this identity primer. Athletic identity, in these cases, proved to be detrimental to the students' test performance and likely, may have influenced how well they did while in college.

Finally, regarding athletic identity and sexual identity, research by Dr. Eric Anderson and colleagues (Anderson and McCormack 2010a, 2010b; Anderson and McGuire 2010) has begun to uncover the historical and contemporary factors that often negatively impact African American athletes, gay athletes, and African American gay athletes. A central thesis throughout much of their work is that African American gay athletes often face stigmas from their own communities and among other heterosexual players regarding their masculinity and its link to their perceptions as good players, particularly in physical contact sports such as football. While much more research is needed in this area to corroborate such claims, the authors' discussion of how intersectionality can be used as a framework for such future studies is an important first step in more fully understanding the association between athletic identity and sexual identity, particularly for African American gay and/or bisexual athletes.

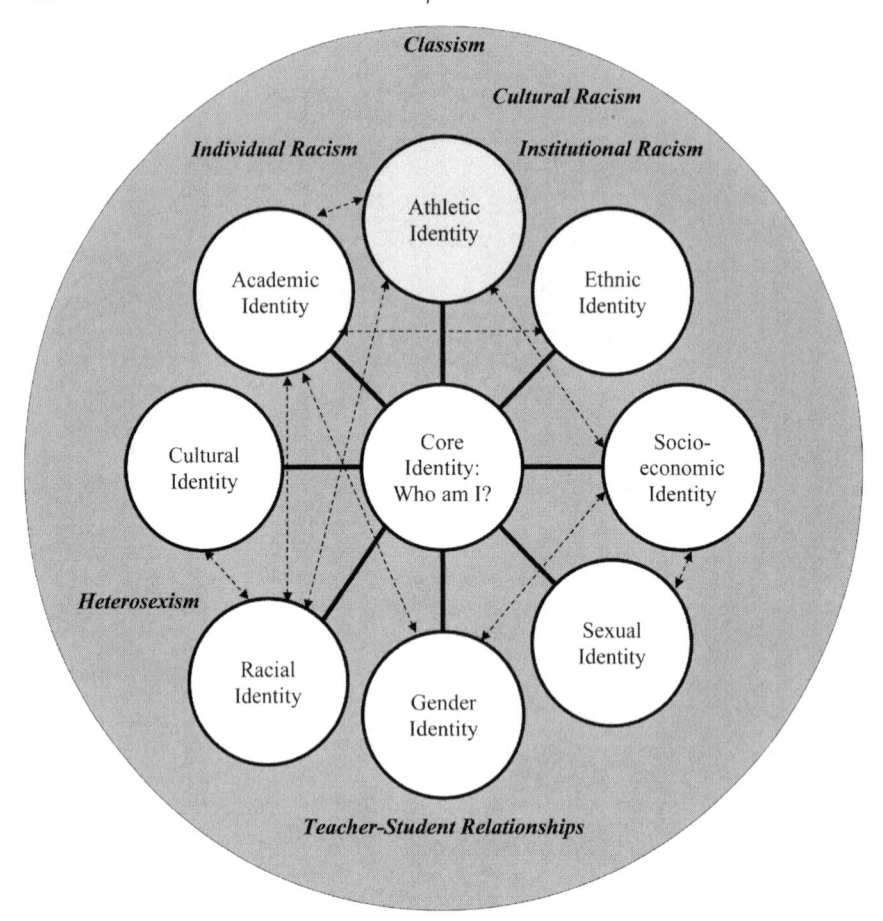

Figure 13.1. Conceptual Model of African American Men's Identity: Compromised Athletic Identity

ILLUSTRATION OF AFRICAN AMERICAN MEN'S IDENTITY INVISIBILITY—ATHLETIC IDENTITY

Figure 13.1 represents athletic identity's interface with the larger, encompassing circle of racism. Unlike other identities, athletic identity is perhaps the only identity to remain somewhat visible within a racist context. That is, the physical prowess of African American men has always been a racist assumption held by most Whites during chattel slavery and by some White persons in the current day (Czopp 2010). Thus, athletic identity or the ability and belief that African American men can excel at physical and athletic feats is an identity that is illuminated within the context of racism. Racism engendered athletic identity for some African American men, to the point where they will also adopt stronger orientations towards athletics and delimit development in other areas such as academics. For some young African American men and their families, particularly those in low-income communities, the development of a strong athletic identity is aligned with a socioeconomic identity and gender identity as well. That is, the desire to develop a solid jumpshot will allow one to go to college, and potentially the pros, which for a very select few, offer opportunities to move beyond possible current socioeconomic identities (i.e., purchase home, take care of parents, live the good life).

FOURTEEN
African American Men's Academic Identity

At this point in the manuscript, I've offered discussion of the lives and experiences of some African American men, including my son, Asa Tyler, Trayvon Martin, President Barack Obama, Kanye West, Tommie Smith and John Carlos, and myself. Among us, there are some commonalities. We are all African American, we are all men, and we all have grown within a society where African American men are viewed as invisible. Yet, an important identity component that we all share that may be missed by some individuals seeking to uncover our commonalities is that of academic identity. Before Asa played football, before Trayvon Martin had purchased candy and a soft drink, before Barack Obama became the 44th president of the United States, before Kanye West emerged as a prolific emcee, before Tommie Smith and John Carlos raised their right and left hands, respectively, at the 1968 Olympics, and certainly before I became a father and a professor, we were all students. All African American men listed here and most, if not all African American men living in the twenty-first century were, at one or several points in their lives, students in formal learning contexts. That is, we, as current or former students in formal learning contexts where our progress and promotion was premised on teachers' social and academic evaluations of us, developed a sense of our own capabilities and shortcomings as thinkers. We, as classroom students gathered, perhaps at earlier ages, our strengths and various forms of intelligence (e.g., Gardner 1995), and in doing so, began to more fully understand ourselves as learners. Throughout our formal learning experiences in the classroom, all of us seemed to more fully comprehend our proclivities toward specific academic domains and our avoidance of others. We learned to "like" different subject matter or perhaps all subject matter. We learned not only that it is important to study and do our best, but also learned more about *how* we actually studied and what qualifies as "doing our best." We garnered a sense of who we were and are as learners, and in doing so, we developed an academic identity.

Though several writers allude to some description of academic identity (Nasir et al. 2009; Osborne 1999; Steele 1997; Zirkel 2002), the term is not clearly operationalized in the psychological or educational literature. More generally, Stets and Harrod (2004) have described academic identity as the degree to which one has the knowledge and skills needed to accomplish an academic task. DeCuir-Gunby (2009) recently discussed the process of academic identification to facilitate discourse on the development of academic identities among African Americans. In particular, DeCuir-Gunby (2009) stated that the process of academic identification involves students feeling that they are positively identified or associated with school and that there is "a meaningful and positive connection between the academic domain and one's sense of identity" (116).

Borrowing from the work of Dr. Albert Bandura (1997), it can be argued that academic identity is comprised of several psychological variables that speak to one's feelings and perceived capabilities as an evaluated participant in the educational process. Some of these variables include self-efficacy (Bandura 1997), academic self-concept (Cokley 2003), self-determination (Cokley 2003), self-esteem (Saunders, Davis, Williams, and Williams 2004), academic motivation (Cokley 2003; Graham 1994) and achievement orientation (Pintrich 2000).

Here, academic identity can be described as how one feels he or she is perceived (by self and social others) as a student or learner across a variety of academic domains. With academic identity, feelings regarding the self or one's self-regard are contingent on successful performance in one, several, or perhaps, all of these domains (Steele 1997). Academic identity asks the question "Who am I as a learner or as a student?" Positive academic identity—as a construct—is typically associated with exposure to effective instructors and strong support networks for all students (Anderman 2003; Bandura 1997; Pintrich 2000).

It is important to point out that much of one's academic identity is contingent on his or her past academic experiences, namely performance and evaluations and also, perceptions of and interactions with school personnel, namely teachers. Returning to the ideas regarding personal and social selves presented in earlier chapters, academic identity is often a self-perception (personal or I-self) as well as a social perception (social or Me-self). Thus, it is likely that many students may believe that they are able to perform at high levels in certain academic domains and may have the past experiences to prove it. While these students may believe that they are able to perform at high levels, while some of their instructors may not hold this position. These perceptions by teachers—particularly when communicated inadvertently or indirectly—may influence the self-perceptions that students have about their academic abilities and thus, reduce their perceptions from highly capable to perhaps, barely capable.

A popular and seminal study in educational psychology literature has corroborated this claim that school age children will perform to the level of expectation held by their classroom teachers (Rosenthal and Jacobsen 1968). In the study, which employed a pre-post test experimental design, elementary students in grades one through six were given a pseudostandardized exam (i.e., I.Q.). Their classroom teachers were informed that roughly 20 percent of the students would likely do better on academic tasks than other students, despite the fact that the faux I.Q. scores were not provided to teachers. The names of these cognitive "growth spurt" or "bloomers" were provided to the teachers, even though there was no evidence to suggest that they would have such a spurt in cognitive ability and intellectual development (i.e., the scores, which were withheld from teachers, were not real I.Q. scores).

Rosenthal and Jacobson (1968) found at the posttest, one year later, when students were given the same I.Q. test again, those identified as "growth spurt" students or "bloomers" showed significantly more cognitive gains than those in the control condition. Given that there was no basis for I.Q. score change among the students in the growth-spurt versus control group, Rosenthal and Jacobsen (1968) concluded that such differences in scores were the result of teachers' higher expectations and subsequent classroom behaviors for students in this condition over the course of a year. Since their initial work examining how classroom teachers interacted with students on the basis of how well they expect students to perform, there have been over 400 studies investigating self-fulfilling prophecy (Rosenthal 1987), some as recent as 2013 (Sorhagen 2013), and most replicating the findings yielded from that seminal 1960s study: that teachers' expectations for students can inform the activities and interactions they maintain with students, which can ultimately impact student achievement.

As Rosenthal and Jacobsen (1968) make clear, many of the negative perceptions of and experiences with public schooling that some students have result chiefly from the teacher-student interaction. Such findings are exacerbated when issues of student race and socioeconomic status are taken into consideration, particularly between low-income students and a predominant middle-class White female teaching force (Ladson-Billings 2005; Neal et al. 2003; Okagaki 2001). For example, research by Neal and colleagues (2003) designed a study investigating the perceptions of 136 (122 White) teachers had regarding the movement styles of African American and White teens. Using an experimental design with video of African American and white students walking with a "stroll"—which may be indicative of gender identity (hypermasculinity) or cultural identity (expressive individualism/hip-hop swag)—it was found that teachers who watched African American and White students stroll versus those exhibiting a more traditional walking style reported that the strolling students were more behaviorally aggressive, and had lower achievement expectations for them. In addition, teachers also reported that the strolling students were in need for special education services, even though roughly only 20 percent of them were special education teachers. For many public school teachers serving predominantly African American students, their expectations for this population's academic success are low (Hauser-Cram, Sirin, and Stipek 2003; Tettegah 1996). For example, one study showed that when teachers of kindergartners from low-income families believe that their educational values were different and higher than their students' parents, they rated the kindergartner students lower on expectations for academic competence and future academic success (Hauser-Cram, Sirin, and Stipek 2003). African American kindergartners constituted 30 percent of the sample, with White (33 percent), Latino (27 percent) and multicultural (10 percent) balancing the sample's ethnicity representation.

While most students seem to have their experiences in school shaped to some degree by interactions with schooling personnel, for young African American men, however, the literature is replete with examples of how their academic identities are most often times shaped by negative interactions, stereotypes, and messages received inadvertently from classroom teachers and school administration, peers, and media (Howard 2001 2002; Osborne 1999; Palmer and Maramba 2011; Stets and Harrod 2004; Whiting 2006). Though discussing the schooling experiences of young African Canadian men, James (2012) highlights those stereotypes that many African American men and male students are exposed to throughout their experiences in school, including, but not limited to teacher-student interactions. These stereotypes include being "fatherless," "athletes," "troublemakers," and/or "underachievers" (James 2012). Harper (2009) extends these stereotypical images to include criminals, descendants of dysfunctional families, self-destructive drug addicts, materialistic lovers of flashy possessions, and other images of this population (Harper 2009, 697).

Indeed, the underachiever stereotype and other damaging social images of this population can shape their academic identities in one of two ways: such experiences can aid in the development of disidentification and disengagement with school or such experiences can aid in the development of increased academic motivation and performance in an attempt to reclaim a compromised academic identity. As Gordon (2012) stated,

> the pathological image of African Americans, particularly African American males, has infiltrated American education so completely that African American advances in socioeconomic status, occupation, and academic achievement in the past decade seem neither to erase nor to mitigate the powerful impact of race. (4)

Despite such a belief, the educational literature is beginning, however, to heed the call of Davis (2003) and Howard and Flennaugh (2011) who encouraged the study of African American male high achievers in an attempt to understand the personal and social/contextual factors that facilitate academic success. To this end, several researchers have highlighted examples of many young African American men who, in spite of negative teacher interactions, racist experiences, negative stereotypes, and other adverse school interactions, have sought a positive academic identity vis-à-vis, strong academic performance and educational attainment beyond secondary and even postsecondary education (Frazier 2012; Gayles 2006; Harper and Davis 2012; Robinson and Werblow 2012; Thompson and Gregory 2011). For example, Gayles' (2006) qualitative research with five high-achieving African American high school seniors found that some participants sought to disprove the negative stereotypes regarding African Americans and their achievement, especially challenging the beliefs that African Americans don't do well in school or they have to adopt a raceless persona (i.e., act White) in order to achieve. More recent research by Gordon (2012) also supported the findings that emerged from Gayles (2006). Specifically, Gordon (2012) conducted a qualitative study of African American male students attending suburban high schools where their own educational experiences as high achievers were examined. All participants reported that they often dealt with negative experiences (e.g., perceptions of low academic potential) by performing at high academic levels. For each of them, the stereotypes regarding a lack of or questionable intelligence actually incentivized them to achieve at high levels (Gordon 2012).

Such findings have also emerged for African American male college students and adult men. For example, a recent qualitative study by Harper and Davis (2012) examined essays among African American male college students who, despite their previous experiences with discrimination, school resource inequity, and racist interactions with school personnel, developed a resolve to pursue higher education because it was considered a great equalizer (i.e., a means to which the participants could enhance their chances of success despite their previous disconcerting schooling experiences).

Similarly, Stinson (2011) used qualitative methodology to uncover the perceptions of four African American adult men ages twenty to twenty-five. Interestingly, the author had his participants read two of Ogbu's works on the cultural diversity and learning and "acting White" and one article by Ogbu's coauthor, Signithia Fordman, on racelessness. After reading, participants answered questions about the veracity of the claims made by the authors concerning African American students and their learning experiences. Specifically, students were asked if the themes present throughout the articles were applicable to their own experiences as former high school students (i.e., What were some occasions when you experienced Ogbu's theory of "acting White"?). Findings revealed that though some felt that they were not expected to pursue academic success, none of the participants felt that they had to "act White' or perceive academic success as being inconsistent with their experiences and conceptualization of themselves as African American men.

Even with the aforementioned research examples discussing how many African American male students use negative stereotypes and school-based racial discrimination experiences to incentivize their efforts toward academic success, much of the literature continues to find that some young African American male students have more adverse outcomes. For example, some African American male students have been said to be tense and uncomfortable at school. Such findings are believed to be the result of the teachers-student relationship (Davis 2003; Ferguson 2001; Noguera 2003; Price 1998). Bakari (2003), for example, cites that teachers of African American students are not content with having to instruct this student population and are less willing to do so. Dusek and Joseph (1985), in a meta-analysis, found that many teachers preferred teaching White, middle-class students than African Americans from low-income backgrounds. Later research found that teachers feel less prepared to instruct African American students (Pang and Sablan 1998). Schultz, Neyhart, and Reck (1996) found that many preservice teachers believed that many African American children bring attitudes to school that hinder effective instruction.

More recent examples include the work of Caton (2012) who interviewed ten African American male high school dropouts. For many participants, the school climate was viewed as punitive and prejudicial against young African American men, with most believing that school personnel viewed them as criminals and untrustworthy. Also, many participants believed that their teachers often focused on their misbehavior, particularly for minor infractions (e.g., classroom disruption) than on their academic and personal strengths (Caton 2012). The emphasis on developing and executing classroom management strategies rather than instruction was viewed as an attempt to reduce or eliminate possible positive teacher-student interactions. In addition to these strategies, the disciplinary practices—which often excluded students from classroom activities via expulsion or in-school or out-of-school suspension—were viewed as another means in which African American male students were subjected to adverse treatment by school officials and therefore, developing an orientation toward disengagement and disidentification with schooling and achievement (Caton 2012).

Addressing the fact that many African American men will encounter negative social images and perceptions held by teachers and school personnel, Allen (2010) captured the sentiment that many African American parents have to convey to their young African American male students when entering and learning within formal learning contexts such as the public school. Specifically, in a study examining racial microaggressions among the schooling experiences of African American high school students, one African American mother explained to her son,

> You're going to have to work twice as hard as anybody else out there just because you've got so many things that you're up against. You need to be brighter. You need to be stronger. You need to be more emotionally intelligent. You need to know where your center is because you're always going to be thrown. (Allen 2010, 136)

In another study by Allen (2012), African American fathers and sons from middle class backgrounds described their microaggressive interactions with school personnel at their sons' high school. Specifically, one respondent described his encounter with a school visitor who, upon being given directions by the respondent, stated, "I can tell you're—what's your GPA?" Respondent indicated 3.6 GPA, to which the visitor replied, "Yeah, I can tell you have a really high GPA because of the way you talk and the way you carry yourself, you carry yourself so well!" After the comment, the respondent stated that "it was just this realization of wow'; this is how the world sees Black men. They don't think that we're smart or talk normal" (Allen 2012, 10). One father indicated significant concern with a parental meeting where he indicated that many of the personnel were police officers and sheriffs who were providing information on how to identify possible deviants. The assumption at the meeting, for the father, was that much of this information was being produced as a result of the perception and assumed deviance of the African American male students at the school and within the larger community (Allen 2012).

Such findings regarding assumed deviant and/or criminal behavior among African American male students were also found in a qualitative study by Henfield (2011) who noted that each of the eighth grade African American male students reported that others assumed that they were criminals at worst, and "rappers and gangbangers" at best. Reinforcing these points is another qualitative study by Lynn and colleagues (Lynn et al. 2010) who showed that even among African American teachers and school personnel participating in focus group research, there often is a feeling that some African American male students are lazy, unmotivated, and oppositional.

Along with qualitative research in this area, some quantitative research has also sought to examine the impact of negative stereotypes on the academic identity vis-à-vis, academic self-concept and academically related behaviors of African American middle grade and high school students. The first study contained two independent investigations that examined the association between endorsement of negative racial stereotypes about intelligence (i.e., academic race stereotypes; "I think in math, Black children do this well.") and reports of academic self-concept. The first study employed 237 middle grade students and results showed that stronger endorsement of academic race stereotypes were predictive of lower academic self-concept. The second investigation in the article employed 290 seventh-grade African American students and found the same association as reported in the first investigation (Okeke, Howard, Kurtz-Costes, and Rowley 2009). Tyler, Thompson, Burris, and Lloyd (under revision) examined a similar association with African American male high school students. Specifically, the authors investigated endorsement of negative intelligence-based stereotypes and its association with academic self-handicapping, which is incongruent with a positive academic identity. Results revealed a positive association between the two factors, with higher endorsement of negative stereotypes about African Americans being predictive of higher academic self-handicapping reports.

INVISIBILITY AND AFRICAN AMERICAN MEN'S ACADEMIC IDENTITY

The messages communicated directly and indirectly from the school context to young African American male students are so potent and omnipresent that simply being informed of upcoming academic evaluation produces enough anxiety among African American students to hinder optimal performance (Steele 1997; Steele and Aronson 1995). These same young African American men in the elementary and secondary grades are primed toward these negative messages about their academic performance and distorted images about their capabilities as learners (Hudley and Graham 2001; Osborne 1999; Thomas, Coard, Stevenson, Bentley, and Zamel 2009). These school-based and societal messages often communicate images and beliefs of intellectual inferiority, which take a toll on African American male students (Ladson-Billings 2011).

That toll is "invisibility syndrome" or feelings of alienation, disrespect, invalidation, and illegitimacy when in the public school classroom. These feelings of invisibility can compromise academic identity. What remains for African American male students is what McMillian and colleagues (2010) refer to as academic disidentification. Here, academic disidentification is described as the association between one's self-esteem and his or her academic achievement becoming virtually nonexistent. More specifically, McMillian et al. (2010) describe a three-step process for academic disidentification. The first component of the process is discounting or the sense that the relationship between a student's self-evaluated achievement and external evidence of said achievement is beginning to diminish. When a student engages in discounting, he or she begins to care less about their own academic performance (i.e., doing well on an exam) and academic performance indices (i.e., grades earned for the exam). McMillian and colleagues (2010) refer to devaluing, the second academic disidentification component, as the diminishing association between a student's global self-worth and perceptions of his or her own ability to successfully carry out academic tasks, particularly in school settings such as the public school classroom. McMillian et al. (2010) refer to full blown disidentification, the final academic disidentification component, as a student's diminished relationship between his or her self-esteem and academic performance and subsequent achievement.

The process of academic disidentification, according to the authors, may be significantly more pronounced for young African American male students than their female counterparts (McMillian et al. 2010; Osborne 1999). For example, when we have African American male students who do not carry out classroom activities because they are psychologically threatened by the social expectation of poor performance (Steele 1997; Steele and Aronson 1995), feelings of invalidation may ensue. With consistent classroom experiences such as this one, it is likely that a compromised sense of academic identity and academic disidentification behaviors will result for the young African American male student. Similarly, when young African American male students are penalized for wanting to learn and work in environments that promote communalism, physical movement and verve or otherwise express themselves in ways that reflect their out-of-school cultural values (Boykin, Tyler, and Miller 2005; Boykin, Tyler, Watkins-Lewis, and Kizzie 2005; Gay 2000; Neal et al. 2003; Parsons 2003; Tyler, Boykin, Miller, and Hurley 2006; Tyler, Boykin, and Walton 2005), they may feel that the integrity of their cultural values is dishonored in the classroom. In this and similar classrooms over time, the academic identity of those African American students is likely compromised and academic disidentification may result.

Academic identity is further compromised when African American male students do not see aspects of their racial and cultural heritage as an integral part of the academic curriculum they are exposed to, or have any role models throughout their schooling experiences who actually look like them (i.e., African American male teachers, professors, etc.) (Bryant and Zimmerman 2003; Dunbar 1999; Prier 2008; Zirkel 2002). That is, when African American male students are consistently demonized in the social science, humanities, and historical literatures, are not represented within the core teaching faculty at the primary, secondary, or postsecondary levels, and when effective and preferred aspects of their preferred learning orientations are not systematically incorporated into the instructional process, it is likely that they will begin to devalue the purpose of and their presence in school. Such devaluing can lead to an eventual disidentification for many African American male students. Moreover, when disciplinary practices and policies demonstrate a disproportionate number of young African American male students being subjected to teacher dismissal from class at best and suspension and expulsion from class at worst, it is likely that the African American male student, in garnering the belief that the school is not a place where he is welcomed, will begin to disengage from academic achievement in particular and schooling in general.

In all, many researchers agree that African American young men are being exposed to learning contexts that ultimately erode aspects of positive academic identity, rendering it invisible (Howard 2008; Ladson-Billings 2005 2011; Lee 2001; Parsons 2003; Prior 2008; Wilson-Jones and Caston 2003). In answering the question, "Who am I as a student?" the findings discussed above indicate that the answer for some African American male students may not be aligned with the types of attitudes and self-beliefs typically predictive of academic success. While there is literature illuminating the fact that not all African American male students begin to devalue schooling or academic achievement or associate such with "acting White" (Gordon 2012; Harper 2006, Stinson 2011), the data regarding African American male student school performance and overall school presence strongly suggest that many young African American men continue to struggle in U.S. public school classrooms and university lecture halls (Harper 2006; Rodney, Crafter, Rodney, and Mupier 1999; Whiting 2006). Much of this struggle may stem from the possibility that they are perceived as inferior or unintelligent students, as lazy, unproductive, and, untrustworthy and criminal. That is, it is likely that their academic identity or perceptions of how well they believe they can work in an academic setting may be made invisible or at least threatened by the destructive racist stereotypical images and messages conveyed directly and inadvertently by social others within the formal learning context such as the public school and by society and media in general.

INTERSECTIONALITY AND AFRICAN AMERICAN MEN'S ACADEMIC IDENTITY

The section above articulates the synergistic nature between race and academic identity for young African American men. From this literature, researchers can glean the important and intricate interactions between issues of race, racial identity, and academic identification for African American men. Yet, an examination of academic identity of this population from an intersectionality framework has not occurred. While some researchers have forwarded tentative hypotheses that juxtapose gender and academic identity (Davis 2003; Majors and Billson 1992; Osborne 1999; Oyserman et al. 2003), no studies to date have uncovered whether the relationship between gender identity (i.e., "being a man") and academic performance (e.g., GPA) is mediated by academic identity. Further, no studies have paired measures of cultural identity or specific cultural values with academic identity in order to determine whether the interaction between these two variables significantly predicts schooling outcomes for African American male students. Finally, no studies have examined the moderation of racial identity by academic identity and their confluence on school performance outcomes.

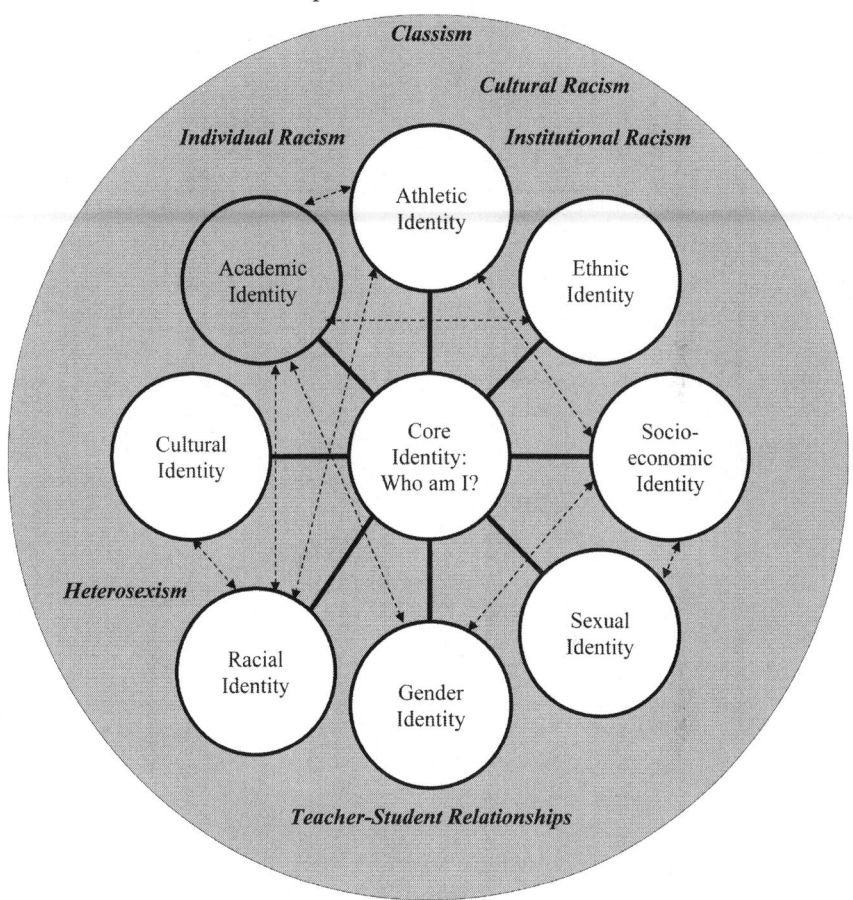

Figure 14.1. Conceptual Model of African American Men's Identity: Compromised Academic Identity

ILLUSTRATION OF AFRICAN AMERICAN MEN'S IDENTITY INVISIBILITY—ACADEMIC IDENTITY

Figure 14.1 illuminates the final identity component for young African American men; academic identity. Per the illustration, it is clear that academic identity is also compromised by the larger circle of racism, to the point where the identity seemingly blends in and is thus, rendered invisible by the larger, racist context. Just like athletic identity, academic identity is influenced by racism in that the stereotypes about the intellectual capacities and capabilities of African Americans emerged roughly at the same time stereotypes regarding athletic superiority emerged. Yet, the academic identity of African Americans, African American men in particular, is not viewed in the same way athletic identity is viewed. The racist stereotype regarding athletic identity focuses on African American men's capabilities, while the racist stereotype regarding academic identity focuses on African American men's inabilities. That is, racism, by and large, makes African American men's academic identity as invisible as much as it makes their athletic identity visible. The same student who will likely be told that he would not perform well in an advanced placement class could be encouraged to try out for the varsity football *and* basketball team. As noted earlier, there is already some evidence suggesting that White persons believe that African American student-athletes are encouraged to pursue sports over academics. In this instance, academic identity was rendered invisible and such is likely due to the persistent and harmful images of African Americans as unintelligent, but athletic.

FIFTEEN
Additional Identity Considerations: Colorism

In 1991, I entered mid-adolescence and was exposed to a film that would eventual provide a significant amount of information and understanding for my naïve interpretation of the so-called drug war. *New Jack City*, a film directed by African American actor Mario Van Peebles and starring several African American artists such as actor Wesley Snipes, hip-hop artist Ice-T, actor and dancer Allen Payne, comedian Chris Rock, and singer Christopher Williams. The movie told the story of New York City at the height of its war against drug lords and their takeover of communities inhabited largely by young African Americans and Latinos. The rise and fall of the Carter empire leader, Nino Brown, is tantamount to the story told in the movie *Scarface*, where Tony Montana, played by actor Al Pacino, reaches the height of his ascent to drug overlord, only to crumble under his own greed and addiction to his own product (cocaine). Nino Brown faces a similar plight. Specifically, on finding out that a former drug addict, Pookie, played by Chris Rock, had made a deal with the cops to have himself wired to infiltrate the Cash Money Brothers (CMB) operation, Nino Brown is forced to shut down the Carter (name of the apartment complex transformed into drug production warehouse). In one of the more elaborate scenes in the film, Brown and his CMB family are shown quickly snatching up floppy disks and burning computer files and other technologies containing years of financial information on the Carter operation.

Wondering how the cover was blown to what proved to be a nearly foolproof operation (working CMB members had to perform tasks in the nude to ensure that no wires or any other activities detrimental to the Carter operation were occurring), Nino Brown, in perhaps the most memorable scene, has all of the CMB, including Gee Money, Nino's right-hand man and most trusted member of CMB (Allen Payne), Duh-Duh Man, a stuttering CMB enforcer/muscle man (Bill Nunn), Keisha, a sly, but beautiful enforcer of CMB (Vanessa L. Williams), and little known banker Kareem Akbar (Christopher Williams) who help to set up all of the financial plans and accounts necessary to keep CMB drug money safe. Nino and the others show up at another undisclosed location to discuss the day's events, all dressed in black.

Nino circles the round table, playfully jumping rope with his dog chain while appearing menacing in his somewhat subtle displeasure with the CMB for allowing such a breach to occur. He begins to ask very brusquely about the day's events. No responses emerge from the clan of CMB brethren. Nino, in disbelief, begins to question the silence in the room before he is assured by his own consciousness and perhaps, suspicion that Gee Money, cofounder of the CMB, may know a little more than he lets on. Convinced of an implicit knowledge withheld by his right hand man, Nino, assuredly, turns to Gee Money, because, as the right hand to Nino, he should have definitely known not to allow something like a breach of the Carter, which brought in millions of dollars to CMB, to occur. Nino goes on to vehemently accuse Gee Money of being incapable of running the operation. In a passionate protest to Nino's accusation, Gee Money promptly stands up only to be shut down with a sword to the throat and the roar of Nino's voice when he commands Gee Money to, well, promptly allow his backside—which to Nino had a monetary value of five dollars—to be seated prior to its inevitable modification.

Uninitiated ears would then have to pay close attention to the next set of events as they provide the spark for this section of this manuscript. Gee Money, in sitting his five dollar behind down, calmly reports that the possible culprit in the ultimate destruction of the Carter was brought to his attention by banker Kareem Akbar. Specifically, Gee Money infers that the downfall of the Carter and the CMB operation overall was the fault of Kareem, who, I believe, brought in Ice-T's character, Scotty Appleton, into the CMB operation, while simultaneously making a deal with rehabbed drug dealer Pookie to infiltrate the Carter on behalf of the New York City police. Earlier in the movie, it is disclosed that Nino Brown actually shot and killed Appleton's mother earlier in his criminal career and thus, Appleton spends his career looking to bring Nino Brown down.

After a few snide remarks by Gee Money, who remained upset that Nino began courting the woman he was longing for, Nino Brown angrily asks Gee Money to repeat the statements made. Gee Money humbles himself in a somewhat regrettable acknowledgement of the facts that 1) Nino Brown has always been in charge of the operation and, 2) even in seeking to possibly speak out against Brown for his escapades with his woman, Money is powerless to do so. Nino Brown, now violently disgruntled resulting from the thoughts of present and future revenue loss, begins to shout at the room that his million-dollar-a-week business has been reduced to virtually nothing. Such a realization sparks outrage within Brown and at this point, Nino, having long unsheathed his sword, violently plunges the weapon into the right hand of Kareem Akbar, accused of having been responsible for the loss of the CMB operation. In addition, upon everyone's collective gasp at the vicious act, including Kareem Akbar's, Nino swiftly secures his dog chain around Akbar's throat, ensuring to everyone that he means business and he is clearly distraught at the outcome of the day's event.

It is understandable that losing a fortune at the hands of an unfortunate gaffe or an irresponsible and somewhat cavalier individual will likely make someone angry enough to engage in violent acts against them. To some degree, Nino Brown's displeasure with Akbar is somewhat warranted, especially if he was in fact the person who did allow the cover to be blown. To Akbar's credit, however, it should be pointed out the manner in which the financial records were secured in banks and the ability to create the Carter—the financial side of it anyway—was largely his doing. Thus, to some degree, he can be credited with the success of the Carter in the same manner as he is accused of its downfall. What is striking, however, is Nino Brown's last words to Kareem Akbar. Soon after loosening the steel noose from Akbar's neck and quickly retrieving his sword from inside Akbar's hand, Nino Brown says—in the most ominous of tones—that he never liked [Akbar] anyway. He, in an exhibited display of disgust and contempt for Akbar, goes on to refer to him as a pretty [expletive].

For me, especially now, that line was an important, but perhaps understudied and unexplored sentiment within the film. Kareem Akbar, a lighter-skinned, curly-haired man played by Christopher Williams, was considered a pretty [expletive] by Nino Brown, a darker-skinned, funky-hairstyled (his choosing) man played by Wesley Snipes. In fact, it would be argued that in much of the movie, there is evidence of an apparent skin color bias. Nino Brown is a darker-skinned, murderer at an earlier age than most (according to his story of killing Appleton's mother for gang initiation), and a drug lord who is disloyal to his closest and trusted friend/colleague, particularly by engaging in sexual relations with his girlfriend. While there is one scene where Brown is shown giving out turkeys during the holidays, Brown, nonetheless, is cast as a menacing and diabolical figure that can kill older women and pour liquor over the younger ones he breaks up with. He's portrayed as a monster. When Appleton beats him toward the end of the movie, neighbors cheer it. When Nino Brown dies at the end of the movie at the hand of an older gentleman with a revolver, there is no remorse, a life that deserves to be taken, it seems. The lighter-skinned detective, who had wanted revenge on Brown as a result of killing his mother, simply dons his sunglasses and walks away.

Gee Money, on the other hand, who is a shade or two lighter than Brown, is the mild, more socially accepted member of CMB. He's casted as having charm, wit, and to some degree, a ladies' man. While he eventually succumbs to crack cocaine addiction and eventually, Nino's gunfire, Gee Money, nonetheless, portrayed the strong wingman to Nino Brown without the dark past and activities which characterized Nino Brown from beginning to end. Gee Money, in the movie, does not appear to kill anyone. At best, he is the individual driving the motorcycle that Nino Brown uses to shoot and kill his rival drug lord adversaries. Gee Money, even in his death at the hands of Nino Brown, who tearfully shoots him out of a sense of betrayal, dies a good man, even with a crack cocaine pipe in his hands.

Other major characters in the movie included Rapper Ice-T's character, Scotty Appleton, who is a seemingly lighter-skinned African American man, sharing a complexion on par with that of Allen Payne's character, Gee Money. Appelton is the good cop/detective whose interest is justice for the public he seeks to protect from drugs, drug traffickers, and the crimes that is characterized these types of activities. His character seeks to take down the likes of Nino Brown in particular and CMB in general.

Another character is Kareem Akbar, who based on appearance, has the lightest complexion among all the film's male characters (with the exception of Judd Nelson, who is white). Akbar is a banker and appears to be in a relationship with CMB's Keisha played by Vanessa L. Williams. Still another character was Pookie, a darker-skinned African American man whose life within the film included petty theft, drug trafficking and preparation, drug addiction, snitch, and perhaps worse of all, a man who is seen beating his wife/significant other in the alleys of New Jack City as a result of their mutual drug addiction. Pookie is violently killed toward the end of the movie.

So, in recapping, it wouldn't be erroneous to conclude that if you were a lighter-skinned African American man in this movie, you likely survived or at least died at the hands of the bad guy while still being perceived as the "decent" guy. If you were a darker-skinned African American man, you died a violent and regretless death at the hands of people who long wanted to see you dead. Clearly, the intricate plot to the film does not simplify the characters or their stories in these ways. There are certainly provided rationales for why these characters either survived or died in *New Jack City*. Yet, it isn't too far off the mark to say that the above synopsis, as simplistic as it is, is somewhat accurate.

More to the point of this section, I always wondered why Nino Brown didn't "like" Kareem Akbar. Sure, he may have ruined the business, but he also help start the business of CMB operations. What was it about Akbar that Brown "never liked"? To say that and then to call him a "pretty [expletive]" must have been at the root of his displeasure with

Akbar (It should be noted that Akbar is accused by Brown in court of being the brains behind the CMB operation. As the financial wizard behind CMB, this is an accurate assessment. Akbar is seen being taken into custody shortly after the admission). With a sword through the hand and the court admission that likely resulted in Akbar doing time, it is clear that Brown had it in for Akbar. Why? Was Brown aware of the privilege afforded to Akbar as a result of his lighter-skin tone? Did Brown see Akbar's relative success as a function of how he looked? Did he see his own difficult pathway to financial freedom differently and more adversely as a result of his own skin tone? More importantly, did society and their perceptions of the differences in these men's skin tone have anything to do with their relative success within mainstream and street culture?

What Nino likely experienced are the effects of colorism or skin bias. Though the term does not have a common usage or presence in most African American communities (Wilder and Cain 2011), it is considered one of several "isms" that affect members of racial minority groups, most notably African Americans (Forster-Scott 2011). Colorism has been defined as the intraracial system of inequality that is rooted in skin color and other physical features such as hair texture and facial characteristics (Wilder and Cain 2011). Despite having less salience than sexism, racism, and even heterosexism, colorism is believed to foster the continuation of dominant versus subordinate group relationships, particularly among members of the same race (Forster-Scott 2011).

Skin color bias can be considered the more immediate manifestation of colorism in that it articulates how such discrimination and prejudice can actually occur and for whom these do occur. Specifically, skin color bias has been defined as a tendency to categorize and thus, behave toward members of a specific racial category based on the lightness or darkness of their skin (Maddox and Gray 2002; Watson, Thornton, and Engelland 2010). As Hill (2002) explains, skin color bias emerged to justify chattel slavery within the United States. White persons were considered civilized and pure and those with much darker skin tones were considered ugly and sinful. As Watson et al. (2010) have noted, the color-caste system in the United States placed darker-skinned persons at the bottom, lighter-skinned persons in the middle, and White persons at the top. Here, the rationale was that light-skinned slaves and eventual African Americans were more valuable than darker-skinned African Americans as a result of their genetic lineage (i.e., having European/White bloodlines). More than just skin tone, other phenotypic characteristics (e.g., nose shape and width, eye color, lip size, hair texture) became markers associated not only with skin tone, but also standards of beauty and social acceptability. Thus, those Africans with physical characteristics such as dark brown eyes, wide noses, larger lips, and coarse hair were not only considered inferior, but also dreadful in the eyes of slave owners.

The rape and sexual assault of many African females slaves led to what would eventually become generations of people whose mixed racial lineage and thus, more European phenotypic characteristics (e.g., lighter skin, narrow nose, lighter eye color) would afford them opportunities to become more greatly accepted within the United States. Based on beliefs such as mixed-race children were genetically superior and more socially desirable, even as slaves, Hill (2002) and others (Coard, Breland, and Raskin 2001; Keith and Herring 1991) note that, children of interracial parents would receive special advantages unlike those whose phenotypic characteristics were not proximal to European physical features. For example, it was widely known that lighter-skinned slaves or mulattos were forced to work inside the slave owner's home, typically as a servant or skilled laborer, while darker-skinned slaves were forced to work outside the home (Hall 1992). The financial value of the mixed-heritage slave/ mulatto, even as a slave, was considered more than that of the darker-skinned slave (Wade and Bielitz 2005).

Since the time of chattel slavery, skin color bias had not only been perpetuated among African Americans themselves, but also had significant implications for the lifestyles and opportunities available and provided to individuals with certain skin tones. (Coard et al. 2001). For example, even after the abolition of slavery in the United States, African Americans engaged in practices that would evidence a Eurocentric characteristic, lighter-skinned preference, both among children and adults. The famous study of Drs. Kenneth and Mamie Clark (1947) expertly showed that many young African American children showed preferences toward White and lighter-skinned persons. Many of these children also held negative beliefs about darker-skinned African Americans (Tyler and Uqdah 2008).

It is likely that many of the preferences exhibited by these children resulted from the inadvertent and perhaps, direct socialization practices of their parents and other adults in their lives. Specifically, Hill (2002) discusses the "brown paper bag" test, which was used to determine the suitability of possible patrons into local churches, fraternities, and other social institutions. The belief was that persons whose complexion was lighter than the brown paper bag possessed a set of characteristics, both physical and cultural, that were aligned with European standards of beauty and conduct. Thus, these persons were admitted into such institutions, whereas those whose complexions were as dark or darker than the brown paper bag were denied admission. Also considered the "blue vein societies," the requirement for inclusion in these social institutions was that possible patrons' skin tone has to be light enough so that blue veins could be viewed, typically through the arm (Thompson and Keith 2001). Though such practices have long since been outlawed and are not at least, overtly presence in the daily lives of many African Americans, it is likely that colorism still persists among African Americans overall.

Consider a fairly recent qualitative study where the authors (Wilder and Cain 2011) used focus group interviews with twenty-six African American women to uncover how these women had been socialized toward issues of race and "color consciousness." Findings reveal that for a majority of the study participants, colorism/skin tone bias was considered a normal part of the socialization messages they received while growing up. Specifically, some participants reported that members of their own families discussed preferences for lighter skin complexions, either in the selection of potential mates or in the birth of a child. One participant, who reported that she was light-skinned, stated that she had an aunt who found darker skin so unattractive, she would typically use the word "black and ugly" simultaneously, to the point where they seemed to merge into one word "blackandugly" (Wilder and Cain 2011). Another participant noted that her mother treated her, a darker-skinned young woman, much differently than she did her sister, who was reportedly much lighter-skinned than she. One participant even reported that her own mother was critical of her dating choices as a result of the possibility that emerging offspring would be darker-skinned—as a result of dating a darker-skinned man. Still another study participant reported that she was "never expected to be smart," which she believed to be the result of her darker skin tone. As Wilder and Cain (2011) concluded, though much had been done within the household of these study participants to prepare them for racism and even sexism, it was clear that the colorism/skin tone bias was not only perpetuated by members of their own families, but these perceptions have significant implications for how the participants thought about themselves and the choices they make regarding dating and their children.

While it is important to underscore the psychological and emotional implications for having such a bias, it is equally important to remember that much of the thinking behind skin tone bias/colorism stems from racist beliefs that have been 1) institutionalized within the larger society and 2) internalized by some persons of color, particularly African Americans. It is likely that many of the family members of the persons in the Wilder and Cain (2011) study have, unfortunately, adopted and maintained a set of racist beliefs regarding skin tone and intelligence and attractiveness that was used to justify slavery in the first place (Forster-Scott 2011). Perhaps even more unfortunate is the fact that, within the United States and perhaps, across the world, the perceptions of lighter-skinned versus darker-skinned persons do have significant implications for the lives they are or are looking to lead. As Harrison and Thomas (2009) wrote, "although Blacks may often be at a disadvantage when applying for jobs, not all Blacks are disadvantaged equally and the burden that Blacks may face is highly dependent on whether they have light or dark skin" (136).

For example, it has been shown that lighter-skinned African Americans complete more years of schooling and have better, more lucrative jobs and promising careers than their darker-skinned counterparts (Keith and Herring 1991; Thompson and Keith 2001). Hochschild (2006), in her report of data from The Multicity Study of Urban Inequality (MCSUI) recorded from 1992 to 1994, found that lighter-skinned African Americans were more likely to have a college degree and earn more income than were darker-skinned African Americans. In the same article (Hochschild 2006), it was shown that across all inmates, irrespective of the actual crime, darker-skinned African Americans received prison sentences that were 15 percent longer than either whites or lighter-skinned African Americans (Blair, Judd, and Chapleau 2004; Burch 2005). In another article, it was shown that, in capital murder cases where the victim was White/Caucasian, darker-skinned African American defendants were twice as likely to receive the death penalty than lighter-skinned African American defendants (Eberhardt et al. 2006).

In a later review article, Hochschild (2007) reported that darker-skinned African Americans were less likely to be married and if they were, they were often married to spouses of lower socioeconomic status (Edwards, Carter-Tellison, and Herring 2004). Additionally, Hughes and Hertel (2000) showed that lighter-skinned African Americans were more likely to have attained more years of education, earn higher salaries, and have more "prominent jobs than darker-skinned African Americans" (Harrison and Thomas 2009). Additionally, some darker-skinned African American students have been discriminated against more than their lighter-skinned counterparts (Hall 1992), even in the workplace (Hunter 2002) and have been reported to have lower self-esteem and self-efficacy than their lighter-skinned African American counterparts (Robinson and Ward 1995; Thompson and Keith 2001). Also, in the larger world of media and broadcast, there is a preference for lighter-skinned African Americans, most often African American women, than for darker-skinned African Americans. These realities have often resulted in significant health issues for this population, including incidence of hypertension (Hall 2007).

Though much of the current literature argues that colorism and skin tone bias has more explicit ramifications for African American women (Forster-Scott 2011; Hill 2002), there is some research to show that African American men are not only victimized by the effects of colorism, (Uzogara, Lee, Abdou, and Jackson, 2014) but are also perpetuators of this social ill. For example, several studies have shown that many African American men have preferences for lighter-skinned African American women and they associate the attributes of these women with beauty standards aligned with mainstream culture (Esmail and Sullivan 2006; Hill 2002;

Maddox 2004; Maddox and Gray 2002). Most recently, an experimental study by Watson and colleagues (2010) found that African American male participants rated portraits of lighter-skinned African American women higher on physical attractiveness than their darker-skinned African American counterparts. In that same journal article, another study reported that African American women, however, rated the portraits of darker-skinned African American women as more physically attractive than the lighter-skinned African American women. The latter finding was consistent with a literature that had long reported that African American women do not often share African American men's preferences for lighter-skinned partners (Hill 2002; Mullins and Sites 1984; Ross 1997; Udry, Bauman, and Chase 1971).

While demonstrating a preference for lighter-skinned African American women in particular and partners in general, this same standard has been used to limit opportunities among African American men as well. For example, Thompson and Keith (2001) showed that self-efficacy is positively associated with movement from darker skin tone to a lighter skin tone. That is, high self-efficacy is found more often among lighter-skin-toned African American men than darker-skin-toned men. This self-efficacy differential may be the result of darker-skinned African American men having fewer or limited opportunities for growth and advancement in the workplace than do lighter-skinned African American men (Thompson and Keith 2001). Lighter-skinned African American men, on the other hand, are viewed to have better job prospects and overall, appear less daunting to White persons than their darker-skinned counterparts. Some authors have concluded that darker-skinned African American men are perceived as dishonest, violent, and are associated with crime and general misconduct, which for many, place them at a disadvantage when applying and/or interviewing for a position. (Hall 1995; Kirschenman and Neckerman 1998).

Recent findings corroborate the racial prejudice experienced by darker-skinned African American men. Uzogara and colleagues (2014) found that light-skinned African American men received more preferential treatment from Whites than their darker-skinned counterparts. Also, in an earlier study, Harrison and Thomas (2009) recruited two hundred and forty undergraduate research participants (nearly 90 percent White, over 70 percent female) to participate in a study where they received a packet containing one picture of a man or a woman and one resume. For the experiment, there were six pictures and two resumes of the same man and woman whose facial skin tones were manipulated using computer software. All other facial characteristics (e.g., hair) remained consistent throughout the pictures. A 2 (gender: male and female) x 2 (resume level: average and above average) x 3 skin tone: light, medium, dark) between subjects design was used.

Study participants, after receiving a packet containing one applicant and one type of resume, reported how strongly he or she would recommend the applicant and whether he or she would hire the fictitious applicant. Results showed two main findings: For hiring decision, the highest ratings (scale range from one to seven) were given to the light-skinned African American woman with the Bachelor's degree listed on the resume and medium-skinned African American woman with the Master's of Business Administration degree listed on the resume. It was also revealed that lowest hiring decision were provided to the darker-skinned African American men with the Master's of Business Administration degree listed on the resume. Another related finding pertaining to hiring decision was that lighter-skinned and medium-skinned African American men who only listed a Bachelor's degree on their respective resumes received a significantly higher rating of hiring favorability than darker-skinned African American men with the Master's of Business Administration listed on their resumes.

Based on findings like these, it is at least tenable to consider the role of colorism in the identity development of young African American men. While there hasn't been any evidence to support a claim that these young men discriminate against each other on the basis of skin tone, some research does support the fact that these young men are discriminated against on the basis of their skin complexion. Along with some scientific evidence reported in this chapter, there has been some anecdotal evidence to support the claim that skin tone bias does pervade the lives of young African American men. Noted scholar Dr. Michael Eric Dyson wrote in his 2008 text that he believed that colorism impacts his life and that of his brother, with the former—a lighter-skinned African American man—growing to become a professor at several prestigious universities and the latter, a darker-skinned African American man serving a life sentence in prison (Wilder and Cain 2011).

Whether the colorism factor could serve as a contextual factor or personal/social identity component for young African American men remains to be seen. It, nonetheless, should be considered in discussion of young African American male identity (Wilder and Cain 2011). When I consider how many darker-skinned African American men are perceived by some members of society, particularly by those who may endorse various stereotypes regarding this population, it seems clear that there needs to be greater research initiatives designed to more fully uncover the role that colorism plays in the lives of young African American men. This issue of skin tone bias may be far more impactful than initially considered.

For example, in returning to the Trayvon Martin tragedy, I wonder if the shooter would have seen him in a somewhat different light had Trayvon been White or a much lighter-skinned African American man? Additionally, consider the 2012 presidential campaign of Barack Obama, particularly in his drive against a Republican party that included a darker-skinned African American man, millionaire and entrepreneur Herman Cain. Specifically, at one point, Cain was leading in the Republican polls during the presidential primaries of 2012. Suddenly, a sex scandal eliminated his candidacy and forced the then front-runner out of the running for the Republican Party presidential nomination. Cain, a darker-skinned African American man, was seemingly placed under the radar and Barack Obama, a lighter-skinned biracial African American man, had a successful run for the second term as president of the United States.

There may be some explanation for this, albeit not directly related to the 2012 presidential election, per se. Specifically, Hochschild (2007) summarized an experiment conducted by her and colleagues on the impact of skin color on the selection of hypothetical Senate candidates among a nationally representative sample of White/Caucasian voting-age participants. Participants were shown hypothetical candidates' advertisements and were asked to complete a survey indicating whether they would likely vote for the candidate. Hypothetical candidates varied by name, political agenda/platform, and skin tone. Results revealed that African American Senate candidates did not achieve the level of favorability that White candidates received. However, more telling was the finding which revealed that, among African American candidates who opposed each other had much different ratings of favorability. Specifically, the lighter-skinned candidate received nearly 20 percentage points more over the darker-skinned African American candidate/opponent. Study participants also rated the light-skinned African American candidate as more intelligent, more experienced, and trustworthier than the darker-skinned African American candidate/opponent (Hochschild 2007)

I can offer nothing more than speculation, but, given the Hochschild (2007) findings, there seems to be some parallel between the story of President Barack Obama and Herman Cain and that offered at the beginning of this section on the movie *New Jack City*. Nino Brown, a darker-skinned African American man, was eliminated at the hands of a vigilante. Herman Cain, a darker-skinned African American presidential candidate, was eliminated due to a sex scandal. Kareem Akbar, a lighter-skinned African American man battered by the darker-skinned man antagonist survives at the end of the film. Barack Obama, a lighter-skinned African American man, also survives a tumultuous campaign season to remain the 44th president of the United States. It is likely that skin tone bias had nothing to do with either of these fictional and reality-based scenarios. It is, plausible, however, that skin tone bias, had everything to do with the outcomes present in both of these scenarios. Our young African American men, particularly those who may be perceived differently on the basis of the actual color of their skin, are worth an investigation of the role of colorism in their lives. Without asking questions regarding the internalization of the perception of darker- and lighter-skinned African American men, researchers and educators may never be in a secure place to actually assist young African American men toward the development of a better life vis-à-vis, a stronger negotiation of the context that, depending on the color of their skin, may not view or treat them fairly.

COLORISM AND INVISIBILITY

Though the research examining whether young African American men in particular and African American men in general adopt feelings of invisibility is scarce, some anecdotal and empirical evidence has been provided to show that, for some African American men, their skin complexion can render them invisible in much of society's eyes. As previously mentioned, it has been documented that darker-skinned African American men are less likely to be hired for a job they are qualified for and instead, are passed up for a lighter-skinned African American male job candidate with lesser credentials (Harrison and Thomas 2009). Additionally, given the omnipresence of darker-skinned African American men in sports and entertainment, they are often rated as more physically and athletic dominant and less intelligent (Wade and Bielitz 2005). In these examples, it is shown that who these men are, specifically, their physical appearance is enough to render them invisible by mainstream society. The irony, however, is that this issue does not *appear* in sports and entertainment fields. When taking stock of NFL players and NBA players and MLB players, there is likely a disproportionate representation of darker-skinned African American men. Yet, there doesn't *appear* to be animosities or perceptions of discrimination on the basis of skin tone. Skin tone does not seem to impact their perceptions as athletics with superior physical prowess as a previous chapter has noted that the athletic identity of young African American men is perceived at much greater levels than, say, academic identity (Czopp 2010). Yet, it would be interesting to know whether, deep down, there was some feeling among darker-skinned African American athletes about whether a lighter-skinned African American athlete received a contract or a commercial or endorsement deal or bonus or more playing time or favorability among coaches because of the color of his skin. Again, we can only speculate because these discussions about colorism are not as prevalent among African Americans as they should be (Hochschild 2006). Yet, Nino Brown, in *New Jack City*, seemed to believe that Kareem Akbar's "prettiness"—as a lighter-skinned African American man—was worthy of him being stabbed in the hand and chain choked. Perhaps underneath that rampage against the light-skinned, curly-haired banker was Nino's own struggle with invisibility; one that may have resulted in him having a much more difficult life experience than Kareem; one that may have resulted from the color of his skin. Given this finding that, among some darker-skinned African American men, the greater the acceptance of the skin color, the lower the self-esteem (Coard, Breland, and Raskin 2001), it is plausible that Nino Brown may have had some underlying self-hatred issues emerging from his exposure to a society that, for the most part, judges him, criminalizes him, and marginalizes him because of his skin tone.

While addressing this and like issues regarding colorism and invisibility, it will also be important to note whether there is a similar reaction among lighter-skinned African Americans and the social perceptions surrounding the color of their skin. Specifically, some research has argued that some light-skinned African Americans are ridiculed because their complexions are not dark or black enough (Coard, Breland, and Raskin 2001; Scales-Trent 1995). Thus, how lighter-skinned African Americans, men in particular, deal with this societal "privilege" is another facet of research that ought to be investigated.

COLORISM AND INTERSECTIONALITY

Similar to research examining the invisibility of skin complexion, particularly among darker-skinned African American men, examining attitudes and behaviors that may be associated with skin color would be a logical next step. President Obama, in his book *Dreams from My Father,* discusses the link between his racial heritages, how it emerges through his physical appearance and the resulting attitudes he adopted in order to negotiate environments that were not often cordial to young African American men. In the same vein, it is likely that self-perceptions, particularly those beginning at the level of the skin complexion, have an impact on how African Americans view themselves and others. Two studies support this claim.

In particular, Robinson (1992) found that as lighter-skinned African American participants had reported preferences for darker skin, the more they endorsed the immersion-emersion stage of Black racial identity. That is, as preference for darker skin emerged among light-skinned African American participants, so too did preferences for all-Black activities, events, and culture. Similarly, Coard and colleagues (2001) examined the reports among 113 African American undergraduates on racial identity (Racial Identity Attitudes Scales; Parham and Helms 1981) and skin color preference (Skin Color Questionnaire, Bond and Cash 1992). Results revealed that among the participants with reported lighter skin tones, there was a higher endorsement of pro-Black/anti-White attitudes.

Across these two studies, it is shown that skin color or color identity may intersect with at least one component of African American identity, namely racial identity. Given that perceptions of skin color/tone may impact social others' beliefs about an individual's intellect, employability, attractiveness, and even leadership capability, it would be important for future research to begin to uncover the role that skin color has in the lives of young African American men, many of whom may be directly or inadvertently judged on their outward physical appearance. With findings such as these reported in this section, where some African American men go to prison for longer sentences or are subjected to capital punishment on the basis of their skin tone, it is conceivable that a lighter-skinned Trayvon Martin, complete with pants, hoodie, candy, soft drink, walk, swag, and cellphone would have likely still been alive today. Perceptions of skin color and color identity in general could be an unlikely, but impactful correlate of many of the difficulties faced by our young African American men. This issue of colorism among our youth, particularly those who may die or suffer adversity because of what they were born with needs to be more thoughtfully and critically addressed by everyone claiming to care about young African American men. Even if it is to make sure that it may not be a significant an issue among them.

SIXTEEN
"One Day It'll All Make Sense"

Examining a Model of African American Men's Identity

Figure 16.1 illustrates what happens when racism impacts each identity component of young African American men. To review, figure 6.1 offers an account of the multiple contextual factors that aid in the shaping of identities among young African American men. Though the list of factors is far from complete, figure 6.1 does seek to illustrate how various identity components of this population are exhibited within societal contexts that will most likely include multiple forms of racism. Figures 7.1 to 14.1 presented in the preceding chapters offer illustrations of how contextual factors such as, but not limited to racism, may impact or render invisible each identity component independently.

Perhaps it is figure 16.1, however, which offers the most comprehensive and accurate visual account of the identities of many young African American men in the United States. Specifically, figure 16.1 details how racism—among other contextual factors—can negatively influence the development and manifestation of young African American men's multiple identities. For many of these young men, it is probable that exposure to societal ills results in several identities being perceived as invisible. For example, racism—in its various manifestations—can shut down or render invisible one's preferences for his own culture (cultural identity), one's public regard for his ethnic group (ethnic identity), one's feelings about being African American (racial identity), one's ability to become a man (gender identity), one's ability to take care of himself and his loved ones (socioeconomic identity), one's sexual preferences, particularly if they are inconsistent with traditional manhood themes (sexual identity), and one's ability and desire to do well in school (academic identity). As it is consistent with racist beliefs and images, the athletic identity would be

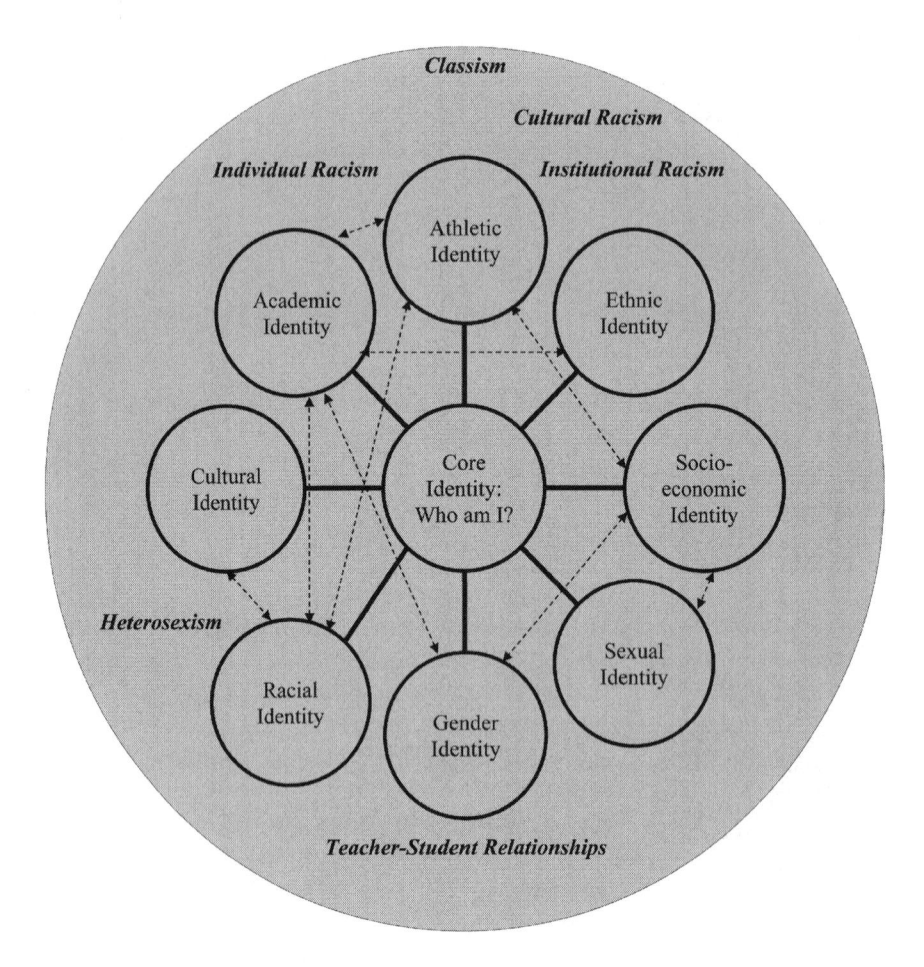

Figure 16.1. Conceptual Model of African American Men's Identity: Overall Compromised Identity

the sole illuminated identity component within the racism circle, although such illumination would be compromised to some degree as the expectation of being athletic and little else is largely consistent with racist stereotypes about young African American men. Thus, it is likely that each identity component can be simultaneously impacted by racism, which may result in an overall compromised core identity for young African American men. Moreover, it is tenable that the maladaptive coping strategies and dangerous behaviors exhibited among some African American men are the result of a fully compromised sense of self; a set of identities that have been rendered invisible through continuous and damaging racist events and encounters, both personally and vicariously within the United States.

IDENTITY MEASURES AND AFRICAN AMERICAN MEN'S IDENTITY

Of course, the writing about overall compromised identity is largely speculative as the research investigating the impact of contextual factors on the intersecting identities of young African American men is beginning to emerge. While the conceptual model hypothesizes that racism and its direct and indirect effects are chiefly accountable in much of the feelings of invisibility many young African American men feel regarding some of their identity components, it will be important for social scientists and education researchers to begin to corroborate this and similar claims through the continuation of research that may not include a conceptual model to facilitate development of research questions and hypotheses. That is, when readers and researchers review much of the behavioral statistics on this population and realize that these behaviors are the result of both a racist environment and a set of personal and social identities possessed by this population, it becomes paramount for those in the research communities to look more fully at the role of identity in the coping responses and behavioral outcomes of young African American men. In addition to studying the intersection of young African American men's multiple identities, the conceptual model described in this text allows for various contextual factors to serve as predictors for each identity component.

Currently, there are several instruments in the literature that can be used as predictor variables in analyses discerning the association between contextual factors and identity formation among young African American men. For instance, it would be interesting to determine whether the development of hypermasculinity attitudes is linked to perceptions of the salience of individual, institutional, and cultural racism (McNeilly, Anderson, Armstead, Clark, Corbett, Robinson, Pieper, and Lepisto 1996). The Perceived Racism Scale, along with various measures assessing masculinity are available in the literature and could be used to address this research question (Burk, Burkhart, and Sikorski 2004; Chesebro and Fuse 2001; Mahalik et al. 2003). In particular, the Auburn Differential Masculinity Inventory (Burk et al. 2004) could be paired with the Perceived Racism Scale (McNeilly et al. 1996) to determine whether racism is predictive of young African American men's orientation toward hypermasculine or androgynous gender attitudes.

From an intersectionality framework, gender identity measures such as the Auburn Differential Masculinity Inventory could be paired with racial identity scales such as the BRIAS (Helms 1990; Trimble, Helms, and Root 2002) to determine whether the interaction term produced has a significant predictive relationship with behavioral outcomes such as risky sexual behaviors and/or academic performance. Regarding the intersection between racial identity and cultural identity, it would be interesting to determine whether immersion scores, for example, interact significantly with African American acculturation scores (Klonoff and Landrine 1999) to predict academic performance and/or psychological well-being for young African American men. Given that racial identity development is viewed largely as how one racially defines self before and after a racist encounter, it would also be interesting to examine whether gender (e.g., masculinity) and sexual identity are equally exacerbated by such an encounter and the stress it produces (Utsey, Chae, Brown, and Kelly 2002). Some work reviewed in this book has determined that the intersection between racial and sexual identity has implications for the psychological health of African American homosexual men (Crawford et al. 2002).

Also noteworthy is the relationship between young African American men's race socialization experiences and their resulting racial identity. This could be assessed empirically using the Teenager Experience with Racial Socialization Scale (Stevenson et al. 2005) and Seller's et al. (1997) MIBI. The interaction term created between race socialization and racial identity could serve as a predictor variable for a host of psychological and performance outcomes, including academic identity. It would also provide a richer understanding of the hypothesis linking school performance to issues of race and racism for young African American men (McWhorter 2000; Ogbu 2003; Steele 1995). Creation of an invisibility syndrome measure would also enable researchers to determine whether invisibility mediates the relationship between perception of a racist event and the multiple identities of young African American men.

In addition, path analytic procedures could offer a statistical analysis of the mediating capabilities of racial socialization in the relationship between racial identity and school achievement. Relevant instrumentation has already been developed and validated for racial identity (Cokley 2007; Helms 1990; Sellers et al. 1997; Vandiver et al. 2001). Also, several measures have been advanced to captures students' reports of their feelings about school, academic self-esteem, academic self-efficacy, task engagement and related psychological factors (see Anderman, Austin, and Johnson 2002; Anderman and Maehr 1994; Dweck and Leggett 1988; Elliot and Harackiewicz 1996; Harackiewicz, Barron, and Elliot 1998; Meece, Blumenfeld, and Hoyle 1988; Pintrich 2000; Urdan 1997).

Regarding ethnic identity, examination of this identity component is best achieved through the use of the Multi-group Ethnic Identity Measure (MEIM) by Phinney and Ong (2007). The empirical literature on ethnic identity shows that Phinney's MEIM measure is, by far, the most relied upon measure of ethnic identity. Not only has there been very little evidence of alternative ethnic identity measures within the literature, but some research has shown the overall robustness of the MEIM in assessing ethnic identity. Specifically, Avery and colleagues (2007) showed that the factor structure of the MEIM remains constant when assessing ethnic identity among White, Hispanic, African American, and Asian American subjects. The ability of the MEIM to show a solid factor structure along with strong psychometric properties (i.e., internal consistency coefficients) across different ethnic groups provides confidence to psychologists and educators regarding the assessment of ethnic identity and therefore, should be used in examination of intersectionality with other identity components. Previously cited research has already demonstrated significant associations between ethnic identity and various psychological outcomes, including racial identity (Cokley 2005; Johnson and Arbona 2006). Thus, examination of ethnic identity using the MEIM would continue in an already established avenue of research on the components and corollaries of ethnic identity.

Regarding cultural identity, the African American Acculturation Scale (Klonoff and Landrine 1999) has been validated with African Americans as a measure to assess the degree to which this population endorses either traditional/mainstream cultural practices or those deemed unique to African Americans. While this measure assesses the presence of what Boykin (2002) refers to as expressive culture (e.g., more tangible elements and artifacts of a given culture), additional cultural identity-based instruments that reflect the axiological, ontological, and cosmological belief systems of African Americans have been found in the literature. Specifically, Gaines and colleagues (1997) validated the Collectivism and Familism scales on a sample of African American college students, while Oyserman and colleagues (2002) have used the Collectivism scale to assess the presence of communal/collectivistic behavioral tendencies among African American and European American samples.

In addition, measures assessing reports of various cultural value-based behaviors of African Americans have been developed, although with limitations regarding their psychometric properties (Boykin and Allen 1998; Grills and Longshore 1996; Kambon 1996; Vandiver et al. 2002). Researchers can refine and use these measures to assess the degree to which cultural identity or endorsement/salience of culturally aligned behaviors are 1) gender specific, 2) more salient among heterosexual or homosexual African American men, 3) linked to specific racial identity subscales (i.e., BRIAS, CRIS or MIBI) or 4) predictive of specific academic outcomes for this population. Also, cultural identity measures could be coupled with identity measures like the Perceived Hyper-masculinity Scale (Chesebro and Fuse 2004) to determine whether the interaction term created between these two identities is predictive of various achievement attitudes and academic motivation. Given the literature suggesting that hypermasculine attitudes do not mesh fully with requisite achievement attitudes and behaviors (Majors and Billson 1992; Osborne 1999), it would also be beneficial for researchers to examine whether hypermasculinity scores mediate the relationship between cultural identity and achievement attitudes for young African American men.

There are several measures in the literature to assess sexual identity. For example, Brady and Busse (1994) offer the Gay Identity Questionnaire to assess the various stages of homosexual identity formation. Also, the measure used by Crawford and colleagues (2002) has demonstrated sound psychometric properties in their study of homosexual identity formation among African American men. Also, links between sexual orientation and specific sex roles have been investigated with the Bem Sex-Role Inventory (1981). Moreover, there is at least one instrument that assesses the salience of heterosexism (Morrison and Morrison 2002) in a given context. This measure could serve as a predictor variable for hypermasculine attitudes reported by African American men. Additionally, researchers could determine among young African American men the degree to which homosexual identity aligns with reports of masculinity and racial identity. Also, it would be interesting to note whether aspects of young African American men's cultural identity, namely spirituality, are associated with their reports of their homosexual identity. Whether this relationship is mediated by racial identity or African American acculturation scores would also be of interest to psychologists and counselors serving this population.

QUANTITATIVE INVESTIGATION OF AFRICAN AMERICAN MEN'S IDENTITIES

In its simplest form, the proposed model allows for bivariate associations between the various factors identified within the core identity of African American males and contextual factors such as racism to be substantiated. It also allows for some empirical investigation of the associations among racial, cultural, ethnic, gender, socioeconomic, sexual, athletic, and academic identities. Furthermore, higher-order statistical analyses such as path analysis and structural equation modeling also provide researchers with the ability to understand the complex associations among context, ecology, identity, and behavioral and psychological outcomes. Though some authors have called for a more qualitative approach to examining the intersectionality of multiple identities (Narvaez et al. 2009), more quantitatively aligned analyses would allow for greater generalizability of study findings.

Given the substantiated importance of race, ethnic identity, and culture to the academic well-being of young African American men (Adelabu 2008; Ferguson 2001; Gay 2000; Graham and Anderson 2008; Ladson-Billings 2005; Noguera 2001), the proposed model could, for example, allow researchers to use hierarchical regression analyses to examine how much variance in academic identity is accounted for by racial, ethnic, and cultural identity, as separate and interactive/synergistic constructs. These basic analyses could furnish researchers with greater understanding of the types of activities, curriculum, and pedagogy necessary to enhance African American male students' academic performance.

Additionally, path analysis could be used to examine the complex associations among gender, cultural, and academic identities. Cultural identity, for example, could serve as a mediator between gender and academic identity. Given that academic identity could be an amalgam between several psychological correlates of academic performance (i.e., self-efficacy, academic motivation, academic self-esteem), structural equation modeling—which allows for the observed variables (e.g., academic self-efficacy, academic motivation) to create a latent variable (e.g., academic identity) and thereby, produce a more robust representation of the construct in question—could be used throughout the analysis (Klem 1995).

As many of the identity constructs outlined above have at least one quantitative measure to assess the salience of corresponding behaviors and beliefs, path analysis and/or structural equation modeling could be used to examine the association among several of the identities presented in the model. Also, these mediation analyses would allow researchers to investigate the relationships among proposed, observed, or latent variables presented in either the full or modified version of the African American male identity model.

Consistent with the African American male identity model, structural equation modeling could also examine whether racism is simultaneously predictive of racial, cultural, ethnic, gender, sexual, socioeconomic, athletic, and academic identities. For instance, McNeilly and her colleagues (1997) have developed a perceived racism scale, with three subscales assessing the perceptions of individual, institutional, and cultural racism. Using SEM, the mediating effects of perceived racism on the relationship between racial identity and sexual identity could be determined. The research question driving such an analysis would ask whether racial identity is predictive of sexual identity (Bem 1981; Brady and Busse 1994) and whether the coefficient indicating a significant relationship between these two factors is reduced when experiences with racism are considered. How racism and the racial, cultural, and academic identities predict academic performance (i.e., GPA) can also be empirically determined.

Along with SEM, hierarchical linear modeling (HLM; Bryk and Raudenbush 1992) could be used with the proposed conceptual model of African American men's identities. In particular, latent growth curve modeling (analyzed typically through HLM software) could be used to examine changes in specific identity reports over time as well as discern which demographic and other identity factors are significant predictors of that change. For example, Sellers and colleagues (1997, 1998) have long determined that African American college students' sense of racial identity—as measured by the MIBI—are predictive of reported academic variables such as efficacy. Yet, these data analyses have typically been performed on data collected at one point in time and thus, provide only limited understanding of the role that racial identity reports have in African American students' academic performance. Some researchers have already called for racial identity research to take a developmental approach to investigating the presence and impact of various racial identity statuses on several academic, cognitive, and behavioral outcomes (Burrow, Tubman, and Montgomery 2006).

With latent growth modeling, researchers would be able to examine predictors of academic identity, for example, at three points in time (the minimal number required to perform growth curve analysis using HLM) (Anderman 2003). Along with demographic variables such as age, SES, and gender, identity reports discussed throughout this book could be entered into growth curve analyses to better understand whether such identities are predictive of academic performance over time.

SEVENTEEN

"Never Say You Can't Survive"

Pragmatics and Future Considerations

CONCLUSION

On July 13, 2013, nearly one year and five months since Trayvon Martin was shot in the chest and killed, his shooter—who racially profiled Trayvon and dismissed instructions not to follow the young African American man—was found not guilty of second-degree murder or manslaughter. While it is clear that the nation went into a tailspin at the announcement of the verdict, with subsequent hours and days of media news coverage, debate, commentary, protest, and vigils, the shooting of Trayvon Martin and the not-guilty verdict provided is but one of several hundred if not thousands of cases where many young African American men were the victims of assault.

For example, at the time of this writing, in the same state as the shooting of Trayvon Martin, another young African American man, Jordan Davis, same age as Trayvon (17) was killed by a shooter who alleged feeling threatened by the words and actions of Davis and his friends who were sitting in an SUV playing loud music. Specifically, as an argument ensued over a request to turn down the music, the shooter claimed that—while in his own vehicle—he felt his life was being threatened, later stating to police after fleeing the crime scene that he believed a shotgun was in the possession of the young men in the SUV. Using the same defense tactic as that provided by Trayvon Martin's shooter (Stand Your Ground), the assailant in this scenario shot at the vehicle ten times, hitting Jordan Davis three times and killing him before pulling off from the parking lot where both vehicles were. Police did not locate any weapons in the vehicle where Jordan Davis died.

Also at the time of this writing, another case was pending against the shooter of Darius Simmons, a young African American man (13 years old) living in Wisconsin who was shot and killed by his neighbor as a result of the shooter believing that the young man burglarized his home, stealing shotguns. As of this writing, the shooter had initially claimed temporary insanity, for which a jury of his peers found erroneous and thus, found the shooter mentally competent to stand trial for the first-degree intentional homicide charge. Police searched the home of Darius Simmons and did not locate any firearms, stolen or otherwise.

The lives of many other young African American men, including Emmitt Till (age 14), Oscar Grant (age 22), Amadou Diallo (age 23), Sean Bell (age 23) and countless other young African American men, many of whom had their lives taken by other young African American men, have been ended much too early. For example, in major urban metropolitan areas such as Chicago and New York and Los Angeles, there is typically a significant loss of life among young African American men at the hands of other young African American men. Former New York Senator Pat Buchanan makes this point in his recent commentary surrounding Trayvon Martin's shooter's case and verdict. Specifically, he cites a report by the Manhattan Institute that shows data stating that 83 percent of all gun assailants in the city of New York within a six-month period were African American. Indeed, data to show that young African American men are often both victim and perpetrator of violent crime, particularly homicide are irrefutable. Yet, it was the Trayvon Martin case that awakened a resurgence of attention to the issues of race, gender, and racial prejudice within the United States in the twenty-first century.

For me, however, the larger question and one that this text looks to address is why is this the case? Specifically, what was it that the shooters of Trayvon Martin, Jordan Davis, Darius Simmons, Amadou Diallo, Sean Bell, Oscar Grant, and hundreds of other young African American men are seeing when they viewed these now deceased individuals? What did Trayvon Martin's shooter perceive 17-year-old Trayvon to be? Who or what did he think he was? Was Trayvon considered a threat? Am I? Why does my 10-year-old grow up in a world where his knowledge of the U.S. president begins with an understanding that he and the president look and perhaps are alike, and yet, there's a chance that he may never, ever make it to age 18 where he would be able to vote for another U.S. president like him?

Regarding Trayvon and other African American male victims of invisibility, were these individuals considered a threat? If so, was such a perception based on the victim's previous documented/observed activities or simply what folks thought persons like him do? Why wasn't there some greater description of young African American men that could have given rise to the thinking that they are much, much more than society's caricature of criminal/menacing/lazy/unintelligent boys? As

Tracy Martin and Sybrina Fulton inferred at the close of the shooter's murder trial, why wasn't Trayvon perceived for whom and what he was that night and every night . . . a kid. Why didn't the shooter, in the face-to-face confrontation, at least see that?

Several scholars have weighed in on this recent issue. Noted columnist Eugene Robinson argued, "Trayvon Martin was fighting more than [shooter] that night. He was up against prejudices as old as American history, and he never had a chance" (Robinson 2013). My good friend and Morehouse College professor Dr. David Rice poignantly argued, "Black boys and black men are conditioned to be invisible. Our visibility scares folks. It scared [shooter]. And [shooter] killed Trayvon Martin because of his fear" (Rice 2013). Even President Barack Obama chimed in on two occasions regarding the issue, the first time when the argument for a criminal case against the shooter of Trayvon Martin was hashed out and the second, when the verdict of not guilty emerged on that night in July. First, the president noted that if he had a son, he would have looked like Trayvon. A week following the verdict, President Obama emphasized that "35 years ago, he could have been Trayvon."

Yet, for this and all other commentary despising both the shooter and the verdict of his actions on the night he shot and killed Trayvon Martin, a looming set of questions still remain. Regarding Mr. Robinson's comments, I am curious about those classic stereotypical prejudices and caricatures relied upon most frequently used to pass judgment on the character of young African American men. Specifically, what have we, as a society, done to change the prevailing image of young African American men? Are there newer images, newer realities of this population that could have been used to gauge just who is Trayvon Martin? Trayvon Martin was initially pursued and eventually shot and killed because, to the shooter, he fit a certain demographic profile, that of a criminal. These prejudicial images of African American men (i.e., shiftless, lazy, criminal, hypersexualized, immoral, unintelligent), which have been around since chattel slavery, had been prevalent in nearly every aspect of American culture, from all genres of media to political and social and educational systems and certainly within many households. Trayvon Martin's shooter relied on these images to profile and eventually antagonize young Trayvon to the point of his untimely death by firearm. Why wasn't there an alternative image—one that is far more prevalent and accurate—than the one chosen by Trayvon Martin's shooter? Why wasn't there better understanding put forth by academics and scholars and reporters to provide a counter image of that which led the shooter toward racially profiling, following, and eventually killing Trayvon Martin? Why didn't the shooter see "scholar" or "scholar-athlete" or "future U.S. president" when he decided to look twice at this young African American man that rainy night in February?

Similarly, to my friend Dr. Rice, who echoes the late Ralph Ellison and Dr. Anderson Franklin in discussing the invisibility of young African American men, I ask "What components of Trayvon Martin were invisible to his shooter?" Was there more to know about young Trayvon? And if so, who is telling that story? Where is that story represented so that persons can pause prior to adopting a stereotypical image of young African American men?

Clearly, the shooter saw race and gender and perhaps aspects of young Trayvon's promotion of his expressive individualism, by way of his dress and appearance. Moreover, given the trial evidence suggesting that many young African American men were at least suspicious in the eyes of the shooter, including a preteen African American male, it is likely that the shooter's perspective was beyond reproach when it came to gathering a newer, more accurate, and comprehensive understanding of young African American men. Sometimes, some folks will always see the bad no matter how much good you do.

For others who may not yet espouse such a racist and unidimensional view of African American men, it is incumbent upon scholars and professionals to not only gather a broader, more comprehensive understanding of young African American men, who they are, how they think, what they feel and how these lead to the behaviors they exhibit, but also, these same scholars and professionals must be the producers of such an image as well. We must provide a greater characterization of young African American men to society. There is one. There are millions. Those stories must be told if we are desiring to change the societal image we African American men fight against and die because of everyday.

Granted, in the minds of the shooters of Trayvon Martin and Jordan Davis and Darius Simmons, I sincerely doubt that there could be any other images of young African American men that were not reflective of traditional stereotypes regarding this population. As Dr. Rice passionately writes in the opinion piece, "[shooter] killed Trayvon Martin because of his fear." That fear was likely associated with the possibility of Trayvon Martin being the type of young African American man who vandalized and burglarized homes, the kind who engages in "apple-picking" (public stealing of Apple's iPhones while in use by the owner) and sells the product for crack or to buy the new pair of Lebrons or shoots and kills to get initiated into a gang, not unlike Nino Brown's character did in New Jack City, where he shot the detective's mother early in his youth to join a gang.

These images not only typecast Trayvon Martin, a young African American man that only a select few Americans had actually known prior to his death, but this image was also used against him in his own death trial. Some reporters have demonstrated an unmitigated gall in maintaining that it was the appearance of the deviant and diabolical "hoodie" that ultimately led to a mischaracterization of Trayvon Martin, his pursuit by a racial profiler and his eventual death at the hands of this racial profiler—turn—shooter (O'Conner 2013). His crime: being African American and male, and for some, an African American man who wore a hooded sweatshirt.

But, was Trayvon more? Many classic and contemporary scholars know that, in fact, most young African American men are far beyond the racist, stereotypical images projected and displayed by media and news outlets. There's been research spanning nearly two decades discussing young African American college-age men. There's been plenty of progress regarding the development of excellence and pursuit of academic and professional career goals among African American men. Yet, on the night Trayvon Martin was killed, it is arguable that this research and these progressions were not entirely accessible. Of course, it is not likely that they would have served much purpose to the shooter, as he sought out Trayvon Martin regardless of who he actually was. It is probable that the shooter would have relied on the negative stereotypes of young African American men anyway.

The bottom line here is, however, academics and professional persons of color, particularly African American social scientists, needed to have done more to eliminate the stigma associated with being a young African American man. As I mentioned to my friend, David, while we—as tenured professors at research-driven institutions—didn't kill Trayvon, nothing we have done in terms of our own research and outreach to the masses was present—in tangible form—to save him. We, as academicians, as reporters and journalists, as faculty members and college students and successful fathers to our children and sons of our own parents, had an obligation to ensure that we are telling the best possible story about who we are as African American men. We have an obligation to ensure not only our own legacies, but the legacies of our son's friends and their kin as well. We've discussed and challenged and endured the contextual factors that, for decades, have influenced the men and scholars and professionals we have become. We knew of our multiple identities and therefore, the requisite code switching and other associated behaviors when we are in given contexts. We knew who Trayvon Martin was. I was Trayvon Martin when I was 17. David was Trayvon as well when he was a teenager. So was Eugene. And admittedly, so was our 44th president of the United States of America.

Yet, in knowing Trayvon's story, for the most part, as our own, in knowing the backdrop to his story (what factors are present to influence who he becomes and the decisions he makes), in knowing how best to negotiate the realms of experiences inherent within Trayvon's story, we did not produce stories that others could reference. We did not offer the complex model of African American male identity that we lived and thereby, have fuller understanding of. Personally, and unfortunately, I took my PhD, secured a professorship at a research institution of higher learning, earned tenure by publishing research on African Americans in journals read by other scholars and scarcely available to practical educational stakeholders like parents and teachers. During this time, I looked out for myself and my own.

In retrospect, I realize that there was more I and others could have done long before Trayvon's death to offer a better, more informed story of not only the identities many African American men have, but also the manner in which these identities develop, are manifested and are influenced by other identities as well as environmental factors such as racism. This could have been done, for the persons who don't fully understand the lives and challenges associated with being an African American man in the racist environment. For those exposed to negative stereotypes about young African American men, may not initially buy into their veracity; a text like this should have been available long ago.

Speaking tangentially for a moment, by now, the reader should have realized that the shooter of Trayvon Martin has remained unidentified and thus, purposefully invisible throughout this text. Bear in mind that the namelessness of Trayvon Martin's shooter and absence of formal identity isn't an attempt to spite this person. In fact, describing him as "Trayvon Martin's shooter" is not an unfounded or unsubstantiated stereotype borne out of racism or prejudice. That he shot Trayvon Martin isn't based on some expectation that people like him go around shooting folks like Trayvon. Referring to him as Trayvon Martin's shooter is entirely accurate. It is based on his actions, not stereotypes about who he is or what his "kind" are like. To refer to him solely as Trayvon Martin's shooter is exact. Unlike the myriad images held by the shooter about Trayvon Martin that cold, rainy night in Florida, the only one with the gun was the shooter. The only one who pulled the gun was the shooter. The only one who had any suspicions based on negative stereotypes about young African American men was the shooter. The only one who stalked another human being walking home while on the phone was the shooter. The only one who killed another human being that night was the shooter. That night, the shooter became everything he thought Trayvon Martin was. A thug, a bully, a bad ass with a gun. Much like his own stereotypes about Trayvon and those like him, the shooter was the one who actually got away with taking the life of another human being. That he is a shooter of a fellow American is a fact. Referring to him as the shooter, then, is fair and balanced.

Returning to what can be done, Dr. Boyce Watkins echoes the fears and beliefs of classic African American scholars (e.g., Carter Woodson, W.E.B. DuBois) who predicted that the production of African American scholars and scholarship might not automatically lead to the uplift of the communities in which they were produced. Specifically, Watkins (2013) notes that "it is perfectly fine for scholars to teach at white universities and do research in journals controlled by white males. But it is also OK for us to re-engage our communities, earn multiple sources of income and find other relevant platforms through which we can share our expertise with our communities." Engaging our communities, on a national scale about the issues concerning the identities of young African American men, has yet to occur. Certainly, there is often discussion of and critique about the behavioral outcomes of this population. However, such has not been done en masse on behalf of African American men and the identities that inform us about how they think about themselves and the world around them. No, there is still a significant preoccupation within U.S. society and within the academy about what African American men are actually doing rather than the self-perceptions that precede these behaviors and activities.

As previously stated, there is much known regarding the behavioral outcomes of young African American men. As Watkins (2013) noted in his Trayvon Martin murder case opinion column, it is true that gun manufacturers are profiting from the facilitation of black genocide. The problem is that there is no clear understanding or explanation of what psychological and affective factors about self and/or race are salient when one young African American man picks up a gun and shoots another. That is, the presence and availability of a firearm for one young African American man does not automatically lead to the shooting of another. That behavioristic line of thinking—where the environment controls the individual's behaviors—has been absent within contemporary psychological research for well over half a century. The black genocide that Watkins speaks of stems from a compromised psychological and affective sense of self and others possessed by one or several African American men holding guns. As stated in the introduction, to date, there are limited discussions of these psychological processes that often precede the maladaptive behaviors of many young African American men. Many African American men shoot and kill other young African American men for the same reasons Trayvon Martin's shooter decided to stalk and eventually shoot him: Who they truly are and what they are capable of representing and becoming are invisible.

While voices such as myself and Rice's and Watkins' champion a greater visibility vis-à-vis, a broader conceptualization of African American manhood and identity, one needn't look too far back in history to pinpoint the efforts of one scholar whose ideas on the topic of African American men and families capture the attention of millions of households. Specifically, one of the greatest examples of this was Dr. William H. Cosby and his NBC network phenomenon, "The Cosby Show." After eight seasons on the network, I could not find one instance where a young African American man did not present himself as upstanding, focused, loving, involved, and compassionate. Granted, there was the occasional goofing off of Theo and his friend, Walter, a.k.a. "Cockroach," but even with their adolescent antics and dilemmas, there was still a drive toward doing well in school and staying out of serious trouble like drugs and gangs. In one episode, the two got into snowball fights with neighborhood kids in order to retrieve a library recording of MacBeth for an exam! In another episode, where "The Enforcer" planted marijuana in Theo's book, Dr. Cosby offers the young man advice and assistance if there is no one available to him (incidentally, Theo semicoerced the young man to his parents' home, despite Dr. Cosby's insistence in the belief that Theo was being truthful about the illegal drug).

A graduate of the University of Massachusetts, Amherst, Dr. Cosby used his research and knowledge of the African American experience to project and showcase an image of African American family values that did not in the least contain or reflect the race-based social stereotypes often used and referred to in more contemporary shows portraying African Americans. Here, in essence, was a scholar, whose research about African Americans was used to portray a positive image of African Americans. Dr. Cosby's spinoff series, "A Different World" which captured, for many, the lives of successful, African American college students, faculty, and staff, was at least partially responsible for many Generation X'ers such as myself wanting to experience college life.

Dr. Cosby, for a time, captured that sense of pride instilled by and exhibited among young African American men. From the presence and influence of both African American grandfathers in the show to the innocent and inquisitive upstanding positionality of young Kenny, Dr. Cosby provided a newer, fresher image of African American men. In "A Different World," indeed, the characterizations of young African American men included those who were motivated by women, those motivated by academic success and career goals, and those motivated by a sense of civic duty, either to college or country. Resonating with these portrayals of young African American men are the comments of my friend David, who writes, "We [African Americans] are whole people, human beings with lived experiences that are of value, and different and sometimes, the same as everyone else." Dr. Cosby's exhibited that for well over a decade across two different television shows.

In the same sentence, however, Rice writes, "Black men and black boys are understood to be a threat to everyone else. He ends that paragraph with a commanding, "We deserve justice." I wholeheartedly agree with Rice (2013). As African American men living in a country where our very existence poses a threat simply by walking down the street or sitting in a parked car or retrieving trash bins from the curb outside our very own homes, there needs to be a stronger orientation toward justice for us. There needs to be less of a reliance on the perpetually negative images of African American men and more of those images that reflect the broader diversity of lived experience as members of the African American community. Even President Barack Obama suggested that the country "spend some time in thinking about how do we bolster and reinforce our

African American boys and give them a sense that their country cares about them and values them and is willing to invest in them."

While we are fortunate to have Dr. Cosby around for possible future discussions on this issue, his goal of and contribution towards promoting a just world for young African American men through the projection of an image that obliterates those stereotypical ones has been accomplished. It is time for additional scholars and professionals to become about the business of promoting a newer, broader conceptualization of our young African American men.

Still, where and how we start to actualize a road toward justice for young African American men and African American men in general is still imprecise. To be fair, there are still far too many instances where the recorded behaviors of some African American men can strike fear in the hearts of not only other African American men, but also persons far removed from this community. As Pat Buchanan wrote in his essay, "Black America's Real Problem isn't White Racism," many Black fathers are having discussions with their sons about what to do in case of being stopped by police or official law authorities. Yet, his discussion of the statistics regarding Black-on-Black crime at least reinforces the idea that many Black fathers, like myself, are also having discussions about which areas of the city to never go into and where to always keep your valuables while out. My son knows, at age 10, that far more African Americans were shot during a holiday weekend in the city of Chicago in 2013 than in a month in his hometown in Kentucky. My occasional solo visits to hang out with my parents and family in my hometown of Chicago typically prompts a "Be careful, daddy" or "Make sure you find cousin John-John" (he knows my cousin is a Chicago police officer).

Like my son already knows, most African Americans are well aware of the adverse social behaviors that not only victimize other African Americans, but also serve to fuel the negative stereotypes about this population. Not only are many of us privy to such activities, but in many cases, we have family members and/or friends who are stuck within the game of criminality, whether the activities are drug and/or substance abuse and trafficking, homicide and various forms of assault, and other crimes (i.e., burglary, theft). Not that these behaviors are germane exclusively to African Americans. In our country, we've got at least three U.S. presidents that have actually mentioned any experimentation with recreational drugs and therefore, evidence of social delinquency during their developmental years. Only one of these men was African American.

Yet, while some African Americans will engage in these deleterious behaviors, the problem for all African American men is that there is a social and societal expectation for us to engage in these kinds of behaviors. That is, the image and expectations of these behaviors are not only held by many non–African Americans (Sue et al. 2003), but they often overshadow any belief or expectation that young African American men can or will display alternative, more socially normative modes of behavior (e.g., doing the right thing). These images and expectations stem from the recorded and overly relied upon behaviors of some African American men, but certainly not all. Yet, the stereotype about these behaviors seemingly apply to all African American men, regardless of dress, social location, socioeconomic status, or even skin tone.

Trayvon Martin was killed in February of 2012 because his shooter chose not to access alternative images of this population and rather, relied on preexisting stereotypes and news and televised media imagery and stories about some members of this population. Given the prevalence of these images and stereotypes within the U.S. context, it, perhaps, was almost easier to assume that Trayvon Martin was the kind of African American man who committed crime and was a menace to society rather than the kind of young African American man Tracy Martin and Sybrina Fulton raised, the one who loved kids and dreamed of being a pilot. Like Trayvon's shooter, we know too much about the negative stereotypes and the preceding deleterious actions of some African American men that inform these stereotypes and not enough of the alternative images and identities actually possessed by this population, particularly those identities and behaviors that typically *do not* lead to hostile outcomes such as crime and victimization.

As Dr. Rice challenged us in his commentary, we deserve justice, but it must be the kind of justice that starts at the level of understanding of who we are before we begin combating those we think are out to get us. Thus, the justice to be served on behalf of this population is the offering of a more comprehensive articulation of the multiple, interrelated identities of young African American men. It is time that, for the sake of our remaining young African American men, we begin to more critically and candidly discuss what these identity components are, the feelings they provide to young African American men, and the behaviors that such feelings and attitudes ultimately lead toward. In other words, this book serves to make the lives of young African American men more visible.

In an effort to reduce some of the psychosocial and academic dilemmas faced by young African American men, researchers in the social sciences and in education, along with professionals across the array of humanities and medical and law disciplines must begin to first see and explore the various identities of this population. In addition to recognizing and unpacking the multiple identities possessed by young African American men, careful attention must be paid to the manner in which these identities intersect. These individuals must also have understanding of how various contextual factors such as racism impact each identity. Specifically, researchers and educational and psychological practitioners and professionals must know that every young African American man has feelings about being African American (racial identity), about being part of the African American community (ethnic identity), about values and customs and behaviors specific to African Americans (cultural identity), about his socioeconomic status and access to resources (socioeconomic identity), about himself and his role in the world as a man (gender identity), about who and what he is sexually attracted to (sexual identity), about his ability to perform athletic feats (athletic identity), and about his ability to excel in the primary, secondary, and postsecondary classrooms (academic identity).

Each of these identities emerges simply as a function of the young African American man being born and existing within the U.S. context. They are based on his social locations within the context of the U.S. They are all social identities to which the young African American man gives significant thought toward. Based on his actions, his socialization with parents, peers, and social others, along with the observation of others' actions, he will also develop feelings and perceptions about each of these identities. Hence, these identities are initially social identities as they are reflective of his social location within the United States, but they quickly become personal identities as well as the young African American man takes stock of his past and current experiences within these identities and thus, reaches certain conclusions about each of them ("I do well in school; therefore, I am a good student").

When these identities are deemed invisible and/or their development into strong, adaptive identities is arrested by social/contextual factors such as racism, the result can be deleterious for members of this population. This invisibility syndrome allows for the self-worth associated with being African American, with being from a specific socioeconomic background, with being homosexual, with being athletic, or even a successful student to be diminished and replaced with actions that reinforce rather than refute the negative stereotypical depictions of young African American men.

Our young African American men deserve more. A new story. A better understanding. A stronger advocacy, not just by politicians catapulted into the fray of African American male survival as a result of a tragic story of one of us being killed by way of racial profiling. Rather, this advocacy begins at home, begins at schools and surrounding communities. It begins with parents and education stakeholders, each of whom is aware of our sons' promising lives and their activities, attitudes, and idiosyncracies. This advocacy begins with understanding who they are from their own perspectives. It begins with their voices and the acknowledgement of the authenticity and veracity of those voices and the things they tell us. It begins with our understanding of their voices which communicate a message about how they are thinking about themselves, about others in the world, and about what they think can be done about any and all of it. It starts with those seeking to enhance the lives of young African American men beginning to more fully understand these lives.

This stronger advocacy requires those who want to create a better tomorrow for our young African American men to understand the multiple identities they bring to the table today. These identities inform what they think, how they feel, and why they do the things they do. It is essentially and literally who they are. Survival for young African American men will mean that those who love them will have to do a much better job of showcasing the fact that they are significantly more than what current stereotypical depictions show. Scholars and professionals in particular must move in the direction of proactively championing the identities of this population and therefore, the lives of our sons if we are to lead the charge in enhancing their lives.

Tracy Martin, Trayvon's father, asked African American Congress members, shortly after the shooter's not-guilty verdict was rendered, "What can we do as parents, what can we do as African American men, to assure our kids that you don't have to be afraid to walk outside your house?"

Several efforts are currently in the works. For example, several divisions in the American Psychological Association (2013) put forth a position paper that spoke to research evidence suggesting that African Americans are stereotyped more often than other ethnic group members and African American male teenagers are viewed as more adultlike. The APA argues that such views supported the rationale held by Trayvon Martin's shooter that deadly force was imminent. To change such views, the Ethnic Minority Issues Caucus, Public Interest Caucus, Society of Counseling Psychology (Division 17), Society for the Psychological Study of Ethnic Minority Issues (Division 45), and the Society for the Psychological Study of Men and Masculinity (Division 51) have called for the American Psychological Association to 1) speak out against "Stand Your Ground" laws, where the authors cite that the odds of a White-on-Black homicide is justified is 281 percent greater than a White-on-White homicide in Stand Your Ground states.

In addition, the authors advocate that the investigation of Stand Your Ground laws by the Department of Justice, use evidence from psychological research to speak out against racial disparities occurring within the criminal justice system, along with pushing for increased funding to support racial stereotyping prevention research (Neville and Rom-Rymer 2013). The last two points are especially poignant considering that in criminal justice research that a disproportionate bias against African Americans exists in jury verdicts (Bucolo and Cohn 2010) and capital sentencing (Eberhardt, Davies, Purdie-Vaughns, and Johnson 2006), the decision to shoot armed and unarmed African Americans (Cornell, Park, Judd, and Wittenblank 2002; Sadler, Correll, Park, and Judd 2012; Sim, Correll, and Sadler 2013) and whether an African American adolescent will be treated as an adult in a criminal case (Rattan, Levine, Dweck, and Eberhardt 2012) some work has shown that college age adults and police officers make the decision to shoot armed African American targets more so than armed white targets and they were slower in their decision to shoot unarmed African American targets than white targets (Correll, Park, Judd, and Wittenbrink 2002; Sadler, Correll, Park, and Judd 2012).

In addition and more directly tied to the lives of young African American men, a website entitled BlackandMarriedwithKids.com has offered four documentaries seeking to promote a much more positive image of African American marriage and African American men. One of the DVD documentaries, Men Ain't Boys (2011) tells the stories of several African American men whose richer conceptualizations of manhood helped them become better at negotiating hostile environments while simultaneously setting the tone and image for their younger brethren to follow. Along with these, in his 2014 State of the Union address, President Obama indicated a plan to launch an initiative aimed at bolstering the lives of young men of color. Called "My Brother's Keeper" and based on the program out of Chicago, Illinois called "Becoming a Man (B.A.M.), his initiatives will seek to bring agencies and institutions together in an effort to examine strategies and policies that support young men of color. In addition, My Brother's Keeper will evaluate public policies that positively impact the lives of this population.

To date, B.A.M. has been shown to have a positive impact on the lives of young African American men with significant decreases in reported violent crime arrests, vandalism, and juvenile justice school attendance. The program, which is based on six core values (integrity, accountability, self-determination, positive anger expression, visionary goal setting, and respect for womanhood) has also evidenced an increase in graduation rates up to 23 percent (Goldfarb 2014). Much like programs like BAM and my Brother's Keeper and on behalf of Trayvon Martin and the hundreds of thousands of young African American men whose identities were not fully understood, it is the intention of this book to be part of the discussions that generate effective solutions to Mr. Martin's fundamental question.

PRAGMATICS

I had always known and accepted that God works in mysterious ways, but I was duly reminded in writing the conclusion of this book. Upon picking up my son, Asa, you know, the football player, from school, I was informed by his teacher and principal of an incident that had occurred between him and three of his friends. Asa, and his three friends were engaged in a classic game of the "dozens." Asa, far too sensitive to engage in talking about another's parent, but always willing to enjoy a good laugh, sat in his seat after finishing his schoolwork and quietly laughed at the jokes exchanged between one White friend and one African American friend.

According to Asa's story, his White friend got upset that Asa's African American friend had bested him on the funniest joke so far. The White friend proceeded to say to the African American friend, "That's why when Abraham Lincoln first saw you, he started jails!" The fourth friend, who was not interacting but spectating as Asa was, became uncomfortable with the statement and proceeded to tell the teacher. Upon hearing, the teacher called all four boys to the principal's office where she graciously discussed how such a statement could be really hurtful to the other boys at the table. The young man apologized and with the other three students, Asa included, went back to class to continue schoolwork.

It was my son's first encounter with a racist event. We talked about racism and perceptions of young African American men, and Trayvon Martin and how some people's perceptions of us have cost us our lives, including other African Americans' perceptions. We talked for close to an hour, which is probably overkill for a ten-year-old. I realized that in talking with him about this important issue, just as I did when Trayvon Martin's case against the shooter was only speculative, that I needed to talk more about actions and activities. As a father, I needed to convey to him the kind of world we live in and the way some people perceive him has implications for what happens to him in life. And yes, he and the young man are all still very good friends. My point wasn't to allow such a statement to promote ill-feelings so that friendships are discontinued and part of the innocence of childhood is lost. My point was to find the lesson in such encounters, expose its history and impact to Asa, and help him decide whether the incident should cost him a friend.

In a similar fashion, I feel that there are things that can be done to increase the visibility of young African American men's identities that go beyond the reading and discussion of this text and the conceptual model presented within it. So, in concluding this text, in much the same way I talked with Asa about what he should do if he ever encounters a more tempestuous episode of racism, I'd like to offer some suggestions or questions for parents and African American media outlets that I think may facilitate the understanding of who our young African American men are. These are far from conclusive or definitive and I'm sure will not work for all parents. The point, however, is to get African American parents to begin thinking and creating plans for their young man's future through his articulation of the things he wants and the perceptions he has of himself as an African American man.

In closing, President Barack Obama, in his announcement of the My Brother's Keeper initiative in late February 2014, reminded the young men on stage with him that he also grew up without a dad, and was angry about it, got high, didn't take school as seriously as he should have and ultimately sold himself short. He also discussed this at the time he met with several young African American men at a school in Chicago near his home. He reminded one of the young men who, in disbelief of hearing such from a sitting president, asked "Are you talking about you?" that not only was he talking about himself, but that all of these feelings and emotions and behaviors were written in his book. He also reminded the youth at the My Brother's Keeper's initiative that he made it because he was given second chances to correct mistakes.

This book was written because, just like President Obama, these young men—a group that has been acknowledged by the president as facing some of the most severe challenges in the twenty-first century—also have stories to tell. They have identities to share, feelings to express, and behaviors to more fully understand and have better understood by those who do and those who don't have their best interests at heart. In reading this text, it is plausible that most young African American men can be given second chances just like President Obama had.

Because they will be better understood.

Parents of Young African American Men (Adolescents and Young Adults)

- Have candid conversations about how your child feels about being African American. In doing so, have discussions about how racism impacts African Americans, personal and vicarious stories are especially important, as they can inform your child that these things can actually happen.
- Embrace their preference for and orientation toward cultural artifacts and expressions that you may not understand. It will likely become more difficult for a child to feel accepted at school if neither his teacher nor his parents want him to listen to 2 Chainz or Kendrick Lamar. Ask them why they like these artists and search the Internet for artists during your era who you feel were similar to the current artist.
- Reinforce the development of both academic and athletic identities, by insisting that he work hard to do well in both areas. Become as vigilant about studying as you may be with free throw shooting or making practice. This allows the young man to understand that he needn't choose between the identities and rather, can work hard to excel in both academic and athletics.
- If the student is college bound, look at schools that have at least one African American male faculty member. Here, you want to have a model of success that goes beyond the court or the field and into the classroom or the office tower. If financially capable, try to visit one school (local, regional, or across the country) long before the young man is seriously considering college. A good way to lower the anxiety about being in college and believing that they should be

is actually going and stepping foot on the campus and allowing the young man to see folks just like him.
- Discuss career goals and allow the young man to discuss at least three types: one he definitely needs to go to college for, one he can get some training in, but does not need a four-year institutional degree, and one he doesn't need college for at all. Help him create a plan of action to achieve each of these goals.
- Discuss with your young man's teacher his learning orientations and preferences and overall, what you know about him and what he knows about himself as a learner (i.e., how he does his homework, what he needs and uses to study better, whether he's a reserved child who doesn't like to ask questions or has a high academic self-efficacy?). This allows teachers to know that you are his advocate while he is in the classroom and you are in support of the learning orientation he brings to the teachers' classrooms.
- Discuss different definitions of what it means to be an African American man in the United States. Allow him to talk about what he believes he can do (even if you don't initially buy into such a belief) and ask him about his plans to achieve these things. Make a pact with the young man indicating what part you will play in the acquisition of these goals and what parts he will play.
- Discuss how love and relationships factor into his overall plan. Whether he plans to wed or be single? What his opinions are about women and/or same-sex attractions?

African American Media Outlets

- In magazines, showcase African American men who are simply good men: Active community members and leaders, scholars, custodians, coaches. *Jet Magazine* has for well over half a century, included a picture of the Jet Beauty of the Week. If we are trying to change the image of African American men, we can start by showcasing those everyday men who bring integrity to manhood. Like the Jet Beauty of the Week, *Jet Magazine* and other publications could do this weekly. Trust me, there are enough of us out there who could qualify as a Jet Man of the Moment.
- In movies, create television and cable programming that reflect the integrity of the positive patriarch and the essence of the professional African American man. Unidimensional characters, which reinforce the negative stereotypes of African American men, are no longer necessary in television or in movies. America has long gotten the message that this is how we are perceived (i.e., criminal, felon, drug dealer/user).
- Among cultural genres, showcase African American authors, poets, dancers, musicians, and other artists who don't necessarily have

contracts, but are excellent in their craft. This would likely change the perception that in order to be successful, you have to project an image of success, even to your own detriment. One simply has to enjoy and be passionate about the work they do.

- Among African American television networks, have an awards show that acknowledges and praises African American athletes who either complete their postsecondary education or who come back to complete their education at the college level. Currently, there is no incentive for African American athletes to complete their education, although they are typically provided some forms of assistance ot attend college. If BET showcased graduating seniors from their respective sports, it would likely be recognized that it is important to go to school for sports and leave there with a degree. Similarly, have awards show that acknowledge the contributions of African American scholars and professionals. If we can do this for "best barbershops" and "best soul food," certainly we can create a category for "best school-based research."
- Also, it would be important to showcase the efforts of scholars and professionals and the work/research they conduct with African American populations. The creation of independent journals geared toward this purpose would aid in the dissemination of ideas and strategies that could enhance the lives of young African American men. Some journals such as the *Journal of Black Psychology*, the *Journal of Negro Education*, the *Negro Educational Review*, and most recently, the *Journal of African American Men in Education*, are excellent examples of these kinds of journal outlets.
- Media such as magazines and periodicals (i.e., *Ebony, Essence, Jet,* and *Upscale*) should contain columns and summaries of actual research studies about young African American men. Articles should be written for lay audiences and should contain implications for parents and young African American men as well as actual tangible recommendations that both can use in an effort to enhance the lives they live. IIVIIIVVIII

References

Abes, E. S., Jones, S. R., and McEwan, M. K. 2007. Reconceptualizing the model of multiple dimensions of identity: The role of meaning-making capacity in the construction of multiple identities. *Journal of College Student Development* 48:1–22.

Adams, T. M., and Fuller, D. B. 2006. The words have changed, but the ideology remains the same: Misogynistic lyrics in rap music. *Journal of Black Studies* 36:938–957.

ADDHealth: The National Longitudinal Study of Adolescent Health 2007. http://www.cpc.unc.edu/projects/addhealth.

Adelabu, D. H. 2008. Future time perspective, hope, and ethnic identity among African American adolescents. *Urban Education* 43:347–360.

Akbar, M., Chambers, J. W., and Sanders-Thompson, V. L. 2001. Racial identity, Africentric values, and self-esteem in Jamaican children. *Journal of Black Psychology* 27:341–358.

Allen, Q. 2010. Racial microaggressions: The schooling experiences of Black middle-class males in Arizona's secondary schools. *Journal of African American Males in Education* 1:125–143.

———. 2012. "They think minority means lesser than": Black middle-class sons and fathers resisting microaggressions in the school. *Urban Education*, 1–27.

Allen, R. L., and Bagozzi, R. P. 2001. Consequences of the Black sense of self. *Journal of Black Psychology* 27:3–28.

Allen-Meares, P., and Burman, S. 1995. The endangerment of African American men: An appeal for social work action. *Social Work* 40:269–274.

Altschul, I., Oyserman, D., and Bybee, D. 2006. Racial-ethnic identity in mid-adolescence: Content and change as predictors of academic achievement. *Child Development* 77:1155–1169.

American Psychological Association. 2012. Guidelines for psychological practice with lesbian, gay, and bisexual clients. *American Psychologist* 67:10–42.

———. 2003. Guidelines on multicultural education, training, research, practice, and organizational change for psychologists. *American Psychologist* 58:377–401.

Anderman, E. M., Austin, C. C., and Johnson, D. M. 2002. The development of goal orientation. In A. Wigfield and J. S. Eccles (Eds.), *Development of achievement motivation. A volume in the educational psychology series* (pp. 197–220). San Diego, CA: Academic Press.

Anderman, E. M., and Maehr, M. L. 1994. Motivation and schooling in the middle grades. *Review of Educational Research* 64:287–309.

Anderman, L. H. 2003. Academic and social perceptions as predictors of change in middle school students' sense of school belonging. *The Journal of Experimental Education* 72:5–22.

Anderson, C. B. 2004. Athletic identity and its relation to exercise behavior: Scale development and initial validation. *Journal of Sport and Exercise Psychology* 26:39–56.

Anderson, E., and McCormack, M. 2010a. Comparing the Black and gay male athlete: Patterns in American oppression. *Journal of Men's Studies* 18:145–158.

———. 2010b. Intersectionality, critical race theory, and American sporting oppression: Examining Black and gay male athletes. *Journal of Homosexuality* 57:949–967.

Anderson, E., and McGuire, R. 2010. Inclusive masculinity and the gendered politics of men's rugby. *Journal of Gender Studies* 19:249–261.

Anderson, K. A., Howard, K., and Graham, A. 2007. Reading achievement, suspensions, and African American males in middle school. *Middle Grades Research Journal* 2:43–63.

Anglin, D. M., and Wade, J. C. 2007. Racial socialization, racial identity, and Black students' adjustment to college. *Cultural Diversity and Ethnic Minority Psychology* 13:207–215.

Anzaldúa, G. E. 2003. "La Conciencia de la Mestiza: Towards a New Consciousness." In C. R. McCann and S. Kim (Eds.), *Feminist Thought Reader: Local and Global Perspectives*, pp 179–189. New York: Routledge

Arias, D. C. 2007. "http://web.ebscohost.com/ehost/viewarticle?data=dGJyMPPp44 rp2%2fdV0%2bnjisfk5Ie46bZMsqeuSLak63nn5Kx95uXxjL6vrUq1pbBIrq2eSbiotFK xp55oy5zyit%2fk8Xnh6ueH7N%2fiVbKmsEqurrZPspzqeezdu33snOJ6u9fugKTq33 %2b7t8w%2b3%2bS7SrKotU%2b0qrI%2b5OXwhd%2fqu37z4ups4%2b7y&hid=106 High rate of incarcerated black men devastating to family health. *Nation's Health* 37:6–8.

Aronson, J., Fried, C., and Good, C. 2002. Reducing the effects of stereotype threat on African American college students by shaping theories of intelligence. *Journal of Experimental Social Psychology* 38:113–125.

Artiles, A. J., Harry, B., Reschly, D. J., and Chinn, P. C. 2002. Over-identification of students of color in special education: A critical overview. *Multicultural Perspectives* 4:3–10.

Ashmore, R. D., Deaux, K., and McLaughlin-Volpe, T. 2004. An organizational framework for collective identity: Articulation and significance of multidimensionality. *Psychological Bulletin* 130:80–114.

Assibey-Mensah, G. O. 1997. Role models and youth development: Evidence and lessons from the perceptions of African American male youth. *The Western Journal of Black Studies* 21:242–252.

Auerbach, J. A., Krimgold, B. K., and Lefkowits, B. 2000. *Improving health: It doesn't take a revolution. Health and social inequality*. Washington, D. C.: Kellogg Foundation.

Avery, D. R., Tonidandel, S., Thomas, K. M., Johnson, C. D., and Mack, D. A. 2007. Assessing the multigroup ethnic identity measure for measurement equivalence across racial and ethnic groups. *Educational and Psychological Measurement* 67:877–888.

Awad, G. 2007. The role of racial identity, academic self-concept, and self-esteem in the prediction of academic outcomes for African American students. *Journal of Black Psychology* 33:188–207.

Azmitia, M., Syed, M., and Radmacher, K. 2008. On the intersection of personal and social identities: Introduction and evidence from a longitudinal study of emerging adults. *New Directions for Child and Adolescent Development* 120:1–16.

Babbie, E. 2005. *The basics of social research*. Belmont, CA: Thomson, Wadsworth

Bailey, A. A. 2006. A year in the life of the African-American male in advertising. *Journal of Advertising* 35:83–104.

Bakari, R. 2003. Preservice teachers' attitudes toward teaching African American students: Contemporary research. *Urban Education* 38:640–654.

Bandura, A. 1997. *Self-Efficacy: The Exercise of Control*. New York: W. H. Freeman.

Banks, J. A. 1994. *Multiethnic education: Theory and practice* (3rd ed.). Boston: Allyn and Bacon.

Barksdale, D. J., Farrug, E. R., and Harkness, K. 2009. Racial discrimination and blood pressure: Perceptions, emotions, and behaviors of Black American adults. *Issues in Mental Health Nursing* 30:104–111.

Baron, R. M., and Kenny, D. A. 1986. The moderator-mediator variable distinction in social psychological research: Conceptual, strategic, and statistical considerations. *Journal of Personality and Social Psychology* 51:1173 - 1182.

Baszile, D. T. 2009. Deal with it we must: Education, social justice and the curriculum of hip hop culture. *Equity and Excellence in Education* 42:6–19.

Battle, J., and Scott, B. M. 1997. Mother-only versus father-only households: Educational outcomes for African American males. *Journal of African American Men* 17:93–116.
BBC News. 1968. *Black athletes make silent protest.* http://news.bbc.co.uk/onthisday/low/dates/stories/october/17/newsid_3535000/3535348.stm.
Beamon, K. 2012. "I'm a baller": Athletic identity foreclosure among African American former student-athletes. *Journal of African American Studies* 16:195–208.
Beamon, K., and Bell, P. A. 2006. Academics versus athletics: An examination of the effects on background and socialization on African American male student athletes. *Social Science Journal* 43:393–403.
Belgrave, F. Z., Brome, D. R., and Hampton, C. 2000. The contribution of Africentric values and racial identity to the prediction of drug knowledge, attitudes, and use among African American youth. *Journal of Black Psychology* 26:386–401.
Bell, R. N., Jones, T. J., Roane, R. A., Square, K. M., and Chung, R. C. 2013. Reflections on the murder of Trayvon Martin. *Journal for Social Action in Counseling and Psychology* 5:88–102
Bell, Y., and Clark, T. 1998. Culturally relevant reading material as related to a comprehension and recall in African-American children. *Journal of Black Psychology* 24:455–476.
Bem, S. L. 1974. http://web.ebscohost.com/ehost/viewarticle?data=dGJyMPPp44rp2%2fdV0%2bnjisfk5Ie46bZMsqeuSLak63nn5Kx95uXxjL6trUqtqK5ItZayUq6vuEqxls5lpOrweezp33vy3%2b2G59q7UbeurlCxq7ZRpOLfhuWz44ak2uBV7un3gKTq33%2b7t8w%2b3%2bS7SbetskWwrbRLr6OuSK%2bc5Ifw49%2bMu9zzhOrK45Dy&hid=8 The measurement of psychological androgyny. *Journal of Consulting and Clinical Psychology* 42:155–162.
———. 1981. *Bem Sex-Role Inventory: Professional manual.* Palo Alto, CA: Consulting Psychologists Press.
Bennett, C. 2001. Added http://web.ebscohost.com/ehost/viewarticle?data=dGJyMPPp44rp2%2fdV0%2bnjisfk5Ie46bZMsqeuSLak63nn5Kx95uXxjL6vrUq1pbBIrq2eSbiqrlKwrZ5oy5zyit%2fk8Xnh6ueH7N%2fiVbKmsEqurrZPspzqeezdu33snOJ6u9fugKTq33%2b7t8w%2b3%2bS7TbautUqwr6R%2b7ejrefKz5I3q4tJ99uoA&hid=104 Genres of research in multicultural education. *Review of Educational Research* 71:171–222.
Bennett, G. G., Merritt, M. M., Edwards, C. L., and Sollers, J. J. 2004. Perceived racism and affective responses to ambiguous interpersonal interactions among African American men. *American Behavioral Scientist* 47:963–976.
Bennett, M. D., and Fraser, M. W. 2000. Urban violence among African American males: Integrating family, neighborhood, and peer perspectives. *Journal of Sociology and Social Welfare* 27:93–117.
Benson, K. F. 2000. Constructing academic inadequacy: African American athletes' stories of schooling. *Journal of Higher Education* 71:223–246.
Bergin, D. A., and Cooks, H. C. 2002. High school students of color talk about accusations of 'acting White.' *The Urban Review* 34:113–134.
Betancourt, H., and Lopez, S. R. 1993. The study of culture, ethnicity, and race in American psychology. *American Psychologist* 48:629–637.
Bigler, R. S., Averhart, C. J., and Liben, L. S. 2003. http://web.ebscohost.com/ehost/viewarticle?data=dGJyMPPp44rp2%2fdV0%2bnjisfk5Ie46bZMsqeuSLak63nn5Kx95uXxjL6trUqtqK5ItZaxUq6vuEquls5lpOrweezp33vy3%2b2G59q7UbeurlCxq7ZRpOLfhuWz44ak2uBV3%2bbmPvLX5VW%2fxKR57LO3T7Our0%2b2nOSH8OPfjLvc84TqyuOQ8gAA&hid=8 Race and the Workforce: Occupational Status, Aspirations, and Stereotyping Among African American Children. *Developmental Psychology* 39:572–581.
Bimper, A. Y., Harrison, L., and Clark, L. 2013. Diamonds in the rough: Examining a case of successful Black male student athlete in college sport. *Journal of Black Psychology,* 1–24. DOI: 10.1177/0095798412454676.
Blumenfeld, W. J. 2007. *Adolescence, sexual orientation and identity: An overview.* http://www.outproud.org/article_sexual_identity.html.

Bohn, A. P. 2003. Familiar voices: Using Ebonics communication techniques in the primary classroom. *Urban Education* 38:688–707.

Bonner, F. A., Lewis, C. W., Bownan-Perrott, L., and Hill-Jackson, V. 2009. Definition, identification, identity, and culture: A unique alchemy impacting the success of gifted African American millennial males in school. *Journal for the Education of the Gifted* 33:176–202.

Bowen-Reid, T. L., and Smalls, C. 2004. Stress, spirituality and health promoting behaviors among African American college students. *The Western Journal of Black Studies* 28:283–291.

Boyd, H and Watson, J. E. 2004. http://web.ebscohost.com/ehost/viewarticle?data= dGJyMPPp44rp2%2fdV0%2bnjisfk5Ie46bZMsqeuSLak63nn5Kx95uXxjL6trUqtqK5I tZawUq%2bvuEiuls5lpOrweezp33vy3%2b2G59q7UbeurlCxq7ZRpOLfhuWz44ak2 uBV3%2bbmPvLX5VW%2fxKR57LOvTa6ttE21raR%2b7ejrefKz5I3q4tJ99uoA&hid= 8 10 PERCENT BEHIND BARS. *New York Amsterdam News*, 11/11/2004 95:1–2.

Boykin, A. W. 1983. The academic performance of Afro-American children. In J. Spence (Ed.), *Achievement and achievement motives*. San Francisco: Freeman.

———. 1986. The triple quandary and the schooling of Afro-American children: In U. Neisser (Ed.), *The school achievement of minority children* (pp 57–92). Hillsdale, NJ: Lawrence Erlbaum.

———. 1994. Harvesting culture and talent: African American children and school reform. In R. Rossi (Ed.), *Schools and students at risk: Context and framework for positive change* (pp. 116–138. New York: Teachers College Press.

———. 2001. The challenges of cultural socialization in the schooling of African American elementary school children: Exposing the hidden curriculum. In W. Watkins, J. Lewis, and V. Chou (eds.) *Race and education: The roles of history and society in educating African American students:* Allyn and Bacon.

———. 2002. Integrity-based approaches to the literacy development of African American children: The quest for talent development. In B. Bowman (ed.), *Love to read: Essays in developing and enhancing early literacy skills of African American children*. National Black Child Development Institute, Inc: Washington, DC.

Boykin, A. W., Albury, A. Tyler, K. M., Hurley, E. A., Bailey, C. T., and Miller, O. A. 2005. The influence of culture on the perceptions of academic achievement among low-income African and Anglo American elementary students. *Cultural Diversity and Ethnic Minority Psychology* 11:339–350.

Boykin, A. W., and Allen, B. A. 1998. Enhancing African American children's learning and motivation: Evolution of the verve and movement expressiveness paradigms. In R. Jones (Ed.), African American youth. Hampton, VA: Cobb and Henry Publishers.

———. 2000. Beyond deficits and difference: Psychological integrity in developmental research. *Advances in Education in Diverse Communities: Research,Policy and Praxis* 1:15–34.

Boykin, A. W., Coleman, S. T., Lilja, A. J., and Tyler, K. M. 2004. Building on children's cultural assets in simulated classroom performance environments: Research vistas in the communal learning paradigm. CRESPAR Technical Report #68.

Boykin, A. W., and Cunningham, R. T. 2001. The effects of movement expressiveness in story content and learning context on the analogical reasoning performance of African American children. *Journal of Negro Education* 70:72–83.

Boykin, A. W., and Ellison, C. M. 1995. The multiple ecologies of Black youth socialization: An Afrographic analysis. In R. L. Taylor's, *African American Youth: Their social and economic status in the United States*. Praeger: Connecticut

Boykin, A. W., Jagers, R. J., Ellison, C. M., and Albury, A. 1997. Communalism: Conceptualization and measurement of an Afrocultural social orientation. *Journal of Black Studies* 27:409–418.

Boykin, A. W., Lilja, A. J., and Tyler, K. M. 2004. The influence of communal versus individual learning context on the academic performance of African-American elementary school students. *Learning Environments Journal* 7:227–244.

Boykin, A. W., Tyler, K. M., and Miller, O. A. 2005. In search of cultural themes and their expressions in the dynamics of classroom life. *Urban Education* 40:521–549.

Boykin, A. W., Tyler, K. M., Watkins-Lewis, K. M., and Kizzie, K. 2005. Culture in the sanctioned classroom practices of elementary school teachers serving low-income African American students. *Journal of Education of Students Placed At-Risk*,11,161–173.

Brady, S., and Busse, W. J. 1994. The Gay Identity Questionnaire: A brief measure of homosexual identity formation. *Journal of Homosexuality* 26:1–21.

Branch, A., and Young, R. 2006. Ethnic identity development of African Americans: Experiences in search of a paradigm. *The Western Journal of Black Studies* 30:160–170.

Bridges, E. M. 2011. Racial identity development and psychological coping strategies of undergraduate and graduate African American males. *Journal of African American Males in Education* 2:150–167.

Bridges, T. 2011. Towards a pedagogy of hip hop in urban teacher education. *The Journal of Negro Education* 80:325–338.

Brody, G. H., Chen, Y., Murry, V., Ge, X., Simons, R. L., Gibbons, F. X., Gerrard, M., and Cutrona, C. E. 2006. Perceived discrimination and the adjustment of African American youths: A five-year longitudinal analysis with contextual moderation effects. *Child Development* 77:1170–1189.

Bronfenbrenner, U. 1986. Ecology of the family as a context for human development: Research perspectives. *Developmental Psychology* 22:723–742.

Brookins, C. C. 1994. http://web.ebscohost.com/ehost/viewarticle?data=dGJyMPPp44r p2%2fdV0%2bnjisfk5Ie46bZMsqeuSLak63nn5Kx95uXxjL6vrUq1pbBIrq2eSbiotFKx p55oy5zyit%2fk8Xnh6ueH7N%2fiVbKmsEqurrZPspzqeezdu33snOJ6u%2bbxkeac8 nnls79mpNfsVa%2bvt0yrqbdNsq%2brSK6npH7t6Ot58rPkjeri0n326gAA&hid=106 The relationship between Afrocentric values and racial identity attitudes: Validation of the Belief Systems Analysis Scale on African American college students. *Journal of Black Psychology* 20:128–142.

Brown, A. L. 2011. "Same old stories": The Black male in social science and educational literature, 1930s to the present. *Teachers College Record* 113:2047–2079.

Brown, D. R., McGregor, K. C., and Gary, L. E. 1997. Sex role identity and depressive symptoms among African American men. *African American Research Perspectives*, 77–82

Brown, E. 2005. We wear the mask: African American contemporary gay male identities. *Journal of African American Studies* 9:29–38.

Brown, E. J., and Smith, F. B. 2006. Drug (Ab)use research among rural African American males: An integrated literature review. *International Journal of Men's Health* 5:191–206.

Brown, T. L., Linver, M. R., Evans, M., and DeGennaro, D. 2009. African American parents' racial and ethnic socialization and adolescent academic grades: Teasing out the role of gender. *Journal of Youth and Adolescence* 38:214–227.

Brunson, J. E. 2011. Showing, seeing: Hip-hop, visual culture, and the show-and-tell performance. *Black History Bulletin* 74:6–12.

Bryant, A. L., and Zimmerman, M. A. 2003. Role models and psychosocial outcomes among African American adolescents. *Journal of Adolescent Research* 18:36–67.

Bryant, N. 1998. African American males: Soon gone? *Journal of African American Men* 14:9–17.

Bryant, W. W. 2011. Internalized racism's association with African American male youth's propensity for violence. *Journal of Black Studies* 42:690–707.

Bryk, A. S., and Raudenbush, S. W. 1992. *Hierarchical linear models: Applications and data analysis methods*. Newbury Park, CA: Sage Publications.

Bryson, S. 1998. Relationship between race and attitudes towards Black men. *Journal of Multicultural Counseling and Development* 26:282–294.

Bucolo, D. O., and Cohn, E. S. 2010. Playing the race card: Making race salient in defence opening and closing statements. *Legal and Criminological Psychology* 15:293–303.

Bullard, R., Mohai, P., Saha, R., and Wright, B. 2007. *Toxic waste and race at twenty, 1987–2007. A report prepared for the United Church of Christ Justice and Witness Ministries.* http://www.ucc.org/assets/pdfs/toxic20.pdf.

Burfew, L. D., and Serface, H. C. 2006. The tricultural experience of older, African American, gay men: Counseling implications. *Adultspan Journal* 5, 81–90.

Burk, L. R., Burkhart, B. R., and Sikorski, J. F. 2004. Construction and preliminary validation of the Auburn Differential Masculinity Inventory. *Psychology of Men and Masculinity* 5:4–17.

Burrow, A. L., Tubman, J. G., and Montgomery, M. J. 2006. Racial identity: Toward an integrated developmental psychological perspective. *Identity: An International Journal of Theory and Research* 6:317–339.

Busby, D. R., Lambert, S. F., and Ialongo, N. S. 2013. Psychological symptoms linking exposure to community violence and academic functioning in African American adolescents. *Journal of Youth and Adolescence* 42:250–262.

Buseh, A. G., Kelber, S. T., Hewitt, J. B., Stevens, P. E., and Park, C. G. 2006. Perceived stigma and life satisfaction: Experiences of urban African American men living with HIV/AIDS. *International Journal of Men's Health* 5:35–51.

Bush, L. V. 1999. Am I a man? A literature review engaging the sociohistorical dynamics of Black manhood in the United States. *The Western Journal of Black Studies* 23:49–57.

———. 2004. Solve for X: Black women + Black boys = X. *Journal of African American Men* 5:31–53.

Bush, L. V., and Bush, E. C. 2013. Introducing African American male theory (AAMT). *Journal of African American Males in Education* 4:6–17.

Bynum, M. S., Best, C., Barnes, S. L., and Burton, E. T. 2008. Private regard, identity protection, and perceived racism among African American males. *Journal of African American Studies* 12:142–155.

Byrd, C. M., and Chavous, T. M. 2009. Racial identity and academic achievement in the neighborhood context: A multilevel analysis. *Journal of Youth and Adolescence* 38:544–559.

Caldwell, C. H., Kohn-Wood, L. P., Schmeelk-Cone, K. H., Chavous, T. M., and Zimmerman, M. A. 2004. Racial discrimination and racial identity as risk or protective factors for violent behaviors in African American young adults. *American Journal of Community Psychology* 33:91–105.

Callahan, J. S. (2008, November). *Twenty-first century mojo: Hip hop identity development among Black college students at a predominantly White university.* Paper presented at the National Association for Gifted Children Research Gala. Tampa Bay, Fl.

———. (2009, November). *"Fresh captures right now": Hip hop music and the ritual practices of bright, Black university students in the Dirty South.* Paper presented at the National Association of the Gifted Children. St. Louis, Mo.

Callahan, J. S., and Grantham, T. C. 2012. "Deeper than rap": Gifted males and their relationship with hip hop culture. *Gifted Child Today* 35:197–207.

Callahan, J. S., Grantham, T. C., and Harris, W. G. (2010, November). *Gifted children in today's hip hop culture: Timely recommendation for parents and teachers.* Poster presentation at the annual meeting of the National Association for Gifted Children, Atlanta, Ga.

Campbell, D. B., and Fleming, J. 2001. Fear of success, racial identity, and academic achievement in Black male college students. *Community Review*, (), 5–18.

Carroll, G. 1998. *Environmental stress and African Americans: The other side of the moon.* Westport, CT: Praeger.

Carter, R., and Helms, J. E. 1988. The relationship between racial identity and social class. *Journal of Negro Education* 57:22–30.

Carter, R. T., Williams, B., Juby, H. L., and Buckley, T. R. 2005. Racial identity as mediator of the relationship between gender role conflict and severity of psychological symptoms in Black, Latino, and Asian men. *Sex Roles* 53:473–486.

Cartwright, A. D., and Henrikson, R. C. 2012. The lived experience of Black collegiate males with absent fathers: Another generation. *Journal of Professional Counseling, Practice, Theory, and Research* 39:29–39.

Carver, P. R., Egan, S. K., and Perry, D. G. 2004. Children who question their heterosexuality. *Developmental Psychology* 40:43–53.

Cass, V. C. 1979. Homosexual identity formation: A theoretical model. *Journal of Homosexuality* 4:219–235.

———. 1984. Homosexual identity formation: Testing a theoretical model. The *Journal of Sex Research* 20:143–167.

Caton, M. T. 2012. Black male perspectives on their educational experiences in high school. *Urban Education*, 1–31.

Centers for Disease Control and Prevention 2005. HIV/AIDS among African Americans. http://www.cdc.gov/hiv/topics/aa/resources/factsheets/aa.htm.

Chang, D. F., and Sue, S. 2003. The effects of race and problem type on teachers' assessment of student behavior. *Journal of Counseling and Clinical Psychology* 71:235–242.

Chavous, T. M., Bernat, D. H., Schmeelk-Cone, K., Caldwell, C. H., Kohn-Wood, L., and Zimmerman, M. A. 2003. Racial identity and academic attainment among African American adolescents. *Child Development* 74:1076–1090.

Chesebro, J. W., and Fuse, K. 2001. The development of a Perceived Masculinity Scale. *Communication Quarterly* 49:203–278.

Chiles, N. 2013. The state of Black boys. *Ebony* 68:122–127

Chung, Y. B. 1995. The construct validity of the Bem Sex-Role Inventory for heterosexual and gay men. *Journal of Homosexuality* 30:87–97.

Clark, R., Anderson, N. B., Clark, V. R., and Williams, D. R. 1999. Racism as a stressor for African Americans: A biopsychosocial model. *American Psychologist* 54:805–816.

Coakley, J. 1994. *Sport in society: Issues and controversies*. St. Louis: Mosby Publishers.

Coard, S. I., Breland, A. M., and Raskin, P. 2001. Perceptions of and preferences for skin color, Black racial identity, and self-esteem among African Americans. *Journal of Applied Social Psychology* 31:2256–2274.

Coates, E. E., Phares, V., and Dedrick, R. F. 2013. Psychometric properties of the Connor-Davidson resilience scale 10 among low-income African American men. *Psychological Assessment* 25:1349–1354.

Cochran-Smith, M. 2005. Studying teacher education: What we know and need to know. *Journal of Teacher Education* 56:301–306.

Cohen, A. B. 2009. Many forms of culture. *American Psychologist* 64:194–204.

Cokley, K. 2002. The impact of college racial composition on African American students' academic self-concept: A replication and extension. *The Journal of Negro Education* 71:288–296.

———. 2002. Testing Cross's revised racial identity model: An examination of the relationship between racial identity and internalized racialism. *Journal of Counseling Psychology* 49:476–493.

———. 2003. What do we know about the motivation of African American students? Challenging the "anti-intellectual" myth. *Added Harvard Educational Review* 73:524–558

———. 2005. http://web.ebscohost.com/ehost/viewarticle?data=dGJyMPPp44rp2%2f dV0%2bnjisfk5Ie46bZMsqeuSLak63nn5Kx95uXxjL6trUqtqK5ItZaxUq6vuEquls5lp Orweezp33vy3%2b2G59q7UbeurlCxq7ZRpOLfhuWz44ak2uBV3%2bbmPvLX5VW %2fxKR57LOvUa6psEy0qaR%2b7ejrefKz5I3q4tJ99uoA&hid=8 Racial(ized) identity, ethnic identity, and Afrocentric values: Conceptual and methodological challenges in understanding African American identity. *Journal of Counseling Psychology* 52:517–526.

———. 2007. Critical issues in the measurement of ethnic and racial identity: A referendum on the state of the field. *Journal of Counseling Psychology* 54:224–234.

Cokley, K., and Chapman, C. 2008. The roles of ethnic identity, anti-white attitudes, and academic self-concept in African American student achievement. *Social Psychology of Education* 11:349–365.

Cokley, K., Komarraju, M., King, A., Cunningham, D., and Muhammad, G. 2003. Ethnic differences in the measurement of academic self-concept in a sample of African American and European American college students. *Educational and Psychological Measurement* 63:707–722.

Cokley, K., and Moore, P. 2007. Moderating and mediating effects of gender and psychological disengagement on the academic achievement of African American college students. *Journal of Black Psychology* 33:169–187.

Cokley, K., and Williams, W. 2005. A psychometric examination of the Africentric scale: Challenges in measuring Afrocentric values. *Journal of Black Studies* 35:827–843.

Cole, E. R. 2009. Intersectionality and research in psychology. *American Psychologist* 64:170–180.

Collins, P. H. 2001. It's all in the family: Intersections of gender, race, and nation. *Hypatia* 13:62–82.

———. 2006. *From Black power to hip-hop.* Philadelphia: Temple University Press.

Comeaux, E., and Harrison, C. K. 2007. Faculty and male student athletes in higher education: Racial differences in the environmental predictors of academic achievement. *Race, Ethnicity, and Education* 10:199–214.

Comeaux, E., Harrison, C. K., and Plecha, M. 2006. Gender, sport, and higher education: The impact of student-faculty interactions on academic achievement. *The Academic Athletic Journal*, 38–54.

Compton, M. T., Thompson, N. J., and Kaslow, N. J. 2005. Social environment factor associated with suicide attempt among low-income African Americans: The protective role of family relationships and social support. *Social Psychiatry and Psychiatric Epidemiology* 40:175–185.

Constantine, M. G., Miville, M. L., Warren, A. K., Gainor, K. A., and Lewis-Coles, M. E.L. 2006. Religion, spirituality, and career development in African American college students: A qualitative inquiry. *The Career Development Quarterly* 54:227–241.

Constantine, M. G., and Sue, D. W. 2006. Factors contributing to optimal human functioning in people of color in the United States. *The Counseling Psychologist* 34:228–244.

Conyers, J. L. 2005. African American males memory, culture, and ethos. *Journal of African American Men*, 19–36.

Cook, K. V. 2000. "You have to have somebody watching your back, and if that's God, then that's mighty big": The church's role in the resilience of inner-city youth." *Adolescence* 35:717–730.

Corby, B. C., Hodges, E. V.E., and Perry, D. G. 2007. Gender identity and adjustment in Black, Hispanic, and White preadolescents. *Developmental Psychology* 43:261–266.

Corneille, M., Fife, J. E., Belgrave, F. Z., and Sims, B. C. 2012. Ethnic identity, masculinity, and healthy sexual relationships among African American men. *Psychology of Men and Masculinity* 13:393–399.

Corprew, C. S., and Cunningham, M. 2012. Educating tomorrow's men: Perceived school support, negative youth experiences, and bravado attitudes in African American adolescent males. *Education and Urban Society* 44:571–589.

Correll, J., Park, B., Judd, C. M., and Wittenbrink, B. 2002. The Police Officer's Dilemma: Using ethnicity to disambiguate potentially threatening individuals. *Journal of Personality and Social Psychology* 83:1314–1329.

Cota-Robles, S., Neiss, M., and Rowe, D. C. 2002. The role of puberty in violent and nonviolent delinquency among Anglo American, Mexican American, and African American boys. *Journal of Adolescent Research* 17:364–376.

Cox, S., and Gallois, C. 1996. Gay and lesbian development: A social identity perspective. *Journal of Homosexuality* 30:1–30.

Crawford, I., Allison, K. W., Zamboni, B. D., and Soto, T. 2002. The influence of dual-identity development on the psychosocial functioning of African American gay and bisexual men. *Journal of Sex Research* 39:179–189.

Cross, W. E. 1971. The Negro-to-Black conversion experience: Toward a psychology of black liberation. *Black World* 20:13–27.

———. 1995. The psychology of nigrescence: Revising the Cross model. In J. G. Ponterotto and J. M. Casas, (Eds.), *Handbook of multicultural counseling* (pp. 93–122). Thousand Oaks, CA: Sage Publishing.

Cubbin, C., Pickle, L. W., and Fingerhut, L. 2000. Social context and geographic patterns of homicide among U.S. Black and White males. *American Journal of Public Health* 90:579–587.

Cunningham, M. 1999. African American adolescent males' perceptions of their community resources and constraints: A longitudinal analysis. *Journal of Community Psychology* 27:569–588.

Cunningham, M., Swanson, D. P., and Hayes, D. M. 2013. School- and community-based associations to hypermasculine attitudes in African American adolescent males. *American Journal of Orthopsychiatry* 83:244–251.

Cunningham, M., Swanson, D. P., Spencer, M. B., and Dupree, D. 2003. The association of physical maturation with family hassles among African American adolescents males. *Cultural Diversity and Ethnic Minority Psychology* 9:276–288.

Czopp, A. M. 2010. Studying is lame when he got game: Racial stereotypes and discouragement of Black student-athletes from schoolwork. *Social Psychology of Education* 13:485–498.

Czopp, A. M., Lasane, T. P., Sweigard, P. N., Bradshaw, S. D., and Hammer, E. D. (1998) Masculine styles of self-presentation in the classroom: Perceptions of Joe Cool. *Journal of Social Behavior and Personality* 13:281–294.

Dade, L. R., and Sloan, L. R. 2000. An investigation of sex-role stereotypes in African Americans. *Journal of Black Studies*, 676–690.

Dale, S. K., and Daniel, J. H. 2013. Talking about the Trayvon Martin case in psychology and counseling training and psychotherapy. *Journal for Social Action in Counseling and Psychology* 5:37–49.

Dancy, T. E. 2010. Faith in the unseen: The intersection(s) of spirituality and identity among African American males in college. *The Journal of Negro Education* 79:416–432.

———. 2011. Colleges in the making of manhood and masculinity: Gendered perspectives on African American males. *Gender and Education* 23:477–495.

Davidson, A. L. 1996. *Making and molding identity in schools*. Albany, New York: State University of New York Press.

Davis, J. E. 2003. Early schooling and academic achievement of African American males. *Urban Education* 38:515–537.

Davis, S., Jenkins, G., and Hunt, R. 2002. *The pact: Three young men make a promise and fulfill a dream*. Riverhead Trade: New York, NY.

Day-Vines, N. L., and Day-Hairston, B. O. 2005. Culturally congruent strategies for addressing the behavioral needs of urban, African American male adolescents. *Professional School Counseling* 8:236–244.

Deaux, K. 1993. Reconstructing social identity. *Personality and Social Psychology Bulletin* 19:4–12.

Debnam, K., Holt, C. L., Clark, E. M., Roth, D. L., and Southward, P. 2012. Relationship between religious social support and general social support with health behaviors in a national sample of African Americans. *Journal of Behavioral Modification* 35:179–189.

DeCuir-Gunby, J. T. 2009. A review of the racial identity development of African American adolescents: The role of education. *Review of Educational Research* 79:103–124.

DeGruy, J., Kjellstrand, J. M., Briggs, H. E., and Brennan, E. M. 2012. Racial respect and racial socialization as protective factors for African American male youth. *Journal of Black Psychology* 38:395–420.

Delpit, L. 1995. *Other people's children*. New York: The New Press.
Derogatis, L. R. 1983. *SCL-90-R: Administration, scoring, and procedures manual II for the (revised) version and other instruments of the psychopathology rating scale*. Towson, MD: Clinical Psychometric Research.
Deyhle, D. 1992. Constructing failure and maintaining cultural identity: Navajo and Ute school leavers. *Journal of American Indian Education* 31:24–47.
———. 1995. Navajo youth and Anglo racism: Cultural integrity and resistance. *Harvard Educational Review* 65:403–444.
Deyhle, D., and LeCompte, M. 1994. Cultural differences in child development: Navajo adolescents in middle schools. *Theory Into Practice* 33:156–178.
Diemer, M. A. 2002. Constructions of provider role identity among African American men: An exploratory study. *Cultural Diversity and Ethnic Minority Psychology* 8:30–40.
———. 2007. Two worlds: African American men's negotiation of predominantly White educational and occupational worlds. *Journal of Multicultural Counseling and Development* 35:2–14.
Dill, E., and Boykin, A. W. 2000. The comparative influence of individual, peer tutoring and communal learning contexts on the text recall of African American students. *Journal of Black Psychology* 26:65–78.
Dilorio, Cl, Hartwell, T., and Hansen, N. 2002. Childhood sexual abuse and risk behaviors among men at high risk for HIV infection. *American Journal of Public Health* 92:214–219.
Din-Dzietham, R., Nembhard, W. N., Collins, R., and Davis, S. K. 2004. Perceived stress following race-based discrimination at work is associated with hypertension in African Americans. The metro Atlanta heart disease study, 1999–2001. *Social Science and Medicine* 58:449–461.
Dixon, P. 2009. Marriage among African Americans: What does the research reveal? *Journal of African American Studies* 13:29–46.
Dixon-Roman, E. J. 2012. The forms of capital and the developed achievement of Black males. *Urban Education*. DOI: 10.1177/0042085912463707
Dotterer, A. M., McHale, S. M., and Crouter, A. C. 2009. Sociocultural factors and school engagement among African American youth: The roles of racial discrimination, racial socialization, and ethnic identity. *Applied Developmental Science* 13:61–73.
Downs, A., Ashton, J. 2009. Vigorous physical activity, sports participation, and athletic identity: Implications for mental and physical health in college students. *Journal of Sports Behavior,* 228–249.
Dressler, J. 1985. Survey of school principals regarding alleged homosexual teachers in the classroom: How likely (really) is discharge? *Dayton Law Review* 10:599–605.
Dube, E. M., and Savin-Williams, R. C. 1999. Sexual identity development among ethnic sexual-minority male youths. *Developmental Psychology* 35:1389–1398.
Dunbar, C. 1999. African American males and participation: Promising inclusion, practicing exclusion. *Theory into Practice* 38:241–246.
Dupree, D., Spencer, M. B., and Bell, S. 1997. The ecology of African-American child development: Normative and non-normative outcomes. In G. Johnson-Powell and Y. Yamamoto, (Eds.), *Transcultural child psychiatry: A portrait of America's children* (pp. 237–268). New York: John Wiley and Sons, Inc.
Durkin, K. 1995. *Developmental social psychology: From infancy to old age*. Oxford: Blackwell Publishers.
Dusek, J. B., and Joseph, G. 1985. The bases of teacher expectancies. In J. B. Dusek (Ed.), *Teacher expectancies* (pp.229–250). Hillsdale, NJ: Lawrence Erlbaum.
Dweck, C. S., and Leggett, E. L. 1988. A social-cognitive approach to motivation and personality. *Psychological Review* 95:256–273.
Eberhardt, J. Davies, P., Purdie-Vaughns, V., and Johnson, S. 2006. "Looking deathworthy: Perceived stereotypicality of Black defendants predicts capital-sentencing outcomes." *Psychological Science* 17:383–386.

Eccles, J. 2009. Who am I and what am I going to do with my life? Personal and collective identities as motivators of action? *Educational Psychologist* 44:78–89.

Eccles, J. S., Midgley, C., Wigfield, A., Miller-Buchanan, C. M., Reuman, D., Flanagan, C., et al. 1993. Development during adolescence: The impact of stage-environment fit on young adolescents' experiences in schools and in families. *American Psychologist* 48:90–101.

Edwards, H. 1992. Are we putting too much emphasis on sports? *Ebony* 47:128–129.

———. 2000. Crisis of Black athletes on the eve of the 21st century. *Society* 37:9–14.

Edwards, K., Carter-Tellison, K., and Herring, C. 2004. "For richer, for pooer, whether dark or light: Skin tone, marital status, and spouse's earnings." In C. Herring, V. Keith, and H. Horton (Ed.), *Skin Deep: How Race and Complexion Matter in the Color-Blind Era* (pp 65–81). Urbana, Il: University of Illinois Press.

Egan, S. K., and Perry, D. G. 2001. Gender identity: A multidimensional analysis with implications for psychosocial adjustment. *Developmental Psychology* 37:451–463.

Eitle, T., and Eitle, D 2002. Race, cultural capital, and the educational effects of participation in sports. *Sociology of Education* 75:123–146.

Eldeib, D. (2010, March 5). Every Urban Prep senior is college-bound. Chicago Tribune. http://www.chicagotribune.com.

Elligan, D., and Utsey, S. O. 1999. Utility of an African-centered support group for African American men confronting societal racism and oppression. *Cultural Diversity and Ethnic Minority Psychology* 5:156–165.

Elliot, A. J., and Harackiewicz, J. M. 1996. Approach and avoidance achievement goals and intrinsic motivation: A mediational analysis. *Journal of Personality and Social Psychology* 70:461–475.

Ellison, C. M., Boykin, A. W., Towns, D. P., and Stokes, A. 2000. Classroom cultural ecology: The dynamics of classroom life in schools serving low-income African American children. Technical Report #44, Center for Research on the Education of Students Placed at Risk (CRESPAR).

Ellison, R. 1952. *Invisible Man*. New York: Random House.

Emdin, C. 2009. Urban science classrooms and new possibilities: Intersubjectivity and grammar in the third space. *Cultural Studies of Science Education* 4:239–254.

Emdin, C., and Lee, O. 2012. Hip-hop, the "Obama effect," and urban science education. *Teachers College Record* 114:1–25.

Engstrom, C. H., Sedlacek, W. E., and McEwen, M. K. 1995. Faculty attitudes toward male revenue and nonrevenue student-athletes. *Journal of College Student Development* 36:217–227.

Epstein, J. N., March, J. S., Conners, C. K., and Jackson, D. L. 1998. Racial differences on the Conners Teacher Rating Scale. *Journal of Abnormal Child Psychology* 26:109–118.

Erikson, E. H. 1968. *Identity: Youth and crisis*. New York: Norton.

Esmail, A., and Sullivan, J. M. 2006. African American college males and females. A look at color mating preferences. *Race, Gender, and Class* 13:201–220.

Essed, P. 1991. *Understanding everyday racism*. Newbury Park, CA: Sage.

Evelyn, J. (2000) The miseducation of hip-hop. *Black Issues in Higher Education* 17:24–29.

Ewing, K. M., Richardson, T. Q., James-Myers, L., and Russell, R. K. 1996. The relationship between racial identity attitudes, worldview, and African American graduate students' experiences of the imposter phenomenon. *Journal of Black Psychology* 22:53–66.

Feist-Price, S., Logan, T. K., Leukefeld, C., Moore, C. L., and Ebreo, A. 2003. Targeting HIV prevention on African American crack and injection drug users. *Substance Use and Misuse* 38:1259–1284.

Felson, R. B., and Painter-Davis, N. 2012. Another cost of being a young Black male: Race, weaponry, and lethal outcomes in assaults. *Social Science Research* 41:1241–1253.

Ferguson, R. F. 2003. Teachers' perceptions and expectations and the Black-White test score gap. *Urban Education* 38:460–507.

Fhagen-Smith, P. E., Vandiver, B. J., Worrell, F. C., and Cross, W. E. 2010. (Re)examining racial identity attitude differences across gender, community type, and socioeconomic status among African American college students. *Identity: An International Journal of Theory and Research* 10:164–180.

Fischer, A. R., and Shaw, C. M. 1999. African Americans' mental health and perceptions of racist discrimination: The moderating effects of racial socialization experiences and self-esteem. *Journal of Counseling Psychology* 46:395–407.

Fisher, C. B., Wallace, S. A., and Fenton, R. E. 2000. Discrimination distress during adolescence. *Journal of Youth and Adolescence* 29:679–695.

Fitzgerald, T. D. 2008. Controlling the Black school-age male: Psychotropic medications and the circumvention of Public Law 94–142 and Section 504. *Urban Education* 44:225–247.

Foley, D. 2005. Elusive prey: John Ogbu and the search for a grand theory of academic disengagement. *International Journal of Qualitative Studies in Education* 18:643–657.

Folkman, S., Chesney, M. A., Pollack, L., and Phillips, C. 1992. http://web.ebscohost.com/ehost/viewarticle?data=dGJyMPPp44rp%2fdV0%2bnjisfk5Ie46bZMsqeuSLak63nn5Kx95uXxjL6trUutqK5ItZavSrintFKxr55oy5zyit%2fk8Xnh6ueH7N%2fiVauor0ixqLNNrqyyPurX7H%2b72%2bw%2b4ti7iPHv5j7y1%2bVVv8Skeeyzr1G3qatIs6q1Squrmkmk3O2K69fyVeTr6oTS2%2faM&hid=15 Stress, coping, and high-risk sexual behavior. *Health Psychology* 11:218–222.

Ford, D. Y., Grantham, T. C., and Whiting, G. 2008. Another look at the achievement gap: Learning from the experiences of gifted African American students. *Urban Education* 43:216–239.

Ford, D. Y., and Harris, J. J. 1997. A study of racial identity and achievement of Black males and females. *Roeper Review* 20:1–12.

Ford, D.Y., and Moore, J.I., (2013). Understanding and reversing underachievement, low achievment and achievement gaps among high-ability African American Males in urban school contexts. *Urban Review* 45, 399–415.

Forster-Scott, L. 2011. Understanding colorism and how it relates to sport and physical education. *Journal of Physical Education, Recreation, and Dance* 82:48–52.

Foster, K. M. 2005. Narratives of the social scientist: Understanding the work of John Ogbu. *International Journal of Qualitative Studies in Education* 18:565–580.

Foster, M. L., Arnold, E., Rebchook, G., Kegeles, S. M. 2011. "It's my inner strength": Spirituality, religion, and HIV in the lives of young African American men who have sex with men. *Culture, Health, and Sexuality* 13:1103–1117.

Franklin, A. J. 1999. Invisibility syndrome and racial identity development in psychotherapy and counseling African American men. *The Counseling Psychologist* 27:761–793.

——— 2004. *From brotherhood to manhood: How Black men rescue their relationships and dreams from the Invisibility Syndrome.* New Jersey: Wiley and Sons.

Franklin, A. J., and Boyd-Franklin, N. 2004. Invisibility syndrome: A clinical model of the effects of racism on African American males. *American Journal of Orthopsychiatry* 70:33–41.

Franklin, C. W., and Mizell, C. A. 1995. Some factors influencing success among African-American men: A preliminary study. *Journal of Men's Studies* 3:191–204.

Frazier, A. D. 2012. The possible selves of high-ability African American attending a residential high school for highly able youth. *Journal for the Education of the Gifted* 35:366–390.

Freeman, H. O., Armor, D., Ross, J. M., and Pettigrew, T. F. 1966. Color gradation and attitudes among middle incomes Negroes. *American Sociological Review* 31:365–374.

French, S. E., Seidman, E., Allen, L., and Aber, J. L. 2006. The development of ethnic identity during adolescence. *Developmental Psychology* 42:1–16.

Freud, S. 1949. *An outline of psychoanalysis*. New York: W. W. Norton and Co.

Gaines, J. S. 2007. Social correlates of psychological distress among adult African American males. *Journal of Black Studies* 37:827–858.

Gaines, S. O., Marelich, W. D., Bledsoe, K. L., Steers, W. N., Henderson, M. C., Granreose, C. S., et al. 1997. Links between race/ethnicity and cultural values as mediated by racial/ethnic identity and moderated by gender. *Journal of Personality and Social Psychology* 72:1460–1476.

Garcia-Coll, C., Lamberty, G., Jenkins, R., McAdoo, H. P., Crnic, K., Wasik, B. H., and Garcia, H. V. 1996. An integrative model for the study of developmental competencies in minority children. *Child Development* 67:1891–1914.

Garcia-Coll, C., and Szalacha, L. A. 2004. The multiple contexts of middle childhood. *The Future of Children* 14:81–97.

Garland, A. F., Lau, A. S., Yeh, M., McCabe, K. M., Landsverk, J. A. 2005. Racial and ethnic differences in utilization of mental health services among high-risk youths. *American Journal of Psychiatry* 162:1336–1343.

Gay, G. 2000. *Culturally responsive teaching*. New York: Teachers College Press.

———. 2002. Preparing for culturally responsive teaching. *Journal of Teacher Education* 53:106–116.

Gayles, J. 2006. "Carrying it for the whole race": Achievement, race, and meaning among five high achieving African American men. *Journal of African American Studies* 10:19–32.

Gibbs, J. T. 1997. http://web.ebscohost.com/ehost/viewarticle?data=dGJyMPPp44rp2%2fdV0%2bnjisfk5Ie46bZMsqeuSLak63nn5Kx95uXxjL6trUutqK5ItZavSLiptlKurZ5Zy5zyit%2fk8Xnh6ueH7N%2fiVauor0ixqLNNrqyyPurX7H%2b72%2bw%2b4ti7ffDf4T7y1%2bVVv8Skeeyzw2Kzq7FMtKqkfu3o63nys%2bSN6uLSffbq&hid=15 African-American suicide: A cultural paradox. *Suicide and Life-Threatening Behavior* 27:68–79.

Gilmore, S., DeLamater, J., and Wagstaff, D. 1996. Sexual decision making by inner city Black adolescent males: A focus group study. *The Journal of Sex Research* 33:363–371.

Goldfarb, Z. A. 2014. President Obama to launch major new effort to help young men of color. The Washington Post. http://www.washingtonpost.com/politics/president-obama-to-launch-major-new-effort-on-young-men-of-color/2014/02/11.

Goodstein, R., and Ponterotto, J. G. 1997. Racial and ethnic identity: Their relationship and their contribution to self-esteem. *Journal of Black Psychology* 23:275–292.

Gordon, B. M. 2012. "Give a brotha a break!": The experiences and dilemmas of middle-class African American male students in White suburban schools. *Teachers College Record* 114:1–26.

Gordon, E. T., and Gordon, E. W., and Nembhard, J. G.G. 1994. Social science literature concerning African American men. *Journal of Negro Education* 63:508–531.

Graham, A., and Anderson, K. A. 2008. "I have to be three steps ahead": Academically gifted African American male students in an urban high school on the tension between an ethnic and academic identity. *Urban Review* 20:472–499.

Graham, S. 1994. Motivation in African Americans. *Review of Educational Research* 64:55–117.

Graham, S., Taylor, A. Z., and Hudley, C. 1998. Exploring achievement values among ethnic minority early adolescents. *Journal of Educational Psychology* 90:606–620.

Grantham, T. C. 2004. Multicultural mentoring to increase Black male representation in gifted programs. *Gifted Education Quarterly* 48:232–245.

———. 2011. New directions for gifted Black males suffering from bystander effects: A call for upstanders. *Roeper Review* 33:263–272.

Grayman-Simpson, N., and Mattis, J. S. 2013. Doing good and feeling good among African Americans: Subjective religiosity, helping, and satisfaction. *Journal of Black Psychology* 39:411–427.

Green, A. I. 2007. On the horns of a dilemma: Institutional dimensions of the sexual career in a sample of middle-class urban, Black, gay men. *Journal of Black Studies* 37:753–774.

Griffin, K. A., Jayakumar, U. M., Jones, M. M., and Allen, W. R. 2010. Ebony in the Ivory tower: Examining trends in the socioeconomic status, achievement, and self-concept of Black, male freshmen. *Equity and Excellence in Education* 43:232–248.

Griffin-Fennell, F., and Williams, M. 2006. Examining the complexities of suicidal behavior in the African American community. *Journal of Black Psychology* 32:303–319.

Grills, C., and Longshore, D. 1996. Africentrism: Psychometric analyses of a self-report measure. *Journal of Black Psychology* 22:86–106

Grimley, D. M., Hook, E. W., DiClemente, R. J., and Lee, P. A. 2004. Condom use among low-income African American males attending an STD clinic. *American Journal of Health Behavior* 28:33–42.

Grinstead, O. A., Peterson, J. L., Faigeles, B., and Catania, J. A. 1997. Antibody testing and condom use among heterosexual African Americans at risk for HIV infection: The National AIDS behavioral surveys. *American Journal of Public Health* 87:857–859.

Gullan, R. L., College, G., Hoffman, B. N., The Children's Hospital of Philadelphia, and Leff, S. S. 2011. "I do, but I don't": The search for identity in urban African American adolescents. *Perspectives on Urban Education*, 29–40.

Guthrie, R. V. 2003. *Even the rat was White. A historical view of psychology*. New York: Pearson.

Guyll, M., Matthews, K. A., and Bromberger, J. T. 2001. Discrimination and unfair treatment: Relationship to cardiovascular reactivity among African American and European American women. *Health Psychology* 20:315–325.

Hall, D. M., Cassidy, E. F., and Stevenson, H. C. 2008. Acting "tough" in a "tough" world: An examination of fear among urban African American adolescents. *Journal of Black Psychology* 34:381–398.

Hall, R. E. 1992. Bias among African Americans regarding skin color: Implications for social work practice. *Research on Social Work Practice* 2:479–486.

———. 1995. The bleaching syndrome: African Americans' response to cultural domination vis-à-vis skin color. *Journal of Black Studies* 26:172–184.

———. 2007. Racism as health risk for African American males: Correlations between hypertension and skin color. *Journal of African American Studies* 11:204–213.

Hall, R. E., and Pizarro, J. M. 2010. Unemployment as conduit of Black self-hate: Pathogenic rates of Black male homicide via legacy of the Antebellum. *Journal of Black Studies* 40:653–665.

———. 2011. Cool pose: Black male homicide and the social implications of manhood. *Journal of Social Service Research* 37:86–98.

Halpin, S. A., and Allen, M. W. 2004. Changes in psychosocial well-being during stages of gay identity development. *Journal of Homosexuality* 47:109–126.

Hammond, W. P., and Mattis, J. S. 2005. Being a man about it: Manhood meaning among African American men. *Psychology of Men and Masculinity* 6:114–126.

Harackiewicz, J. M., Barron, K. E., and Elliot, A. J. 1998. Rethinking achievement goals: When are they adaptive for college students and why? *Educational Psychologist* 33:1–21.

Harper, B. E., and Tuckman, B. W. 2006. Racial identity beliefs and academic achievement: Does being Black hold students back? *Social Psychology of Education* 9:381–403.

Harper, C. E. (2011) Identity, intersectionality, and mixed-methods approaches. *New Directions for Institutional Research* 151:103–115.

Harper, S. R. 2005. Inside the experiences of high-achieving African American male students. *About Campus*, 8–15.

———. 2006. Peer support for African American male college achievement: Beyond internalized racism and the burden of "acting White." *The Journal of Men's Studies* 14:337–358.

———. 2009. Niggers no more: A critical race counternarrative on Black male student achievement at predominantly White colleges and universities. *International Journal of Qualitative Studies in Education* 22:697–712.

Harper, S. R., and Davis III, C. H. F. 2012. They (don't) care about education: A counternarrative on Black male students' responses to inequitable schooling. *Educational Foundations,*

Harper, S. R., and Griffin, K. A. 2010. Opportunity beyond affirmative action: How low-income and working-class black male achievers access highly selective, high-cost colleges and universities. *Harvard Journal of African American Public Policy* 17:43–60.

Harrell, J. P., Hall, S., Taliaferro, J. 2003. Physiological responses to racism and discrimination: An assessment of the evidence. *American Journal of Public Health* 93:243–248.

Harrell, S. P. 2000. A multidimensional conceptualization of racism-related stress: Implications for the well-being of people of color. *American Journal of Orthopsychiatry* 70:42–57.

Harris, A. L. 2006. I (don't) hate school: Revisiting oppositional culture theory of Blacks' resistance to schooling. *Social Forces* 85:797–834.

———. 2008. Optimism in the face of despair: Black-White differences in beliefs about school as a means for upward social mobility. *Social Science Quarterly* 89:608–630.

———. 2010. Is a raceless identity an effective strategy for academic success among Blacks? *Social Science Quarterly* 91:1242–1263.

Harris, F., Palmer, R. T., Struve, L. E. 2011. "Cool posing" on campus: A qualitative study of masculinities and gender expression among Black men at a private research institution. *Journal of Negro Education* 80:47–62.

Harris, O. 1997. The role of sport in the Black community. *Sociological Focus* 30:311–319.

Harris, S. M. 1995. Psychosocial development and black male masculinity: Implications for counseling economically disadvantaged African American male adolescents. *Journal of Counseling and Development* 73:279–287.

———. 2002. Father absence in the African American community: Towards a new paradigm. *Race, Gender, and Class* 9:111–133.

Harris-Britt, A., Valrie, C. R., Kurtz-Coates, B., and Rowley, S. J. 2007. Perceived racial discrimination and self-esteem in African American youth: Racial socialization as a protective factor. *Journal of Research on Adolescence* 17:669–682.

Harrison, C. K. 1998. Themes that thread through society: Racism and athletic manifestation in the African American community. *Race, Ethnicity, and Education* 1:63–74.

———. 2008. Athleticated versus educated: A qualitative investigation of campus perceptions, recruiting, and African American male student-athletes. *Challenge: A Journal of Research on African American Men* 14:39–60.

Harrison, L. A., and Esqueda, C. W. 2000. Race stereotypes and perceptions about Black males involved in interpersonal violence. *Journal of African American Men,* 81–92.

Harrison, L., Sailes, G., Rotich, W. K., and Bimper, A. 2011. Living the dream or awakening from the nightmare: Race and athletic identity. *Race, Ethnicity, and Education* 14:91–103.

Harrison, M. S., and Thomas, K. M. (2009) The hidden prejudice in selection: A research investigation on skin color bias. *Journal of Applied Social Psychology* 39:134–168.

Harvey, A. R. 2004. The plight of the African American male in the United States: An Africentric human service provider analysis and intervention strategy. *Journal of African American Studies* 8:37–51.

Harvey, I. S., and Silverman, M. 2007. The role of spirituality in the self-management of chronic illness among older African Americans and Whites. *Journal of Cross Cultural Gerontology* 22:205–220.

Hauser-Cram, P., Sirin, S. R., and Stipek, D. 2003. When teachers' and parents' values differ: Teachers' ratings of academic competence in children from low-income families. *Journal of Educational Psychology* 95:813–820.

Hawkins, R. 1992. *Athletic investment and academic resilience among African American females and males in the middle grades.* Urban Child Research Center. Cleveland, Oh: CSU.

Helms, J. E. 1989. Considering some methodological issues in racial identity counseling research. *The Counseling Psychologist* 17:227–252.

———. 1990. *Black and White racial identity: Theory, research, and practice.* Westport, CT: Greenwood.

———. 1997. Implications of Behrens (1997) for the validity of the White Racial Identity Attitude Scale. *Journal of Counseling Psychology* 44:13–16.

———. 2007. Some better practices for measuring racial and ethnic identity constructs. *Journal of Counseling Psychology* 54:235–246.

Helms, J. E., Jernigan, M., and Mascher, J. 2005. The meaning of race in psychology and how to change it: A methodological perspective. *American Psychologist* 60:27–36.

Helms, J. E., and Parham, T. A. 1996. The development of the racial identity attitude scale, In R. L. Jones (Ed.), *Handbook of tests and measurement for Black populations.* Berkeley, CA: Cobb and Henry.

Helms, J. E., and Talleyrand, R. M. 1997. Race is not ethnicity. *American Psychologist,* 1246–1247.

Heinzmann, D. 2012. *Homicide numbers reveal stark contrast: African Americans hardest hit by spike in violence, deaths in Chicago.* http://articles.chicagotribune.com/2012-07-12/news/ct-met-chicago.

Henfield, M. S. 2011. Black male adolescents navigating micro aggressions in a traditionally White middle school: A qualitative study. *Journal of Multicultural Counseling and Development* 39:141–155.

Herek, G. M., and Capitanio, J. P. 1995. http://web.ebscohost.com/ehost/viewarticle?data=dGJyMPPp44rp2%2fdV0%2bnjisfk5Ie46bZMsqeuSLak63nn5Kx95uXxjL6trU utqK5ItZavSLiptlKurZ5Zy5zyit%2fk8Xnh6ueH7N%2fiVauor0ixqLNNrqyyPurX7H%2b72%2bw%2b4ti7ee7epIzf3btZzJzfhruvs0i3p7ZMt6uuPuTl8IXf6rt%2b8%2bLqb OPu8gAA&hid=15 Black heterosexuals' attitudes toward lesbians and gay men in the United States. *Journal of Sex Research* 32:95–105.

Herek, G. M., and Glunt, E. K. 1993. Interpersonal contact and heterosexuals' attitudes toward gay men: Results from a national survey. *Journal of Sex Research* 30:239–244.

Herndon, M. K. 2003. Expressions of spirituality among African American college males. *Journal of Men's Studies* 12:75–86.

Hill, M. E. 2000. Color differences in the socioeconomic status of African American men: Results of a longitudinal study. *Social Forces* 78:1437–1460.

———. 2002a. Skin color and the perception of attractiveness among African Americans: Does gender make a difference? *Social Psychology Quarterly* 65:77–91.

———. 2002b. Skin color and intelligence in African Americans: A reanalysis of Lynn's data. *Population and Environment* 24:209–218.

Hill, S. A. 1999. *African American children: Socialization and development in families.* Thousand Oaks, CA: Sage Publications.

Hill, S. A., and Sprague, J. 1999. Parenting in Black and White families: The interaction of gender with race and class. *Gender and Society* 13:480–502.

Hines, E. M., and Holcomb-McCoy, C. 2013. Parental characteristics, ecological factors, and the academic achievement of African American males. *Journal of Counseling and Development* 91:68–77.

Hochschild, J. 2006. When do people not protest unfairness? The case of skin color discrimination. *Social Research* 73:473–498.

Hochschild, J. L., and Weaver, V. 2007. The skin color paradox and the American racial order. *Social Forces* 86:643–670.

Hoffman, R. M. 2004. Conceptualizing heterosexual identity development: Issues and challenges. *Journal of Counseling and Development* 82:375–380.

Hollins, E. R., and Spencer, K. 1990. Restructuring schools for cultural inclusion: Changing the schooling process for African American youngsters. *Journal of Education* 172:89–100.

Holmes, K. J., and Lochman, J. E. 2009. Ethnic identity in African American and European American preadolescents: Relation to self-worth, social goals, and aggression. *The Journal of Early Adolescence* 29:476–496.

Holt, C. L., Wang, M. Q., Caplan, L., Schulz, E., Blake, V., Southward, V. L. 2011. Role of religious involvement and spirituality in functioning among African Americans with cancer: Testing a meditational model. *Journal of Behavioral Modification* 34:437–448.

Holt, C. L., Wynn, T. A., Litaker, M. S., Southward, P., Jeames, S., and Schulz, E. 2009. A comparison of a spiritually based and non-spiritually based educational intervention for informed decision making for prostate cancer screening among church-attending African American men. *Urologic Nursing* 29:249–258.

Honora, D. 2003. Urban African American adolescents and school identification. *Urban Education* 38:58–72.

Hopkins, D. N. 2002. A new Black homosexual male. *Black Theology in Britain* 4:214–227.

Horvat, E. M., and Lewis, K. S. 2003. Reassessing the "Burden of Acting White": The importance of peer groups in managing academic success. *Sociology of Education* 76:265–280.

Houle J. L.W., Brewer, B. W., Kluck, A. S. 2005. Developmental trends in athletic identity: A two-part retrospective study. *Journal of Sport Behavior*, 146–159.

Howard, M., Davis, J., Evans-Ray, D., Mitchell, M., and Apomah, M. 2004. Young males' sexual education and health services. *American Journal of Public Health* 94:1332–1335.

Howard, T. C. 2001. Telling their side of the story: African-American students' perceptions of culturally relevant teaching. *The Urban Review* 33:131–149.

———. 2002. Hearing footsteps in the dark: African American Students' descriptions of effective teachers. *Journal of Education for Students Placed At Risk* 7:425–444.

———. 2008. Who really cares? The disenfranchisement of African American males in PreK-12 schools: A critical race theory perspective, *Teachers College Record* 110:954–985.

Howard, T.C. (2013). How does it feel to be a problem? Black male students, schools, and learning in enhancing the knowledge base to disrupt deficit frameworks. *Review of Research in Education*, 37, 54–86.

Howard, T. C., Flennaugh, T. K., and Terry, C. L. 2012. Black males, social imagery, and the disruption of pathological identities: Implications for research and teaching. *Educational Foundations* 26:85–102.

Hoyt, E. H., Schiraldi, V., Smith, B. V., and Ziedenberg, J. 2002. Pathways to juvenile detention reform: Reducing racial disparities in juvenile detention. http://www.justicepolicy.org/reports/Pathway8.pdf.

Hudley, C., and Graham, S. 2001. Stereotypes of achievement striving among early adolescents. *Social Psychology of Education: An International Journal* 5:201–224.

Huebner, D. M., and Davis, M. C. 2007. Perceived antigay discrimination and physical health outcomes. *Health Psychology* 26:627–634.

Hughes, A., and Saxton, P. 2006. Geographic micro-clustering of homosexual men: Implications for research and social policy. *Social Policy Journal of New Zealand* 28:158–178.

Hughes, D., Rodriguez, J., Smith, E. P., Johnson, D. J., Stevenson, H. C., and Spicer, P. 2006. Parents' ethnic-racial socialization practices: A review of research and directions for future study. *Developmental Psychology* 42:747–770.

Hunter, A. G., and Davis, J. E. 1994. Hidden voices of Black men: The meaning, structure, and complexity of manhood. *Journal of Black Studies* 25:20–40.

Hunter, M. A. 2010. All the gays are white and all the blacks are straight: Black gay men, identity and community. *Sex Research and Social Policy* 7:81–92.

Hunter, M. L. 2002. "If you're light, you're alright": Light skin color as social capital for women of color. *Gender and Society* 16:175–193.

Hurley, E. A., Boykin, A. W., and Allen, B. A. 2005. Communal versus individual learning of a math-estimation task: African American children and the culture of learning contexts. *The Journal of Psychology* 139:513–527.

Hurtado, S., Inkelas, K. K., Briggs, C., and Rhee, B. 1997. Differences in college access and choice among racial/ethnic groups. Identifying continuing barriers. *Research in Higher Education* 38:43–75.

Hwang, Y. S., Echols, C., and Vrongistinos, K. 2002. Multidimensional academicmotivation of high achieving African American students. *College Student Journal* 36:544–554.

Icard, L. 1986. http://web.ebscohost.com/ehost/viewarticle?data=dGJyMPPp44rp2% 2fdV0%2bnjisfk5Ie46bZMsqeuSLak63nn5Kx95uXxjL6trUutqK5ItZavSrintFKxr55oy 5zyit%2fk8Xnh6ueH7N%2fiVauor0ixqLNNrqyyPurX7H%2b72%2bw%2b4ti7iPHv 5j7y1%2bVVv8Skeeyzr1G2ratLr6iwSaumrkmk3O2K69fyVeTr6oTS2%2faM&hid=15 Black gay men and conflicting social identities: Sexual orientation versus racial identity. *Journal of Social Work and Human Sexuality* 4:83–93.

Irvine, J. J. 1985. Teacher communication patterns as related to the race and sex of the student. *Journal of Educational Research* 78:338–345.

Irving, M. A., and Hudley, C. 2005. Cultural mistrust, academic outcome expectations, and outcome values among African American adolescent men. *Urban Education* 40:476–496.

———. 2008. Cultural identification and academic achievement among African American males. *Journal of Advanced Academics* 19:676–698.

Isom, D. A. 2007. "Performance, resistance, caring: Racialized gender identity in African American boys." *The Urban Review* 39:405–423.

Ispa-Landa, S. (2013). Gender, race, and justifications for group exclusion: Urban Black Students bussed to affluent suburban schools. *Sociology of Education,* 86, 218–233.

Jackson, C. C., and Neville, H. A. 1998. Influence of racial identity attitudes on African American college students' vocational identity and hope. *Journal of Vocational Behavior* 53:97–113.

Jagers, R. J., and Mock, L. O. 1993. Culture and social outcomes among inner-city African American children: An Afrographic exploration. *Journal of Black Psychology* 19:391–405.

———. 1995. The communalism scale and collectivistic-individualistic tendencies: Some preliminary findings. *Journal of Black Psychology* 21:153–167.

James, C. E. 2011. Students "at risk"" Stereotypes and the schooling of Black boys. *Urban Education*, 1–31.

James, J. 2003. TRIOS: A psychological theory of the African legacy in American culture. *Journal of Social Issues* 59:217–242.

Jamil, O. B., Harper, G. W., Fernandez, M. I., and Adolescent Trials Network for HIV/ AIDS Interventions. Sexual and ethnic identity development among Gay-Bisexual-Questioning (GBQ) male ethnic minority adolescents. *Psychology of Men and Masculinity* 15:203–214.

Jamison, D. R. 2006. The relationship between African Self-Consciousness, cultural misorientation, hypermasculinity, and rap music preference, *Journal of African American Studies* 9:45–60

Jenkins, T. S. 2013. A beautiful mind: Black male intellectual identity and hip-hop culture. *Journal of Black Studies* 42:231–251.

Jett, C. C. 2010. "Many are called, but few are chosen": The role of spirituality and religion in the educational outcomes of "chosen" African American male athematics majors. *The Journal of Negro Education* 79:324–334.

Joe, E. M., and Davis, J. E. 2009. Parental influence, school readiness, and early academic achievement of African American boys. *Journal of Negro Education* 78:260–276.

Joe, S., and Marcus, S. C. 2003. Trends by race and gener in suicide attempts among U.S. adolescents, 1991–2001. *Psychiatric Services* 54:454.

Joe, S., Marcus, S. C., and Kaplan, M. S. 2007. Racial differences in the characteristics of firearm suicide decedent in the United States. *American Journal of Orthopsychiatry* 77:124–130.

Johnson, B. 2010. Toward an anti-sexist black American male identity. *Psychology of Men and Masculinity* 11:182–194.

Johnson, E. P. 2003. The specter of the Black fag: Parody, Blackness and hetero/homosexual B(r)others. *Journal of Homosexuality* 45:217–234.

Johnson, J. 2011. The state of today's Black men. *Ebony* 66:100–102.

Johnson, S. C., and Arbona, C. 2006. The relation of ethnic identity, racial identity, and race-related stress among African American college students. *Journal of College Student Development* 47:495–507.

Johnson, T. S., and Migliaccio, T. A. 2009. The social construction of an athlete: African American boy's experience in sport. *The Western Journal of Black Studies* 33:98–106.

Johnson, V. D. 2003. A comparison of European and African-based psychologies and their implications for African American college student development. *Journal of Black Studies* 33:817–829.

Johnson, W. E. 2010. *Social work with African American males: Health, mental health, and social policy.* Oxford University Press, New York, NY.

Jones, J. M. 1997. *Prejudice and racism* (2nd ed.). New York: McGraw-Hill.

———. 2003. TRIOS: A psychological theory of the African legacy in American culture. *Journal of Social Issues* 59:217–242.

Jones, S. R. 2009. Constructing identities at the intersections: An autoethnographic exploration of multiple dimensions of identity. *Journal of College Student Development* 50:287–304.

Jones, S. R., Kim, Y. C., and Skendall, K. C. 2012. (Re-)framing authenticity: Considering multiple social identities using autoethnographic and intersectional approaches. *The Journal of Higher Education* 83:698–723.

Jones, S. R., and McEwan, M. K. 2000. A conceptual model of multiple dimensions of identity. *Journal of College Student Development* 41:405–414.

Kambon, K. 1996. The African self-consciousness scale. In R. L. Jones (Ed.), *A handbook of tests and measurements for Black populations.* Hampton, VA: Cobb and Henry Publishers.

———. *The Cultural Misorientation Scale manual.* Tallahassee, Fl. Florida Agricultural and Mechanical University.

Karenga, M. 1998. *Kwanzaa: A celebration of family, community, and culture:* Los Angeles, CA: University of Sankore Press.

Kashima, Y., Gurumurthy, A. K., Ouschan, L., Chong, and Mattingly, J. 2007. Connectionism and self: James, Mead, and the stream of enculturated consciousness. *Psychological Inquiry* 18:73–96.

Kelly, L. L. 2013. Hip-hop literature: The politics, poetics, and power of hip-hop in the English classroom. *English Journal* 102:51–56.

Kendrick, L., Anderson, N. L.R., and Moore, B. 2007. Perceptions of depression among young African American men. *Family and Community Health* 30:63–73.

Kennedy, S. B., Nolen, S., Applewhite, J. Pan, Z., Shamblen, S., and Vanderhoff, K. J. 2007. A quantitative study on the condom-use behaviors of eighteen-to twenty-four-year old urban African American males. *AIDS Patient Care and STDs* 21:306–320.

Kessler, R. C., Mickelson, K. D., and Williams, D. R. 1999. The prevalence, distribution, and mental health correlates of perceived discrimination in the United States. *Journal of Health and Social Behavior* 40:208–230.

Kim, B. S. K., Li, L. C., and Ng, G. F. 2005. The Asian American Values Scale–Multidimensional: Development, reliability, and validity. *Cultural Diversity and Ethnic Minority Psychology* 11:187–201.

King, A. E. O., and Allen, T. T. 2009. Personal characteristics of the ideal African American marriage partner. *Journal of Black Studies* 39:570–588.

King, C. S. 1987. *The words of Martin Luther King, Jr.* New York: Newmarket Press.

King, J. L. 2004. http://www.oprah.com/tows/booksseen/200404/tows_book_20040416_jking.jhtmlOn the down low: A journey into the lives of "straight" black men who sleep with men.

Kirschenman, J., and Neckerman, K. M. 1998. We'd love to hire them, but... In A. S. Wharton (ed.), *Continuity, conflict, and and change*. Mountain view, CA: Mayfield.

Kistner, J. A., David, C. F., and White, B. A. 2003. http://web.ebscohost.com/ehost/viewarticle?data=dGJyMPPp44rp2%2fdV0%2bnjisfk5Ie46bZMsqeuSLak63nn5Kx9 5uXxjL6trUqtqK5ItZawUq%2bvuEiuls5lpOrweezp33vy3%2b2G59q7UbeurlCxq7Z RpOLfhuWz44ak2uBV3%2bbmPvLX5VW%2fxKR57LOvSLapr1C2q6R%2b7ejrefKz 5I3q4tJ99uoA&hid=8 Ethnic and sex differences in children's depressive symptoms: Mediating effects of perceived and actual competence. *Journal of Clinical Child and Adolescent Psychology* 32:341–351.

Kitwana, B. 2002. *The hip-hop generation: Young Blacks and the crisis in African American culture*. New York: Basic Civitas Books.

Klem, L. 1995. Structural equation modeling. In L. G. Grimm and P. R. Yarnold (Ed.), *Reading and understanding more multivariate statistics*. Washington DC: American Psychological Association.

Klonoff, E. A., and Landrine, H. 1999. Revising and improving the African American Acculturation Scale. *Journal of Black Psychology* 26:235–261.

Klonoff, E. A., Landrine, H., and Ullman, J. B. 1999. Racial discrimination and psychiatric symptoms among Blacks. *Cultural Diversity and Ethnic Minority Psychology* 5:329–339.

Kogan, S. M., Lei, M., Grange, C. R., Simons, R. L., Brody, G. H., Gibbons, F. X., and Chen, Y. 2013. The contribution of community and family contexts to African American young adults' romantic relationship health: A prospective analysis. *Journal of Youth and Adolescence* 42:878–890.

Kohatsu, E. L., and Richardson, T. Q. 1996. Racial and ethnic identity assessment. In L. A. Suzuki, P. J. Meller, and J. G. Ponterotto (Eds.), *Handbook of multicultural assessment: Clinical, psychological and educational applications* (pp. 611–650). San Francisco: Jossey-Bass.

Kohlberg, L. A. 1966. A cognitive-developmental analysis of children's sex role concepts and attitudes. In E. E. Maccoby (Ed.), *The development of sex differences*, (pp.82–173). Stanford, CA: Stanford University Press.

Kowalski, R. M. 2000. Including gender, race and ethnicity in psychology content courses. *Teaching of Psychology* 27:18–24.

Krieger, N., and Sidney, S. 1996. Racial discrimination and blood pressure: The CARDIA study of young Black and White adults. *American Journal of Public Health* 86:1370–1378.

Kubrin, C. E., Wadsworth, T., and DiPietro, S. 2006. Deindustrialization, disadvantage, and suicide among young Black males. *Social Forces* 84:1559–1579.

Kulkin, H. S., Chauvin, E. A., and Percle, G. A. 2000. Suicide among gay and lesbian adolescents and young adults: A review of the literature. *Journal of Homosexuality* 40:1–29.

Ladson-Billings, G. 2005. Is the team all right? *Journal of Teacher Education* 56:229–234.

———. 2011. Boyz to men: Teaching to restore Black boys' childhood. *Race, Ethnicity, and Education* 14:7–15.

Lapchick, R. 1982. *The Black athlete in contemporary American sport*. Paper presented at the annual meeting of the North American Society for the Sociology of Sport. Boston, November.

Lee, C. 2001. Is October Brown Chinese? A cultural modeling activity system for underachieving students. *American Educational Research Journal* 38:97–143.

Lee, C., and Slaughter-Defoe, D. 1995. Historical and sociocultural influences on African American education. In J. A. Banks and C. M. Banks (Eds.), *Handbook of research on multicultural education* (pp. 348–371). New York: Macmillan.

Lemelle, A. J., and Battle, J. 2004. Black masculinity matters in attitudes towards gay males. *Journal of Homosexuality* 47:39–51.

Lemon, R. L., and Waehler, C. A. 1996. A test of stability and construct validity of the Black Racial Identity Attitude scale, form B and the White Racial Identity Attitude scale. *Measurement and Evaluation in Counseling and Development* 29:77–86.

Letiecq, B. L. 2007. African American fathering in violent neighborhoods: What role does spirituality play? *Fathering* 5:111–128.

Lewis, D. K. 1975. The black family: Socialization and sex roles. *Phylon* 36:221–237.

Lewis, L. M. 2008. Spiritual assessment in African Americans: A review of measures of spirituality used in health research. *Journal of Religious Health* 47:458–475.

Lindberg, C., Lewis-Spruill, C., and Crownover, R. 2006. Barriers to sexual and reproductive health care: Urban male adolescents speak out. *Issues in Comprehensive Pediatric Nursing* 29:73–88.

Lindsey, M. A., Joe, S., and Nebbitt, V. 2010. Family matters: The role of mental health stigma and social support on depressive symptoms and subsequent help-seeking among African American boys. *Journal of Black Psychology*,

Lindsey, M. A., Korr, W. S., Broitman, M., Bone, L., Green, A., and Leaf, P. J. 2006. Help-seeking behaviors and depression among African-American adolescents boys. *Social Work* 51:49–58.

Littrell, J., and Beck, E. 2000. http://web.ebscohost.com/ehost/viewarticle?data=dGJyMPPp44rp2%2fdV0%2bnjisfk5Ie46bZMsqeuSLak63nn5Kx95uXxjL6trUqtqK5ItZawUq%2bvuEiuls5lpOrweezp33vy3%2b2G59q7UbeurlCxq7ZRpOLfhuWz44ak2uBV3%2bbmPvLX5VW%2fxKR57LOzT6%2busUywnOSH8OPfjLvc84TqyuOQ8gAA&hid=8 Do inner-city, African-American males exhibit 'bad attitudes' toward work? *Journal of Sociology and Social Welfare* 27:3–24.

Lockett, C. T., and Harrell, J. P. 2003. Racial identity, self-esteem, and academic achievement: Too much interpretation, too little supporting data. *Journal of Black Psychology* 29:325–336.

Loiacano, D. K. 1989. Gay identity issues among Black Americans: Racism, homophobia, and the need for validation. *Journal of Counseling and Development: JCD* 68:21–25.

Loewen, J. 2008. *Lies my teacher told me. Everything your American history textbook got wrong.* New York: Touchstone.

Lynn, M., Bacon, J. N., Totten, T. L., Bridges, T. L., and Jennings, M. 2010. Examining teachers' beliefs about African American male students in a low-performing high school in an African American school district. *Teachers College Record* 112:289–330.

Maddox, K. B. 2004. Perspectives on racial phenotypicality bias. *Personality and Social Psychology Review* 8:383–401.

Maddox, K. B., and Gray, S. A. 2002. Cognitive representations of Black Americans: Re-exploring the role of skin tone. *Personality and Social Psychology Bulletin,28*, 250–259.

Madhubuti, H. R. (1991) *Black men: Obsolete, single, dangerous? The Afrikan American family in transition.* Third World Press: Chicago, IL.

Mahalik, J. R., Locke, B. D., Ludlow, L. H., Diemer, M. A., Scott, R. A., Gottfried, M., and Freitas, G. 2003. Development of the Conformity to Masculine Norms Inventory. *Psychology of Men and Masculinity* 4:3–25.

Majors, R., and Billson, J. M. 1992. *Cool pose: The dilemmas of Black manhood in America.* New York: Lexington Books.

Maliski, S. L., Connor, S. E., Williams, L., and Litwin, M. S. 2010. Faith among low-income, African Ameircan/Black men treated for prostate cancer. *Cancer Nursing* 33:470–478.

Mandara, J. 2006. The impact of family functioning on African American males' academic achievement: A review and clarification of the empirical literature. *Teachers College Record* 108:206–223

Mandara, J., and Murray, C. B. 2006. Father's absence and African American adolescent drug use. *Journal of Divorce and Remarriage* 46:1–12.

Mandara, J., Murray, C. B., and Joyner, T. N. 2005. The impact of fathers' absence on African American adolescents' gender role development. *Sex Roles* 53:207–220.

http://www.garfield.library.upenn.edu/classics1984/A1984TR91100001.pdf Marcia, J. E. 1966. Development and validation of ego identity status.http://en.wikipedia.org/wiki/Journal_of_Personality_and_Social_Psychology *Journal of Personality and Social Psychology* 3:551–558.

———. 1980. Identity in adolescence. In J. Adelson, (Ed.), *Handbook of adolescent psychology* (pp. 159–187). New York: Wiley.

Marks, B. Settles, I. H., Cooke, D. Y., Morgan, L., and Sellers, R. M. 1996. African American racial identity: A review of contemporary models and measures. In R. L.Jones, *Handbook of Tests and Measurements for Black Populations* (pp. 383–404). Hampton, Va: Cobb and Henry.

Marryshow, D., Hurley, E. A., Allen, B. A., Tyler, K. M., and Boykin, A. W. 2005. The impact of learning orientation on African American children's attitudes toward high achieving peers. *American Journal of Psychology* 118:603–618.

Martin, B., Harrison, C. K., and Bukstein, S. 2010. "It takes a village" for African American male scholar-athletes. *Journal for the Study of Sports and Athletes in Education* 4:277–296.

Martin, B. E., Harrison, C. K., Stone, J., and Lawrence, S. M. 2010. Athletic voices and academic victories: A phenomenological investigation of African American male student-athlete academic experiences. *Journal for Sport and Social Issues.*

Martin, C. L., Ruble, D. N., and Szkrybalo, J. 2002. Cognitive theories of early gender development. *Psychological Bulletin* 128:903–933.

Mattis, J. S. 2000. African American women's definitions of spirituality and religiosity. *Journal of Black Psychology* 26:101–122.

Mattis, J. S., Beckham, W. P., Saunders, B. A., Williams, J. E., McAllister, D., Myers, V., et al. 2004. Who will volunteer: Religiosity, everyday racism, and social participation among African American men. *Journal of Adult Development* 11:261–272.

Mattis, J. S., Eubanks, K., Zapata, A. A., Grayman, N., Mitchell, N. K., and Cooper, S. 2004. Factors influencing religious non-attendance among African American men: A multimethod analysis. *Review of Religious Research* 45:386–403.

Mattis, J. S., Hearn, K. D., and Jagers, R. J. 2002. Factors predicting communal attitudes among African American men. *Journal of Black Psychology* 28:197–214.

Mattis, J. S., Murray, Y. F., Hatcher, C. A., Hearn, K. D., Lawhon, G. D., Murphy, E. J., and Washington, T. A. 2001. Religiosity, spirituality, and the subjective quality of African American men's friendships: An exploratory study. *Journal of Adult Development* 8:221–230.

May, V. M., Chatters, L. M., Cochran, S. D., and Mackness, J. 1998. African American families in diversity: Gay men and lesbians as participants in family networks. *Journal of Comparative Family Studies* 29:73–87.

Mays, V. M., Johnson, D., Coles, C. N., Gellene, D., Cochran, S. D. 2013. Using the science of psychology to target perpetrators of racism and race-based discrimination for intervention efforts: Preventign another Trayvon Martin tragedy. *Journal for Social Action in Counseling and Psychology* 5:11–36.

Mbiti, J. S. 1970. *African religions and philosophy.* New York: Doubleday.

McCall, L. 2005. The complexity of intersectionality. *Signs: Journal of Women in Culture and Society* 30:1771–1800.

McCready, L. T. 2004. Understanding the marginalization of gay and gender non-conforming Black male students. *Theory into Practice* 43:136–143.

McGee, E.D. (2013). Threatened and placed at risk: High achieving African American Males in Urban high schools. *Urban Review*, 45, 448–471

McGee, E., and Martin, D. B. 2011. From the hood to being hooded: A case study of a Black male PhD. *Journal of African American Males in Education* 2:46–65.

McMillian, M. M., Frierson, H. T., and Campbell, F. A. 2010. Do gender differences exist in the academic identification of African American elementary school-aged children? *Journal of Black Psychology*, 1–21.

McNeilly, M., Anderson N. B., Armstead C. A., Clark, R., Corbett, M., Robinson, E. L., Pieper C. F., and Lepisto, E. M. 1996. The perceived racism scale: A multidimensional assessment of the experience of white racism among African Americans. *Ethnicity Discourse* 6:154–166.

McWhorter, J. 2001. *Losing the Race: Self-Sabotage in Black America*. New York: Free Press.

Meece, J. L., Anderman E. M., and Anderman, L. H. (in press). Educational psychology: Structures and goals of educational settings. *Annual Review of Psychology, Vol. 56*. Stanford, CA: Annual Reviews.

Meece, J. L., Blumenfeld, P. C., and Hoyle, R. H. 1988. Students' goal orientations and cognitive engagement in classroom activities. *Journal of Educational Psychology* 80:514–523.

Melendez, M. C. 2008. Black football players on a predominantly White college campus: Psychological and emotional realities of the Black college athlete experience. *Journal of Black Psychology* 34:423–451.

Meyers, M. 2004. African American women and violence: Gender, race and class in the news. *Critical Studies in Media Communication* 21:95–118.

Miller, D. B. 1999. Racial socialization and racial identity: Can they promote resiliency for African American adolescents? *Adolescence* 34:1–14.

Miller, R. L. 2005. An appointment with God: AIDS, Place, and spirituality. *The Journal of Sex Research* 42:35–45.

———. 2007. Legacy denied: African American gay men, AIDS and the Black church. *Social Work* 52:51–61.

Miller-Cribbs, J. E., Cronen, S., Davis, L., and Johnson, S. D. 2002. An exploratory analysis of factor that school engagement and completion among African American students. *Children and Schools* 24:159–175.

Miller-Johnson, S., Winn, D. C., Coie, J. D., Malone, P. S., and Lochman, J. 2004. Risk factors for adolescent pregnancy reports among African American males. *Journal of Research on Adolescence* 14:471–495.

Milliones, J. 1980. Construction of a Black consciousness measure: Psycho-therapeutic implications. *Psychotherapy: Theory, Research, and Practice* 17:175–182.

Milner, H. R. 2006. Culture, race and spirit: a reflective model for the study of African Americans. *International Journal of Qualitative Studies in Education (QSE)* 19:367–385.

Mizell, A. C. 1999. Life course influences on African American men's depression: Adolescent parental composition, self-concept, and adult earnings. *Journal of Black Studies* 29:467–480.

Moemeka, A. A. 1998. Communalism as a fundamental dimension of culture. *Journal of Communication* 48:118–141.

Mohr, J. M. 2009. Oppression by scientific method: The use of science to "other" sexual minorities. *Journal of Hate Studies*, 21–45.

Moore, A. L. 2002. African-American early childhood teachers' decisions to refer African American students. *International Journal of Qualitative Studies in Education* 15:631–652.

Moore, S. E., Madison-Colmore, O., and Moore, J. L. 2003. An Afrocentric approach to substance abuse treatment with adolescent African American males: Two case examples. *The Western Journal of Black Studies* 27:219–230.

Morgan, H. 1980. How schools fail Black children. *Social Policy* 11:49–54.

Morrison, M. A., and Morrison, T. G. 2002. Development and validation of a scale measuring modern prejudice toward gay men and lesbian women. *Journal of Homosexuality* 43:15–37

Mosher, D., and Sirkin, M. 1984. Measuring a macho personality constellation. *Journal of Research in Personality* 18:150–163.

Moul, J. W. 1998. Prostate cancer in African American men. *Prostate Cancer and Prostatic Diseases* 1:109–118.

Moynihan, D. P. 1965. *The Negro family*. Washington, DC: Office of Policy Planning and Research, U.S. Department of Labor.

Mullins, E. I., and Sites, P. 1984. The origins of contemporary eminent Black Americans: A three-generation analysis of social origin. *American Sociological Review* 49:672–685.
Murry, V. M., Simons, R. L., Simons, L. G., and Gibbons, F. X. 2013. Contributions of family environment and parenting processes to sexual risk and substance use of rural African American males: A 4–year longitudinal analysis. *American Journal of Orthopsychiatry* 83:299–309.
Mutisya, P. M., and Ross, L. E. 2005. Afrocentricity and racial socialization among African American college students. *Journal of Black Studies* 38:235–247.
Myers, L. W. 2004. African American males speak: The lifelong process. *Journal of African American Studies* 8:62–68.
Nario-Redmond, M. R., Biernat, M., Eidelman, S., and Palenske, D. J. 92004). The social and personal identities scale: A measure of the differential importance ascribed to social and personal self-categorizations. *Self and Identity* 3:143–175.
Narvaez, R. F., Meyer, I. H., Kertzner, R. M., Ouellette, S. C., and Gordon, A. R. 2009. A qualitative approach to the intersection of sexual, ethnic, and gender identities. *Identity: An International Journal of Theory and Research* 9:63–86.
Nasco, S. A., and Webb, W. M. 2006. Toward an expanded measure of athletic identity: The inclusion of public and private dimensions. *Journal of Sport and Exercise Psychology* 28:434–453.
Nasir, N. S., McLaughlin, M. W., and Jones, A. 2009. What does it mean to be African American? Constructions of race and academic identity in an urban public high school. *American Educational Research Journal* 46:73–114.
Neal, L. I., McCray, A. D., Webb-Johnson, G., and Bridgest, S. T. 2003. The effects of African American movement styles on teachers' perceptions and reactions. *The Journal of Special Education* 37:49–57.
Neblett, E. W., Philip, C. L., Cogburn, C. D., and Sellers, R. M. 2006. African American adolescents' discrimination experiences and academic achievement: Racial socialization as a cultural compensatory and protective factor. *Journal of Black Psychology* 32:199–218.
Neville, H. A., Heppner, P. P., Ji, P., and Thye, R. 2004. The relations among general and race-related stressors and psychoeducational adjustment in Black students attending predominantly White institutions. *Journal of Black Studies* 34:599–618.
Neville, H., and Rom-Rymer, B. 2013. Taking a stand against racism: A time to act. American Psychological Association. http://www.peacepsych.org/newsletter.htm.
Niemi, N. S. 2005. The emperor has no clothes: Examining the impossible relationship between gendered and academic identities in middle school students. *Gender and Education* 17:483–497.
Nobles, W. W. 1991. African philosophy: Foundations of black psychology. In R. L. Jones (Ed.) *Black Psychology* (3rd. ed., pp. 180–192). Berkeley, CA: Cobb and Henry.
Noguera, P. A. 2003. The trouble with black boys: The role and influence of environmental and cultural factors on the academic performance of African American males. *Urban Education* 38:431–459.
Norton, N. E.L. (2008) Singing in the spirit: Spiritual practices inside public school classrooms. *Education and Urban Society* 40:342–360.
Nyborg, V. M., and Curry, J. F. 2003. The impact of perceived racism: Psychological symptoms among Black boys. *Journal of Clinical Child and Adolescent Psychology* 32:258–266.
Obama, B. H. 2004. *Dreams from my father: A story of race and inheritance*. New York: Three Rivers Press.
Ochse, R. and Plug, C. 1986. Cross-cultural investigation of the validity of Erikson's theory of personality development. *Journal of Personality and Social Psychology* 50:1240–1252.
O'Connor, C. 2001. Making sense of the complexity of social identity in relation to achievement: A sociological challenge in the new millennium. *Sociology of Education*, 159–168.

Ogbar, J. O.G., and Prashad, V. 2000. Black is back. *The Unesco Courier* 53:31–32.
Ogbu, J. 2003. *Black students in an affluent suburb: A study of academic disengagement.* New York: Lawrence Erlbaum.
———. 2004. Collective identity and the burden of "acting White" in Black history, community, and education. *The Urban Review* 36:1–35.
Okagaki, L. 2001. Triarchic model of minority children's school achievement. *Educational Psychologist* 36:9–20.
Okech, A. P., and Harrington, R. 2002. The relationships among Black consciousness, self-esteem, and academic self-efficacy in African American men. *The Journal of Psychology* 136:214–224.
Okeke, N. A., Howard, L. C., Kurtz-Costes, B., and Rowley, S. J. 2009. Academic race stereotypes, academic self-concept, and racial centrality in African American youth. *Journal of Black Psychology* 35:366–387.
Oliver, W. 1984. Black males and the tough guy image: A dysfunctional compensatory adaptation. *The Western Journal of Black Studies* 8:199–203.
———. 2006. "The streets": An alternative Black male socialization institution. *Journal of Black Studies* 36:918–937.
Olneck, M. 2006. Economic consequences of the academic achievement gap for African Americans. *Marquette Law Review* 89:95–104.
O'Neill, J. M., Helms, B. J., Gable, R. K., David, L., and Wrightsman, L. S. 1986. Gender role conflict scale: College men's fear of femininity. *Sex Roles* 14:335–350.
Oparanozie, A., Sales, J. M., DiClemente, R. J., and Braxton, N. D. 2013. Racial identity and risky sexual behaviors among Black heterosexual men. *Journal of Black Psychology* 38:32–51.
Ornelas, I. J., Arnell, J., Tran, A. N., Royster, M., Armstrong-Brown, J., and Eng, E. 2009. Understanding African American men's perceptions of racism, male gender socialization and social capital through photovoice. *Qualitative Health Research* 19:552–565.
Osborne, J. W. 1999. Unraveling underachievement among African American boys from an identification with academics perspective. *Journal of Negro Education* 68:555–565.
Osborne, J. W., and Jones, B. T. 2011. Identification with academics and motivation to achieve in school: How the structure of the self influences academic outcomes. *Educational Psychology Review* 23:131–158.
Oseguera, L. 2010. Success despite the image: How African American male student-athletes endure their academic journey amidst negative characterizations. *Journal for the Study of Sports and Athletes in Education* 4:297–324.
Oware, M. 2011. Brotherly love: Homosociality and Black masculinity in gangsta rap music. *Journal of African American Studies* 15:22–39.
———. 2012. Decent daddy, imperfect daddy: Black male rap artists' views of fatherhood and the family. *Journal of African American Studies* 15:327–351.
Owens, T. J., Robinson, D. T., and Smith-Lovin, L. 2010. Three faces of identity. *Annual Review of Sociology* 36:477–499.
Oyserman, D., Bybee, D., and Terry, K. 2003. Gendered racial identity and involvement with school. *Self and Identity* 2:307–324.
Oyserman, D., Coon, H. M., and Kemmelmeier, M. 2002. Rethinking individualism and collectivism: Evaluation of theoretical assumptions and meta-analyses. *Psychological Bulletin* 128:3–73.
Oyserman, D., Elmore, K., and Smith, G. 2012. Self, self-concept, and identity. In M. R. Leary and J. P. Tangery (2nd ed.), *Handbook of self and identity* (pp. 69–104). New York, NY: The Guilford Press.
Oyserman, D., Gant, L., and Ager, J. 1995. A socially contextualized model of African American identity: Possible selves and school persistence. *Journal of Personality and Social Psychology* 69:1216–1232.
Oyserman, D., Harrison, K., and Bybee, D. 2001. Can racial identity be promotive of academic efficacy? *International Journal of Behavioral Development* 25:379–385.

Page, H. E. 1997. "Black male" imagery and media containment of African American men. *American Anthropologist* 99:99–111.

Palmer, R. T., and Maramba, D. C. 2011. African American male achievement: Using a tenet of critical theory to explain the African American male achievement disparity. *Education and Urban Society* 43:431–450.

Pang, V., and Sablan, V. 1998. Teacher efficacy: How do teachers feel about their abilities to teach African American students? In M. Dilworth (Ed.), *Being responsive to cultural differences: How teachers learn* (pp.39–60). Thousand Oaks, CA: Corwin Press.

Parham, T. A. 1999. Invisibility syndrome in African descent people: Understanding the cultural manifestations of the struggle for self-affirmation. *The Counseling Psychologist* 27:794–801.

Parham, T., and Helms, J. E. 1981. The influence of Black students' racial identity attitudes on preferences for counselor's race. *Journal of Counseling Psychology* 28:250–257.

———. 1985. Relation of racial identity attitudes to self-actualization and affective states of Black students. *Journal of Counseling Psychology* 32:432–440.

Parsons, E. C. 2003. Culturalizing instruction: Creating a more inclusive context for learning for African American students. *The High School Journal* 86:23–30.

Paschall, M. J., Ringwalt, C. L., and Flewelling, R. L. 2003. Effects of parenting, father absence, and affiliation with delinquent peers on delinquent behavior among African-American male adolescents. *Adolescence* 38:15–34.

Pastrana, A. 2004. Black identity constructions: Inserting intersectionality, bisexuality, and (Afro-) Latinidad into Black studies. *Journal of African American Studies* 8:74–89.

Patchen, L. M., Bernstein, B. A., Szalacha, L. A., and Garcia-Coll, C. 2010. Perceived racism and discrimination in children and youths: An exploratory study. *Health and Social Work* 35:61–69.

Patchen, L. M., Szalacha, L. A., Bernstein, B. A., and Garcia-Coll, C. 2010. Perceptions of racism in children and youth (PRaCY): Properties of a self-report instrument for research on children's health and development. *Ethnicity and Health* 15:33–46.

Patton, L. D., and Simmons, S. L. 2008. Exploring complexities of multiple identities of lesbian in a Black college environment. *The Negro Educational Review* 59:197–215.

Patton, T. O., and Snyder-Yuly, J. 2007. Any four Black men will do: Rape, race, and the ultimate scapegoat. *Journal of Black Studies* 37:859–895.

Paxton, K. C., Robinson, W. L., Shah, S., and Schoeny, M. E. 2004. Psychological distress for African-American adolescent males: Exposure to community violence and social support as factors. *Child Psychiatry and Human Development* 34:281–295.

Payne, Y. A. 2008. "Street Life" as a site of resiliency: How street life-oriented Black men frame opportunity in the United States. *Journal of Black Psychology* 34:3–31.

Perna, L. W. 2000. Differences in the decision to enroll in college among African Americans, Hispanics, and Whites. *Journal of Higher Education* 71:117–141.

Peters, M. F. 1997. Parenting of young children in Black families. In H. P. McAdoo (Ed.), *Black families* (pp. 227–241). Newbury Park, CA: Sage Publications.

Peterson, E. (1992, September 2). What's so funny? http://www.webcom.com/~erique/writing/funny/html.

Pettit, B., and Western, B. 2004. Mass imprisonment and the life course: Race and class inequality in U.S. incarceration. *American Sociological Review* 69:151–169.

Pfeifer, C. M., and Sedlacek, W. E. 1974. Predicting black student grades with nonintellectual measures. *Journal of Negro Education*, 67–77.

Phelps, R. E., Taylor, J. D., and Gerard, P. A. 2001. Cultural mistrust, ethnic identity, racial identity, and self-esteem among ethnically diverse Black university students. *Journal of Counseling and Development* 79:209–216.

Phillips, J. A. 1997. Variation in African-American homicide rates: An assessment of potential explanations. *Criminology* 35:527–560.

Phinney, J. 1990. Ethnic identity in adolescents and adults: Review of research. *Psychological Bulletin* 108:499–514.

———. 1996. When we talk about American ethnic groups, what do we mean? *American Psychologist* 51:918–927.

Phinney, J., and Ong, A. D. 2007. Conceptualization and measurement of ethnic identity: Current status and future directions. *Journal of Counseling Psychology* 54:271–281.

Piaget, J., and Inhelder, B. 1969. *The psychology of the child*. Paris, France: Basic Books.

Pierre, M. R.and Mahalik, J. R. 2005. Examining African self-consciousness and Black racial identity as predictors of Black men's psychological well-being. *Cultural Diversity and Ethnic Minority Psychology* 11:28–40.

Pillay, Y. 2005. Racial identity as a predictor of the psychological health of African American students at a predominantly White university. *Journal of Black Psychology* 31:46–66.

Pintrich, P. R. 2000. Multiple goals, multiple pathways: The role of goal orientation in learning and achievement. *Journal of Educational Psychology* 92:544–555.

Polzer, R. L., and Miles, M. S. 2007. Spirituality in African Americans with diabetes: Self-management through a relationship with God. *Qualitative Health Research* 17:176–188.

Pope-Davis, D. B., Liu, W. M., Ledesma-Jones, S., and Nevitt, J. 2000. African American acculturation and Black racial identity. *Journal of Multicultural Counseling and Development* 28:41–52.

Price, J. N. 1998. Accommodation and critique in the school lives of six young African American men. *Curriculum Inquiry* 28:443–471.

Prier, D. 2008. A relevant Black male curriculum. *ENCOUNTER: Education for meaning and social justice*. 25–26.

Prier, D., and Beachum, F. 2008. Conceptualizing a critical discourse around hip-hop culture and Black male youth in educational scholarship and research. *International Journal of Qualitative Studies in Education* 21:519–535.

Raffaele Mendez, L. M., and Knoff, H. M. 2003. Who gets suspended from school and why: A demographic analysis of school and disciplinary infractions in a large school district. *Education and Treatment of Children* 26:30–32.

Ratele, K. 2003. We black men. *International Journal of Intercultural Relations* 27:237–249

Rattan, A., Levine, C. S., Dweck, C. S., and Eberhardt, J. L. 2012. Race and the fragility of the legal distinction between juveniles and adults. *PLoSONE 7*, 1–5.

Rebollo-Gil, G., and Moras, A. 2012. Black women and black men in hip hop music: Misogyny, violence, and the negotiation of (White-owned) space. *The Journal of Popular Culture* 45:118–132.

Reed, E., Silverman, J. G., Ickovics, J. R., Gupta, J., Welles, S. L., Santana, M. C., and Raj, A. 2010. Experiences of racial discrimination and relation to violence perpetration and gang involvement among a sample of urban African American men. *Journal of Immigrant Minority Health* 12:319–326.

Reese, L., Balzano, S., Gallimore, R., and Goldenberg, C. 1995. The concept of *educación*: Latino family values and American schooling. *International Journal of Educational Research* 23:57–81.

Reese, L., and Gallimore, R. 2000. Immigrant Latinos' cultural model of literacy development: An evolving perspective on home-school discontinuities. *American Journal of Education* 108:103–134.

Reid, P. T. 2002. Multicultural psychology: Bringing together gender and ethnicity. *Cultural Diversity and Ethnic Minority Psychology* 8:103–114.

Resnicow, K., Soler, R. E., Braithwaite, R. L., Selassie, M. B., and Smith, M. 1999. Development of a racial and ethnic identity scale for African American adolescents: The survey of Black life. *Journal of Black Psychology* 25:171–188.

Reynolds, A. L., and Pope, R. L. 1991. The complexities of diversity: Exploring multiple oppressions. *Journal of Counseling and Development* 70:174–180.

Reynolds, R. 2010. "They think you're lazy, " and other messages Black parents send their Black sons: An exploration of critical race theory in the examination of educational outcomes for Black males. *Journal of African American Males in Education* 1:144–163.

Rice, D. W. 2008. *Balance: Advancing identity theory by engaging the Black male adolescent.* Lexington Books, Lanham, MD.

Richardson, J. B. 2012. Beyond the playing field: Coaches as social capital for inner-city adolescent African-American males. *Journal of African American Studies* 16:171–194.

Riggins, R. K., McNeal, C., and Herndon, M. K. 2008. The role of spirituality among African American colleges males attending a historically Black university. *College Student Journal* 42:70–81.

Riina, E. M., Martin, A., Gardner, M., and Brooks-Gunn, J. 2013. Context matters: Links between neighborhood cohesion and African American adolescents' adjustment. *Journal of Youth and Adolescence* 42:136–146.

Rivas-Drake, D., Syed M., Umana-Taylor, A., Markstorm, C., French, S., Schwartz, S.J. and Lee, R (2014). Feeling good, happy, and proud: A meta-analysis of positive ethnic-racial affect and adjustment. Child Development, 85, 77–102.

Robinson, Q. L., and Werblow, J. 2012. Beating the odds: How single Black mothers influence the educational success of their sons enrolled in failing schools. *American Secondary Education* 40:52–66.

Robinson, T. 1993. The intersections of gender, class, race, and culture: On seeing clients whole. *Journal of Multicultural Counseling and Development* 21:50–58.

Robinson, T. L., and Ward, J. V. 1995. African American adolescents and skin color. *Journal of Black Psychology* 21:256–274.

Roderick, M. 2003. What's happening to the boys? Early high school experiences and school outcomes among African American male adolescents in Chicago. *Urban Education* 38:538–607.

Rodney, H. E., and Mupier, R. 1999. Behavioral differences between African American male adolescents with biological fathers and those without biological fathers in the home. *Journal of Black Studies* 30:45–61

Rodney, L. W., Crafter, B., Rodney, H. E., and Mupier, R. M. 1999. Variables contributing to grade retention among African American adolescent males. *The Journal of Educational Research* 92:185–190.

Rodriguez, J., Jones, E. B., Pang, V. O., and Park, C. D. 2004. Promoting academic achievement and identity development among diverse high school students. *The High School Journal* 87:44–54.

Rodriguez, M. S. 2008. Perceived discrimination: Multiple measures and the intersections of race and gender. *Journal of African American Studies* 12:348–365.

Rogoff, B. 2003. *The cultural nature of cognitive development.* Oxford University Press: New York.

Rogoff, B., and Chavajay, P. 1995. What's become of research on the cultural basis of cognitive development? *American Psychologist* 50:859–877.

Romero, A. J., and Roberts, R. E. 1998. Perception of discrimination and ethnocultural variables in a diverse group of adolescents. *Journal of Adolescence* 21:641–656.

Rosenthal, R. 1987. Pygmalion effects: Existence, magnitude, and social importance. *Educational Researcher* 16:37–41.

Rosenthal, R., and Jacobsen, L. 1968. *Pygmalion in the classroom: Teacher expectation and pupil's intellectual development.* New York: Holt, Rinehart, and Winston.

Ross, L. E. 1997. Mate selection preferences among African American college students. *Journal of Black Studies* 27:554–569.

Rotherman-Borus, M. J., Rosario, M., Van-Rossem, R., Reid, H., and Gillis, R. 1995. Prevalence, course, and predictors of multiple problem behaviors among gay and bisexual male adolescents. *Developmental Psychology* 31:75–85.

Rowley, S. J., Sellers, R. M., Chavous, T. M., and Smith, M. A. 1998. The relationship between racial identity and self-esteem in African American college and high school students. *Journal of Personality and Social Psychology* 74:715–724.

Roy, K. M., and Dyson, O. 2010. Making daddies into fathers: Community-based fatherhood programs and the construction of masculinities for low-income African American men. *American Journal of Community Psychology* 45:139–154.

Rushton, J. P., and Jensen, A. R. 2005. Thirty years of research on race differences in cognitive ability. *Psychology, Public Policy and Law* 11:235–294.

Sadler, M. S., Correll, J., Park, B., and Judd, C. M. 2012. The world is not Black and White: Racial bias in the decision to shoot in a multiethnic context. *Journal of Social Issues* 68:286–313.

Sailes, G. A. 1996. Betting against the odds: An overview of Black sports participation. *Journal of African American Men*, 11–22.

Sampson, E. E. 1977. Psychology and the American ideal. *Personality and Social Psychology* 35:767–782.

Sanchez, D., and Carter, R. T. 2005. Exploring the relationship between racial identity and religious orientation among African American college students. *Journal of College Student Development* 46:280–295.

Sanders-Thompson, V., and Akbar, M. 2003. The understanding of race and the construction of African American identity. *The Western Journal of Black Studies* 27:80–88.

Sankofa, B. M., Hurley, E. A., Allen, B. A., and Boykin, A. W. 2005. Cultural expression and black students' attitudes towards high achievers. *The Journal of Psychology* 139:247–259.

Santos, C. E., Galligan, K., Pahlke, E., and Fabes, R. A. 2013. Gender-typed behaviors, achievement, and adjustment among racially and ethnically diverse boys during early adolescence. *American Journal of Orthopsychiatry* 83:252–264.

Saunders, J., Davis, L., Williams, T., and Williams, J. H. 2004. Gender differences in self-perceptions and academic outcomes: A study of African American high school students. *Journal of Youth and Adolescence* 33:81–90.

Savin-Willams, R. C. 1994. Verbal and physical abuse as stressors in the lives of lesbian, gay male, and bisexual youths: Associations with school problems, running away, substance abuse, prostitution, and suicide. *Journal of Consulting and Clinical Psychology* 62:261–269.

———. 2001. A critique of research on sexual-minority youths. *Journal of Adolescence* 24:5–13.

Savin-Williams, R. C., and Ream, G. L. 2003. Suicide attempts among sexual-minority male youth. *Journal of Clinical Child and Adolescent Psychology* 32:509–522.

Schmader, T., Major, B., and Gramzow, R. H. 2001. Coping with ethnic stereotypes in the academic domain: Perceived injustice and psychological disengagement. *Journal of Social Issues* 57:93–111.

Schultz, E. L., Neyhart, K., and Reck, U. M. 1996. Swimming against the tide: A study of prospective teachers' attitudes regarding cultural diversity and urban teaching. *The Western Journal of Black Studies* 20:1–7.

Schwartz, S. 2001. The evolution of Eriksonian and Neo-Eriksonian identity theory and research: A review and integration. *Identity: An International Journal of Theory and Research* 1:7–58.

Scott, D. A., and Robinson, T. L. 2001. White male identity development: The Key model. *Journal of Counseling and Development* 79:415–421.

Scott, L. D. 2003a. The relation of racial identity and racial socialization to coping with discrimination among African American adolescents. *Journal of Black Studies* 33:520–538.

———. 2003b. Cultural orientation and coping with perceived discrimination among African American youth. *Journal of Black Psychology* 29:235–256.

Scott, L. D., and House, L. E. 2005. Relationship of distress and perceived control to coping with perceived racial discrimination among Black youth. *Journal of Black Psychology* 31:254–272.

Scott, L. D., Munson, M. R., McMillen, J. C., and Snowden, L. R. 2007. Predisposition to seek mental health care among Black males transitioning from foster care. *Children and Youth Services Review* 29:870–882.

Scottham, K. M., and Sellers, R. M. 2008. A measure of racial identity in African American adolescents: The development of the multidimensional inventory of Black identity—Teen. *Cultural Diversity and Ethnic Minority Psychology* 14:297–306.

Sealey-Ruiz, Y., and Greene, P. 2011. Embracing urban youth culture in the context of education. *Urban Review* 43:339–357.

Sears, J. T. 1989. Personal feelings and professional attitudes of prospective teachers toward homosexuality and homosexual students: Research findings and curriculum recommendations. ERIC Accession # ED312222

Seaton, E. K., Caldwell, C. H., Sellers, R. M., and Jackson, J. S. 2008. The prevalence of perceived discrimination among African American and Caribbean Black youth. *Developmental Psychology* 44:1288–1297.

Seaton, E. K., Neblett, E. W., Upton, R. D., Hammond, W. P., and Sellers, R. M. 2011. The moderating capacity of racial identity between perceived discrimination and psychological well-being over time among African American youth. *Child Development* 82:1850–1867.

Seaton, E. K., and Yip, T. 2009. School and neighborhood contexts, perceptions of racial discrimination, and psychological well-being among African American adolescents. *Journal of Youth and Adolescence* 38:153–163.

Sellers, R. M., Caldwell, C. H., Schmeelk-Cone, K. H., and Zimmerman, M. A. 2003. Racial identity, racial discrimination, perceived stress, and psychological distress among African American young adults. *Journal of Health and Social Behavior* 43:302–317.

Sellers, R. M., Copeland-Linder, N., Martin, P. P., and Lewis, R. L. 2006. Racial identity matters: The relationship between racial discrimination and psychological functioning in African American adolescents. *Journal of Research on Adolescence* 16:187–216.

Sellers, R. M., Rowley, S. A.J., Chavous, T. M., Shelton, J. N., and Smith, M. A. 1997. Multidimensional inventory of Black identity: A preliminary investigation of reliability and construct validity. *Journal of Personality and Social Psychology* 73:805–815.

Sellers, R. M., and Shelton, J. N. 2003. The role of racial identity in perceived racial discrimination. *Journal of Personality and Social Psychology* 84:1079–1092.

Serpell, Z. N., Boykin, A. W., Madhere, S., and Nasim, A. 2006. The significance of contextual factors in African American students' transfer of learning. *Journal of Black Psychology* 32:418–441.

Shah, S., and Sato, G. 2012. Where do we go from here? Philanthropic support for Black men and boys. Downloaded at http://foundationcenter.org/gainknowledge/research/pdf/osf_bmb.pdf

Shann, M. H. 2001. Added Students' use of time outside of school: A case for after school programs for urban middle school youth. *Urban Review* 33:339–357.

Silverman, I. J., and Dinitz, S. 1974. Compulsive masculinity and delinquency: An empirical investigation. *Criminology* 11:498–515.

Silverstein, L. B. 2006. Integrating feminism and multiculturalism: Scientific fact or science fiction? *Professional Psychology: Research and Practice,* 37, 21–28.

Simons, H. D. 2003. Race and penalized sports behaviors. *International Review for the Sociology of Sport.* 38, 5–22.

Simons, H. D., Bosworth, C., Fujita, S., and Jensen, M. 2007. The athlete stigma in higher education. *College Student Journal* 41:251–274.

Simons, R. L., Murry, V., McLoyd, V., Lin, K., Cutrona, C., and Conger, R. D. 2002. Discrimination, crime, ethnic identity, and parenting as correlates of depressive symptoms among African American children: A multilevel analysis. *Development and Psychopathology* 14:371–393.

Sims, J. J., Correll, J., and Sadler, M. S. 2013. Understanding police and expert performance: When training attenuates (vs. exacerbates) stereotypic bias in the decision to shoot. *Personality and Social Psychology Bulletin* 39:291–304.

Slaney, R. B., and Brown, M. T. 1983. Effects of race and socioeconomic status on career choice variables among college men. *Journal of Vocational Behavior* 23:257–269.

Smith, E., and Hattery, A. 2007. *African American families.* Los Angeles: Sage Publications.

Smith, T., and Steele, D. 2007. *Silent gesture – Autobiography of Tommie Smith.* Philadelphia, PA: Temple University Press.

Sneed, J. R., Schwartz, S. J., and Cross, W. E. 2006. A multicultural critique of identity status theory and research: A call for integration. *Identity: An International Journal of Theory and Research* 6:61–84.

So, D. 2003. Psychosocial HIV/AIDS prevention for high-risk African American men: Guiding principles for clinical psychologists. *Clinical Psychology: Science and Practice* 10:468–480.

Sorhagen, N. S. 2013. Teacher expectations in the first grade disproportionately affect poor children's high school performance. *Journal of Educational Psychology* 105:465–477.

Spander, A. (Feb, 2006). A moment in time: Remembering an Olympic protest. http://www.cstv.com/sports/c-track/stories/022406aas.html.

Spencer, M. B. 1995. Old issues and new theorizing about African American youth: A phenomenological variant of ecological systems theory. In R. L. Taylor (Ed.), *Black youth: Perspectives on their status in the United States* (pp. 37–69). Westport, CT: Praeger.

———. 2000. Identity, achievement orientation and race: "Lessons learned" about the normative developmental experiences of African American males. In W. Watkins, et al. (Eds.), *Race and education* (pp. 100–127). Needham Heights, MA: Allyn and Bacon.

———. 2001. Resiliency and fragility factors associated with the contextual experiences of low resource urban African American male youth and families. In A. Booth and A. Crouter (Eds.), *Does it take a village?: Community effects in children, adolescents and families* (pp. 51–77). Mahwah, NJ: Lawrence Erlbaum Associates.

Spencer, M. B., Dupree, D., Cunninghman, M., Harpalani, V., and Munoz-Miller, M. 2003. Vulnerability to violence: A contextually-sensitive, developmental perspective on African American adolescents. *Journal of Social Issues* 59:33–49.

Spencer, M. B., Dupree, D., and Hartmann, T. 1997. A phenomenological variant of ecological systems theory (PVEST): A self-organization perspective in context. *Development and Psychopathology* 9:817–833.

Spencer, M. B., Noll, E., Stoltzfus, E. N., and Harpalani, V. 2001. Identity and school adjustment: Revisiting the "acting White" assumption. *Educational Psychologist* 36:21–30.

Steele, C. M. 1997. A threat in the air: How stereotypes shape intellectual identity and performance. *American Psychologist* 52:613–629.

Steele, C. M., and Aronson, J. 1995. Stereotype threat and the intellectual test performance of African Americans. *Journal of Personality and Social Psychology* 69:797–811.

Steinbugler, A. C., Press, J. E., and Dias, J. J. 2006. Gender, race, and affirmative action: Operationalizing intersectionality in survey research. *Gender and Society* 20:805–825.

Steinfeldt, J. A., Reed, C., Steinfeldt, M. C. 2010. Racial and athletic identity of African American football players at Historically Black Colleges and Universities and Predominantly White Institutions. *Journal of Black Psychology* 36:3–24.

Steinfeldt, M., and Steinfeldt, J. A. 2012. Athletic identity and conformity to masculine norms among college football players. *Journal of Applied Sport Psychology* 24:115–128.

Stets, J. E., and Harrod, M. M. 2004. Verification across multiple identities: The role of status. *Social Psychology Quarterly* 67:155–171.

Stevens, J. W. 1997. African American female adolescent identity development: A three-dimensional perspective. *Child Welfare* 66:145–172.

Stevens-Watkins, D., and Graves, S. L. 2011. Risk and protective factors among African American adolescent males that predict adult involvement in the criminal justice system: Evidence from a national sample. *Journal of Ethnicity in Criminal Justice* 9:136–151.

Stevenson, H. C. 2002. Wrestling with destiny: The cultural socialization of anger and healing in African American males. *Journal of Psychology and Christianity* 21:357–364.

Stevenson, H. C., McNeil, J. D., Herrero-Taylor, and Davis, G. 2005. Influence of Perceived Neighborhood Diversity and Racism Experience on the Racial Socialization of Black Youth. *Journal of Black Psychology* 31:273–290.

Stewart, A. J., and McDermott, C. 2004. Gender in psychology. *Annual Review of Psychology* 55:519–544.

Stewart, D. L. 2008. Being all of me: Black students negotiating multiple identities. *The Journal of Higher Education* 79:183–207.

Stewart, R. 2000. African American males' reported involvement in the criminal justice system: A descriptive analysis. *Journal of African American Men* 5:55–70.

Stinson, D. W. 2011. When the "burden of acting White" is not a burden: School success and African American male students. *Urban Review* 43:43–65.

Stirratt, M. J., Meyer, I. H., Ouellette, S. C., and Gara, M. A. 2008. Measuring identity multiplicity and intersectionality: Hierarchical classes analysis (HICLAS) of sexual, racial, and gender identities. *Self and Identity* 7:89–111.

Stone, J., and Harrison, C. K., and Mottley, J. 2012. "Don't call me a student-athlete": The effect of identity priming on stereotype threat for academically engaged African American college athletes. *Basic and Applied Social Psychology* 34:99–106.

Storms, M. D. 1980. Theories of sexual orientation. *Journal of Personality and Social Psychology* 38:783–792.

Stovall, D. 2006. "We can relate: Hip-hop culture, critical pedagogy, and the secondary classroom." *Urban Education* 41:585–602.

Street, J., Harris-Britt, A., and Walker-Barnes, C. 2009. Examining relationships between ethnic identity, family environment, and psychological outcomes for African American adolescents. *Journal of Child and Family Studies* 18:412–420.

Sue, D. W. 2004. Whiteness and ethnocentric monoculturalism. Making the 'invisible' visible. *American Psychologist* 59:759–769.

Sue, D. W., Capodilupo, C. M., Tirono, G. C., Bucceri, J. M., Holder, A. M.B., Nadal, K. L., Esquilin, M. 2007. Racial microaggressions in everyday life: Implications for clinical practice. *American Psychologist* 62:271–286.

Swanson, D. P., Cunningham, M., and Spencer, M. B. 2003. Black males' structural conditions, achievement patterns, normative needs, and opportunities. *Urban Education* 38:608–633.

Swim, J. K., Hyers, L. L. Cohen, L. L., Fitzgerald, D. C., and Bylsma, W. H. 2003. African American college students' experiences with everyday racism: Characteristics of and responses to these incidents. *Journal of Black Psychology* 29:38–67.

Tajfel, H., and Turner, J. C. 1979. An integrative theory of intergroup conflict. In W. G. Austin and S. Worchel (Eds.), *The social psychology of intergroup relations* (pp. 33–47). Monterey, CA: Brooks/Cole.

Task Force on the Education of Maryland's African American males 2006. http://www.arylandpublicschools.org//11495/AfricanAmericanMaleTaskForceReportDecember06.pdf.

Tatum, A. W. 2003. All "degreed" up and nowhere to go: Black males and literacy education. *Journal of Adolescent and Adult Literacy* 46:620–623.

Tatum, A. W., and Muhammad, G. E. 2012. African American males and literacy development in contexts that are characteristically urban. *Urban Education* 47:434–463.

Tatum, B. D. 2004. Family life and school experience: Factors in the racial identity development of Black youth in White communities. *Journal of Social Issues* 60:117–135.

Terrell, F., Terrell, S. L., and Miller, F. 1993. Level of cultural mistrust as a function of educational and occupational expectations among Black students. *Adolescence* 28:573–578.

Teti, M., Martin, A. E., Massie, J., Malebranche, D. J., Tschann, J. M., and Bowleg, L. 2012. "I'm a keep rising. I'm a keep going forward, regardless": Exploring Black men's resilence amid sociostructural challenges and stressors. *Qualitative Health Research* 22:524–533.

Tettegah, S. 1996. The racial consciousness attitudes of White prospective teachers and their perceptions of the teachability of students from different racial/ethnic backgrounds: Findings from a California study. *Journal of Negro Education* 65:151–163.

Thomas, A. J. 2000. Impact of racial identity on African American child-rearing beliefs. *Journal of Black Psychology* 26:317–329.

Thomas, A. J., and Speight, S. L. 1999. Racial identity and racial socialization attitudes of African American parents. *Journal of Black Psychology* 25:152–170.

Thomas, C. 1971. *Boys no more.* Beverly Hills, CA: Glenco Press.

Thomas, D. E., Coard, S. I., Stevenson, H. C., Bentley, K., and Zamel, P. 2009. Racial and emotional factors predicting teachers' perceptions of classroom behavioral maladjustment for urban African American male youth. *Psychology in the Schools* 46:184–196.

Thomas, D. E., Townsend, T. G., and Belgrave, F. Z. 2003. The influence of cultural and racial identification on the psychosocial adjustment of inner-city African American children in school. *American Journal of Community Psychology* 32:217–228.

Thomas, P. A., Krampe, E. M., and Newton, R. R. 2008. Father presence, family structure, and feelings of closeness to the father among adult African American children. *Journal of Black Studies* 38:529–546.

Thomas, R. M. 2000. *Comparing theories of child development.* Stamford, CT: Wadsworth.

Thompson, A. R., and Gregory, A. 2011. Examining the influence of perceived discrimination during African American adolescents' early years of high school. *Education and Urban Society* 43:3–25.

Thompson, C. E., and Neville, H. A. 1999. Racism, mental health and mental health practice. *The Counseling Psychologist* 27:155–223.

Thompson, E. H., Pleck, J. H., and Ferrera, D. L. 1992. Men and masculinities: Scales for masculinity ideology and masculinity-related constructs. *Sex Roles* 27:573–607.

Thompson, L. R., and Lewis, B. F. 2005. Shooting for the stars: A case study of the mathematics achievement and career attainment of an African American male high school student. *The High School Journal*, 6–18.

Thompson, M. S., and Keith, V. M. 2001. The blacker the berry: Gender, skin tone, self-esteem, and self-efficacy. *Gender and Society* 15:336–357.

Thompson-Robinson, M., Weaver, M., Shegog, M., Richter, D., Usdan, S., and Saunders, R. 2007. Perceptions of heterosexual African American males' high-risk sex behaviors. *International Journal of Men's Health* 6:156–166.

Torres, V., Jones, S. R., and Renn, K. A. 2009. Identity development theories in student affairs: Origins, current status, and new approaches. *Journal of College Student Development* 50:577–596.

Tover-Murray, D., and Munley, P. H. 2007. Exploring the relationship between race-related stress, identity, and well-being among African Americans. *The Western Journal of Black Studies* 31:58–70.

Tovar-Murray, D., and Tovar-Murray, M. 2012. A phenomenological analysis of the invisibility syndrome. *Journal of Multicultural Counseling and Development* 40:24–36.

Trimble, J. E. 2007. Prolegomena for the connotation of construct use in the measurement of ethnic and racial identity. *Journal of Counseling Psychology* 54:247–258.

Trimble, J., Helms, J., and Root, M. 2002. Social and psychological perspectives on ethnic and racial identity. In G. Bernal, J. Trimble, K. Burlew, and F. Leong (Eds.), *Handbook of racial and ethnic minority psychology* (pp. 239–275). Thousand Oaks, CA: Sage.

Troiden, R. R. 1979. Becoming homosexual: A model of gay identity acquisition. *Psychiatry* 42:362–373.

———. 1989. The formation of homosexual identities. In G. Herdt (Ed). *Gay and lesbian youth.* New York: Harrington Park Press

Tucker, C. M., and Herman, K. C. 2002. Using culturally sensitive theories and research to meet the academic needs of low-income African American children. *American Psychologist* 57:762–773.

Tucker, C. M., Herman, K. C., Pedersen, T., Vogel, D., and Reinke, W. M. 2000. Student-generated solutions to enhance the academic success of African American youth. *Child Study Journal* 30:205–222.

Tyler, K. M. (in preparation). Validating the Cultural Activities and Values Scales. To be submitted to *Education and Urban Society*.

Tyler, K. M., Boykin, A. W., Boelter, C. M., and Dillihunt, M. L. 2005. Examining mainstream and Afrocultural value socialization in African American households. *Journal of Black Psychology* 31:291–311.

Tyler, K. M., Boykin, A. W., Miller, O. A., and Hurley, E. A. 2006. Cultural values in the home and school experiences of low-income African American students. *Social Psychology of Education* 9:363–380.

Tyler, K. M., Boykin, A. W., and Walton, T. R. 2005. Cultural considerations in teachers' perceptions of student classroom behavior and achievement. *Teaching and Teacher Education* 22:998–1005.

Tyler, K. M., Dillihunt, M. L., Boykin, A. W., Coleman, S. T., Scott, D. M., Tyler, C. M.B., and Hurley, E. A. 2008. Cultural socialization activities within African and European American families. *Cultural Diversity and Ethnic Minority Psychology* 14:201–204.

Tyler, K. M., Thompson, F. A., Burris, J., and Lloyd, H. (under revision). Believing the hype: Examining the Association between Internalized Racist Stereotypes and Academic Self-Handicapping among African American Male High School Students. *Journal of African American Males in Education*.

Tyler, K. M., and Uqdah, A. L. 2008. Kenneth B. Clark. In E., anderman and L., anderman (Ed.), *Psychology of Classroom Learning: An Encyclopedia*. Farmington Hills, MI: Thomson Gale Publishing. Fall 2008

Tyler, K.M., Uqdah, A.L., Dillihunt, M.L., Beatty-Hazelbaker, R., Conner, T., Gadson, N.C., Henchy, A.M., Hughs, T., Mulder, S., Owens, E., Roan-Belle, C., Smith, L and Stevens, R. (2008). Cultural discontinuity: Towards the empirical inquiry of a major hypothesis in education. *Education Researcher*. 37, 280–297.

Tyree, T. C. M. 2008. Lovin' momma and hatin' on baby mama: A comparison of misogynistic and stereotypical representations in songs about rappers' mothers and baby mamas. *Women and Language* 32:50–58.

Umana-Taylor, A.J., Quintana, S.M., Lee, R.M., Cross, W.E., Rivas-Drake, D., Schwartz, Syed. M., Yip. T., Seaton, and Ethnic and Racial Identity in the twenty-first century Study Group. Ethnic and racial identity during adolescence and into young adulthood: An Integrated conceptualization. *Child Development*, 85, 21–39.

Udry, J. R., Bauman, K. E., and Chase, C. 1971. Skin color, status, and mate selection. *American Journal of Sociology* 76:722–733.

Urdan, T. 1997. Achievement goal theory: Past results, future directions. In M. L. Maehr and P. R. Pintrich (Eds.), *Advances in motivation and achievement* (Vol. 10, pp. 99–141). Greenwich: JAI Press.

U.S. Bureau of Justice Statistics. 2007. Corrections statistics. http://www.ojp.usdoj.gov/bjs.htm.

Utsey, S. O., Chae, M. H., Brown, C. F., and Kelly D. 2002. Effect of ethnic group membership, ethnic identity, race-related stress and quality of life. *Cultural Diversity and Ethnic Minority Psychology* 8:366–377.

Vandiver, B. J., Cross, W. E., Worrell, F. C., and Fhagen-Smith, P. E. 2002. Validating the Cross Racial Identity Scale. *Journal of Counseling Psychology* 49:71–85.

Van Hoof, A. 1999. The identity status field re-reviewed: An update of unresolved and neglected issues with a view on some alternative approaches. *Developmental Review* 19:497–556.

Varner, F., and Mandara, J. 2013. Discrimination concerns and expectations as explanations for gendered socialization in African American families. *Child Development* 84:875–890.

Vygotsky, L. S. 1978. *Mind in society: The development of higher psychological processes.* (M. Cole, V. John-Steiner, S. Scribner, and E. Souberman, Eds). Cambridge, MA: Harvard University Press

Wade, J. C. 1996. African American men's gender role conflict: The significance of racial identity. *Sex Roles* 34:17–33.

Wade, T. J., and Bielitz, S. 2005. The differential effect of skin color on attractiveness, personality evaluations, and perceived life success of African Americans. *Journal of Black Psychology* 31:215–236.

Waldner, L. K., and Magruder, B. 1999. Coming out to parents: Perceptions of family relations, perceived resources, and identity. *Journal of Homosexuality* 37:83–101.

Walker, K. L., and Dixon, V. 2002. Spirituality and academic performance among African American college students. *Journal of Black Psychology* 28:107–121.

Walker, K. L., and Satterwhite, T. 2002. Academic performance among African American and Caucasian college students: Is the family still important. *College Student Journal* 36:113–128.

Walker, M. A. 2006. Enrolling in hip-hop 101. *Diverse: Issues in Higher Education* 23:22–23.

Walker, R. 2007. Acculturation and acculturative stress as indicators of suicide risk among African Americans. *American Journal of Orthopsychiatry* 77:386–391.

Wallace, B. C., and Constantine, M. G. 2005. Africentric cultural values, psychological help-seeking attitudes, and self-concealment in African American college students. *Journal of Black Psychology* 31:369–385.

Walpole, M. 2003. Socioeconomic status and college: How SES affects college experiences and outcomes. *Review of Higher Education* 27:45–73.

Walsemann, K. M., Bell, B. A., Maitra, D. 2011. The intersection of school racial composition and student race/ethnicity on adolescent depressive and somatic symptoms. *Social Science and Medicine* 72:1873–1883.

Ward, E. G. 2005. Homophobia, hypermasculinity, and the US black church. *Culture, Health, and Sexuality* 7:493–504.

Ward, E., and Mengesha, M. 2013. Depression in African American men: A review of what we know and where we need to go from here. *American Journal of Orthopsychiatry* 83:386–397.

Ward, L. M. 2004. Wading through the stereotypes: Positive and negative associations between media use and Black adolescents' conceptions of self. *Developmental Psychology* 40:284–294.

Warikoo, N., and Carter, P. 2009. Cultural explanations for racial and ethnic stratification in academic achievement: A call for a new and improved theory. *Review of Educational Research* 79:366–394.

Warren, J. 2012. Woodson Academy in Fayette County tries to close testing gap for black males. Downloaded at http://www.kentucky.com/2012/10/14/2371231/new-academy-in-fayette-county.html.

Watkins, D. C., Green, B. L., Goodson, P., Guidry, J., and Stanley, C. 2007. Using focus groups to explore the stressful life events of Black college men. *Journal of College Student Development* 48:105–118.

Watkins, D. C., Walker, R. L., and Griffith, D. M. 2010. A meta-study of Black male mental health and well-being. *Journal of Black Psychology* 36:303–330.

Watson, L. W. 2006. The role of spirituality and religion in the experiences of African American male college students. In M. J. Cuyjet (Ed.), *African American men in college*, (pp. 112–127). San Francisco: Jossey-Bass.

Watson, S., Thornton, C. G., and Engelland, B. T. 2010. Skin color shades in advertising to ethnic audiences: The case of African Americans. *Journal of Marketing Communications* 16:185–201.

Watts, R. J., and Abdul-Adil, J. K. 1998. Promoting critical consciousness in young, African American men. *Journal of Prevention and Intervention in the Community* 16:63–86.

Watts, R. J., Abdul-Adil, J. K., and Pratt, R. 2002. Enhancing critical consciousness in young African American men: A psycho-educational approach. *Psychology of Men and Masculinity* 3:41–50.

Waymer, D. 2008. A Man: An autoethnographic analysis of Black male identity negotiation. *Qualitative Inquiry* 14:968–989.

Webb-Johnson, G. 2002. Are schools ready for Joshua? African American culture among students identified as having behavioral/emotional disorders. *Qualitative Studies in Education* 15:653–671.

Weddle-West, K., Hagan, W. J., Norwood, K. M. 2013. Impact of college environments on the spiritual development of African American students. *Journal of College Student Development* 54:299–314.

Wessel, R. D., and Wallaert, K. A. 2011. Student perceptions of the hip hop culture's influence on the undergraduate experience. *Journal of College Student Development* 52:167–179.

West, K. 2004. *All Falls Down*. The College Dropout. New York, NY: Sony Music Studios.

Wester, S., Vogel, D. L., Wei, M., and McLain, R. 2006. African American men, gender role conflict, and psychological distress: The role of racial identity. *Journal of Counseling and Development* 84:419–429.

Whaley, A. L. 2003. Cognitive-cultural model of identity and violence prevention for African American youth. *Genetic, Social, and General Psychology Monographs* 129:101–151.

Whatley, P. R., Allen, J., and Dana, R. H. 2003. Racial identity and the MMPI in African American male college students. *Cultural Diversity and Ethnic Minority Psychology* 9:345–353.

White, J. L., and Cones, J. H. 1999. *Black man emerging. Facing the past and seizing a future in America*. Routledge: New York, Ny.

Whiting, G. W. 2006. From at risk to at promise: Developing scholar identities among Black males. *The Journal of Secondary Gifted Education* 17:222–229.

———. 2009. The Scholar Identity Institute: Guiding Darnel and other Black males. *Gifted Child Today* 32:53–63.

Wilder, J., and Cain, C. 2011. Teaching and learning color consciousness in Black families: Exploring family processes and women's experiences with colorism. *Journal of Family Issues* 32:577–604.

Williams, D. R., Neighbors, H. W., and Jackson, J. S. 2003. Racial/ethnic discrimination and health: Findings from community studies. *American Journal of Public Health* 93:200–208.

Williams, J. M. 2013. Moving from words to action: Reflections of a first year counselor educator for social justice. *Journal for Social Action in Counseling and Psychology* 5:79–87.

Willis, L. A., and Clark, L. F. 2009. Papa was a rolling stone and I am too: Paternal caregiving and its influence on the sexual behavior of low-income African American men. *Journal of Black Studies* 39:548–569.

Wilson, B. D. M., Harper, G. W., Hidalgo, M. A., Jamil, O. B., Torres, R. S., Fernandez, M. I., and Adolescent Medicine Trials Network for HIV/AIDS Interventions. 2010. Negotiating dominant masculinity ideology: Strategies used by gay, bisexual, and questioning male adolescents. *American Journal of Community Psychology* 45:169–185.

Wilson, B. D. M., and Miller, R. L. 2002. Strategies for managing heterosexism used among African American gay and bisexual men. *Journal of Black Psychology* 28:371–391.

Wilson, P. A. 2008. A dynamic-ecological model of identity formation and conflict among bisexually-behaving African American men. *Archives of Sex Behavior* 37:794–809.

Wilson-Jones, L., and Caston, M. C. 2002. Cooperative learning on academic achievement in elementary African American males. *Journal of Instructional Psychology* 31:280–283.

Wilton, L. 2008. Correlates of substance use in relation to sexual behavior in Black gay and bisexual men: Implications for HIV prevention. *Journal of Black Psychology* 34:70–93.

Wingate, L. R., Bobadilla, L., Burns, A. B., Cukrowicz, K. C., Hernandez, A., Ketterman, R. L., Minnix, J., Petty, S., Richey, J. A., Sachs-Ericsson, N., Stanley, S., Williams, F. M., and Joiner, T. E. 2005. Suicide and African American men. *Suicide and Life-Threatening Behavior* 35:615–629.

Wise, S. J. 2004. Redefining Black masculinity and manhood: Successful Black gay men speak out. *Journal of African American Men* 40:3–22.

Witherspoon, K. M., Speight, S. L., and Thomas, A. J. 1997. Racial identity attitudes, school achievement, and academic self-efficacy among African American high school students. *Journal of Black Psychology* 23:344–357.

Wood, J. L., and Essein-Wood, I. 2012. Capital identity projection: Understanding the psychosocial effects of capitalism on Black male community college students. *Journal of Economic Psychology* 3:984–995.

Wood, L. J., and Hilton, A. A. 2013. Moral choices: Towards a conceptual model of Black male moral development (BMMD). *The Western Journal of Black Studies* 37:14–27.

Wood, P. B., and May, D. C. 2003. Racial differences in perceptions of the severity of sanctions: A comparison of prison with alternatives. *Justice Quarterly* 20:605–631.

Woods, T. A., Kurtz-Costes, B., and Rowley, S. 2004. The development of stereotypes about the rich and poor: Age, race, and family income differences in beliefs. *Journal of Youth and Adolescence* 34:437–445.

Worrell, F. C., Vandiver, B. J., Cross, W. E., and Fhagen-Smith, P. E. 2004. Reliability and structural validity of Cross Racial Identity Scale Scores in a sample of African American adults. *Journal of Black Psychology* 30:489–505.

Worthington, R. L., Savoy, H. B., Dillon, F. R., and Vernaglia, E. R. 2002. Heterosexual identity development: A multidimensional model of individual and social identity. *The Counseling Psychologist* 30:495–531.

Wright, B. L. 2011. I know who I am, do you? Identity and academic achievement of successful African American male adolescents in an urban pilot high school in the United States. *Urban Education* 46:611–638.

Wyatt, G. E. 1999. Beyond invisibility of African American males: The effects on women and families. *The Counseling Psychologist* 27:802–809.

Xu, S. H. 2001. Teachers' full knowledge of students' popular culture and the integration of aspects of that culture in literacy instruction. *Education* 122:721–730.

Yakushko, O., Davidson, M. M., and Williams, E. N. 2009. Identity salience model: A paradigm for integrating multiple identities in clinical practice. *Psychotherapy Theory, Research, Practice, and Training* 46:180–192.

Yanico, B. J., Swanson, J. L., and Tokar, D. M. 1994. A psychometric investigation of the Black racial identity attitude scale—Form B. *Journal of Vocational Behavior* 44:218–234.

Yarhouse, M. A., Nowacki-Butzen, S., and Brooks, D. F. 2009. Multiple identity considerations among African American Christian men experiencing same-sex attraction. *Counseling and Values* 54:17–31.

Yeh, C. J. 1999. Invisibility and self-construal in African American men: Implications for training and practice. *The Counseling Psychologist* 26:810–819.

Yeh, C. J., and Huang, K. 1996. The collectivistic nature of ethnic identity development among Asian American college students. *Adolescence* 31:645–661.

Yip, T., Seaton, E. K., and Sellers, R. M. 2006. African American racial identity across the lifespan: Identity status, identity content and depressive symptoms. *Child Development* 77:1504–1517.

Yoo, H. C., and Lee, R. M. 2005. Ethnic identity and approach-type coping as moderators of the racial discrimination/well-being relation in Asian Americans. *Journal of Counseling Psychology,* 52,497–506.

Yopyk, D. J.A., and Prentice, D. A. 2005. Am I an athlete or a student? Identity salience and stereotype threat in student-athletes. *Basic and Applied Social Psychology* 27:329–336.

Zaytoun, K. 2006. Theorizing at the borders: Considering social location in rethinking self and psychological development. *NWSA Journal* 18:52–72.

Zimmerman, M. A., Ramirez-Valles, J., Zapert, K. M., and Maton, K. I. 2000. A longitudinal study of stress-buffering effects for urban African American male adolescents problem behaviors and mental health. *Journal of Community Psychology* 28:17–33.

Zinn, M. B., and Dill, B. T. 1996. Theorizing difference from multiracial feminism. *Feminist Studies* 22:321–323.

Zirkel, S. 2002. Is there a place for me? Role models and academic identity among White students and students of color. *Teachers College Record* 104:357–376.

Index

Academic difficulties, 19
Academic disidentification, 206
Acting "white," 136
Adolescence, 8
African American men, 5
African American racial identity models: nigrescence, 116, 116–117; multidimensional model of Black identity, 117–118
Afrocultural themes, 144
American Journal of Orthopsychiatry, 12

Bandura, Dr. Albert, 200
Black Entertainment Television, 9
Boykin, Dr. Wade, 143
Bronfenbrenner, Dr. Urie, 36
Brown, Nino, 211–215
Bullard, Dr. Robert, 48

Capital identity projection, 172
Cain, Herman, 220
Carlos, John, 192
Cass, Dr. Vivienne, 102–103
Chronosystem, 36
Clark, Dr. Kenneth, 216
Collins, Jason, 98
Common, 151
Cool pose, 91
Colorism, 215
Cosby, Dr. William, 239
Cross, Dr. William, 116

Dee, Kool Moe, 152
Down low, 97
Drug Abuse, 26

Ebony Magazine, 58; The Black Man's Game of Life, 59; The State of Black Boys, 62; The State of Today's Black Men, 58

Ecological Systems Theory, 36
Ego identity, 32
Ellison, Ralph, 65
Erikson, Dr. Erik, 27, 30
Ethnic identity, 129
Ethnic identity development, 130–132
Ethnicity, 129
Ethnocentric monoculturalism, 47, 164
Exosystem, 36

Franklin, Dr. Anderson, 67

Garcia-Coll, Dr. Cynthia, 37
Gender identity, 87
Group membership-based identity, 33

Harris-Perry, Dr. Melissa, 12
Helms, Dr. Janet, 117
Heterosexism, 107
Heterosexual identity development, 100
Hip-hop culture, 149
Homicide, 23
Homosexuality, 104
Hypermasculinity, 91

I-self, 30
Identities: academic, 7, 200; athletic, 7, 185; differential status, 170; Category-based, 33; cultural, 7, 143; ethnic, 7; gender, 7; personal, 32; racial, 7, 115; role, 33; sexual, 7, 99; social, 32; socioeconomic, 7
Identity development, 8
Intersectionality, 16, 74–76
Invisibility syndrome, 16, 67–72

James, Dr. William, 30
Jay-Z, 150
Jones, Dr. Susan, 76

Journal of African American Men in Education, 63
Journal of Early Adolescence, 15
Journal of Social Action on Counseling and Psychology, 12

Kohlberg, Dr. Lawrence, 87
Kohlberg's identity development theory: gender consistency, 87; gender labeling, 87; gender stability, 87

Macrosystem, 36
Mainstream cultural themes, 144
Martin, Trayvon, 3, 9, 52–53, 78, 122, 220, 233; parents of, 242, 244
Masculinity, 97
Mattis, Dr. Jacqueline, 154
Me-self, 30
Mead, Dr. George, 30
Mesosystem, 36
Microsystem, 36
Model of Multiple Dimensions of Identity (MMDI), 76, 77

Nas, 153
National Association for Gifted Children, 153
National Basketball Association (NBA), 98, 185, 190
National Football League (NFL), 98, 185, 190
Neville, Dr. Helen, 45
New Jack City, 211

Obama, First Lady Michelle, 38
Obama, President Barack, 4, 9, 29, 43, 153, 221; My Brother's Keeper, 245
Ogbu, Dr. John, 135–136

Phenomenological Variant of Ecological Systems Theory, 37
Phinney, Dr. Jean, 129

Racism: cultural racism, 14, 47, 164; definition, 46; effects of, 45; environmental racism, 48; forms, 51; individual racism, 14, 46; institutional racism, 14, 47

Racist stereotypes about African American men, 5
Rice, Dr. David, 235
Robinson, Eugene, 235
Rosenthal and Jacobsen, 201

Sam, Michael, 98
Scott, Jill, 57–58
Sellers, Dr. Robert, 117
Sexually Transmitted Infections (STIs), 25
Sharpton, Reverend Al 12
Skin color bias, 215
Social class, 169
Social cognitive theory, 26
Social identity theory, 8
Socioeconomic status, 167
Spencer, Dr. Margaret Beale, 37
Spirituality, 154
Stereotype threat, 133; research, 133–135
Steele, Dr. Claude, 133, 135
Suicide, 24

Tajfel, Dr. Henri, 30
The Cosby Show, 239
The Plight of Young Black Males is Worse Than You Think, 11

Thompson, Dr. Chalmer, 45
Tommie Smith, 192
Traditional gender roles, 87–88
Troiden, Dr. Richard, 103
Triple Quandary framework, 143; afrocultural realm, 144; mainstream culture, 144; minority culture, 143, 151

United States Supreme Court, 97
Urban Prep Academy, 22

Watkins, Dr. Boyce, 238
West, Kanye, 151, 173–176
Wood, Dr. Luke, 172

Young African American men, 3, 13

About the Author

Kenneth Maurice Tyler is associate professor of educational psychology in the College of Education at the University of Kentucky. His research interests include examinations of the link between culture and cognitive development, Intersectionality, and contextual and interpersonal predictors of academic performance and related factors among African American school-age children and college students. Born and raised on the West Side of Chicago, Tyler attended Whitney Young Magnet High School and the University of Illinois at Chicago, where he double majored in Psychology and African American Studies. Tyler went on to earn masters' and doctoral degrees in developmental psychology under the tutelage of A. Wade Boykin, a leading scholar on African American culture and achievement. Tyler has one son, Asa McKenzey Tyler, who loves to play football and is a bit of a science whiz.